Livestock
Legacy

NUMBER TWENTY-SEVEN
The Centennial Series of the Association of Former Students,
Texas A&M University

LIVESTOCK
LEGACY

The Fort Worth Stockyards

1887–1987

J'NELL L. PATE

Texas A&M University Press
COLLEGE STATION

Library of Congress Cataloging-in-Publication Data
Pate, J'Nell L.
    Livestock legacy : the Fort Worth stockyards, 1887–1987 / J'Nell
L. Pate. — 1st ed.
        p.   cm. — (The Centennial series of the Association of Former
Students, Texas A&M University ; no. 27)
    Bibliography: p.
    Includes index.
    ISBN 0-89096-277-4 (cloth); 0-89096-530-7 (paper)
    1. Stockyards—Texas—Fort Worth—History.   2. Cattle trade—
Texas—Fort Worth—History.   I. Title.   II. Series.
HD9433.U5F675   1988
388.1'760831—dc19
                                                      88-1116
                                                        CIP

For my husband, Kenneth

Contents

Illustrations

Foreword

FORT WORTH—what a name in the history of the livestock industry. Cowtown—a city built around livestock. I first began hearing of the Fort Worth Stockyards when I started working at the stockyards in Sioux City in 1933. It was one of the giants ranked along with Chicago, Kansas City, Saint Louis, and Saint Paul. Because they were all larger than Sioux City, I looked with awe at the great number of cattle and sheep they handled. It seemed that Texas was a great sea of cattle. Many, including some longhorns, even made it as far north as Sioux City. Over the following years, I had many opportunities to observe personally much of the history of the Fort Worth Stockyards that the author has here so faithfully recorded.

I was assigned to the Fort Worth Army Air Base in 1943, and my wife who joined me there about January 1, 1944, went to work for the Texas Livestock Marketing Association, the largest commission firm at the yards. The year of 1944 saw the Fort Worth Market first in the nation in sheep receipts and a solid fourth in total receipts. Many times she had to work until midnight and past. I visited the yards several times, and we both retain many memories of that unbelievable busy place and the many fine friends we made there. The city of Fort Worth was known among servicemen for its friendliness.

John Lewis, who served as president of the Fort Worth Stockyards from 1960 to 1971, was a close friend of mine and a man I respected very much. I had worked with him at Sioux City and Sioux Falls. He was known as a very honest man and for his ability to get a job done under difficult circumstances. John was doing very well at Sioux Falls. He was well liked (something unusual for a Stock Yards president), and under his leadership a steady growth in receipts was started that has now carried that market to first place in the nation in the last several years.

He wanted the challenge of running a "major" market, however. Fort Worth with its acres and acres of cattle pens, sheep facilities second to none, and a beautiful impressive Exchange Building was certainly that. But the market had already started its decline, and despite his efforts to reverse the tide, there was no way to stop it, just adapt facilities and procedures to slow it. I'm sure he never thought that his problems would be compounded because he was a "Damn Yankee." It is only human nature that when things are going wrong, people must blame somebody.

In the late 1960s, I had the opportunity to spend a full week at the Fort Worth Stockyards as a member of a committee composed of the vice-presidents of several of United Stockyards Corporation's largest yards. We had the responsibility of studying each yards we visited and giving recommendations for improving operations and increasing receipts. Fort Worth was well into its decline by then and not a major market, but John had specifically requested we visit his market. He was looking for the magic bullet. We were of very little help—just keep cutting down on the size of the yards and reducing expenses so that United Stockyards would not close the yards completely.

One must marvel at the tremendous amount of research and work put into this history of the Fort Worth Stockyards by the author, literally thousands of hours over many years. She became as deeply involved in the industry as those of us who, taking a part-time job as a youth, ended up spending our lifetimes there. Of particular interest was the very thorough and understandable story on government regulation in chapter 8. The most entertaining is chapter 9, "A Day at the Yards." The people at every yards remember anecdotes of a similar nature. The stories gathered are so typical.

J'Nell Pate has considered writing an overall history of all stockyards in the nation. She does not need to. In this most comprehensive history of Fort Worth she has told the story of all. Livestock markets developed around methods of transportation and buyer demand. First the animals were driven on foot over the trails to the city market square. Then came water transportation over the rivers and canals. Some markets developed when the owners of hotels for livestock drovers built pens to hold the animals overnight while the men got their rest. Buyers in need of supplies were attracted along with the fact livestock people are natural traders. So the markets developed. Bourbon Stockyards in Louisville, Kentucky, which celebrated its 150th year in 1984, is a good example of that. Livestock first came by foot and by river, and the market started among the pens at the drovers' hotel.

Railroads brought the greatest growth in stockyards. Refrigerated rail cars for hauling meat brought the concentration of packers at terminal points, and stockyards developers seeking to build buying power offered unbelievable inducements to packers as a reward for operating plants at their markets. Outright gifts of already built plants or substantial and sometimes majority ownership interests in the stockyards were quite common. Fort Worth and Sioux City offer excellent examples.

Then came highways, trucks, and automobiles. The stockyards over the nation did adapt by building truck facilities and by more country solicitation by commission firms, but the highways also helped build country auction markets closer to the farm or ranch and made it more practical for the buyers to come to the livestock rather than the livestock come to the buyers.

The story of all stockyards is right here in this history of the Fort Worth Yards: long periods of struggle, triumphs, disappointment, government regulation, fires, floods, and strikes. But most important of all, the wonderful, interesting stockyards people that brought Fort Worth and all stockyards through those many years. They were, as one Sioux City advertising program was titled, "The Livestock Breed."

It's very few businesses that have lasted long enough to celebrate, as many stockyards now are doing, 100-year anniversaries. The livestock industry is indebted to J'Nell Pate for a job well done. Thank you from all of us.

L. V. Kuhl, President
American Stock Yards Association

Preface

WHEN PEOPLE CONSIDER the history of the cattle industry in the American West, they think first of the long cattle drives. Romanticized stories of cowboys, chuck-wagon cooks, and rags-to-riches Texas cattlemen are pervasive, and the celebrations in Kansas cowtowns at the end of the trail are special favorites. Though obviously less glamorous, the meat-packing facet of the cattle industry has received its share of attention, too. Near the turn of the century Upton Sinclair attacked the Chicago meat entrepreneurs in *The Jungle*, and J. Ogden Armour quickly came to the defense of his industry in *The Packers, the Private Car Lines and the People*. Few people who do not live near them, however, have ever given a thought to the industry that developed between the long drive and the packing plant: the holding pens for cattle awaiting slaughter. These stockyards or terminal markets—so called because they represented the end of the line, often a railroad line—constituted a vital part of the livestock industry.

As meat packers built stockyards and arranged for rail service into them, they created the large markets scattered throughout the livestock-producing areas of the country. These stockyards where producers could sell (through commission agents) and packers and others could buy constituted the major arena for marketing the nation's livestock for nearly eighty years.

The stockyards provided a place where two or three million head of livestock a year could receive "hotel" accommodations—"lodging," food, and water — as well as services necessary for marketing them — weighing, identification, and health inspections to comply with state and federal laws. Stockyards owners, livestock dealers, and commission men all hoped to make a profit by providing at stockyards the facilities where others could buy and sell.

The Fort Worth Stockyards is typical of large terminal livestock markets and thus offers insights into the workings of all. It was the largest market in the Southwest, the third- to fourth-largest in the nation. Its story is not yet complete, for active trading still continues there. But its heyday has passed, as has that of the other great markets, some of which, like that in Chicago, have closed.

The publication of this book caps off ten years of research on the Fort Worth market, which began when I chose it as my doctoral dissertation topic at North Texas State University. I began my study knowing nothing about the Fort Worth Stockyards except that my father and brother had often sold cattle there in the late 1940s and early 1950s and that I had seen and smelled a lot of cattle there every time I had ridden over the Twenty-eighth Street bridge as a youngster.

I have learned that at least two viewpoints toward stockyards exist. Some view the meat moguls Armour and Swift, who owned the Fort Worth Stockyards and other yards, as monopolists exploiting the public and producers alike. Others, notably Fort Worth old-timers, remember only the pride they felt in their market in its boom days and realize the meat packers made it possible. They emphasize the integrity of all concerned, including the buyers for Armour and Swift. I have tried to see both sides and to present them as accurately as possible from the facts uncovered. Mainly, I have enjoyed learning how it was that Fort Worth came to be known as Cowtown.

Acknowledgments

THE FIRST TWO PEOPLE I want to thank are the ones who gave me the idea of researching the history of the Fort Worth Stockyards. In 1975 Wilford "Butch" Saxton and Jack Shannon spoke before a committee of which I was a member explaining the work of the Stockyards Area Restoration Committee (SARC). Saxton served as senior city planner on the project and Shannon chaired SARC for over a decade. One of them said in passing that the stockyards would make somebody a great dissertation topic.

Secondly, I wish to acknowledge the untiring efforts of Dr. A. Ray Stephens, western historian at North Texas State University and my major advisor during the long course of my research. His knowledge of the West and the role of livestock in it kept me on the right path.

While serving as vice-president of the Fort Worth Stockyards, Ron Brown helped save a truckload of old letters and stockyards files. He also carried the books of the Corporate Record out of the vault for me those numerous times I came by the office. Thanks also to Elmo "Mo" Klingenberg, president of the stockyards during the time I was doing most of my research, for putting up with my nosing around so much.

Rosemary and Ted Gouldy of the *Weekly Livestock Reporter* didn't know I would spend every day from eight to five for six weeks in their office when they gave me permission to go through the back files of the *Reporter.* Many thanks to them for graciously making

xvii

a place for me and to Tommy Brown in their office, who lugged all those heavy volumes out of the storeroom. I also appreciate Ted Gouldy's reading of the chapters that covered the years when he was working closely with the Fort Worth Stockyards.

Thanks also to Roy Weeman, head cattle buyer for Swift for many years, for reading a chapter and for all his help with information and photographs. Patsy Cooper and Kathy Rainey of the Fort Worth Stockyards staff provided invaluable information and assistance during recent years, as their jobs changed with the drastic transitions of the stockyards.

Additional thanks go to William E. Jary, Jr., for letting me use his files on the stockyards; to Ruth Alexander, assisant city secretary for Fort Worth and the women in her office; to Don King and Steve Munday at the Texas and Southwestern Cattle Raisers Association; to David Murrah, director of the Southwest Collection at Texas Tech University; to Milan Hughston, Amy Simon, Nancy Wynne, and Ron Tyler of the Amon Carter Museum of Western Art for the use of their library facilities and to Carol Roark of the Museum's photography department; to Charlcia Bullard, Wanda McCleskey, and Hettie Arleth of the *Fort Worth Star Telegram*'s Reference Library; to Anne McDermott and Ruby Hardy, Texas Christian University Library Special Collections; to Charles Hughes, state archivist at the Texas Christian University Library; to Charles Hickox, Tarrant County Junior College Library; to Paul Campbell, Patricia Chadwell Jackson, Jerry Parr, and Phillip Hallmark, Fort Worth Public Library; to Ellen Warthoe and Richard Himmel of the North Texas State University Library Archives; to Mrs. Frances Perry, Tarrant County Law Library; to Carolyn Snyder, Stockyards Redevelopment Office; and to Gary Havard, Janie Reid, Charlie McCafferty, and Sue McCafferty of the North Fort Worth Historical Society.

Not all of the people still hold the positions they did six or eight years ago when I did the bulk of my research. One whose affiliation has remained constant, however, is my husband of twenty-eight years, Kenneth Pate. His continuing patience has enabled me to devote much of my energy to research and writing over these years.

I gratefully acknowledge the assistance of these people and the many persons I interviewed whose names will appear in the book.

These interviewees represent only a portion of the hundreds of persons closely associated with the stockyards. They were the ones still around whom I found willing to help me tell the story; that these were mentioned and others omitted does not imply that they were more important than others. From any whose names I may inadvertently have left out of my acknowledgments, I ask indulgence.

Any errors in fact or interpretation must, of course, remain my responsibility.

Livestock
Legacy

City Fathers Conspire
1870–90

BOSTON CAPITALIST and meat-packing entrepreneur Greenlief W. Simpson gazed with amazement at the glut of cattle that had arrived one crisp fall day in October, 1892, at the Union Stock Yards north of Fort Worth. "This is some market," he told his lawyer, William Johnson.[1]

Not long afterward Simpson instructed Johnson to handle the legal arrangements to buy out the Union Stock Yards. The new company, called the Fort Worth Stock Yards, was chartered in March, 1893, in West Virginia.

Back home in Boston, Simpson talked to one of his neighbors, Louville V. Niles, about investing in stockyards and meat packing right in the heart of the livestock country. Niles too had been active in the meat-packing industry, so he, along with some Chicago businessmen, bought stock in the Fort Worth company.

What Simpson did not know when he saw the overstocked pens in Fort Worth was that several washouts and a railroad strike had caused more livestock than usual to be housed in the yards that day. The Union Stock Yards Company had built the pens to handle the load from 150 railroad cars, but workers had crowded 500 carloads into them that day. Simpson, Niles, and their associates faced

---

1. Written transcript of 1915 interview with Verner S. Wardlaw (1861–1924), "The History of the Packing Plant Industry in Fort Worth" (copy in author's possession), p. 4.

nearly a decade of struggle before their fledgling Fort Worth Stock Yards Company would begin the period of tremendous growth that would make it the largest market in the entire Southwest and even a challenger to the big markets in Chicago, Saint Louis, and Kansas City.

Simpson and Niles also had little knowledge of the years of Herculean efforts already put forth by local Fort Worth businessmen to make a cattle market out of their frontier community—to bring first a railroad and then a stockyards and meat-packing concern to their town. The arrival of these Boston capitalists with their money and influence would herald the out-of-state ownership and control of the Fort Worth livestock market that would characterize it throughout nearly all its history and assure its success, but none of the later growth could have been achieved without the years of struggle local business leaders had endured. In fact, the overriding influence during Fort Worth's early days as a livestock market would be the promotion of that market by its citizens.

The success the Fort Worth Stock Yards Company finally achieved was in stark contrast to the heartbreaking failures of these early decades despite the efforts of local men like John Peter Smith, Khleber M. Van Zandt, B. B. Paddock, and others. By the age of thirteen, John Peter Smith was an orphan who had gone to live with a cousin in Kentucky. Upon graduating from college in 1853, he came west to make his fortune and chose the four-year-old community of Fort Worth as his home. There he taught school, surveyed land, and practiced law. During the Civil War he led fellow Fort Worthians in battle. Colonel Smith returned to Fort Worth and practiced law, and in 1874 he invested in banking. He acquired a great deal of land while it remained cheap and contributed much of the wealth he gained to a variety of enterprises that he hoped would help Fort Worth grow.

Major Khleber Miller Van Zandt moved from East Texas to Fort Worth late in 1865 and opened a mercantile establishment on the square in January, 1866. Soon he bought the entire block bounded by Main and Houston and Third and Fourth streets, plus a farm west of the Clear Fork of the Trinity River. In 1874 Van Zandt joined with John Peter Smith and one of his own brothers-in-law to purchase a share in a financial house that later became the Fort Worth National Bank. Van Zandt became the bank's president, a position he held for more than fifty years. He was not an outspoken booster and promoter, but instead he worked behind the scenes as a quiet underwriter of practically every major event in Fort Worth's early growth, including the coming of the railroad.

Twenty-eight-year-old Buckley B. Paddock arrived in Fort Worth in November, 1872, with the intention of settling there. K. M. Van Zandt, who had been recommended to Paddock, had started a newspaper, the *Fort Worth Democrat,* a year before, but had had trouble finding a good editor. Paddock turned out to be so good that he soon bought the paper from Van Zandt. The young editor's main goal seems to have been to make Fort Worth the greatest town in Texas. "God makes the country, but man makes the town," Paddock wrote in his newspaper early in 1873. He set out to help make Cowtown, pushing especially for a railroad, for stockyards, and for meat-packing plants.[2]

Captain Ephraim M. Daggett was another of the city's early promoters. Captain Daggett had sought his fortune in Fort Worth only a year after the military post was established in 1849. He easily acquired much land both north and south of the downtown area. By 1870 he began giving free lots south of Tenth and Main to people who would choose Fort Worth for their home and build on their lot.

Fort Worth may have been called "Cowtown" as early as 1862. Certainly after the Civil War, and after the Chicago Union Stock Yards opened in 1865, Tarrant County occupied a strategic position in the booming cattle industry. At that time South Texas ranchers began gathering up the herds of longhorns that had run wild and multiplied during the Civil War. Worth only three to four dollars in Texas, these animals would bring forty to fifty dollars in the northern slaughter houses. Railroads had not yet extended into South Texas, so the cattlemen walked their animals to market. Fort Worth was the last Anglo village betwen Texas and the Kansas railheads. It was the last stop in Texas on the Great Trail, or Texas Trail, which later would be called the Chisholm Trail because of its connection with a route in Indian Territory used by an old trader named Jesse Chisholm.

2. Julia Kathryn Garrett, *Fort Worth: A Frontier Triumph,* p. 337.

A longhorn herd belonging to Colonel J. J. Myers of Lockhart, Texas, apparently the first herd to travel through Fort Worth on its way north, approached the village in April, 1866. Colonel Myers rode ahead of the herd to find the best place to cross the Trinity. Charles B. Daggett, brother of Ephraim, and some others led him to a spot just east of present-day Samuels Avenue Railway Bridge, which became known as Daggett's Crossing. Once he reached Kansas, Myers talked to Joseph McCoy, who was wrestling with the problems the 1866 trail drivers faced when traveling through settled communities. McCoy was proposing the opening of a cattle depot at the small village called Abilene, Kansas, where the Kansas-Pacific Railroad would extend by the spring of 1867. For nine years, until the railroad reached Dodge City in 1876, Abilene remained the chief cattle market for Texas herds. Fort Worth became a major stop along the way.

During the last three or four years of the 1860s Fort Worth was just a small village of one or two business houses and about twenty families. With the burst of activity associated with the cattle drives, though, new businesses began to open. Many saloons catered to the cowboys, and other new establishments, even banks, cashed in on the cattle business as well. After the Civil War, Captain M. B. Loyd, a veteran of the Battle of Vicksburg, spent about five years gathering and marketing South Texas cattle. With his profits, he opened a loan office on the square in Fort Worth at the start of the 1870s. He later would be a charter shareholder in the First National Bank (now Interfirst).

Drovers estimated that it took three-fourths of a pound of bacon, the same amount of flour, and a good supply of coffee, beans, and dried fruit to sustain a cowhand each day. Cattlemen needed to take on supplies in Fort Worth to last a month for each of their drovers. Local businessmen took advantage of that ready opportunity for profit. Then after the herds reached Abilene, the cowboys turned right around and rode back down the trail toward home, so Fort Worth became the first place they could spend their money (after their initial spree in Abilene itself). New businesses like saddleries and bath houses, as well as keno parlours and saloons, appeared by 1872.

Remembering those days, one old-timer later professed that "Fort Worth was less conscious of her morals than some of her neighbors." Some city fathers encouraged the somewhat boisterous cattle trade for the money it attracted. As could be expected, the more conservative citizens expressed displeasure with what they considered disreputable elements, but those who saw the need for a strong economic base for the community prevailed.[3]

By the early 1870s, Tarrant County also became a supply center for a ranching district developing to the west. In addition, aggressive cattle buyers from the North soon began to come to Fort Worth to meet herds on their way to Kansas and thus gain an advantage over other buyers. They would persuade some of the already weary drovers to sell out early and save themselves the trouble of going on into the dangerous Indian Territory. The danger was exaggerated considerably, no doubt. The buyers then grouped several herds together and finished the trip to Kansas.

While Fort Worth grew in population and developed as a cowtown supplying the trail herds headed toward the meat-packing plants of the North, an indigenous meat-packing industry already existed along the Texas coast. Beginning in 1854, men there slaughtered cattle for their hides and tallow; later they began salting and packing the meat in large barrels. In 1870 fifteen of these Texas plants in places like Indianola, Fulton, and Rockport grossed over a million dollars and produced over two-thirds of all factory-packed beef in the United States. However, South Texas eventually lost its early advantage in this industry to northern states because of the mildness of its climate in an age when natural ice had to be used as a refrigerant. Also, the Texas plants were far from the nation's great meat-consuming centers; products had to be shipped by sea—a long and expensive route—and the railroads came too late to help. Cattlemen could gain quicker profits by trailing cattle northward, and they could do so with little capital risk. Had barbed-wire fences which prevented the trail drives, come into use ten years earlier, the coastal packing plants might have retained their lead.

The Fort Worth story would not have developed as it did had not the community seen the advantages of packing meat in Texas. As early as 1875 they urged that a packing plant be built in Fort Worth

3. Verna Elizabeth Berrong, "History of Tarrant County from Its Beginning until 1875" (Master's thesis, Texas Christian University, 1938), p. 59.

to slaughter the large numbers of cattle in the state.[4] A railroad, however, had to be an even higher priority for Cowtown. As early as November 13, 1858, a dream of bringing a railroad to town began to form, when citizens in a mass meeting in the county courthouse adopted a resolution to ask the Houston and Texas Central and the Southern Pacific to make Fort Worth a junction for their lines. Captain Ephraim Daggett served as chairman of the meeting, and Captain Joseph C. Terrell became the secretary. Captain Terrell had first visited in Fort Worth in 1857 and had opened a law office there soon afterward. Being an early settler, he had invested in cheap land that later brought him wealth.

During the next few years, the rumors of a railroad's coming helped double the population of Fort Worth to about twelve hundred. The U.S. Congress on March 3, 1871, granted a charter to a new railroad company, the Texas and Pacific, to be built along the thirty-second parallel from Marshall, Texas, to San Diego, California. The Texas legislature then gave cities and counties the power to grant bonuses to railroads.

Colonel Thomas A. Scott, president of the Texas and Pacific Railroad, came to Fort Worth on June 20, 1872, with one of the company's directors, John W. Forney, to look for roadsites and to get the citizens to pledge $100,000 to bring the train to their city. Colonel Scott told the Fort Worthians that he wanted 320 acres of land south of town. By that evening four citizens had signed a note pledging that amount.[5]

Fort Worth citizens began bragging about several proposed railroad lines going out from the city, and editor Paddock placed a map in the *Democrat* on June 26, 1873, showing Fort Worth as a large circle in the center of several North Texas cities. Seven railroad lines led into the circle. Writers in many other Texas papers ridiculed Paddock's map, which they claimed resembled a tarantula, especially

4. Troy Jesse Cauley, "Early Business Methods in the Texas Cattle Industry," *Journal of Economics and Business* 4 (May, 1932): 465. See also Jimmy M. Skaggs, *The Cattle-Trailing Industry between Supply and Demand, 1866–1890*, pp. 100–101; and "Texas Cattle," *Fort Worth Democrat*, April 21, 1875.

5. John W. Forney, *What I Saw in Texas*, pp. 71–78. The four signers were Capt. E. M. Daggett, Maj. K. M. Van Zandt, Col. Thomas J. Jennings, and Judge H. G. Hendricks (Howard M. Peak, "Recollections of Early Northwest," in *Research Data*, Fort Worth and Tarrant County, Texas, Federal Writers' Project, I, 224).

after Jay Cooke's banking empire, a primary financer of rail ventures, failed in the fall of 1873, halting railroad building. Paddock called the Cooke collapse a "dark day for Fort Worth." Business and development died; in fact, the spring cattle drive remained as the only business left to the aspiring city. The population dropped from four thousand to less than one thousand within only a few months.[6]

Major K. M. Van Zandt headed a delegation of Fort Worth citizens who traveled to Marshall to interview the Texas and Pacific officials. The railroad men told the Fort Worth group that, although they could purchase rails on credit, the company could not complete the work, since the railroad did not have the money for grading. Major Van Zandt decided to enlist the people of Fort Worth to do the grading, with a lien on the railroad as their compensation. To carry out the project, several local men in October, 1875, created a company, the Tarrant County Construction Company, with Van Zandt as president.

The State of Texas offered a land grant of sixteen sections to the railroad for each mile of track laid, on the condition that the line be completed from Dallas to Fort Worth by January 1, 1874. The legislature later extended the deadline for a year. The Constitutional Convention of 1875 eventually extended the cut-off date even further but, impatient with the lack of progress, issued an ultimatum that unless the railroad began serving Fort Worth by the day in 1876 that the first legislature held under the new constitution adjourned, the state would reclaim the right-of-way.[7]

In order to meet the challenge, the Tarrant County Construction Company planned to grade the line of the railroad along the course of the survey from Fort Worth eastward until they met the existing railroad. By May, 1876, the Texas and Pacific Railroad had disposed of sufficient bonds to lay the rails and equip the part of the road graded by the local company.

Fort Worth's dream of a railroad hung in the balance as the Texas legislature neared adjournment in July, before the railroad had reached the city limits. The state Senate passed and sent to

6. B. B. Paddock, *Early Days in Fort Worth, Much of Which I Saw and Part of Which I Was*, pp. 6–7.

7. *Tex. Gen. Laws*, 1873, ch. 108, sect. 2 at 318, vol. 7; H. Gammel, *Laws of Texas* (1898), 1018. See also Paddock, *Early Days in Fort Worth*, p. 10.

the House a bill that would extend the time for completion thirty days past adjournment. But Fort Worth did not need it. The first train reached Fort Worth's Main and Front (now Lancaster) streets at 11:23 A.M. on July 19, 1876, with the legislature still in session. Most of the citizens of the town had pitched in to help, with the men working around the clock and the women bringing coffee and food to the workers. When the train arrived, a twelve-piece band and a huge crowd greeted it.[8]

Twenty-three head of cattle owned by John F. Swayne left the town in a cattle car September 6, 1876, apparently the first load of cattle ever shipped out of Fort Worth. Swayne received a little over ten dollars a head for them. Swayne had arrived in Fort Worth in 1872 and had formed a law partnership with Captain Joseph C. Terrell. He soon resigned to deal in real estate and the cattle business, eventually raising registered Jersey cattle. The same month that Swayne shipped his cattle, Texas and Pacific officials began building cattle pens in Fort Worth to take care of animals delayed in transit because of lack of cars. When drivers saw that a place to hold cattle existed, they halted herds they had started up the trail, ordering them to be sold and shipped from Fort Worth. Cattle commission firms were quickly developed by city businessmen. With all this activity around the stock pens near the railroad, Fort Worth could boast of its first stockyards.[9]

One of the first commission men and cattle dealers after the railroad came was Colonel E. M. "Bud" Daggett, a nephew of Captain Daggett. Bud Daggett had been only four years old when the

8. *Fort Worth Democrat*, July 22, 1876, July 26, 1876. Paddock, editor of the *Democrat* at the time the railroad arrived, should have looked back into his own newspaper files when he wrote his books about early Fort Worth some three decades later. In his books he related the story that the representative to the state legislature from Tarrant County, Nicholas Darnell, was ill and had to be carried onto the House floor on a cot each day for fifteen days to vote "no" to adjournment until the railroad reached Fort Worth. Darnell may well have voted that way on something crucial, but not every day on adjournment. The legislature had much business that it did not complete until August 21, 1876, over a month after the first train arrived in Fort Worth (Paddock, *Early Days in Fort Worth*, pp. 11–12; *Daily Fort Worth Democrat*, August 23, 1876).

9. "Old Sales Slip Tells Story of First Carload of Cattle from Ft. Worth," *Stockman-Journal*, December 30, 1908, p. 3. See also B. B. Paddock, ed., *A Twentieth Century History and Biographical Record of North and West Texas*, II, 64–65.

family came to Fort Worth from Shelby County, Texas. He handled cattle and other livestock on the Fort Worth market for sixty years, in later years as a senior member of the Daggett-Keen Commission Company.[10]

The city trebled its population within ninety days after the arrival of the railroad. By late 1876 two small, mule-drawn streetcars made continuous round trips from the courthouse to the Texas and Pacific station, in all about 160 trips per day. The town also grew in other ways than population. By 1876 the "wide-open" town could attract cowboys to no fewer than thirteen saloons: the Waco Tap, the Headlight Bar, the Tivoli Saloon, the Occidental, Our Friends, the Red Light, Our Comrades, the Beer Garden, the Bon Ton, the Cattle Exchange, the Horse Head, the White Elephant, and the Trinity.

In 1877, the first full year Fort Worth had a railroad, 51,923 head of cattle, only a small fraction of the trail herds that came through, left the city by rail. The railroads did not have enough stock cars to carry any more. A more important factor, however, in limiting the rail shipments was cost; it remained cheaper to walk cattle to Kansas. Some people still dreamed of making Fort Worth a meat-packing center, even though the city had grown as a shipping point once the railroad came.

Gustavus Swift had successfully pioneered the idea of slaughtering cattle and shipping the fresh meat eastward in a refrigerator car a decade earlier than Fort Worth men began their own local attempt to do so on May 13, 1877. That same year, one of the largest cattle commission companies in the nation, Hunter, Evans and Company, opened a branch office in Fort Worth. With the railroad in town, things seemed to be looking up for Fort Worth, but competition from farther west created problems.[11]

Although in 1876 twice as many cattle went through Fort Worth on trail drives as through Fort Griffin, which was located almost one hundred miles due west in Shackelford County, by 1877 and 1878 Fort Griffin was emerging as a strong competitor. The railroad in

10. "E. M. Daggett, Veteran Cowman Reviews City's Early History," *North Fort Worth Sunday News*, December 17, 1911. Some sources say that Daggett loaded out the first trainload of cattle from the Texas and Pacific yards in 1876.

11. Skaggs, *Cattle-Trailing Industry*, p. 82.

Kansas had moved west from Abilene to Dodge City by 1876, and Dodge City was situated due north of Fort Griffin. In 1879 nearly half the cattle that trailed northward passed through Fort Griffin. In the spring of 1879, Fort Worth leaders sent men down the trail to get cattlemen to use the old Fort Worth route; solicitors for the big grocery stores of the city met the herd on the trail south of Fort Worth with bottles of whiskey and boxes of cigars as gifts. Businessmen instructed the city's representatives to talk up Fort Worth's advantages over Fort Griffin: a larger community, an established route northward, and the railroad. As a result of their efforts, Fort Worth retained a bare majority of the trade. Fort Worthians had worked too desperately for the railroad to allow the cattle traffic to bypass them one hundred miles to the west. Moreover, their dreams of larger stockyards and packing plants for their city would evaporate unless they could keep the cattle coming through.

As northern quarantine laws against Texas cattle began to restrict herdsmen from driving their cattle into Kansas, for fear of Texas fever, the need grew for some type of packing plant in North Texas. In addition, the excessive railroad rates hampered small shippers, livestock prices on northern markets were uncertain and often proved unsatisfactory, and shrinkage posed a problem for cattle shipped long distances by rail. More and more, Texas producers wished to escape from what they began to call the domination of the meat trust, centered in Chicago. Three or four of the largest packers seemed to control the industry.

Newspaper editor Paddock in 1875 had begged for a packing plant to be built in Fort Worth. "There is no reason why Fort Worth should not become the great cattle center of Texas," he had proclaimed in the *Democrat*. The first answer to his plea came in 1881, when W. E. Richardson, a capitalist from East Saint Louis, came to North Texas. Richardson first traveled to Dallas to establish a pork packery; hearing of this, Paddock went to Dallas to lure him to Fort Worth. Richardson was asking for six acres of free land for his plant, but the people of Dallas apparently showed little interest. Paddock told Richardson that if he would come to Fort Worth, all he need do was select the site. Paddock promised that the deed to the land would be in his hands within an hour—with a $10,000 bonus to boot. Richardson followed Paddock westward across the Trinity and picked out the land he wanted. Fortunately for Paddock and his promise, the land belonged to John Peter Smith, who immediately deeded it over to Richardson. The packery received its first shipment of hogs on December 11, 1881. Since Richardson planned to slaughter only hogs, and they remained somewhat scarce in Texas, his plant soon closed.[12]

Late in 1881 the Santa Fe Railroad reached Fort Worth. With the Texas and Pacific and the Missouri, Kansas and Texas, this made three lines into the city. The arrival of the Santa Fe came largely through the efforts of Paddock and Major Van Zandt, who had called a town meeting that raised a bonus of seventy-five thousand dollars to attract the railroad. The Santa Fe reached Fort Worth at a time when the number of cattle being driven northward was dwindling. Fences, settlement, the railroad itself, and Texas fever were among the factors that stemmed the flow of cattle from the southern ranges. An estimated three hundred fifty thousand head passed through Fort Worth in 1882, and cattlemen expected the number to drop to two hundred forty thousand the next year.[13]

A packing plant in Texas was a dream that was not exclusive to Fort Worth businessmen. In Austin in 1882 members of a Central Texas cattle raisers' association decided to build a refrigerated packing house somewhere in Texas. That same year David Higgs of Cincinnati proposed to ship refrigerated and slaughtered beef east from various points in Texas. He named one of his relatives, A. F. Higgs, to head the Texas operation. The Higgses agreed to build a refrigerator plant at Victoria for $50,000 and to ship the processed meat to New Orleans. In July, 1883, the Victoria Packing Company announced plans to establish a second plant in Fort Worth. City business leaders proposed a subscription of $60,000, the actual cost of the Victoria works. Two months later Fort Worth's subsidiary of the Victoria plant, the Continental Beef Company, raised its capital stock to $120,000 and began plans for immediate construction of the works. The company purchased twenty-seven acres in the southeast part of the city and began to build. Slaughtering was to

12. "Texas Cattle," *Fort Worth Democrat*, April 21, 1875, p. 3. See also Charter No. 1490, The Fort Worth Packing Company, filed December 29, 1881, Office of Secretary of State, Austin, Texas.

13. *Texas Live Stock Journal*, May 5, 1883, p. 12.

begin in January, 1884. Most cattle would arrive by rail, for the long drives were ending.[14]

Plans called for the Fort Worth plant to turn out three hundred dressed beeves, one hundred sheep, and one hundred calves per day to be shipped first to New Orleans, then to points in the southeast. Six Fort Worth men, including John Peter Smith, served as directors for the Fort Worth branch of the company. The plant opened for business February 4, 1884, but went into receivership before the end of the year. When the Victoria plant ceased operations a little later, Fort Worth stockholders suspected that the Victoria plant had been in financial trouble and had recruited the Fort Worth stockholders only to prop their own business up a little longer. Local men insisted that excessive freight rates and discrimination against Fort Worth had hurt their refrigerator works; they knew that cattle were still available if they could get a competent packing company to process them.[15]

A local Fort Worth man named Isaac Dahlman leased the refrigerator works from the defunct company and planned to reopen it on May 15, 1885. Dahlman was a relative of the Dahlman brothers — Henry, Aaron, and David—whose store at Houston and First was the oldest clothing establishment in Fort Worth. Dahlman's plant shut down in late 1885 and remained closed the next year.[16]

While Isaac Dahlman had negotiated to buy the refrigerator and reopen it, other local citizens were moving into action. By June, 1885, they had raised sufficient subscriptions to assure the construction of a railroad to Waxahachie that would connect with the Huntington railroad system. They also planned a railroad to Brownwood. In addition, Fort Worthians furnished money to underwrite the con-

14. Delia Ann Hendricks, "The History of Cattle and Oil in Tarrant County" (Masters thesis, Texas Christian University, 1969), pp. 15–16.

15. "Fort Worth Refrigerator Beef," *Texas Live Stock Journal,* August 18, 1883, p. 2; "The Texas Continental Refrigerator Company," ibid., November 17, 1883, p. 8; "The Meat Company," ibid., February 9, 1884, p. 2; "The Refrigerator," ibid., October 18, 1884, p. 4; "The Defunct Texas Continental," ibid., October 31, 1885, p. 4; "Refrigerated Beef," ibid., December 20, 1884, p. 4.

16. "The Refrigerator," ibid., April 25, 1885, p. 4; "Dahlman Brothers," ibid., October 4, 1890, p. 9. See also Mack Williams, *In Old Fort Worth* (Fort Worth: News-Tribune, 1977), pp. 20–64; and "About the Refrigerator," *Texas Live Stock Journal,* June 26, 1886, p. 4.

struction of a cotton mill, and energetic entrepreneurs built more stockyards near the railroads. That same year, 1885, George and June Polk, two brothers, built the first commercial stockyards, locating their pens about a mile south of the Texas and Pacific station, east of the railroad tracks and about three blocks east of Main Street. In fact, four different stockyards existed near the railroads by mid-April, 1886.[17]

In March of 1886, cattle shippers in Fort Worth faced a crisis as the Knights of Labor staged a nationwide railroad strike over higher pay. When strikers tried to prevent the Missouri Pacific trains from moving, a gunfight erupted between them and law enforcement officers, including City Marshall Jim Courtright. The clash occurred south of the downtown area at a place called Buttermilk Junction, located about the present 2200 block of South Main Street. After the gunfight, Mayor John Peter Smith wired Governor John Ireland asking for one or two companies of Texas Rangers. Governor Ireland sent five companies and even came to Fort Worth himself. The trains moved.[18]

The city still did not have a successful meat-packing concern in late 1887. To try to remedy that, thirteen Texas cattlemen, ten of whom lived in or near Fort Worth, raised $100,000 to capitalize the Fort Worth Refrigerating and Export Meat Company, which they incorporated at Austin on June 16, 1888.[19]

Meanwhile, Isaac Dahlman kept trying. He talked to agents of a Metropolitan Trading Company of London, England, who wanted to purchase two hundred dressed Texas beeves a day. The agents had also negotiated with a packing plant in Columbus and the owners of the defunct Continental Beef plants in Victoria and Fort Worth.

17. "Fort Worth Enterprise," *Texas Live Stock Journal*, June 13, 1885, p. 4; "New Stock Yards," ibid., April 17, 1886, p. 4.
18. Leonard Sanders and Ronnie C. Tyler, *How Fort Worth Became the Texas-most City*, pp. 72–76. Luke Short shot Jim Courtright on February 8, 1887, in front of Short's White Elephant Saloon. Following the shooting the mayor led a campaign to clean up the saloon and red-light district, which was called Hell's Half Acre. By 1889 things were fairly quiet.
19. "The Refrigerator Question," *Texas Live Stock Journal*, September 3, 1887, p. 12; Charter No. 3772, The Fort Worth Refrigerating and Export Meat Company, filed June 16, 1888, Office of Secretary of State, Austin, Texas. See also *Fort Worth Daily Gazette*, June 17, 1888.

All three concerns discussed joining together to fulfill the British contract. At a cattlemen's convention in March, 1890, Dahlman explained his situation and asked the livestock producers to help support his meat-packing project. They agreed and formed a committee —Charles Goodnight, H. B. Stoddard, Ike T. Pryor, and R. E. Maddox, who was from Fort Worth—to examine the three refrigerator plants. The cattleman planned to buy all three plants and issue stock for a new company, to be called the Texas Dressed Beef and Packing Company. Deeming Dahlman's plant less valuable than the Victoria and Columbus plants, the committee offered him so little money that he refused to sell. They then began planning a new plant north of the city. Dahlman pulled out of the combination and attempted to fill one-third of the London contract by himself. After someone killed the owner of the Columbus plant, the cattlemen lost interest and gave up on the new company. This left Dahlman with the entire contract from the Metropolitan Trading Company of London to supply two hundred head of dressed cattle per day. Dahlman went east, got financing, formed the Dahlman Dressed Beef Company, and repaired the old Continental Beef Company plant. He began operations the first week of November, 1890, shipping the dressed beef to Liverpool via Galveston. Unfortunately, the meat spoiled, and he lost the contract, ending his meat-packing career.[20]

Other efforts continued, however, and somewhat offset Dahlman's failure. Local businessmen incorporated the Union Stock Yards and a little later chartered a packing company, which they called the Fort Worth Dressed Meat and Packing Company. They estimated that 1.5 million cattle ranged within a hundred-mile radius of Fort Worth, probably more than in any other comparable area in the nation. The packing company, established partly in cooperation with the cattlemen's association, and the Union Stock Yards formed the nucleus of facilities north of Fort Worth that attracted Boston capitalists and that later became the Fort Worth Stock Yards Company.[21]

20. "Refrigeration in Texas," *Fort Worth Daily Gazette*, November 5, 1890; "The Refrigerators," *Texas Live Stock Journal*, March 29, 1890, p. 11; "The Refrigerators," ibid., April 12, 1890, p. 10.
21. "Fort Worth Union Stock Yards," *Texas Live Stock Journal*, March 24, 1888, p. 13.

The Union Stock Yards obtained its charter first, on July 26, 1887. In late December of that year, businessmen and railroad interests raised $30,000 in just a few hours to complete the $200,000 capital fund for the yards. Officers of the Union Stock Yards Company included Colonel J. W. Burgess, president, and Colonel Robert E. Maddox, secretary. Colonel Burgess had come to Tarrant County in 1884, had bought four thousand acres of land twelve miles north of Fort Worth, and had engaged in stock breeding and farming, raising mostly registered shorthorn cattle. Maddox was a prominent Fort Worth businessman who in 1888 was president of the electric light company and the Fort Worth Ice Company and who built four brick buildings on Main Street that year alone.[22]

A series of problems made progress slow and forced the men to reorganize their company late in 1888. The Fort Worth Union Stock Yards entered into an agreement with the Fort Worth and Denver City Railway to give it a right-of-way for one dollar if it would build to the stockyards. Officials made the same agreement with the Saint Louis, Arkansas, and Texas Railway in Texas on January 22, 1889. Not until mid-summer, 1889, were the yards ready to receive stock for feeding. New officers named at that time were John R. Hoxie, president; H. C. Holloway, superintendent; and Andrew T. Byers, secretary. On Hoxie's arrival in Fort Worth in 1889 from Chicago earlier that year, he had immediately organized the Farmers and Mechanics National Bank with a capital of one million dollars and had built the city's first skyscraper, a three-story building at Fourteenth and Main. Loaning money too indiscriminately, Hoxie eventually exhausted the bank's resources and lost control. Under other leadership, it was later reorganized into a sound institution. Meanwhile, as president of the stockyards, Hoxie instructed Superintendent Holloway, a rugged six-footer in his early fifties, to buy land

22. Charter No. 3402, Fort Worth Union Stock Yards Company, filed July 26, 1887, Office of Secretary of State, Austin, Texas. Incorporators included John Peter Smith, Morgan Jones, and J. W. Burgess. Also "Fort Worth Notes," *Texas Live Stock Journal*, July 28, 1888, p. 10; "He Crows Loud," *Fort Worth Daily Gazette*, December 24, 1887, p. 8; "The Union Stock Yards," *Texas Live Stock Journal*, December 31, 1887, p. 8; and *History of Texas, Together with a Biographical History of Tarrant and Parker Counties*, pp. 423–24.

for stock pens, to build fences for the stockyards, and to construct an exchange building.[23]

When completed, the Union Stock Yards occupied 258 acres of land along three-quarters of a mile of Trinity River frontage and had a capacity of five thousand cattle, ten thousand sheep, and twenty thousand hogs. A two-story exchange building, 64 feet wide and 174 feet long, housed a bank, livestock offices, a kitchen, a dining room, a wash room, and overnight accommodations for one hundred guests. The company leased out twelve offices for commission operators.

Byers, secretary of the Union Stock Yards, had come to Fort Worth about 1888, already successful as a lawyer and businessman in the North. Along with several others, he invested in fourteen hundred acres of land north of the courthouse, the site on which the stockyards and packing plants would later be built. Both to develop his property and to provide transportation to the stockyards, Byers extended the streetcar northward and substituted electricity for the horsedrawn power that had been in use on downtown streets. Thus by July 15, 1889, electric street cars ran to the yards. This became one of the first electric railway systems in the Southwest.[24]

Two Fort Worth newspapers even called for a livestock show to be held at the new stockyards in mid-summer, 1889, but the call went unheeded. Promoters remained busy trying to get the new facilities ready to open. Finally, on September 1, 1889, the sale of horses, mules, cattle, hogs, and sheep began.[25]

Members of the Fort Worth business community continued to try to secure a packing plant locally after attempts by the thirteen cattlemen to open a meat packery in 1888 fell through. The direc-

23. Copy of an agreement between Fort Worth Union Stock Yards and Fort Worth and Denver City Railway, August 5, 1890, Fort Worth and Denver City Railroad folder, Gary Havard Personal Collection, Fort Worth, Texas; "Union Stock Yards at Fort Worth, Texas," *Texas Live Stock Journal*, April 13, 1889, p. 10; "A Southern Acady—the Park City of the Southwest," clipping in North Fort Worth file in Fort Worth Public Library; B. B. Paddock, ed. *Fort Worth and the Texas Northwest*, II, 632, 659.

24. Paddock, *Fort Worth and Texas Northwest*, III, 102–103.

25. "Fort Worth," *Texas Live Stock Journal*, July 6, 1889, p. 10; "Packing," *Fort Worth Daily Gazette*, July 15, 1889; "Union Stock Yards," *Texas Live Stock Journal*, June 29, 1889, p. 8, and "Union Stock Yards," Advertisement, *Texas Live Stock Journal*, July 20, 1889, p. 6.

tors of the recently opened Union Stock Yards met on February 6, 1890, at the Farmers and Mechanics Bank and formed the Fort Worth Dressed Meat and Packing Company. The place of business would be at the Union Stock Yards, and the men agreed upon a charter that would run for fifty years, providing a capital of $500,000. Incorporators included Robert McCart, R. E. Maddox, John R. Hoxie, Tobe Johnson, J. C. McCarthy, M. G. Ellis, A. T. Byers, E. B. Harold, and S. D. Rainey. They voted that a majority of the capital stock should be held in Fort Worth "in order that no buying-out scheme" could be worked by outside interests. They planned to let the contracts in March to construct the largest fertilizer, smokehouse, and packery in the Southwest at an estimated cost of $350,000.[26]

Seven men at the February 6 meeting subscribed $115,000 of the stock of the new company. After the meeting they called on enough other interested businessmen to raise the total to $190,000. They optimistically believed they could obtain the authorized $500,000 capital, but apparently problems developed, for later most of these men joined in chartering a new company, the Fort Worth Packing Company, on April 30, 1890, with a reduced capital stock of $200,000.[27]

Colonel Hoxie, president of the stockyards, met a young man named Verner S. Wardlaw in Kansas City, where Wardlaw clerked in the Armour Banking Company. Hoxie persuaded him to move to Fort Worth as office manager of the new packing plant. The young man arrived in Fort Worth shortly afterwards to help oversee construction of five large stone buildings.[28]

The Fort Worth Packing Company opened for business on November 21, 1890, only two weeks after Isaac Dahlman reopened his doomed plant. Although the new packery did not run to full capacity, in the first month it processed 8,340 hogs worth $50,000 as well as some cattle. The local newspaper boasted that the plant

26. The men ran into problems getting the $500,000 in capital stock and never filed a charter for the Fort Worth Dressed Meat and Beef Company (Patricia Camtrell, Certifying Clerk, Secretary of State's Office, Austin, Texas, to author, May 22, 1981). See "It Is a Go," *Fort Worth Daily Gazette,* February 7, 1890; "The Packery," *Texas Live Stock Journal,* February 22, 1890, p. 10.

27. Charter No. 4581, The Fort Worth Packing Company, filed April 30, 1890, Office of Secretary of State, Austin, Texas.

28. Wardlaw interview typescript.

gave "the stockraisers a market equal to Chicago or St. Louis."[29]

An early problem emerged—not enough hogs. The Fort Worth Packing Company considered slaughtering only hogs, leaving beef packing to the refrigerator in the southeast part of the city, the Dahlman facility. Dahlman had not yet suffered the disastrous spoilage of his shipment to Liverpool. There were never enough hogs in the area, however, to keep a packing plant in full operation. A local editorial warned, "If the farmers of Texas do not raise the hogs to keep their packeries running and maintain their markets, the loss will be their own." Managers of the Fort Worth Packing Company sent circulars to the farmers and stockmen of Texas pointing out the advantages of the local market and urging them to go more largely into the swine business. They assumed that in a few years Texas would become one of the leading swine-producing states in the union.[30]

Packing facilities also existed in Dallas. The plants in Fort Worth and Dallas had a combined capacity of one thousand to fifteen hundred hogs a day and could handle all the hogs offered for sale in Texas. The Fort Worth Packing Company did not completely abandon beef packing, either; in December, 1890, the company killed four hundred cattle and eleven hundred hogs.[31]

A year later a local stock journal editor lamented that the Fort Worth packing concern reluctantly paid from $75,000 to $100,000 monthly to Kansas farmers for their hogs in order to keep the packing company open. They would rather pay the money to Texas farmers who "should plant less cotton and more corn."[32] Colonel Hoxie hired a man named Len Hackett to canvass Texas for hogs for the packing plant. He found a number in Llano County and shipped 250 to 300 head per car to Fort Worth. The small native hogs could escape from the pens, so the stockyards company had to rebuild all the hog pens.

Good news came early in April, 1891, when the Fort Worth Pack-

29. "Livestock News," *Fort Worth Gazette*, December 21, 1890.

30. "The Packing House," *Texas Live Stock Journal*, March 29, 1890, p. 11; editorial, ibid., May 17, 1890, p. 8; and "The Pork Packery," ibid., July 5, 1890, p. 10.

31. *Texas Live Stock Journal*, July 12, 1890, p. 8; "Latest Reports from the Live Stock Centers—Fort Worth," ibid., January 3, 1891, p. 14.

32. "Plant Hogs," ibid., December 19, 1891, p. 3.

ing Company obtained a meat contract to supply beef to Texas military posts. On April 11 work began on an addition to the local plant in anticipation of larger receipts. The company operated on borrowed capital at 12 percent interest during this time.

To celebrate the first anniversary of the Fort Worth Packing Company, Colonel Hoxie gave a free barbecue for more than a thousand persons on November 21, 1891, at the Union Stock Yards. Despite Hoxie's celebration, his receipts of cattle in 1891 remained poor, and all fall the packing plant begged in the stock journals for more cattle. Owners recapitalized the Fort Worth Packing Company at $400,000 one week after the party, on November 28, 1891, and added two more directors.[33]

Clearly something else had to be done. The Fort Worth businessmen had invested a great deal of their own money in these meat-packing and stockyards projects. They had used the tactic of overlapping directorships in the stockyards company, the packing company, and even a stockyards bank. Still they struggled, and Dallas remained a rival.[34]

Although the men of vision such as Daggett, Paddock, Van Zandt, and John Peter Smith knew that their hard work had changed Fort Worth from a frontier village to a city, their efforts could not yet cease. The new decade of the 1890s brought continued challenges.

33. "Personal Mention," *Texas Live Stock Journal*, November 28, 1891, p. 10; Charter No. 1490, Fort Worth Packing Company, amended, filed November 28, 1891, Office of Secretary of State, Austin, Texas.
34. Wardlaw transcript, p. 2.

New Company Faces Struggle
1893–1901

OLD DAN WAGGONER, who had created a cattle empire in Wise County and points westward, saw Fort Worth as the city of the future at the beginning of the 1890s. Waggoner, who with his son W. T. (Tom) operated one of the three largest ranches in northwest Texas, moved to the growing cattle center from Decatur in 1891.

The community began to spruce up a bit as people planted more trees and shrubbery about their homes and voted for the city to construct sidewalks. Wealthy families like the Waggoners built fancy residences, hosted an increasing number of social affairs, and encouraged more and more cultural activities. Property values soared as newcomers recognized the city as the gateway to ranches in the Texas Panhandle to the northwest.

In 1890 five local grain elevators held a full capacity of 850,000 bushels a day. The actual trade territory of Fort Worth in 1890 stretched some four hundred by six hundred miles, larger than that of any other Texas city. The North Side developed into the factory area of Fort Worth, with the refrigerator-packery, a roller mill, a shoe factory, a wagon factory, and a barrel manufacturer. A Fort Worth Board of Trade that had begun operations on May 31, 1882, evolved into the more permanent Chamber of Commerce in 1892.[1]

Fort Worth's 1880 population of 6,663 more than tripled, to 23,076, by 1890. During that same decade the state's beef produc-

---

1. *Fort Worth Daily Gazette*, February 17, November 27, 1890.

tion also increased sharply, by 51 percent. Registered breeds finally outnumbered the longhorns. So much interest developed in livestock that the *Texas Live Stock Journal*, published in Fort Worth for members of the cattle raisers' organization, reached a circulation of eighteen thousand by September, 1890. The newspaper editor noted during that year that the White Elephant Saloon remained the favorite gathering place for stockmen when they came to town.[2]

Events of the decade, however, would destroy many of the optimistic hopes Fort Worth businessmen held as the nineties opened. Perhaps the accidental burning of the Spring Palace on May 30, 1890, in only its second cultural season forecast the gloomy days that would plague the city before things got better.

Former newspaperman B. B. Paddock had been the prime mover for the Spring Palace idea. Commenting that Toronto and Saint Paul had "Ice Palaces" and Sioux City a "Corn Palace," he had suggested that Fort Worth call attention to the products of the field, forest, orchard, and garden that Texas produced. Besides, no other major exhibition seemed to be planned for the spring of 1889 anywhere in the country. Paddock became president of a company to raise $50,000 to build the Spring Palace, although it eventually cost $100,000. The 225-foot by 375-foot green wooden building was shaped like a Saint Andrews cross and possessed a massive central dome. Four towers stood two stories high and eight towers three stories high; the roofs were covered with shelled corn and oats. Fort Worth advertised her Spring Palace extensively, and special trains came from as far away as Boston and Chicago to see it.

Although the Palace company showed a deficit the first season, it proved financially successful in its second year. During a dress ball on the next-to-last night of the second season, May 20, an estimated seven thousand people were moving about the building, mostly the ballroom, when fire suddenly erupted. The people moved calmly to the sixteen exits and escaped. Thirty injuries and only one death resulted. Alfred S. Hayne, who returned to the building several times to help others escape, became the one casualty. The

2. "Advertisement for Subscribers," *Texas Live Stock Journal,* September 20, 1890, p. 2, February 20, 1892, p. 7.

building crashed to the ground after only eleven minutes, and promoters never determined the cause of the fire. A memorial statue in the center of Lancaster and Main streets honors Hayne.[3]

A business depression that began in Fort Worth in the summer of 1890 prevented the rebuilding of the Spring Palace. It foreshadowed for Fort Worthians the 1893 financial panic that swept the entire country. Uneven supplies of cattle contributed to the depressed situation in Fort Worth, particularly during the spring of 1892. The packing plant seemed at the mercy of the large Chicago packers who "not only control the principal markets of the United States, but also manipulate railroad rates to the detriment of our home institution," according to a writer in the local stock journal. The frequent unavailability of refrigerator cars when needed also created problems.[4]

Stockyards president John R. Hoxie, who had headed the Fort Worth Packing Company since its beginning, retired in April, 1892, citing health reasons. Mike C. Hurley, a prominent citizen and railroad contractor, replaced him. Hurley, a resident of Fort Worth since childhood, had made his money in railroad construction. The next year he would intervene to get the Rock Island Railroad to build to Fort Worth instead of to Dallas, but in 1892 Hurley apparently decided that the packing plant needed more money than local interests could supply. He traveled to Boston to urge a wealthy capitalist to visit, hoping that he would invest. Hurley, therefore, was responsible for the visit of Greenlief W. Simpson and his entourage the last week of October, when the unusually high number of cattle gathered there because of several washouts and the railroad strike convinced Simpson and his lawyer that Fort Worth represented a burgeoning market. Simpson had served as trustee of the Bay State Cattle Company of Boston as early as 1884 and had made frequent trips to Washington to urge legislation favorable to the industry. He had apparently later sold out to an English syndicate at a large profit. Quite possibly he intended to buy the Fort Worth plant, build it

3. Colby D. Hall, *Gay Nineties*, p. 122; Leonard Sanders and Ronnie C. Tyler, *How Fort Worth Became the Texasmost City*, pp. 103–104.

4. "Slaughtering and Refrigerating in Texas," *Texas Live Stock Journal*, February 13, 1892, p. 3; "Market Reports," ibid., August 19, 1892, p. 11.

up, and then resell. The panic of the mid-1890s disrupted any such plans for profit.[5]

The local owners did not really want to sell, but financial necessity forced them to do so. Hoxie held the entire note on the Union Stock Yards for $125,000 plus interest, and when he retired, he required payment. "It is now generally known that the packing company have [sic] lost heavily and that unless a sale can be made the establishment will soon close and suspend operation," stated the local livestock paper.[6] Owners offered both the packing plant and the Union Stock Yards below cost. Local citizens recognized the value to Fort Worth if someone could make a success of the stockyards and packing enterprises. Therefore, when the buyers and sellers of the Fort Worth Packing Company still differed over the price by $100,000, the people of Fort Worth began trying to raise one-half the amount in hopes that that would induce Simpson and his associates to accept the deal. By late December citizens had subscribed $40,000.

In order to conclude the sale of the property, the original stockholders of the stockyards and packing plant eventually surrendered their stock without remuneration to the Farmers and Mechanics National Bank of Fort Worth, which held Hoxie's note. They had little choice. They could only hope that with the plant in successful operation they somehow would make their money back in various ways.[7]

Simpson, in the meantime, attended a meeting of the Cattle Raisers Association of Texas in the spring of 1893. He told the men that many Texas cities had to secure their fresh pork and beef dur-

5. "Market Report," ibid., April 23, 1892, p. 10; "Market Reports Fort Worth," *Texas Live Stock and Farm Journal*, October 28, 1892, p. 11; written transcript of 1915 inverview with Verner S. Wardlaw (1861–1924), "The History of the Packing Plant Industry in Fort Worth" (copy in author's possession), p. 4; copy of a history of the livestock industry in Fort Worth, W. L. Pier Correspondence, Texas Industry folder, Fort Worth Stock Yards Company Collection, North Texas State University Archives, Denton (hereafter cited as FWSY Co. Coll.).

6. Ross, Chapman and Ross to Greenlief W. Simpson, April 28, 1893, Fort Worth Stock Yards Company Records, Gary Havard Personal Collection, Fort Worth. See also "The Packing House Deal," *Texas Live Stock Journal*, December 16, 1892, p. 3, and December 23, 1892, p. 3.

7. Wardlaw interview typescript, p. 4.

ing the summer from Kansas City because of uneven markets in Texas. He implied that a lack of cooperation between producers and their markets had caused the preceding plant to fail. Simpson promised the Texas cattle producers that if they would ship their cattle to the Fort Worth yards instead of to Kansas City, where most had been sending them, he would pay fifty cents a head more than the ruling market in Kansas City. He also promised to start a stable bank at the yards and to get experienced management for the stockyards and to improve them. Simpson asked the cattlemen to sign pledges that they would market all their cattle at Fort Worth until January 1, 1895. Texas cattleman C. C. Slaughter of Dallas, whose ranching empire at its largest stretched over a million acres from northwest of Big Spring to the New Mexico border, rose to speak to the cattlemen. Slaughter moved that the cattlemen sign the pledges Simpson asked for and invite the "Yankee" entrepreneurs to Texas. "We know New England people are thinkers, and they look out for the pennies. If you invite them here, we will have all the money we want. I say ask them to come here, and if we fail, we lose nothing," he said.[8]

Enough cattlemen signed pledges to satisfy Simpson. The Cattle Raisers Association even voted in 1893 to move its headquarters from Jacksboro to Fort Worth, apparently believing Fort Worth was destined to become the outstanding livestock center of the Southwest.[9] In fulfilling one of the promises he had made, Simpson organized the Stock Yards National Bank on March 27, 1893, as its initial capital with $250,000.[10] Simpson and his associates bought both the Union Stock Yards and the Fort Worth Packing Company. When he purchased the Union Stock Yards Company on April 27, 1893, he paid only $133,333.33.

At the same time he was moving ahead locally, Simpson was or-

8. Proceedings of the Seventeenth Annual Convention of the Cattle Raisers Association of Texas, March 14–15, 1893, Fort Worth, pp. 6, 8, 10, Waggoner Library, Texas and Southwestern Cattle Raisers Foundation, Fort Worth.

9. Ibid., p. 8. The organization, begun under a tree in Graham in 1877, changed its name to Texas and Southwestern Cattle Raisers Association in 1921; it is still headquartered in Fort Worth.

10. Board of Directors Meeting, August 8, 1893, *Corporate Record*, I, 36; "New Bank of Fort Worth," *Austin Daily Statesman*, March 28, 1893, in *Research Data*, Fort Worth and Tarrant County, Texas, Federal Writers' Project, II, 441.

ganizing his eastern base of operations. He chartered an entirely new corporation, which he and his advisors called the Fort Worth Stock Yards Company, in West Virginia, where the tax laws for corporations were more favorable than in Texas. Five Chicago men who organized the new company with Simpson subscribed only $500 in capital stock. If the deal had fallen through, they would not have lost much. The charter, issued March 23, 1893, authorized the company to increase the capital to one million dollars and allowed the officers to construct buildings and to lease and operate railroads, electric light and power plants, and waterworks. The six original organizers met April 24 and selected Simpson as president. Two of the original directors then resigned; two Boston men replaced them, and four other new directors joined the company. Among the new names added was Louville V. Niles, a neighbor of Simpson in Boston. Niles became prominent in the company and eventually spent more time in Fort Worth overseeing his interests than the other stockholders. Since the 1860s he had been a leader in the Boston meat business and was president of the Boston Packing and Provision Company.[11]

The first stock certificates for the Fort Worth Stock Yards Company, issued April 29, 1893, listed Boston as the headquarters. The first five hundred shares went to Greenlief W. Simpson.[12] Then the newly organized company purchased both the Union Stock Yards and the packing plant from Simpson in early August for a combined price of $350,066.66.

Several weeks before Simpson concluded his purchase, the packing company closed its doors. Simpson and his partners planned to begin their operations in mid-May. Then they announced a July 1

11. Copy of an agreement by which G. W. Simpson bought the Fort Worth Union Stock Yards April 27, 1893, Union Stock Yards Folder, Havard Coll.; Board of Directors Meeting, April 24, 1893, *Corporate Record*, I, 27–38.

12. Certificate of Incorporation, Fort Worth Stock Yards Company, Financial Records, FWSY Co. Coll.; *Corporate Record*, Fort Worth Stock Yards Company, Fort Worth, I, 1–2. On March 23, 1893, the same five Chicago men also incorporated a packing company, which they called Fort Worth Packing Company, a West Virginia corporation, for $500 capital stock, which they planned to increase to $1 million (Certificate of Incorporation, Fort Worth Packing Company, filed March 23, 1893, Office of Secretary of State, State of West Virginia, copy in author's possession; Certificates of Capital Stock, Fort Worth Stock Yards Company, Havard Coll.).

date, but problems delayed the actual opening until December 4, 1893. Local citizens believed Simpson and his associates to be "thoroughly familiar with all details of operation." A writer in the local stock journal called Simpson a "bright, active, thorough-going young man, who seems to fully understand the work in hand." Simpson said he could buy all hogs offered. He could not buy all cattle, but promised to bring buyers from eastern markets who would be able to purchase them. The local livestock journal predicted that "the success of this enterprise depends mainly on the cooperation of the stock raiser, and nothing which has ever been done in the state would be of such an advantage to the stock growers as the establishment of a permanent home market." Simpson also made contacts with commission firms to come to Fort Worth in 1893.[13]

Simpson and his associates faced such problems as the management mistakes of the previous owners, financial depression, scarcity of hogs in Texas, unjust discrimination in railroad freight rates, opposition of rival concerns, and the public's general lack of confidence in a new enterprise. Many local people feared that Simpson and his friends had only bought the stockyards for speculation. Simpson claimed that he "took Omaha out of a worse position than the Fort Worth plant had ever been in and put her on her feet." To complicate Simpson's problems, rumors circulated that Armour planned to establish a packing plant in Dallas, just thirty miles to the east.[14]

While Simpson continued to operate the packing plant at a loss, the stockyards fared better. A stockyards made its profits from the feed sold while cattle remained in pens and from various other yardage fees, somewhat like a hotel for livestock. Even cattle in transit to other markets had to be taken off railroad cars and fed. Commission houses and traders also paid for use of the pens that the stockyards owned and rented out. In addition, the company owned the central exchange building and leased office space. Even large-scale

13. "A Home Market," *Texas Live Stock and Farm Journal*, March 31, 1893, p. 3; "Home Markets," ibid., June 2, 1893, p. 3; "Personal Mention," ibid., p. 7; and "The Packing Company," ibid., December 15, 1893, p. 8.

14. Proceedings of the Eighteenth Annual Convention, Cattle Raisers Association of Texas, March 13–15, 1894, Fort Worth, p. 58. See also "Fort Worth Live Stock Market," *Texas Live Stock and Farm Journal*, July 27, 1894, p. 1; and "Must Be A Rumor," ibid., June 22, 1894, p. 1.

livestock producers who still preferred to sell to representatives of northern packing houses for the better prices they offered quite frequently used the facilities at the stockyards. In fact, the lunch counter at the Stockyards Hotel began remaining open all night in March, 1894.[15]

Despite all the activity at the new Fort Worth Stock Yards, the directors naturally worried about their ability to make their investment work. Consequently, in the summer of 1894 they brought in an experienced manager for the company, W. E. Skinner, formerly of the Union Stock Yards of South Omaha. Skinner originally came from Hamilton, Ontario, and even while living in Fort Worth made frequent visits back to Canada. Upon his arrival in Fort Worth, Skinner immediately wrote an open letter in the area stock journal urging Texas stockmen to support the Fort Worth market. He assured them that the owners wanted to build up the market, citing the money they had poured into it. A man referred to as Ward became the new head of the packing house.[16]

Summer receipts in 1894 seemed promising; on several occasions the Fort Worth market sold more livestock in one day than Chicago did. Farmers in Texas, however, hesitated to go all out to raise hogs that year because they could not be sure the packing plant would be permanent. They remembered that the previous ones had closed. They feared that no market would exist when their hogs became fat and ready. Had they realized it, Fort Worth already ranked as one of the major Western markets. The others prominent at this time were Chicago, Kansas City, Saint Louis, Omaha, Sioux City, and Saint Joseph.[17]

Simpson sold stock certificates in the Fort Worth Stock Yards Company to Texas cattlemen from various parts of the state in 1894–95, but they usually purchased only token amounts, from one to ten shares. Ike T. Pryor, a rags-to-riches cattleman of Columbus, bought one share. Winfield Scott, who by the 1880s had become one of the largest cattle owners in Texas and who had moved to Fort

15. "Market Report," *Texas Live Stock and Farm Journal,* March 9, 1894, p. 9.
16. "Fort Worth Live Stock Market," ibid., July 27, 1894, p. 1.
17. "Markets," ibid., July 13, 1894, p. 7; "Swine," ibid., January 19, 1894, p. 7; and Proceedings of the Nineteenth Annual Convention, Cattle Raisers Association of Texas, Fort Worth, Texas, March 12–13, 1895.

Worth from Colorado City in 1889, purchased ten shares. So did Burk Burnett, also of Fort Worth, and C. C. Slaughter of Dallas. These shares sold for $100 each. Burnett, whose family had moved to Denton Creek from Missouri when he was ten, bought land near Wichita Falls in the 1870s for 25 cents per acre and kept expanding, leasing Indian lands as well as buying land outright. The oft-told story that Burnett acquired his ranch and wealth overnight in a poker game in which he held a hand of four sixes, is exaggerated. He won some land with that hand and even named his ranch after it, but he built up his holdings with shrewd investments and business connections, and even through his marriage. Burnett's first wife was Margaret Loyd, daughter of Captain M. B. Loyd who started the First National Bank in Fort Worth in the 1870s. Burnett became an investor in the bank and remained a director for over thirty years. Burnett did not invest heavily in the Fort Worth Stock Yards, however.[18] Greenlief Simpson and Louville Niles, both still in Boston, retained most of the shares of stock.

Local residents invested in their new stockyards in other ways. William Hunter, George Beggs, and James D. Farmer incorporated one of the earliest local commission companies for the purpose of buying and selling livestock on the local market. Their company began as the Fort Worth Live Stock Commission Company, organized in 1895.[19]

If Simpson did not own railroad stock, he should have, for he traveled frequently between Boston, Chicago, and Fort Worth. On one of these visits late in 1895 he told the local stock journal that Texas ranked as the largest cattle-feeding state in the nation and in 1894 had been fourth in hog production. He estimated that during the current year Texas would rank second in hogs. Simpson believed Texas could be first in hogs in less than three years and even pre-

18. Certificates of Capital Stock, Fort Worth Stock Yards Company, Havard Collection. See also T. J. Powell, *Samuel Burk Burnett: A Sketch*, pp. 5–7; C. L. Douglas, *Cattle Kings of Texas*, pp. 351, 353, 357; and *History of the Cattlemen of Texas*, p. 79.

19. William Hunter McLean to Tom B. Saunders, February 7, 1974, Tom B. Saunders, Jr., Collection, Texas Christian University Special Collections, Fort Worth.

dicted that Texas would become a "second Chicago in the packing and provision business."[20]

Simpson's glowing pronouncements constituted a pep talk to encourage more business and also to introduce a new packing concern to operate the old Fort Worth Packing Company. At an October 30 board of directors meeting, held as usual in Chicago, Simpson and the other directors drafted a contract between the Fort Worth Stock Yards Company and a new company to be named the Chicago and Fort Worth Packing Company. William J. Dee, a vice-president of the Chicago Packing and Provision Company, jobbers of packing-house products, agreed to organize the new packing concern on or before January 1, 1896.[21]

The Chicago firm agreed to take over Simpson and Niles's plant and operate it and the stockyards for five years. At the end of that time the Chicago company would receive the packing plant and Simpson and Niles the stockyards. Joseph B. Googins, son of one of the vice-presidents of the parent Chicago company, became head buyer for the new Chicago and Fort Worth Packing Company. Young Googins, only twenty-one and a native Chicagoan, had come to Texas the previous year for his health and had worked on a ranch in Tom Green County. Five years later he would become associated with Swift in Chicago as a cattle buyer and then later come to Fort Worth to oversee Swift's interests for two decades.[22]

Dee, head of the new Fort Worth branch, wasted no time. By mid-November he sent out news releases that the new packing company would employ three hundred people at $12 per week, making a payroll of $3,600 per week or $200,000 per year for the city. The plant would need one thousand cattle a week and one thousand hogs per day, Dee announced. He explained that the packing plant could handle twenty thousand hogs a week if it received them, so farmers need never fear not having a market.

"North Fort Worth expects to be a city of 5,000 population within

20. "Texas Second in Hogs," *Texas Stock and Farm Journal,* November 8, 1895, p. 3.

21. Board of Directors Meeting, October 30, 1895, *Corporate Record,* I, 66, 74.

22. B. B. Paddock, ed., *Fort Worth and the Texas Northwest* IV, 586; and "History of the livestock industry in Fort Worth," FWSY Co. Coll., p. 5.

the next five years," stated a spokesman. He even accurately predicted that "in a few years Fort Worth will be the third largest livestock market in the United States." Unfortunately, Dee's company would not be the one to make those predictions come true. The dark days of the 1890s decade were not over for Fort Worth yet. Dee put all his energy into the effort, however. He supervised construction of four-story rock buildings on twelve acres near the stockyards and railroad, hiring two hundred people by mid-February, 1896.[23]

At a June, 1896, board of directors meeting in Boston, Simpson, still president of the Fort Worth Stock Yards Company, asked directors for authority to build a belt railroad consisting of tracks, engines, and switching facilities to connect with the Texas and Pacific and the Missouri-Kansas-Texas railways at a price not to exceed $15,000. Directors also gave Simpson permission to spend $85 per week to publish a semi-weekly newspaper at the stockyards. Soon the first number of the *Fort Worth Live Stock Reporter* appeared July 16, 1896, with the general manager of the company, W. E. Skinner, as ex-officio general manager of the newspaper. Simpson became president, and Skinner became general manager of the newly constructed railway.[24]

The year 1896 became a year of new beginnings, for in addition to the belt railway and the newspaper, the Fort Worth Stock Yards Company began a fat stock show, which continues to the present day as the Southwestern Exposition and Livestock Show and Rodeo.

The first Fort Worth stock show owed its existence to Charles C. French, who had been a public relations agent for the Fort Worth Stock Yards Company almost from its beginning. Early in 1896, as French made his usual contacts with livestock producers, he discussed the depressing cattle situation with Charles McFarland of Weatherford. McFarland suggested a fat stock show to encourage

23. *Texas Stock and Farm Journal*, November 15, 1895, p. 4; and "The Fort Worth Packing House," ibid., February 14, 1896, p. 2.

24. Board of Directors Meeting, June 9, 1896, *Corporate Record*, I, 85; copy of agreement between St. Louis Southwestern Railway Company of Texas and the Fort Worth Stock Yards Belt Railway Company, September 25, 1896, Havard Coll.; "Souvenir of the Past," *Fort Worth Daily Live Stock Reporter*, August 27, 1903, p. 1; "Skinner and the Exchange," *Texas Stock and Farm Journal*, October 9, 1896, p. 4; and "Fort Worth Market," *Texas Stock and Farm Journal*, July 10, 1896, p. 2.

business. French, who related the conversation later, confessed that the idea did not at first appeal to him because the yards had no fat stock to exhibit. Few cattle were on feed at the time. McFarland overcame French's objections by promising to bring in a couple of loads out of his herd and to persuade others to do the same. The two agreed they would do it if funds could be raised for premiums such as hats, spurs, bridles, boots, and windmills.

Both French and McFarland met with Skinner, manager of the stockyards, who soon enthusiastically took the matter up with the owners. They liked the idea. Skinner and French made arrangements for a one-day show in March to coincide with the Cattle Raisers convention, which was meeting in Fort Worth. Workers constructed a small grandstand near a big pecan grove east of North Main Street and west of the railroads.[25]

Actually, few exhibitors contributed stock for the first show. Mc-Farland, as he had promised, brought some of his cattle, as did Burk Burnett, W. S. Ikard, I. J. Kimberlin, J. W. Burgess, E. M. Daggett, James Day, J. F. Hovencamp, John Maloney, and B. C. Rhone. These Texans preferred cattle and did not exhibit hogs or sheep at this first show. The night before the show a sleet storm struck. The cattle, tied under the trees along Marine Creek, looked "a pitiable sight" when found covered with ice the next morning. As is typical in Texas, however, by noon the sun had melted the ice, so the appearance of the cattle and the spirits of the promoters both improved.[26]

Actually, the Fort Worth Stock Yards Company held two stock shows in 1896. Stockyards officials knew that the National Live Stock Exchange planned to hold its eighth annual convention in Fort Worth October 12–13, expected to have the highest attendance ever. That would be a good time to host a fat stock show "in order that those composing this important organization may have some idea of what

25. C. C. French, "The History of a Great Fort Worth Institution, The Southwestern Exposition and Fat Stock Show," C. C. French Manuscripts, as cited in *Research Data*, LXII, 24582.

26. "The Cattlemen's Convention," *Fort Worth Gazette*, March 10, 1896, p. 4; "Fifty Years of Rodeo in Fort Worth," 1946 program, bound copies of rodeo programs at Amon Carter Museum of Western Art Library, Fort Worth, II, 17; C. C. French, "Blizzard Hit First Stock Show; Exhibit Is Weatherford Man's Idea," *Fort Worth Star Telegram and Sunday Record*, March 11, 1928, Live Stock Section, part 1, p. 7.

Texas can do in the way of furnishing what there is most demand for in livestock markets," said a local stock journal. This time promoters planned to offer premiums for the best carloads and wagon lots of cattle, steers, hogs, and sheep. Local cattlemen and the Fort Worth Stock Yards Company invited the Cattle Raisers Association of Texas, the Texas Live Stock Association, the Texas Swine Breeders Association, livestock associations from North Dakota, South Dakota, Montana, Wyoming, Arizona, and two associations from New Mexico. The convention gave the local market the opportunity to demonstrate to the thousands of visitors the progress Texas had made in the improvement of breeds. They wanted to show outsiders that they were not still "raising the long horn and the razor back of former days."[27]

Manager Skinner reported to the members of the National Live Stock Exchange that he had handled ninety-seven thousand hogs already that year, while three years earlier only five thousand hogs suitable for slaughter could be found in the area around Fort Worth. The exchange elected Skinner as one of its seven vice-presidents for the coming year and placed two Fort Worth men, J. D. Farmer and A. S. Reed, on the executive committee.[28]

In later years Mrs. Lillie Burgess Hovencamp recalled having driven around town in a buggy with her father to collect merchandise donations for livestock prizes for some of these early fat stock shows. She said a parade opened the show, and businessmen entered floats. Rancher Burk Burnett furnished steers for a free barbecue.[29]

What made a livestock show successful for producers, besides having it during the National Live Stock Exchange convention, was the opportunity to buy good breeding stock. At either the first or second show (accounts differ), I. J. Kimberlin made a deal with Robert Kleberg of the King Ranch in South Texas to sell Kleberg all his bull calves for the next five years at fifty dollars a head. This probably represented the first-ever sale of "futures" in bulls in Texas.[30]

27. "Fat Stock Show," *Texas Stock and Farm Journal*, June 12, 1896, p. 4; "The Coming Fat Stock Show," ibid., July 24, 1896, p. 1.
28. *Proceedings of the National Live Stock Exchange at Fort Worth, Texas, October, 1896*, pp. 3, 34.
29. "Fifty Years of Rodeo in Fort Worth," 1946 Program, II, 19.
30. "Background of Stock Show," *Fort Worth* 29 (January, 1954): 15, says Kle-

Prominent citizens met at the Worth Hotel in mid-June, 1897, to consider whether to hold a fat stock show that year and if so to determine the most suitable time. They decided that a March date to coincide with the convention of the Cattle Raisers Association of Texas the following spring would be the most appropriate. They apparently sponsored no show in 1897, and held the second annual one (thus, actually the third show) March 8–10, 1898, simultaneously with the convention.[31]

By 1897 construction workers finished the Fort Worth Stock Yards Belt Railway Company; the stockyards company ran it. The livestock market that year continued strong on anything fat, and "the demand far exceeds the supply," hinted the stock journal.[32]

That year a feud developed between the two rival livestock newspapers published in the city, both of which promoted the local market. The Cattle Raisers Association had published *The Texas Stock and Farm Journal* since 1880. The Fort Worth Stock Yards Company authorized and subsidized the *Live Stock Reporter* beginning in 1896. The *Journal* editor accused the *Reporter* editor of exaggerating the number of livestock handled by the Fort Worth market. The *Reporter* countercharged that such *Journal* articles would hurt the local market. The *Journal* retaliated that it had supported the local market for years but that the "habitual misrepresentation and exaggeration of the management" of the Fort Worth Stock Yards would make Fort Worth a "by-word and a laughingstock in the eyes of Texas cattlemen."[33]

Part of the information Simpson and Skinner released to the press obviously was hoopla calculated to obtain more business, which would benefit both the owners of the local yards and, in the long run, the cattle producers. Texas farmers and cattlemen possessed

---

berg made the deal at the first show. C. C. French in "The History of a Great Fort Worth Institution," p. 24586, says the second show.

31. "Fat Stock Show," *Texas Stock and Farm Journal*, June 23, 1897, p. 8; "Cattle Raisers Association," ibid., March 2, 1898, p. 24.

32. Memo from W. E. Skinner to W. O. Johnson, February 11, 1897, Fort Worth Stock Yards Company Records, Havard Coll.; "Fort Worth Market," *Texas Stock and Farm Journal*, February 24, 1897, p. 8.

33. "The Fort Worth Stock Yards Management," *Texas Stock and Farm Journal*, January 27, 1897, p. 4. No copies of the *Live Stock Reporter* from 1896–1903 exist. The feud can be detected in the pages of the *Journal*.

the raw material to help create a better market, and the *Reporter* used overly optimistic reports to persuade them to support it more fully.

Stockyards profits were increasing, in fact, as evidenced by the owners' inserting into the minutes of their special stockholders meeting May 1, 1897, a motion that "in order that rival companies may not know how successful the Company has been . . . [it is] ordered that the same be not spread upon the minutes." Stockholders who wanted to see figures, which presumably were profits, could view them at the Boston office where the accounts would be on file.[34]

When Skinner took a job in Chicago, William N. Babcock of Omaha, Nebraska, became the new manager of the Fort Worth Stock Yards Company in October, 1897, at a salary of $6,000 per year. His contract also called for him to get 4 percent of the net annual earnings of the company up to $150,000 per year and 3 percent of company earnings from $150,000 to $250,000. Either somebody was being optimistic, or current profits justified the generous terms.[35]

The Stock Yards Company constantly sought to promote its market and in 1897 found a unique way. Recognition came to the company concerning its cooperation with the federal government in tick eradication. Earlier, farmers of Kansas, Missouri, and other states had complained that Texas longhorns driven up the trails brought a disease to their domestic cattle, causing them to sicken and die. Although many ideas existed about what caused this Texas fever, no one actually knew for sure in the early days. When the British and later the Germans threatened to cut off American livestock shipments because of diseased animals, the federal government finally decided to take some steps for inspecting and quarantining cattle. The Bureau of Animal Industry created in 1884 soon went to work to discover the cause of Texas fever. Dr. Theobald Smith and Dr. Fred L. Kilborne, bureau scientists, proved conclusively in 1889 and 1890 that particular cattle ticks caused it.[36]

Dr. Victor A. Norgaard, who later became chief of the Pathologi-

34. Stockholders Meeting, May 1, 1897, *Corporate Record*, I, 89.
35. Board of Directors Meeting, October 11, 1897, ibid., I, 90–91.
36. T. R. Havins, "Texas Fever," *Southwestern Historical Quarterly* 52 (July, 1948): 153–54; also U.S. Congress, House, *Cattle Tick Fever*, H. Doc. 527, 77th Cong., 2d sess., reprinted in *1942 Yearbook of Agriculture*, U.S. Dept. of Agriculture,

cal Division of the Bureau of Animal Industry, began conducting dipping experiments in Texas. Robert J. Kleberg, manager of the Santa Gertrudis (King) Ranch in Nueces County, designed and built the first vat used by the bureau in its dip investigations. He had been using it to dip for mange and itch. Kleberg offered his vat to the bureau early in 1895, together with the infested cattle on the ranch. During the next five years, twenty-five thousand cattle passed through this vat in testing the tick-destroying properties of various disinfecting preparations. The best results during the first year came from the use of two coal-tar preparations.

Ever with an eye to helping business and calling attention to their market, the Fort Worth Stock Yards Company, early in the summer of 1897, offered to build vats and furnish the cattle for experimental purposes if the bureau would do their dipping at Fort Worth. Bureau officials agreed, so the Fort Worth sponsors built a battery of dipping vats on the property that later would become the site of the Swift and Company packing plant.[37]

The government transferred the experiments from the South Texas ranch to the Fort Worth yards, in August, 1897, and began testing some so-called paraffin lubricating oils. The results obtained with these oils from the first proved so satisfactory that in September officials called a meeting at Fort Worth to demonstrate dipping with this substance. Delegates attended from Illinois, Missouri, Nebraska, Kansas, Colorado, Texas, and the Indian Territory.

Rancher Kleberg made a motion at the March, 1898, Cattle Raisers Association convention to thank the Fort Worth Stock Yards Company "for providing and arranging for the Fat Stock Show, and especially for the dipping of cattle. They have gone to great expense; not less than $5,000 or $6,000 have been expended there in order to make these experiments."[38]

Officials resumed the experiments with paraffin oil at the King Ranch on April 1, 1898, where they found more tick-infested cattle available. That June government officials experimented again at Fort

---

p. 574; also Fred Wilbur Powell, *The Bureau of Animal Industry: Its History, Activities, and Organization,* p. 4.

37. Havins, "Texas Fever," p. 161.

38. Proceedings of the Twenty-second Annual Convention of the Cattle Raisers Association of Texas March 8–9, 1898, at Fort Worth.

Worth, using "extra dynamo oil." After a few trials they added sulphur to this oil. The results seemed so promising that officials decided to test it on quite a large number of cattle and then ship them north immediately after dipping. Accordingly, they dipped 311 cattle on July 22 and shipped them to Rockford, Illinois, the following day. The hot weather caused the cattle to suffer severely in transit. The oil killed the ticks, but eight cattle died en route, and eight "downers" (diseased cattle that would lie down and refuse to get up) were left behind at unloading stations.

Scientists tried other dips containing carbolic acid, tobacco extract, sodium sulphate, glycerine, or a combination of lime and sulfur. Finally crude petroleum oil from Beaumont gave better results than any other crude oil or dip, and cattlemen used it almost exclusively from 1903 to 1911 as a spray, a smear, and a dip for freeing cattle of ticks.[39]

The state of Texas made its own attempts to help solve the cattle tick problem, as the state legislature, on April 20, 1893, created the Texas Livestock Sanitary Commission. The Fort Worth Stock Yards became the state headquarters for the commission almost from the beginning. The legislature gave the commission so little power, however, that it accomplished little until 1917, when the legislature conferred upon the commission the authority to enforce compulsory dipping of cattle. After that, when many counties neglected or refused to provide for the dipping of infested cattle, the commission forced the issue by clamping a state quarantine on the counties until they dipped all cattle twice.[40]

Conservative Texas cattlemen were slow to accept the scientific results of the dipping tests. They formed anti-dipping groups and even blew up dipping vats in both Texas and the Indian Territory. Texas ranchers, understandably, worried more about how many cattle died after being dipped than how fast the ticks disappeared. A

39. U. G. Houck, *The Bureau of Animal Industry of the United States Department of Agriculture: Its Establishment, Achievement and Current Activities,* pp. 324–26.

40. T. R. Havins, "Livestock and Texas Law," *Yearbook of the West Texas Historical Association* 36 (1960): 31–32. See also Mary Whatley Clarke, *A Century of Cow Business: A History of the Texas and Southwestern Cattle Raisers Association,* p. 64.

man from Quanah reported that he dipped 321 head of cattle at the Fort Worth Stock Yards on October 28, 1898. Six died, 10 heifers lost their calves, and the rest of the cattle became stiff and sore. The owner feared that one norther would kill them. All the letters quoted by the *Texas Live Stock Journal* in the same issue as the Quanah man's account opposed the dipping.[41]

Although the Fort Worth Stock Yards Company gained national attention for its participation in the dipping experiments, business still faced problems. The Chicago and Fort Worth Packing Company enjoyed good business only until 1897, when a drought depleted the hog supply. The plant shut down in 1898, and the owners became so discouraged that they turned the entire packing operation and yards back to Simpson and Niles. They should have held out a little longer, for the economic situation in Fort Worth soon began to improve after being depressed nearly all of the decade. Excitement over the Spanish-American War spurred some activity.[42] Competition from the two packing houses and the stockyards in Dallas did not help, however. In an attempt to encourage business, the board of the Fort Worth Stock Yards Company approved a motion in March, 1899, to donate four acres of land, for only one dollar in compensation, to persons who planned to construct a complete oil mill, providing they would build it within the year.[43]

Simpson and Niles reopened their plant in April, 1899. L. V. Niles, one of the major stockholders in the Fort Worth Stock Yards Company, organized and operated it as the Fort Worth Packing and Provision Company. He had practical business experience and fared reasonably well, continuing operations until 1901. Men of the city became better acquainted with Niles than with the other stockholders because he commuted frequently between Fort Worth and Boston. He spent about six months out of each year from 1899 through 1901 in Fort Worth, living at the Stockyards Hotel. Many credit Niles with bringing meat packers Armour and Swift to Fort Worth in 1902. Niles, who with his brothers had owned the Boston

41. "Disastrous Effects of Dipping," *Texas Stock and Farm Journal*, December 14, 1898, p. 4.

42. "History of livestock industry in Fort Worth," FWSY Co. Coll.

43. Board of Directors Meeting, March 24, 1899, *Corporate Record*, I, 103.

Packing and Provision Company, was sixty when he came to Fort Worth for his first six-month stint in 1899.[44]

His partner Greenlief Simpson stayed busy, too. He attended the annual conventions of the Cattle Raisers Association of Texas every year from the time he created the Fort Worth Stock Yards Company in 1893 until the end of the decade. "Gentlemen, you have a market," Simpson told the cattlemen. "You can make it just as big as you want to, and every man that has sold cattle, like Mr. [Samuel Burk] Burnett, will tell you that it is best to sell them as near home as you can," Simpson advised.[45]

A setback for Simpson and Niles occurred when a stable and wagon sheds at the stockyards burned in November, 1899, but insurance covered the losses. With so much hay and other feed available for the animals they serviced, fires would remain a continuing threat at the Fort Worth market.[46]

Much of what happened to stockyards and packing in Fort Worth depended on decisions by the absentee owners of the Fort Worth Stock Yards Company, who held their monthly directors meetings, when they could get a quorum, in either Boston or Chicago. But developments were not entirely in their hands; city fathers of Fort Worth always remained willing to promote their market, for that promoted Fort Worth, too. In March, 1900, for example, these local citizens and businessmen held two conferences with an eastern meat-packing expert named Jacob Dold. The Dold interests wanted to build a million-dollar packing plant but wanted Fort Worthians to take $250,000 in stock. One prominent cattleman reportedly offered to take $25,000 if three others would do likewise. The deal fell through, however.[47]

By the turn of the century, meat packing in Fort Worth had not

44. Board of Directors Meeting, July 1, 1899, ibid., I, 125; Wardlaw interview transcript, p. 5; W. L. Pier to Ross Brown, December 26, 1955, W. L. Pier Correspondence, General Correspondence, FWSY Co. Coll.

45. Proceedings of the Twenty-first Annual Convention of the Cattle Raisers Association of Texas, March 9–10, 1897, in San Antonio, p. 71. See also Proceedings, 1893–99, at Waggoner Library, Texas and Southwestern Cattle Raisers Association Headquarters, Fort Worth.

46. Board of Directors Meeting, November 27, 1899, *Corporate Record*, I, 126.

47. "Centers: Fort Worth," *Texas Stock and Farm Journal*, March 21, 1900, p. 6.

yet achieved stability, but the relative success of the stockyards, the railroad shipping facilities, and other businesses made Fort Worth a cattle center of importance, nonetheless. Wealthy cattlemen who owned ranches as far away as one hundred miles to the west called Fort Worth home and built mansions on Samuels and Grand avenues and elsewhere in the city. In 1900 they hosted the meetings of the National Live Stock Association, which had originated two years earlier.[48]

Then, on October 24, 1901, numerous cattlemen joined together with officials of the Fort Worth Stock Yards Company and commission firms to incorporate the Fort Worth Livestock Exchange, to be headquartered in the exchange building of the stockyards company. The exchange, a common feature of stockyards, existed as sort of an exclusive club for promoting the local livestock industry. It provided some organization and protection for all concerned, for members could enforce certain rules of procedure and discipline wrong-doers.

Fort Worth had finally emerged as a promising livestock center, just as early citizens had wanted. But not until packing plants could be established near the stockyards that would convince Texas cattlemen that a continuing market existed comparable to Chicago and Saint Louis would the ambitions of the community leaders be completely fulfilled. Not until then would Fort Worth really rank among the nation's major livestock markets. Such success awaited the arrival of two of the Big Four Chicago meat packers early in the twentieth century.

48. C. C. Cummings, "Fort Worth, the Cattle Center of Texas," *Bohemian* 2 (December–January, 1900–1901): 90.

Reorganization:
Swift and Armour Arrive
1901–1903

OLD-TIME TRAIL DRIVER George W. Saunders of San Antonio knew most of the older cattlemen of Texas and they knew him, for they often saw each other at cattlemen's conventions. Saunders remained a smart old cowman. When trail driving ended, he opened a commission firm in 1886 to handle the stock of his friends when they wanted to sell. Cattle business changed, so he changed with it. When he learned that the two biggest meat packers of the nation had negotiated a deal to open large modern packing plants in Fort Worth, he called in his son-in-law William E. Jary and his nephew Tom B. Saunders, Jr.

"Boys, Fort Worth is the coming market. We've got to have a George W. Saunders Commission Company there," he told them.

The two young men, both around thirty, hurried up to Fort Worth to get the company going. Before the year was out they moved their young families to Fort Worth. George W. Saunders knew what a lot of people knew: the arrival of the packers in Fort Worth meant a booming cattle business. He wanted in on it.[1]

On any list of red-letter dates in the history of Fort Worth, the year the packers came, 1902, stands out as one of the most prominent turning points ever. With their backing, Fort Worth finally would become a stable and wealthy livestock center, the goal for

1. Interview with William E. Jary, Jr., July 12, 1983.

which her business leaders had been struggling for a quarter-century.

Fort Worth residents certainly knew about all the construction going on north of the Trinity River once the packers came. They relished the new jobs it created, but they became distracted by other events happening in Fort Worth that year. Old Dan Waggoner died in September and was buried in North Side's Oakwood Cemetery. After an around-the-world tour, Waggoner's granddaughter Electra got married. Electra's daddy, W. T. (Tom), built her a Fort Worth mansion on Pennsylvania Avenue called Thistle Hill as a wedding present so she would stay in Texas and not go off to the Philadelphia home of her new bridegroom, Albert B. Wharton. Tom Waggoner's ploy worked, and Electra stayed in Fort Worth.

Just about everything else worked for Fort Worth in 1902 as well. To see why, one must examine just how big the two Big Four meat packers, Armour and Swift, really had become by the time they built plants in Fort Worth. The two original Chicago meat entrepreneurs, Armour and Swift were also the largest two of the nation's Big Four packers, which many called a meat-packing trust. The other two in 1902 were Morris and Cudahy.

In defending his business against charges of monopoly, J. Ogden Armour, son of Philip Armour who founded the company, explained that before his father and others developed the packing business in Chicago, only a local market for beef cattle existed in any part of the country. "As invariably happens in our country, when an imperative demand arises for new ways of doing things, somebody steps forward promptly and points out the necessary effective means by which to do them." In other words, the packers provided a market for western beef cattle where no market had existed previously. Armour claimed that the number of beef cattle marketed at the four principal centers increased from 1880 to 1900 by 500 percent.[2]

Armour and Company in 1875 handled no beef or mutton at all, only pork, while Gustavus Swift gained the head start in beef and remained the largest slaughterer throughout the nineteenth century. Near the close of the 1880s Swift began building branch plants in the West and Southwest nearer the source of supply than Chicago.

2. J. Ogden Armour, *The Packers, the Private Car Lines and the People*, pp. 291, 304, 321.

He reasoned that he could save as much money by slaughtering them near their points of origin as he saved when he first dressed beef at Chicago instead of in the East where as a young man he had started as a fledgling butcher.[3]

Thus Armour and Swift, as well as others, gained prominence in the last two decades of the nineteenth century in the slaughter-house industry in Chicago. Some called them the "overlords of beef" as they bought out the smaller packing concerns to eliminate competition. Critics accused the four principal packers of arriving at a "gentlemen's agreement" that also ended all competition among themselves.[4] By 1886 ranchers were talking of a packers' monopoly in Chicago, which could set livestock prices pretty much as it pleased, and they mentioned Philip D. Armour specifically. Both large and small producers soon called for federal supervision of railroad rates, meat packing, and stockyards. Even in Fort Worth local stockmen accused "combinations at the different livestock markets" of "dictating" to cattlemen what they should receive for cattle. They believed that some cattle raisers had been ruined and driven out of the business by this manipulation of the market. Supply and demand did not appear to regulate prices because even when the cattle supply declined beef prices dropped.[5]

The local livestock journal published by the Cattle Raisers Association sided with the cattlemen upon most occasions, but not always. The editor told livestock raisers that men who ship "none but thick fat cattle" do not complain about the Big Four. Only those who shipped scalawags lost out, and they looked for somebody else to blame. "Ship none but good fat stock and you will soon be prosperous, and no longer abuse your benefactors and best friends."[6] Butchers, on the other hand, charged the Big Four with illegal combinations to reduce not only the profits of cattle raisers, but also the profits of retail butchers. The butchers charged that the beef

3. Louis F. Swift with Arthur Van Vlissingen, Jr., *Yankee of the Yards: The Biography of Gustavus Franklin Swift*, pp. 131, 204–205.

4. Matthew Josephson, *The Robber Barons*, pp. 285, 324.

5. Lewis Atherton, *The Cattle Kings*, pp. 118–19; "Refrigeration in Texas," *Fort Worth Daily Gazette*, November 5, 1890.

6. "The Big Four," *Texas Live Stock Journal*, June 13, 1891.

trust's motto was, "Keep the price low to producers but high to consumers."[7]

A public outcry continued. Therefore, in 1888 the U.S. Senate appointed a committee headed by Senator George G. Vest of Missouri to investigate the meat-packing industry, particularly the four largest dealers, for indications of collusion. When the committee met in Chicago early in its investigation, all the Big Four meat packers and their leading subordinates ignored the subpoenas to testify. Later when Philip D. Armour finally appeared, he blamed the decline in prices on overproduction and overmarketing, as well as a quarantine that frightened foreign countries into placing embargoes on American beef and thus limited the export trade.[8]

The Supreme Court in 1898 ruled in favor of the meat packers, but in 1903 the court sustained an injunction charging that the largest meat packers constituted a monopoly. By that time a company named Schwarzchild and Sulzberger had become large enough to be considered a part of the meat trust, making it the Big Five. Just before the injunction was served Swift, Armour, and Morris had incorporated the National Packing Company, with some recently purchased interests (Hammond) as a nucleus. In an attempt at merger, they transferred the ownership of firms they had bought or contracted to buy to this company. Consolidation appeared to be the pattern then, for United States Steel had just emerged in 1901 as the first billion-dollar corporation. Thus the packers believed they could succeed, but a public outcry arose, and a court order later dissolved the company.[9]

A contemporary muckraking book accused the beef trust of controling or influencing the price of "one-half the food consumed by the nation." The author claimed that the trust ignored the 1903 court order enjoining them from acting as a monopoly. He argued that a

7. James Cox, ed., *Historical and Biographical Record of the Cattle Industry and the Cattlemen of Texas and Adjacent Territory*, pp. 727–28.

8. Chester McArthur Destler, "The Opposition of American Businessmen to Social Control during the 'Gilded Age,'" *Mississippi Valley Historical Review* 39 (May, 1953): 644; U.S. Congress, Senate, *Transportation and Sale of Meat Products*, S. Rep. 829, 51st Cong., 1st sess., 1890, pp. 5, 414.

9. *Hopkins* v. *U.S.*, 171 U.S. 578 (1898), and *Swift* v. *U.S.*, 196 U.S. 375 (1905); Swift, *Yankee of the Yards*, p. 209.

producer who got a bid so low for his cattle he could make no profit and who therefore refused to sell would, when he shipped to another market, receive exactly the same bid at the second market as he had at the first. From this he concluded collusion must exist. Texas cattleman C. C. Slaughter testified before the Vest committee that this very sequence had happened to him numerous times. He would refuse a bid for his cattle in Kansas City because the price was too low and take them on to Chicago in hopes of a better price; then after bearing the expense of railroad rates to Chicago, he would receive the same low bid he had received earlier. It appeared someone had wired ahead. Slaughter said no one would look at the cattle or make an offer except agents of the company that had made the offer at the earlier market.[10]

Despite some local complaints against the meat trust, in the spring of 1901 Simpson and Niles began negotiations to bring one or two meat packers to Fort Worth to establish plants. Armour seemed most interested. Texans soon learned that Swift and Armour would come to Texas only if cities subsidized construction of the plants, just as Fort Worth had done for the railroads. By mid-June citizens had raised $50,000 for Armour, and cattlemen planned to raise another $50,000 to attract Swift. Armour and Swift also requested that the Fort Worth Livestock Commission Company ship them a load of hogs each day for a certain length of time so that they might test Texas hogs.[11]

J. Ogden Armour testified many years later that his company had agreed to come to Fort Worth first and Swift had been intending to go to Dallas. Armour offered Swift 50 percent of the business to come to Fort Worth, for that would save Armour from having to build a plant in Dallas, too. Part of the deal included the agreement that if Swift got in on the market at Fort Worth, Armour could get a permit in Saint Louis, where Swift had held exclusive rights.[12]

10. Charles Edward Russell, *The Greatest Trust in the World*, pp. 4, 6, 58, 103. See also Senate, *Transportation and Sale of Meat Products*, pp. 92–93.

11. Oliver Knight, *Fort Worth: Outpost on the Trinity* (Norman: University of Oklahoma Press, 1953), p. 173; "For Big Packery," *Texas Stock Journal*, June 12, 1901, p. 1; transcript of 1915 interview with Verner S. Wardlaw (1861–1924), "The History of the Packing Plant Industry in Fort Worth" (copy in author's possession), p. 5.

12. U.S. Congress, Senate, Committee on Agriculture and Forestry, *Hearings*

Armour and Swift both seemed eager to come, because Texas, New Mexico Territory, and Indian Territory together produced one-fifth of all cattle in the United States. It cost from three to five dollars to transport a beef steer from the Texas ranges to Chicago, Kansas City, or Saint Louis, so it would pay packers to relocate near the raw material.[13]

The Board of Directors of the Fort Worth Stock Yards Company met in Chicago on August 9, 1901, to approve contract offers to both Armour and Company and Swift and Company. In identical contracts, the Fort Worth Stock Yards Company agreed to increase its capital stock from one million to two million dollars and to take over the Fort Worth Packing Company and the entire capital stock and other belongings and assets of the Belt Railroad.[14]

When directors increased the capital stock of the company, they divided it with $680,000 to the stockholders of the original Fort Worth Stock Yards Company (primarily Simpson and Niles), $660,000 to Armour and Company, and $660,000 to Swift. The Fort Worth Stock Yards Company promised to organize a bank, a townsite company, and any other businesses "as are usual at stockyards" to be owned one-third by present stockholders, one-third by Swift, and one-third by Armour. All proceeds of such businesses would go into the treasury of the stockyards company to pay off bonded indebtedness first.[15]

In their visit to Fort Worth in September, 1901, representatives of Armour and Swift encouraged the local citizens' committee to get busy in raising the additional $50,000 subscription from cattlemen and others. With $15,000 remaining to be subscribed, the committee called a meeting of citizens on October 7, 1901, in the

---

on *Government Control of Meat Packing Industry on S. 5305,* 65th Cong., 3d sess., 1919, p. 664; G. O. Virtue, "The Meat Packing Investigation," *Quarterly Journal of Economics* 34 (August, 1920): 671; "History of the Livestock Industry in Fort Worth," W. L. Pier Correspondence, Fort Worth Stock Yards Company Collection, North Texas State University Archives, Denton (FWSY Co. Coll.).

13. "The Great Packeries and Their Benefit to Fort Worth, to Texas and the Southwest," *Bohemian* 4 (1902): 75.

14. Board of Directors Meeting, August 9, 1901, *Corporate Record,* Fort Worth Stock Yards Company, Fort Worth, I, 137–39.

15. Ibid., p. 140; Certificates of Stock 1–250, Fort Worth Stock Yards Company Records, Havard Coll.

city hall auditorium. That evening they raised $15,778. Pandemonium reigned as the audience cheered, threw hats in the air, waved handkerchiefs, and shook hands. Committee members sent telegrams to Swift and Armour. The next morning the local newspaper proclaimed: "Fort Worth started on her road to greatness last night."[16]

Swift and Company (and no doubt Armour, too) sent their lawyers to Fort Worth in October, 1901, to examine numerous papers, including the deeds of the North Fort Worth Land Company, owned by the Fort Worth Stock Yards Company, before signing the agreement. According to the document finally signed in January, 1902, the Fort Worth Stock Yards Company promised to give Swift a deed to 21.8 acres, 6,600 shares of stock worth $660,000, and $300,000 in bonds, in return for Swift's pledge that all livestock slaughtered at their packing plant would "pass through the stock yards of said first party" and that Swift would "pay the customary yardage and other charges thereon." The stockyards would not charge Swift any higher yardage rates than they charged anyone else.[17]

The company made a similar agreement with Armour. Such arrangements had become common throughout the nation among the big packers and stockyards. The stockyards in Oklahoma City had made a comparable agreement, but with packers Morris and Sulzberger. Morris and Swift had signed similar contracts in Saint Louis, and Swift actually owned nearly all of the Saint Joseph stockyards.[18]

In the spring of 1902, J. Ogden Armour became president of the reorganized Fort Worth Stock Yards Company; Edward Swift, vice-president; and Greenlief W. Simpson, second vice-president. Andrew Nimmo served as secretary-treasurer, and W. O. Johnson, Simpson's lawyer since at least 1893, became assistant secretary. Directors chose

16. "Packers at Fort Worth," *Texas Stock Journal,* October 8, 1901, p. 1; "The Bonus Raised," ibid., October 8, 1901, p. 1; "Both Packing Houses Now Assured," *Fort Worth Register,* October 8, 1901.

17. "Agreement," North Fort Worth Land Company Folder, Havard Coll. See also contract between Fort Worth Stock Yards Company and Swift and Company, January 25, 1902 (copy), unmarked folder, Havard Coll.

18. Agreement between Fort Worth Packing and Provision Company and Armour and Company and Swift and Company, January 28, 1902 (copy), Fort Worth Packing and Provision Co. folder, Havard Coll.; "History of Livestock Industry in Fort Worth," Pier Correspondence, FWSY Co. Coll.; "Why the Packers Own Stockyards," *Cattleman* 6 (November 1919): 21.

W. B. King as general manager of the Fort Worth Stock Yards Company as of February 15, 1902, at a monthly salary of $375, or $4500 a year. The new owners were not paying the manager as much as the previous ones had.[19]

Construction of the two packing plants began March 13, 1902. Officials planned for ground breaking ceremonies during the meeting of the Cattle Raisers Association of Texas in Fort Worth. Workers cut down a large tree on the bank of Marine Creek, site of the first stock show, to make room for the packing plants. They also filled in the east branch of Marine Creek and diverted the water to the west.[20]

An Armour official told the story many years later that in 1902 representatives of Armour and Swift tossed a coin for the choice of locations. Swift won and naturally chose the site closest to downtown. This disappointed Armour because Armour employees would have to walk farther from the trolley line and Armour horses would have a longer haul from Fort Worth to the plant. Soon the Armour men got even. When they started to excavate for their plant, they uncovered a fine gravel pit. Swift had to buy all of the sand and gravel for its buildings from Armour.[21]

Workers leveled the old hotel and exchange building that local businessmen had erected in 1889 for the Union Stock Yards. They needed to make room for all the new construction, for Swift alone planned a floor space of 658,785 square feet, or approximately 15.5 acres. New stock pens for the Fort Worth Stock Yards Company soon covered a forty-acre tract west of the packing houses. All eventually would be paved with brick—most of which was brought from Thurber, Texas—laid out in various patterns, some diagonal, some perpendicular.[22]

---

19. Board of Directors Meeting, January 25, 1902, *Corporate Record*, I, 217–18.
20. "Big Packeries at Fort Worth," *Texas Stock Journal*, March 4, 1902, p. 1; "Fort Worth Packing Industry Celebrates 50 Years of Progress," Fifty Years of Rodeo in Fort Worth, (bound rodeo programs), vol. 3, 1952 Program, p. 34, Local History Collection, Amon Carter Museum Library.
21. "Armour President, Fred W. Specht, Speech for Fort Worth Audience," *Weekly Live Stock Reporter*, April 17, 1952, p. 1.
22. "The Packing Plants," *Texas Stock Journal*, June 10, 1902, p. 1; "Big Packeries at Fort Worth," *Texas Stock Journal*, March 4, 1902, p. 1; Board of Directors Meeting, March 12, 1903, *Corporate Record*, 1st bound volume, p. 25.

While work progressed in North Fort Worth, the Fort Worth Stock Yards Company invited more than one hundred editors from Texas and Indian Territory (Oklahoma) newspapers to a banquet and to visit the packeries under construction. Several local men made speeches, including Marion Sansom of Alvarado, who would move to North Fort Worth in November, 1902, and invest in land west of the stockyards. The lieutenant governor of Texas, James M. Browning of Amarillo, and a state senator had also been invited. One farmer who spoke at the gathering expressed the feeling of many citizens when he said that the packers might belong to the beef trust, "but when they do so much good for others as is being done by these institutions here, there is bound to be some good in them." The editors ended their day-long tour of the stockyards and packeries with a visit to Texas Brewing Company's plant and free refreshments.[23]

Directors of the company discussed establishing a newspaper at the yards at their board meeting on November 12, 1902. Either the paper established by the Fort Worth Stock Yards Company in 1896 had ceased publication for a time, or the Chicago men did not know of its existence. In any event, in January, 1903, the *Live Stock Reporter* published volume seven; it eventually became a daily.[24]

Contracts called for the packing plants to open November 1, 1902, but construction progressed slowly. In January, 1903, Armour and Swift wrote a joint open letter in the *Live Stock Reporter* to Texas stock producers. It promised what they would do: buy half a million cattle, half a million sheep, and one and a half million hogs each year and pay the highest market price, saving producers the cost of shrinkage and transportation to ship to northern markets.

23. B. B. Paddock, ed., *A Twentieth Century History and Biographical Record of North and West Texas*, II, 144; "Editors at the Yards," *Texas Stock Journal*, August 5, 1902, p. 1; "The Banquet Complimentary to the Editors by the Fort Worth Stock Yards Co., Aug. 4, 1902," *Bohemian* 4 (Fall, 1902): 78. See also "Editors at Stock Yards," *Texas Stock Journal*, July 15, 1902, p. 1; and "Editors at Fort Worth," *Texas Stock Journal*, July 22, 1902, p. 1.

24. Board of Directors Meeting, November 12, 1902, *Corporate Record*, 1st bound vol., p. 241, and "What the Packing Houses Will Do," *Fort Worth Daily Live Stock Reporter*, January 19, 1903. Back files of the *Reporter* for 1896–1902 are lost.

"If the stockmen will raise and supply the stock, the packing houses will do the rest," the packers assured.[25]

The packing plants opened formally on March 4, 1903, during the annual fat stock show. W. E. Skinner, former manager of the Fort Worth yards and in 1903 with the Chicago Union Stock Yards, came back to town to help celebrate. He urged farmers "to provide the raw material for the packeries to work upon." S. S. Conway, superintendent of the Armour plant, expressed no doubt about Fort Worth's becoming a second Chicago. "The packing plants are now in a position to handle all the cattle, hogs, and sheep that can be shipped here," he said. The daily runs when the plants first opened provided too few animals to keep plants operating at full capacity all day, however.[26]

The Armour plant, which claimed to be the "best equipped packing plant in the world," had a daily capacity of fifteen hundred cattle, three thousand hogs, and fifteen hundred sheep. The big packers called themselves pioneers in the assembly-line technique and claimed that Henry Ford, who later got the credit for assembly lines, gained his inspiration from packing-house methods. Actually, the packing house was a "dis-assembly" line because the animal carcass kept getting smaller as it traveled through the process.[27]

When the new $125,000 Spanish-style, tan stucco exchange building opened in April, 1903, it housed stockyards offices, the Stockyards National Bank, and offices for five railroads and twelve commission companies. Two white marble staircases in the inner gallery led to a common landing on the second floor. A big marble fountain in the lobby spurted water upward and would eventually refresh many a sweating cowboy on sweltering summer days. A dining room on the north ran the width of the building. Patrons of the market also found inside a post office and a telegraph office. So excited were local citizens about all this growth that rumors even started flying in June, 1903, that Cudahy planned to build a packing plant at Fort Worth, too. Fort Worthians envisioned a packing center with five

25. *Fort Worth Daily Live Stock Reporter*, January 19, 1903.
26. "The Great Packing Plants," *Texas Farm Journal*, March 10, 1903, p. 2; "Opinion of Armour's Superintendent as to Future of Fort Worth," *Citizen*, March 7, 1903, p. 3.
27. *A 1903 Packing House*, (pamphlet), p. 6.

or six huge plants in operation and their market eventually surpassing Chicago.[28]

Armour and Swift began operations on a grand scale, each purchasing daily more than all other buyers combined. In categories like calves, sheep, and hogs, they sometimes were the only buyers. In fact, in the first ten months of business, the two packers bought 265,279 cattle, 128,934 hogs, and 40,160 sheep, and paid out six million dollars into the local economy for them. They succeeded where others had failed because they were large enough to handle the thousands of head that came through the Fort Worth yards; they met their obligations promptly and in cash, and they obtained the trade of the other Texas cities. As part of the Big Five, Armour and Swift could also meet the price competition, whereas the earlier packing concerns had not.[29]

Quite clearly, the meat-packing trust had arrived in Fort Worth. The years 1901 to 1903 were busy ones; events in Fort Worth fit a pattern that also existed elsewhere, as the record of Armour and Company shows. In 1901 Armour received four thousand shares of the capital stock of the Sioux City Stockyards Company and 12.5 acres of land for locating their plant there. In 1901 Armour received over $300,000 in stock bonuses from the Saint Louis stockyards and 20 acres of land for constructing packing facilities nearby. In 1902 the company completed its deal with Fort Worth. Then in 1903 the Saint Louis Stockyards Company paid Armour $388,000 in cash, and in 1916 Armour received $1 million from the Saint Paul Union Stockyards Company, of which $400,000 was paid in cash and $600,000 in bonus stock, for locating a plant adjacent to those stockyards. Less than 25 percent of the stock represented actual purchases; most of the rest took the form of stock gifts and stock dividends. The other large meat packers engaged in similar activities.[30]

Consistent with their pattern of operation elsewhere, Armour

28. "The Live Stock Exchange," *Texas Stock Journal,* April 28, 1903, p. 1; "Live Stock Exchange Elects," ibid., July 22, 1903, p. 1; "Is Cudahy Coming?" ibid., June 17, 1903, p. 1.

29. *Fort Worth Daily Live Stock Reporter,* April 5, 1904, p. 1; "Review of the Live Stock Market for the Year 1903. . . ," *Citizen* (Fort Worth), January 1, 1904, p. 1.

30. U.S. Congress, Senate, Committee on Agriculture and Forestry, *Hearings on a Bill to Amend the Packers and Stockyards Act, S. 2089,* 68th Cong., 1st sess., 1924, p. 15.

and Swift soon engaged in a number of related businesses in North Fort Worth. Besides each owning one-third of the Fort Worth Stock Yards Company, the two giant meat packers jointly owned the Reporter Publishing Company, which published the *Live Stock Reporter*; the Belt Railway Company; the Stockyards National Bank of North Fort Worth; the Fort Worth Cattle Loan Company; and the North Fort Worth Townsite Company. For the Townsite Company, Joseph B. Googins, a Swift official, bought almost thirty-four hundred acres from the North Fort Worth Land Company on November 1, 1901, with $175,000 "furnished to him in equal parts by J. Ogden Armour and Gustavus F. Swift." Googins, vice-president of the Townsite Company, had been a buyer for the Chicago and Fort Worth Packing Company in the 1890s, but by 1902 he headed the Swift plant in Fort Worth. The Townsite Company land was located north of the stockyards area, in the present Diamond Hill addition. Old-timers claim that the name came from the head of the surveying team, a retired British army officer who had been wounded on Diamond Hill in South Africa during the Boer War.[31]

Swift bought a cotton oil mill at Alvarado, a small community south of Fort Worth, for $100,000 cash, and planned to purchase others. After farmers living on the Trinity River below Fort Worth sued the stockyards company and the packers for damages from the waste dumped into the water by the packing plants, the Fort Worth Stock Yards Company in 1903 constructed a sewage plant, costing $70,000.[32]

Fort Worth intentionally excluded North Fort Worth from the city's boundary in order to offer a tax advantage to businesses. Therefore, the packing and stockyards interests were free to incorporate

31. Agreement between North Fort Worth Land Company vendor and Joseph B. Googins, purchaser, October 24, 1901 (copy), North Fort Worth Land Co. folder, Havard Coll. See also statement by Gustavus F. Swift and J. Ogden Armour, June 6, 1902 (copy), unmarked folder, Havard Coll.; O. W. Matthews to A. H. Veeder, November 24, 1903, Belt Railway folder, Havard Coll.; Reporter Publishing Co. information from personal interview with Mrs. Nita McCain, October 28, 1977, Fort Worth; B. B. Paddock, ed., *Fort Worth and the Texas Northwest*, IV, 586; Jon McConal, "Smell of Livestock Was Pleasant Odor to City's Economy," *Fort Worth Star-Telegram*, August 6, 1978.

32. "Swift Buys Oil Mills," *Texas Stock Journal*, September 9, 1902, p. 1; "To Purify the Sewage," *Weekly Citizen*, May 6, 1904, p. 2.

the city of North Fort Worth in 1902; citizens chose J. D. Farmer, a commission man, as the first mayor. By April, 1904, the area around the stockyards and packing plants had grown from an open prairie with a few scattered houses in a loose community called Marine to a town of five thousand people. Some earlier prophecies finally began to come true. Paddock's "Tarantula Map," which had brought ridicule back in the 1870s, became a reality, for shortly after the turn of the century twelve trunk lines reached Fort Worth. The city's switchyards soon handled one and a half million cars annually.[33]

Soon after the packers came, Fort Worth became one of the leading grain storage and milling centers of the Southwest. Pharmaceutical firms sprang up to combat livestock diseases. Cattlemen's associations moved their permanent homes to the city. Thus, the city's cattle industry became "the catalytic agent that propelled Fort Worth toward industrial greatness." The packing plants of Swift and Armour soon drew nearly all the cattle of West Texas to Fort Worth for sale. When cattlemen came to town, they often brought their wives along to shop, thus magnifying the prosperity of Fort Worth.[34]

So important to Fort Worth was the coming of Armour and Swift that for many years officials of the local Fort Worth Stock Yards Company thought their own company had originated in 1902, when the packers arrived, instead of the actual 1893, nine years earlier. As late as 1962 two-color letterhead stationery proclaimed their "60 years of leadership, 1902–1962." Of course, 1902 was a critical year for the company, for Armour and Swift's acquisition of two-thirds ownership of the stockyards company through reorganization assured Fort Worth's position as livestock leader in the entire Southwest.[35]

Excitement prevailed in North Fort Worth after the packers came.

33. Mack Williams, "State of Mind Now, It Was N. Fort Worth Then," *Fort Worth Star-Telegram*, November 12, 1951, in North Fort Worth file, Fort Worth Public Library. Boundaries of North Fort Worth were Marine Creek on the north, the Trinity River on the south, the Santa Fe tracks on the east, and Grand Avenue on the west. See also "Advertisement to Fairview Addition," *Weekly Citizen*, April 15, 1904, p. 5.

34. "A Brief Historical Backglance at Fort Worth's Original Major Industry and Its 60 Years of Prosperity," *Fort Worth* 38 (March, 1962): 9.

35. T. H. Hard to J. A. Lovell, December 11, 1962, Dies Correspondence, FWSY Co. Coll. Company advertisements through the years cited the 1902 date as well, particularly in the *Cattleman* magazine.

Promise of Greatness
1903–1909

An electric streetcar stopped at the corner of Main and Exchange avenues; an excited group of strangely dressed young men emerged. Each carried a suitcase and spoke to his companions in a foreign tongue as he looked eagerly eastward down Exchange Avenue toward the Armour and Swift plants. These immigrants had come from Eastern Europe, traveling directly from New York by train to find jobs. They had reached Fort Worth on one of thirty passenger trains that arrived daily. This scene recurred almost continually after 1905, as more and more workers came, attracted by the booming livestock center in North Fort Worth.

What newcomers found in Fort Worth in the first decade of the twentieth century were a few fancy stores outshining their many plain neighbors, more dirt streets than paved ones, and more horses raising dust than automobiles. In fact, the stockyards and packing plant managers drove some of the first "horseless carriages" in town. Things began happening both north and south of the Trinity River because of the livestock center and because Fort Worth possessed, as at most stages in her history, men who promoted change. One of these wandered out to the stockyards one afternoon to watch a demonstration.

Always eager to publicize their market, stockyards officials agreed early in 1906 to host an experiment of pouring fuel oil over dried cow chips. They hoped to provide a more efficient substance for heating than coal or fuel oil alone. Among the group of visitors viewing the demonstration that afternoon was a man who later would make a lot of things happen for Fort Worth, Amon G. Carter. Previously a successful salesman for a nationwide portrait firm, Carter in 1906 headed his own advertising agency in Fort Worth. He talked with A. G. Dawson, a correspondent for the *Dallas Morning News,* and D. C. McCaleb, city editor of the *Fort Worth Record.* After the three men agreed that the only afternoon newspaper in Fort Worth, the *Telegram,* needed some competition, they shook hands over a deal to form a new paper. Carter knew he could sell advertising for it. He had been selling things even before he left home at age eleven, when his mother died. The three men called their paper the *Star.* Three years later they bought out the *Telegram* and merged the two newspapers. Carter called Fort Worth "the city where the West begins" on the masthead of the newspaper, apparently originating the epithet. Amon Carter's biographer declared that the immensely successful *Star-Telegram,* which continually boosted Fort Worth and its livestock market, was the only newspaper ever conceived and founded in a stockyards "over a pile of burning cow manure." As did most onlookers that day, however, Carter decided not to invest in the new fuel because of the smell.[1]

The first decade of the twentieth century witnessed great growth in livestock-related industries in Fort Worth, including the newspapers. The Fort Worth Stock Yards Company became the hub around which everything else revolved. Even problems such as a strike, a flood, federal regulation, excessive railroad rates, and the state of Texas' outlawing of the local livestock exchange could not hamper for long the enthusiasm, the business boom, or the increased cattle receipts. After more than twenty years of struggle to gain a prosperous stockyards and packery, Fort Worth and the livestock industry began to boom.

A bustling Exchange Avenue, with eight to ten saloons, two or three eating houses, a couple of hotels, and two dry goods stores all within three or four blocks of each other, testified to the increased activity. Horses and wagons clattered over the wooden bridge that

1. Jerry Flemmons, *Amon: The Life of Amon Carter, Sr., of Texas,* pp. 48–49, 126, 137.

spanned Marine Creek just a few hundred yards southwest of the exchange building. Because commission firms gave free meal tickets to ranchers and herdsmen coming into the stockyards with livestock, the dining room in the exchange building stayed busy.

When newcomers to the stockyards area turned east from Main Street onto Exchange Avenue, they traveled only a block before encountering wooden horse and mule barns on the south side of the street and the two-story Spanish-style exchange building on the north. North and east of the exchange building stretched the newly constructed brick-floored pens, with a capacity of 24,500 animals. Railroad tracks separated the pens from the huge plants of Armour and Swift located farther east. A sign reading "Armour and Company," which covered the west wall of the long row of Armour refrigerator buildings, stretched four hundred feet long and eighty feet high. It was said to be the largest sign in the entire state. Before the decade ended, additional commission agents needed office space in the exchange building, so the stockyards company constructed offices out of the dining hall that had formerly occupied the entire north part of the lower floor of the building. Ten commission companies quickly snatched them up.[2]

The value of the Fort Worth Stock Yards and packing property interests in 1904 reached $2.5 million. Values rapidly increased. The stockyards company spent large sums for advertising during these early years — over $4,500 in 1903 and over $7,000 in 1904 — their third largest expense, totaling nearly as much as office salaries.[3]

Within a year after Armour and Swift opened their doors, twelve commission companies operated on the yards, and their numbers increased steadily. Northern livestock newspapers, however, remained slow to recognize the growing Fort Worth market. The local market paper complained that the northern interests still cited as the six leading markets Chicago, Kansas City, Omaha, Saint Louis,

2. Board of Directors Meeting, March 12, 1902, Fort Worth Stock Yards Company, *Corporate Record*, 1st bound vol., pp. 225–26; "Fort Worth Stock Yards," *Texas Stockman-Journal*, March 8, 1904, p. 6.

3. *Annual Reports*, Fort Worth Stock Yards Company, 1903, 1904, Fort Worth Stock Yards Company Collection, North Texas State University Archives, Denton (FWSY Co. Coll.).

Saint Joseph, and Sioux City, even though in 1904 Fort Worth showed greater total receipts than either Saint Joseph or Sioux City.[4]

J. Ogden Armour even predicted in 1904 that Fort Worth might surpass Chicago and become number one. Armour actually wanted to run the Chicago stockyards out of business. The big packers did not own the Chicago stockyards; the Vanderbilts did. The packers therefore built large, well-equipped stockyards and packing plants in the Southwest and West. If the Vanderbilts refused to sell the Chicago yards, Armour and the other packers planned to divert trade. The packers did not own the Kansas City yards either and wanted to see Fort Worth outstrip it. In his 1906 book, Armour commented favorably on the growth of Fort Worth: "Last year, with other markets holding their own, the Fort Worth market showed a larger increase in the actual number of cattle handled than any other market in the country. Its percentage of increase in cattle receipts was more than three times that of any other market." From 1904 to 1906, hog receipts increased by 60 percent. The calf market at Fort Worth ranked second only to Chicago by 1906. That same year Texas ranked as the premier cattle state in America, as the state's producers raised eight million range cattle. No wonder J. Ogden Armour believed Fort Worth could become number one.[5]

Both Swift and Armour added canning factories to their Fort Worth plants in the spring of 1906. The canneries brought increased receipts by attracting the cheaper grades of cattle used in canning to the local market. The low-cost meat products could then be sold to those who could not afford fresh meat. The livestock yards would also benefit since Texas cattle producers would no longer have to ship the cheaper grades farther north as they had been doing. In 1906 the livestock industry of North Fort Worth, with its packing and canning facilities, provided over twice as many jobs and produced nearly five times the value of products as the larger city of Fort Worth

4. "One of the Big Markets," *Fort Worth Daily Live Stock Reporter*, February 6, 1904, p. 1. The United States Department of Agriculture Marketing Service cites specific figures for each of the stockyards of the nation beginning in 1917 but no earlier.

5. J. Ogden Armour, *The Packers, the Private Car Lines and the People*, p. 336; "Local Market Grows," *Fort Worth Daily Live Stock Reporter*, January 1, 1907, p. 1.

could boast. With 3,350 workers, North Fort Worth's output totaled $27 million, while Fort Worth's labor force of 1,423 produced less than $6 million for the year.[6]

The panic of 1907 depressed business and industry nationwide, especially cattle receipts at the large terminal markets. Despite that, Fort Worth for the first time reached the one million-cattle point that year, counting calves. The *Live Stock Reporter* bragged that it took Fort Worth less than five years to reach the million mark. Chicago had taken eleven years; Saint Louis, twenty-eight; Kansas City, seventeen; and Omaha, seventeen. Of course, the writer chose to date the beginning of the Fort Worth market as 1902, when the packers came, and to forget all those previous years of struggle. General Manager W. B. King expressed his satisfaction at the excellent 1907 showing in cattle receipts, but he said he would feel a good deal better if he had a million hogs to "jubilate over." Local cattleman and real estate investor Winfield Scott believed that Fort Worth would have done even better that year had it not been for the panic, "but as it is, there is a great deal of improvement going on, and new people coming in every day. With all the buildings I have to rent, there are none vacant."[7]

Directors of the stockyards company voted to increase the capacity of their pens to eighteen thousand cattle and fourteen thousand hogs and sheep in 1908. The packers enlarged their plants that year, too. They added beef coolers, an oleo plant, fertilizer plants, and calf and sheep coolers; Swift even enlarged the hog killing floors and pork and curing cellars. All these enlargements practically doubled their capacity.

In 1908 the directors authorized dividends of $1.25 per share to be paid in May and August and planned regular quarterly dividends of the same amount per share in February, May, August, and November each year after that until further notice. J. Ogden Armour, who held more than six thousand shares, earned over thirty thousand dollars from the Fort Worth Stock Yards Company that next

6. "Comparison of Fort Worth and North Fort Worth Industries," *Fort Worth Daily Live Stock Reporter*, April 14, 1906, p. 1.

7. "Past the Million Mark," *Southwestern Farmer and Breeder*, December 20, 1907, p. 4; Winfield Scott to his daughter Georgia, March 17, 1908, as cited in Roze McCoy Porter, *Thistle Hill: The Cattle Baron's Legacy*, p. 293.

year. He held a comparable amount of stock in several other major stockyards, as did other owners of the Big Five companies.[8]

Again in 1908 Fort Worth was the only large market in the nation to make a considerable gain in receipts of cattle. All others lost heavily, except Saint Louis, which remained constant. Although hog receipts increased steadily, the stockyards needed more swine to meet the market demand. Even so, the Fort Worth Stock Yards Company made a profit of $194,698.64 in 1908 and authorized quarterly dividends of $1.50 per share for the next year. In March, 1909, the directors increased the capital stock of the company from $2 million to $2.5 million. By the end of 1909, the assets and liabilities of the Fort Worth Stock Yards Company balanced at over $4 million, and profits reached $247,583.13.[9]

Stockyards officials in Fort Worth, along with Armour and other packers, continued to dream that the market would rank number one. They had little real chance of ever surpassing Chicago, however, because cattle receipts always outnumbered swine, whereas the situation would have to have been reversed for Fort Worth to predominate. Part of the fault lay with the packers; they should primarily have built facilities to slaughter cattle in Texas. Nonetheless, the dream persisted. When stockyards officials realized in May, 1908, that for the previous four months they had topped Saint Louis in cattle sales, the market newspaper gloated: "We passed St. Joseph last year. We will pass St. Louis this year. Now we are after Omaha. . . ." Then they cited figures showing that the gap between Fort Worth and Omaha was narrowing. "We are going to pass Omaha next year. . . . And then we are going after Kansas City." In January, 1910, figures for the previous year showed that Fort Worth had indeed equalled Saint Louis in receipts of cattle and calves and tallied receipts behind only Chicago and Kansas City. In 1909 Fort Worth again had been the only market in the nation showing a gain in every class of stock—cattle, calves, hogs, sheep, horses, and mules. By March, 1910, five packers besides Armour and Swift maintained buyers on the Fort Worth market: Morris, Cudahy, Schwarzchild and

8. Board of Directors Meeting, January 14, 1908, *Corporate Record*, 1st bound vol., p. 251.

9. Board of Directors Meeting, January 12, 1909, March 15, 1909, January 11, 1910, *Corporate Record*, 1st bound vol., pp. 269, 273, 287, 300.

Sulzberger, Independent Packing Company, and Dold Packing Company. The market newspaper chided them, "Why not come here and do your slaughtering, gentlemen?"[10]

As a result of all the increased livestock receipts, packing activity, and additional jobs in North Fort Worth, the population of that area and of the city of Fort Worth increased tremendously. During the decade Fort Worth increased its population 173 percent, from 26,688 in 1900 to 73,312 in 1910. The Fort Worth Stock Yards Company and its related enterprises stimulated this remarkable growth. Cowtown had established itself as a market to watch in the future.

The tremendous progress did not come without numerous problems. The packing plants and the Fort Worth Stock Yards remained so closely interwoven that anything which affected one inevitably affected the other, as a butchers' strike during the summer of 1904 illustrates. Packinghouse workers nationwide had been attempting to make the Amalgamated Butchers Union a viable force under the presidency of Michael Donnelly since before the turn of the century. Locally, the butchers had just organized on June 6, 1904, when six days later Donnelly ordered a general strike. Other employees of the packing plants and stockyards did not walk out, but they could not work with butchers idle. The commission men sent letters to their regular shippers telling them to hold their stock until further notice. The dispute at Chicago centered on the wage scale and a desire by workers that packers hire only union men. The packers would not agree, especially concerning the union shop. Soon the local plants began hiring other butchers, and Fort Worth production continued more steadily than at any other of the packing centers. In fact, Fort Worth increased production to compensate for the slowdown at the other markets. No violence occurred at Fort Worth, but some erupted at Chicago, Saint Louis, and Saint Paul. Rumors circulated that other packing plant workers would go out and that even railroad employees would refuse to haul cars containing packinghouse products, but in Fort Worth this did not happen.[11]

Numerous local citizens opposed the activity of the strikers.

10. "St. Louis in the Rear," *Fort Worth Daily Live Stock Reporter*, May 2, 1908, p. 1; "Fort Worth Receipts for 1909," January 1, 1910, and "They All Buy Here," *Fort Worth Daily Live Stock Reporter*, March 21, 1910, p. 1.
11. "Butchers Go on Strike," *Fort Worth Daily Live Stock Reporter*, July 12,

Some proposed an ordinance against crowds' gathering and loitering as the strikers had been doing, but none was passed. When the strike finally ended October 10, 1904, the big packers won. Of 700 to 800 local men who had gone out on strike, only about 250 were re-employed by the companies; the rest sought work elsewhere. The nationwide strike cost packers eight million dollars and the strikers about five million in wages. A local striker complained, "There were too many scabs in Texas, and the people had not been sufficiently educated on the principles of the union." No nationwide threat of a meat shortage materialized as the strikers had hoped, because the Big Five packers continued operations, even though curtailed, and the independent packers increased production. The packers broke the power of the national union, and it went underground for years.[12]

Another labor problem occurred during the busy decade of growth at the Fort Worth market center. This involved the hundreds of immigrants from central and eastern Europe who came to the area to work in the packing plants. After a mass protest gathering, a citizens' committee met with packing officials in December, 1907, complaining that they did not like to see "Bohunks" hired while "white" residents of North Fort Worth and Fort Worth remained unemployed. Most of the foreign workers were Bohemians, Polish, Serbians, or Czechoslovakians, but local citizens made no distinction, even in newspaper accounts. Many of them had come to Fort Worth originally because immigration and employment agents, for a large commission, encouraged their work in packing plants.

Packers told the committee that their plants hired foreign workers when labor was scarce and that, because of the export trade, they could not afford to discriminate against foreigners. The packers, however, promised to give work at the first opportunity to those who were suffering and to "cooperate" with the citizens. At the time of the complaints, 160 of these immigrants worked at Swift and 40 at Armour. Swift manager Joe Googins explained that he employed

1904, p. 1; "No Settlement in Sight," *Fort Worth Daily Live Stock Reporter*, July 16, 1904, p. 1.

12. "Strike Is Over Here," *Fort Worth Daily Live Stock Reporter*, July 28, 1904, p. 1, "Effects of the Strike," ibid., September 10, 1904, p. 1, and "The Strike Is Over But Effect Is Yet to Come," *Texas Stockman-Journal*, September 14, 1904, p. 1.

the immigrant workers only to do the jobs the "whites" would not do. The committee disagreed and said that local citizens had held every job there and would do so again to feed their wives and children. William G. Cargill, superintendent of Armour, said that he hired the foreigners because in the fall many of Armour's black employees left the plant to go to the cotton fields. Workers would stand at the gate and the foreman would go and hire what he anticipated he would need that day. Often the foreigners rushed up and got ahead of the "timid white laborer," he said.[13]

Citizens also complained of the unsanitary conditions in which the foreigners lived and insisted the situation represented a danger to all of North Fort Worth. The city health officer reported that they lived twenty in a room, all dipping stale bread into the same pot of soup. The wife of the editor of the *North Fort Worth News* later remembered seeing immigrants living in squalor in tents and going around to schools to eat out of their garbage cans.[14]

The local stock journal indicated that after the complaints surfaced, the packers began turning away foreigners, not employing them. In addition, rowdies attacked the foreigners' quarters, upon at least three occasions breaking windows. The immigrants became frightened, and most left town. Some remained, however, and became substantial citizens of North Fort Worth.

Labor relations did not present the only problem; officials continually feared federal regulation of the meat-packing industry, the stockyards, and the railroads that carried their products. The Vest Committee of 1888 had led to the Sherman Antitrust Act and attempts to regulate railroad rates. The Federal Meat Inspection Act of 1906 directly regulated meat packers. Regulation of stockyards would come a decade and a half later.

Other early efforts at federal controls on the industry concerned tick-infested cattle, which remained a problem after the turn of the century. Conservative estimates in the early 1900s placed the losses directly and indirectly from tick fever at $40 million annually. The Fort Worth Stock Yards built a new brick dipping vat fifty-five feet

13. "Committee Tells Packers Bohunks Are Not Wanted," *Texas Stockman-Journal*, December 25, 1907, p. 6.
14. Interview with Mrs. Nita McCain, Fort Worth, Texas, October 28, 1977.

long in April, 1904. To keep a cow from turning around, the vat measured eighteen inches wide at the bottom and three feet wide at the top. Attendants drove the cattle in; then the animals would slide to a deep part over their heads. Unable to turn around, they kept walking to the steps to climb out. A dripping pen followed. The vat had a capacity of a thousand cattle a day.[15]

In October, 1904, a German doctor who worked in his nation's meat inspection department came to Fort Worth and inspected the stockyards and packing plants. He said that he had been told the modern dipping vats there were the first of their kind in the world and he had come to America especially to see them. He seemed properly impressed.[16]

The federal government renewed its efforts to eradicate the ticks in July, 1906, placing the Inspection Division of the Bureau of Animal Industry in charge. The Inspection Division divided the infested territory into five quarantined districts and allocated the first federal appropriation of $82,500. Texas ranges represented one-fourth of the total area under quarantine in the United States. Not surprisingly then, the majority of the cattle arriving at the Fort Worth Stock Yards carried ticks. A solid board fence separated the tick-infested cattle from the smaller section where the clean pens stood.[17]

Besides tick eradication, other federal regulatory efforts involved six antitrust suits filed against Swift, Armour, Cudahy, Morris, S & S, and a number of their associates in the years from 1902 to 1910. The Supreme Court dismissed most cases and acquitted the defendants in the others. In 1905 the government charged a number of meat packers with a conspiracy to fix livestock prices in the stockyards.

15. U.S. Congress, House, *Cattle Tick Fever*, H. Doc. 527, 77th Cong., 2d sess., reprinted in *1942 Yearbook of Agriculture*, U.S. Department of Agriculture, p. 572. See also "The New Dipping Vat," *Fort Worth Daily Live Stock Reporter*, April 13, 1904, p. 1.

16. "First Dipping Test Is a Success," *Texas Stockman-Journal*, May 18, 1904, p. 8; "Fort Worth Dipping Vats," *Fort Worth Daily Live Stock Reporter*, October 4, 1904, p. 1.

17. U. G. Houck, *The Bureau of Animal Industry of the United States Department of Agriculture: Its Establishment, Achievement and Current Activities*, p. 330; J. E. Boog-Scott, "Fever Tick Eradication in Texas in 1923," *Cattleman* 10 (August, 1923): 41.

The court refused to consider local transactions as separate from interstate commerce, and it made only a vague distinction between sales and production. In *U.S.* v. *E. C. Knight Co.* (1895), the court had ruled that production had only an incidental effect on commerce and so could not be regulated by the federal government. This Knight doctrine remained in force until the 1930s. A proposed piece of anti-trust legislation, the Hepburn Act, failed to pass in 1908, but in the debates on it Congress laid the groundwork for the Clayton Act and the Federal Trade Commission Act, both of which would come in the next decade.

Antipacker discussions were most likely to surface at cattlemen's meetings in Colorado, South Dakota, or other places far from Texas. Local producers seemed too happy about their good market at Fort Worth to do much complaining against the Big Five. Managers of the Armour and Swift plants in Fort Worth naturally denied the existence of filthy conditions such as Upton Sinclair, in his muckraking novel *The Jungle,* described for the Chicago packing plants, and local citizens apparently believed them. When a reporter from the local *Southwestern Farmer and Breeder* toured the Fort Worth plants, the manager urged him to let him know about anything unclean. The reporter said he found nothing suspect. Fort Worth citizens expressed sympathy for the packers. Several of them even sent a telegram to J. Ogden Armour in which they said they represented "the prevailing sentiment." They believed the "persecution" was "conducted more for political purposes than for a sincere desire to improve . . . conditions." Local cattleman Winfield Scott said he believed the packing houses had done more than any other enterprise "towards developing the country."[18]

A few Texans disagreed, however. A. B. Robertson, in a speech to the Cattle Raisers Association of Texas, complained that in the big markets one buyer frequently got precedence one day to stock up and the following day another big packer obtained the same opportunity "in order that there be no competition." As would be expected, the *Live Stock Reporter,* owned by the Fort Worth Stock Yards

18. "Fort Worth Packing Houses Use Utmost Care," *Southwestern Farmer and Breeder,* June 15, 1906, p. 1. See also "Confidence in Mr. Armour," *Fort Worth Daily Live Stock Reporter,* November 29, 1911, p. 1, and "Two Cattlemen's Views," *Fort Worth Daily Live Stock Reporter,* March 27, 1905, p. 1.

Company, defended the packers, calling the attacks against them "untruthful and vicious," and warned that such criticism would "hurt the cattle trade."[19]

To combat the bad publicity jointly a group of small packers met at the Grand Pacific Hotel in Chicago on October 1, 1906, and formed the Association of American Meat Packers. The small meat packers reasoned that what affected the big packers hurt the little ones even more. A man from Morris appeared to be the only representative of a Big Five packer present. Organizers invited the big packers to join, and eventually they did.

While meat packers were organizing, cattle producers were also trying to form a stronger alignment. The American Stock Growers Association and the National Live Stock Association merged on January 30, 1906, to become the American National Cattlemen's Association. Their goals were to unite against the packing and railroad trusts and to influence national politics. That same year cattlemen, predominantly from Iowa, Kansas, Missouri, and Colorado, organized the Cooperative Livestock Commission Company to avoid the excessive rates charged by regular commission companies at livestock exchanges. The commission company did well at first, but intimidation from the exchanges later led producers to boycott it. It ceased operations in 1909. The cooperative retaliated by suing the packers. The producers won a lower court suit in Missouri, but the Missouri Supreme Court overturned the decision, saying the defendants had not engaged in a conspiracy to put the cooperative out of business. One historian has concluded that the cooperative failed partly because "Wyoming sheepmen, Texas cattle raisers, and Iowa cattle and hog farmers were not sufficiently aware of their common interests to stand together."[20]

The meat packers and their stockyards won that round, but they continued to fear federal regulation of their industry. Restrictive action came from the state level as well. Texas at this time possessed

19. A. B. Robertson, "Effects of Packing Industry on Extension of Markets," *Texas Stockman-Journal*, March 29, 1905, p. 14; "Vicious Attacks on Packers Have Baneful Effect," *Fort Worth Daily Live Stock Reporter*, May 25, 1906, p. 1.

20. Keach Johnson, "Struggle in the Stockyards: The Rise and Fall of the Cooperative Livestock Commission Company," *Arizona and the West* 18 (1976): 315, 332.

a climate favorable to reform. All four major candidates for governor in 1906 opposed the trusts. Even as the Kansas Supreme Court was deliberating on a case to consider whether the Kansas City Livestock Exchange constituted a trust, the Texas governor, S. W. T. Lanham, and his attorney general decided to investigate the Fort Worth Live Stock Exchange. Judge Jewell P. Lightfoot, an assistant in the state attorney general's office, made a secret visit to Fort Worth during the first week of March, 1906, announced only after he was back in Austin. The state attorney general then filed antitrust suits against the exchange, the Fort Worth Stock Yards Company, Armour, Swift, commission companies, and some cattlemen, asking for forfeiture of their right to do business in Texas and for penalties totaling $17 million. In brief, the charges alleged that members of the local exchange were fixing prices of livestock as well as slaughtered meat, keeping the former low and the latter high. The suit asked that they be ordered to cease.[21]

Even the *Stockman-Journal*, a newspaper supported by cattle interests, lamented that it "would be a real misfortune to have the packeries at Fort Worth closed" and argued that they could "obey the law and make money" just as small packing houses in Waco, Dallas, and other places were doing.[22]

Members of the exchange, which included the stockyards, commission companies, order buyers, and many Texas cattlemen, protested that the suits against them were political in motivation. Someone noted that every fact in the possession of the state attorney general had been recently threshed over by the Tarrant County grand jury, which "found nothing in the premises that would warrant an indictment." Of course, the writer did not mention that the local grand jury might be loath to destroy the industry that was making Fort Worth wealthy.[23]

Naturally, the *Live Stock Reporter*, owned by the packers and

21. "Atty General after Local Stock Exchange," *Texas Stockman-Journal*, April 11, 1906, p. 3; *State of Texas* v. *Fort Worth Livestock Exchange, et al.,* Case No. 23,941 filed April 24, 1906, 26th Judicial District Court, Travis County, Texas (Austin). See also "Those Exchange Suits," *Texas Stockman-Journal*, May 2, 1906, p. 4.

22. "An Outside View," *Texas Stockman-Journal*, May 2, 1906, p. 4.

23. "Commission Men Plan Action to Test Law," *Texas Stockman-Journal*, May 2, 1906, p. 8.

stockyards, defended the industry. The editor reported that commission men regarded as "laughable" the idea that they would work out a deal to set prices; their interests opposed those of the packers. Packers bought livestock at the market, while commission men worked as agents for sellers. Fort Worth businessmen even started a fund to help the packers defray the costs and penalties in the case in order to show the packers their appreciation for what they had done for the city. Suspense ended in October, 1907, when the attorney general agreed to drop the suit against the exchange if the members would pay $17,500 to the state and legal costs. In addition, the state terminated the Live Stock Exchange charter, which had been issued October 24, 1901, and ordered the exchange to do no further business in the state. Actually, the exchange had been out of business since April, 1906, when litigation began. All defendants, comprising a virtual "who's who" of Texas cattlemen, as well as the stockyards, commission agents, and packers, were enjoined from making contracts or agreements to regulate charges. The Kansas exchange won its case and was declared not to be a trust; this left Fort Worth the only major livestock market without an exchange. Business could continue, but without the beneficial structure that a member-operated livestock exchange provided. No organization existed for long-range planning or even policing of the market other than the stockyards management.[24]

Not only did the state of Texas effectively end the cooperation among the various livestock interests at Fort Worth by disallowing their livestock exchange; in 1907 the state legislature attempted to reduce yardage and feed charges at stockyards. Naturally, the Fort Worth Stock Yards Company fought it. The company asked legislators to visit the yards to examine the costs of operation. A subcommittee of the House Committee on State Affairs toured the yards

24. "State Sues Exchange," *Fort Worth Daily Live Stock Reporter*, April 26, 1906, p. 1. See also judgment dated October 7, 1907, Case No. 23,941, *The State of Texas v. The Fort Worth Livestock Exchange, et al.*, copy included in a letter from William Hunter McLean to Tom B. Saunders, Jr., February 7, 1974, in Tom B. Saunders, Jr., Collection, Texas Christian University Special Collections, Fort Worth, Texas; "Not Considered a Trust," *Fort Worth Daily Live Stock Reporter*, January 9, 1911, p. 1.

on February 16, 1907. While the company extended them every courtesy, it could not show the legislators the financial records because the secretary-treasurer was out of town. The committee members asserted that they opposed any state legislation that would cripple the industry. Since charges indeed seemed unreasonably high, however, they favored federal regulation to place the large operators outside Texas under the same restrictions. Only federal legislation would help, the committee reasoned, because out-of-state packers controlled the local stockyards.[25]

Two years later yardage fees at the local stockyards were still bringing complaints from cattlemen. The Fort Worth Stock Yards Company reduced yardage fees by one-third on January 1, 1909, after a committee from the Cattle Raisers Association of Texas visited company officials and threatened to place the matter before the next legislature if the company made no changes.[26]

Another frustrating setback for the stockyards included a flood on April 17–18, 1908, in the low area between the Trinity River and Marine Creek, which cut off streetcar transportation between Fort Worth and North Fort Worth. The Fort Worth and Denver City Railroad put on a special train service to carry workers to the stockyards area. Old-timers remembered a similar flood in July, 1889. People did not have to wait another nineteen years for the next, however, for only five weeks later, on the night of May 23, flood waters again ravaged North Fort Worth, covering the lawn in front of the exchange building and the floor of a new coliseum. Across Exchange Avenue, on the south, water rose in the buildings of the *Live Stock Reporter* and the Simmons-Team Mule Company to a height of three feet. Both packing houses, located on higher ground to the east, escaped damage, but the area west of the stockyards did not fare as well. Marion Sansom lost all but two hundred of twenty-five hundred sheep in his pasture. Waters swept away the bridge on Ex-

---

25. "Legislators Coming," *Fort Worth Daily Live Stock Reporter*, February 14, 1907, p. 1; "Report Is Favorable," *Texas Stockman-Journal*, February 27, 1907, p. 7; "Report of Committee on Regulation of Stockyards in Texas," *Fort Worth Daily Live Stock Reporter*, February 22, 1907, p. 1.

26. "Yardage Fees Are Cut One-Third," *Texas Stockman-Journal*, December 23, 1908, p. 1.

change Avenue, but the stockyards company soon replaced it with a foot bridge.[27]

Construction and expansion at the yards continued during the decade, despite the floods, threatened state regulation, and legal hassles. Nonetheless, the board did delay some decisions to await the results of state action. In late November, 1905, the board of directors authorized the construction of covered pens costing between $4,000 and $5,000 to connect with existing hog pens. In January, 1906, the board considered a suggestion by General Manager King to build a pavilion or auditorium at the stockyards for the annual stock show. If subscriptions by Fort Worth citizens reached $20,000 or $30,000, King wanted to know, would the company agree to furnish the balance and construct the building? The board preferred to wait.[28]

The directors authorized the officers to dig a new artesian well to a lower stratum than the existing wells, at a cost of about $5,000. At the same meeting they also decided to purchase a suitable tent for the cattle show to be held at the stockyards in March, 1907, and to guarantee the premium list up to $7,500. They arranged for advance sales of tickets for the show, gate receipts, and income from all other sources to be applied to the premium, and the Fort Worth Stock Yards Company would be liable only for the deficit, if any.[29]

The directors continued in the fall of 1906 to discuss building a coliseum or pavilion. They learned that local citizens had pledged $42,000 toward the project. With that much guaranteed, directors were willing to commission an architect. At the same meeting they also decided that as soon as practicable the stockyards company should control the horse business and that leases to outside companies should no longer be made. The needs for cavalry animals

27. "Flood Reaches Records," April 18, 1908, p. 1; and "Stockyards District Ravaged by High Water," *Fort Worth Daily Live Stock Reporter*, May 25, 1908, p. 1.

28. Board of Directors Meeting, November 15, 1905, Fort Worth Stock Yards Company, *Corporate Record*, 1st bound vol., p. 161, and January 25, 1906, p. 181.

29. Ibid., October 25, 1906, p. 187. After the show the following March a directors' meeting revealed that receipts from the show were $10,136.85 and disbursements $13,500.00, so the deficit the Fort Worth Stock Yards Company paid was only $3,363.15 (ibid., March 28, 1907, p. 219).

by foreign governments, particularly the British, had made the horse and mule trade in Fort Worth quite lucrative.[30]

Edward Swift complained at the January, 1907, directors meeting that switching facilities at the stockyards were inadequate. The board also voted to continue negotiations for the control or acquisition of the Hodge Yards, the stockyards located on property of the Texas and Pacific Railroad and the Missouri-Kansas-Texas Railroad in Fort Worth.[31]

Officials also agreed to expand the existing stockyards facilities. General Manager King indicated that commission men and others needed more office space, which would cost $21,000. The directors approved the addition and granted permission to build a three hundred-ton hay barn and granary. Directors delayed the start of construction for the projected coliseum for several months, however, while they waited to see what the state legislature intended to do about regulating stockyards' charges. Finally, in mid-1907 they told King to go ahead. While King always maintained final control over any expansion project, Kennerly Robey, the chief engineer and architect of the Fort Worth Stock Yards Company during these early years, directly supervised the coliseum construction and other additions. He planned the stock show facility to complement the Spanish-style architecture of the exchange building adjacent to it on the east and to ventilate the building with windows in the roof, which let the hot air out and caught the prevailing breezes. A cornerstone ceremony was held on October 3, 1907. Plans called for the coliseum to be the "largest, most elegant and perfectly appointed live stock exhibition building in the South, and one without superior in the United States."[32]

By October, 1907, $37,000 of a $50,000 subscription eventually promised by the local citizens had already been raised, but the nationwide recession slowed down subscriptions. Prime movers in the effort included officials of the local fat stock show: S. Burk Burnett,

30. *Corporate Record*, November 14, 1906, p. 195.

31. Ibid., January 16, 1907, p. 209.

32. Ibid., March 28, 1907, and June 20, 1907, pp. 219, 227; "Will Triple Hog Supply," *Texas Stockman-Journal*, May 22, 1907, p. 12; "New Home of Texas Feeders and Breeders," *Southwestern Farmer and Breeder*, October 4, 1907, p. 1.

president; T. T. D. Andrews, manager and secretary; Marion Sansom, vice-president; and C. C. French, publicity agent for the stockyards and assistant secretary. Burk Burnett helped raise the money by sending out a letter to the cattlemen of Texas.[33]

Show officials promised the Fort Worth Stock Yards that they would hold at least one show each year for the coming ten years if the stockyards company would erect the building. They promised to deposit $50,000 as a guaranty with the stockyards company that they would hold the show. The $50,000 would stay in escrow. If the show continued for ten successful years, the money would go back to the cattlemen; if not, the stockyards company would keep it as partial compensation for the expense of constructing the building. Stockholder L. V. Niles objected to the projected $130,000 cost of the coliseum and to the liberal terms offered the National Feeders and Breeders organization, which hosted the show.[34]

Several changes had occurred in the stock show since the Fort Worth Stock Yards Company had begun it in 1896. The name had changed three of its ultimate five times, from the Texas Fat Stock Show to the Fort Worth Fat Stock Show and in 1906 to the National Feeders and Breeders Show. Officials had added a horse show and poultry show in 1906. With poultry added, they felt the title "fat stock show" was misleading. C. C. French, public relations agent for the stockyards, later noted that promoters had voted down three years in a row a resolution to have a poultry show in connection with the fat stock show. He quoted Frank Hovencamp, a veteran Texas cattleman, as to why: "We don't want six bit roosters crowing in the early morning and waking up $1,000 bulls."[35] The show, always popular with out-of-town visitors, attracted Chief Quanah Parker

33. "Men Prominent in the Upbuilding of This Live Stock Market," *Fort Worth Daily Live Stock Reporter*, March 24, 1908, pp. 10–11; *History of the Cattlemen of Texas* (Dallas: Johnston Printing & Advertising Co., 1914), p. 79.

34. The agreement was presented and put into the record at the meeting (Board of Directors Meeting, December 17, 1907, *Corporate Record*, 1st bound vol., p. 239).

35. C. C. French, "The History of a Great Fort Worth Institution, the Southwestern Exposition and Fat Stock Show," C. C. French Manuscripts, pp. 26, 32, as cited in *Research Data*, Fort Worth and Tarrant County, Texas, Federal Writers' Project, LXII, 24587, 24593 (hereafter cited as *Research Data*).

and two of his wives in March, 1907, while he was in the city to attend the annual cattlemen's convention.[36]

The opening of the new coliseum during the 1908 stock show marked an innovation. The first indoor cutting horse contest ever held under electric lights took place on March 14. L. V. Niles came nearly every year to visit the stockyards during the stock show, and in 1908 Greenlief Simpson came as well. Winfield Scott took Simpson and his wife for a drive. "He [Simpson] said he never saw such a change in a town in his life, the people walked different, acted different and was [sic] different."[37]

Unbelievably, following the 1908 show, S. Burk Burnett, Marion Sansom, and Fort Worth Stock Yards Company manager W. B. King traveled to Chicago to tell Armour and Swift that the show had grown too big for the new coliseum and they needed more room. Subsequently, King submitted plans to the directors for covered sheds or pens with a capacity of 700 cattle, which would cost $23,000 to $25,000 to build, and for open pens with a capacity of thirty-two railroad cars of livestock, to cost about $5,000. The pens would be used for housing overflow show cattle during the fat stock show and for other purposes at other times. King also submitted drawings for the extension of pens in the quarantine division, which he estimated would cost between $6,000 and $7,000 and which would increase the capacity of the yards by about fifty railroad cars. Directors, especially Niles and Simpson, responded that cheaper ways were needed to build the pens. Suggesting that an effort should be made to get the local people to help build the pens for the fat stock show, they appointed a committee to explore the possibility.[38]

The board also in 1908 made an important decision to hire two

36. "Quanah Parker, Great Chief of the Comanches," *Fort Worth Record,* March 17, 1907, p. 1.

37. Tom B. Saunders, "How the Word Rodeo Originated as Applied to Western Events," *Quarter Horse Journal* 20 (June, 1968): 30. The first cutting horse contest ever was in Haskell, Texas, at the Texas Cowboy Reunion (now held in Stamford) on July 29, 1898 (Winfield Scott to daughter Georgia, November 17, 1908, as cited in Porter, *Thistle Hill,* p. 293).

38. "More Room Is Needed," *Fort Worth Daily Live Stock Reporter,* March 28, 1908, p. 1; Board of Directors Meeting, August 11, 1908, *Corporate Record,* 1st bound vol., p. 255.

men to promote hog raising by Texas farmers. The possibility of more hog receipts on the local market increased that year when railroads crossing Oklahoma lowered the tariff from seven cents to two cents on the hundred on hogs shipped from points in Oklahoma to the Fort Worth market. Commission men found the lower rate exciting because it obviously would mean more business.[39]

Directors authorized General Manager King to construct a concrete bridge over Marine Creek at a cost not to exceed $8,000. Directors learned later that the bridge would cost $16,000 and approved that sum as well as authorizing the construction of a brick building on the north side of the bridge at a cost of $34,000 and a brick building on the south side for $25,000. They also decided to colonize and incorporate a village comprising the stockyards and packing houses and authorized $25,000 to $35,000 to construct rentable houses. The directors further gave the general manager authority to spend $16,000 to build more cattle pens in the southern division of the stockyards.[40]

Obviously then, mushrooming growth represented the major theme of the first decade of the twentieth century for the Fort Worth stockyards. Market officials and others understandably expected that growth to continue and for other of the Big Five packers to build plants at the stockyards. Almost from the time that Armour and Swift opened their doors, rumors circulated in the city that other packers would construct plants, too—Nelson Morris or the Schwarzchild and Sulzberger Company. An enthusiastic speaker at a tick dipping ceremony predicted that instead of supporting two great packers, Fort Worth soon would boast three, four, or even half a dozen. City leaders remained always ready to encourage them to come. When local citizens heard a rumor that Nelson Morris might open a packing plant in Oklahoma City, longtime Fort Worth promoter B. B. Paddock met with Morris's lawyers and offered a bonus to lo-

39. Board of Directors Meeting, August 11, 1908, *Corporate Record*, 1st bound vol., p. 257; "Lower Rates to This City on Hogs," *Texas Stockman-Journal*, August 19, 1908, p. 12.
40. Board of Directors Meeting, March 24, 1909, November 23, 1909, *Corporate Record*, 1st bound vol., pp. 293, 294-95. The bridge and two brick buildings still stand: Theo's Saddle and Sirloin Cafe is on the south, and Finchers Western Wear is on the north.

cate at Fort Worth instead of the Oklahoma site, for a plant there would draw off some of Fort Worth's business. Morris's lawyers informed former Mayor Paddock that the packer was not expanding to either location at present.[41]

Cattlemen and local businessmen created a committee in 1907 to raise a bonus to get another packer. Their hopes soared the next year that Schwarzchild and Sulzberger or even Jacob Dold and Company might come. The newspaperman who printed the hopes for another packer admitted that Fort Worth would have grown faster if the market received more hogs. Cattle interests would benefit too, he said, if Texas got more hogs, because more packers would come. A packing house cannot run on beef alone, the writer reminded his readers. The consuming public at this time ate more pork than beef, so packers naturally utilized more.[42]

Fort Worth businessmen made the offer in November, 1908, of a bonus of $100,000 to the first packer who would build, equip, and operate a plant like the existing two. In just a few hours on November 6 they subscribed $51,000. A committee composed of Winfield Scott, S. Burk Burnett, George T. Reynolds, Marion Sansom, and W. T. (Tom) Waggoner planned to go to Chicago and call on the packers to present their proposition. The men felt certain that at least one packer would come. Citizens raised the remainder of the $100,000 bonus, but officials still held it as of June 5, 1909, for no packer had accepted their offer. Rumors continued that Schwarzchild and Sulzberger would build a plant in Texas and one in Oklahoma. When two members of the Cudahy Packing Company came to Fort Worth July 7, 1909, to look over the area, they asked about the supply of cattle and hogs. Citizens felt so certain that one or more new packing plants would be built in the city in 1909 that they stated the information in a souvenir program published that year relating facts about Fort Worth. The next year some citizens even attempted to acquire an interest in the stockyards and give that

41. "Nelson Morris Rumor," *Fort Worth Daily Live Stock Reporter*, March 21, 1904, p. 1; "First Dipping Test Is a Success," *Texas Stockman-Journal*, May 18, 1904, p. 8; "Nels Morris Not Coming," *Fort Worth Daily Live Stock Reporter*, June 14, 1907, p. 1.
42. "Plan Bonus for Packing House," *Texas Stockman-Journal*, March 13, 1907, p. 15.

holding to a packer as an inducement to establish a new packing house, but they failed. No other major packers came to Fort Worth, although the bonus later was given to a smaller company.[43]

While critics might claim that the two Big Five packers already in Fort Worth, Armour and Swift, exerted pressure to keep others away, the overriding factor seemed to be the absence of a sufficient number of hogs to interest a third major packer in coming. Even the Armour and Swift plants never operated to capacity in hogs. C. C. French, the Fort Worth Stock Yards Company promotional agent, told of a conversation with packer Nelson Morris in Chicago in which French urged Morris to build a packing plant in Fort Worth. Morris asked, "How soon will you have hogs enough?"[44]

The supply of hogs in Texas became the one major factor on which the continued growth of the Fort Worth market depended. Whether the Fort Worth Stock Yards Company would become number one and surpass Chicago quite definitely depended on Texas hog production rather than on cattle production.

43. "More Packing Houses," *Fort Worth Daily Live Stock Reporter*, November 7, 1908, p. 1; "More Talk of S & S," ibid., June 5, 1909, p. 1; "Cudahys Looking Around," ibid., July 8, 1909, p. 1; Official Souvenir Programme, Thirty-third Annual Convention, Cattle Raisers Association of Texas, Fort Worth, Texas, March 1909; "Livestock: Packing House Prospects Bright," *Fort Worth Record*, January 16, 1910, as cited in *Research Data*, XIX, 7596–97.

44. C. C. French Manuscripts, in *Research Data*, LXII, 24565.

Hogs! Hogs! Hogs!

1909–10

CHARLES C. FRENCH became a "pork preacher" for the Fort Worth Stock Yards Company in 1909, when he became the major figure in the stockyards' new campaign to "preach the gospel" of hogs to farmers in Texas, the South, and the Southwest. French certainly qualified for the job: he knew most of the cattlemen of Texas from long years in the business, and he was an inveterate talker. One newspaper writer labeled his "talking proclivities . . . second only to the oily-tongued railroad live stock agent."[1]

French, who had come to Texas from Pennsylvania as a boy, started out a cowman, trailing herds northward as a cowboy in the 1870s. By 1888 he had a job traveling in Texas handling cattle successively for three commission companies: McIlhany, James H. Campbell, and then Evans-Snider-Buel. By 1896 he had become the promotional agent of the Fort Worth Stock Yards Company, for in that year he helped organize the first fat stock show. He apparently quit or was laid off near the turn of the century when business slowed, for he worked again for Evans-Snider-Buel. He returned to the stockyards by the time the packers came. Then in 1909 at age fifty-six French tackled his most ambitious promotional effort, one that would take him on thousands of miles of travel to speak to tens of thousands of farmers and their youngsters, the state's re-

---

1. "Personal Mention," *Texas Live Stock Journal,* September 5, 1891, p. 10.

source for the future. His task: talk them into raising more hogs.[2]

The job proved difficult because southern cotton farmers and plantation owners had migrated into East Texas, bringing their agricultural habits with them; cotton provided the one money crop. Other foodstuffs and animals they raised—including hogs—only supplemented the family food supply. Sons and grandsons followed their ancestors' habits even into the twentieth century. With no reliable market until Swift and Armour opened at Fort Worth, few farmers considered raising hogs as a money crop. West Texas and the Panhandle area of the state developed as cattle ranches, often with midwesterners and even British and Scottish syndicates as owners. These West Texas cattlemen resisted hog production even more strenuously than the farmers of East Texas. Neither group cared that the one factor most vital to the growth of the Fort Worth market during its first half-century was the need for more hogs.

While packers and others should have expected that West Texas cattlemen would be difficult to convince, persuading Texas farmers to shift from cotton to pork once an excellent market existed would, on the face of it, have seemed an easier task. Fort Worth stood practically on the borderline between east and west, between the Cross Timbers of the East Texas farming district on one side and the plains of West Texas cattle country stretching out on the other.

Had Fort Worth gathered a large enough supply of hogs to attract two or three other big packers, the local market would have had a reasonable chance to surpass Kansas City and Chicago and to lead the nation. That was what local citizens, packer J. Ogden Armour, and other officials desired. The tremendous effort of the Fort Worth Stock Yards Company to increase hog receipts, especially in the second decade of the twentieth century, constitutes an exciting

2. French worked for the stockyards until the mid-1930s except for about five years with the extension service of Texas A&M. In fact, he was being "carried gratuitously" on the payroll at $162 per month in July, 1936. Rossie Beth Bennett, "History of the Cattle Trade in Fort Worth, Texas" (Master's thesis, George Peabody College for Teachers, 1931), p. 4; "General Range & Stock Notes," *Texas Live Stock Journal*, September 14, 1889, p. 10; *Texas Stock and Farm Journal*, July 31, 1896, p. 4; ibid., October 31, 1898, p. 8; W. C. Walker to L. V. Niles, May 18, 1921, L. V. Niles to W. C. Walker, May 10, 1921, and A. G. Donovan to W. K. Wright, July 11, 1936, Dies Correspondence, Fort Worth Stock Yards Company Collection, North Texas State University Archives, Denton (FWSY Co. Coll.).

story. Company officials' optimism soared, and they accomplished a great deal because of their publicity efforts, but they never attained number-one status. Hogs, not cattle, are the reason why.

Perhaps the two Big Five meat packers, Armour and Swift, erred in expecting to create more hog production in Texas than cattle. They should have planned their slaughtering activities at Fort Worth more closely around cattle and utilized their plants in the Midwest for hogs. Unfortunately for the continued growth of the Fort Worth market, they did not. Yet, even if not up to packers' expectations, local swine receipts did increase dramatically. In the early years of the twentieth century, the stockyards were receiving 75,000 hogs a month, but officials wanted at least twice that many.[3]

In practically every issue of the local stock journal from the 1890s on, a stockyards advertisement begged for more hogs. About a month after Armour and Swift opened their large modern plants, an editorial in the *Live Stock Reporter* comparing hog prices revealed that Fort Worth offered a few cents more than Kansas City or Saint Louis. The editor again urged farmers to ship to Fort Worth.[4]

G. W. Simpson of the stockyards told the local livestock newspaper that by July, 1903, Fort Worth already ranked as the sixth largest cattle market in the country and handled more cattle in its first year than Chicago, Kansas City, or Omaha had in their first. He believed Fort Worth would eventually lead them all "if the people will raise hogs to the extent of their ability." Another local stock journal described the swine industry of Texas as "in its infancy" but believed it "capable of remarkable development" given the opening of the new Texas market. From the outset packers told Texas farmers, "Texas cannot raise more hogs than the Fort Worth market will care for." They assured stockmen that if supply ever did exceed the packers' demand, other companies would come that could handle it.[5]

Livestock writers even tried to convince cattlemen to raise hogs

3. "Now Will You Raise Hogs?" *Fort Worth Daily Live Stock Reporter*, March 5, 1906.
4. "Hogs and Packing House," *Fort Worth Daily Gazette*, February 12, 1890; "Fort Worth the Best Market," *Fort Worth Daily Live Stock Reporter*, April 6, 1903.
5. "Fort Worth Market Comparison of Business with That of Other Markets," *Fort Worth Daily Live Stock Reporter*, July 13, 1903; "Big Packeries at Fort Worth," *Texas Stock Journal*, March 4, 1902, p. 1; "Hog Supply in Texas," *Texas Stockman-Journal*, October 12, 1904 p. 11.

along with their beeves in order to increase cattle prices. They argued that the market continually paid lower prices than the producers desired for their cattle because packers were getting all they could accommodate in present facilities. Because packers never got all the hogs they needed, however, they did not expand. If producers raised more hogs, other packing plants would be built, increasing the demand for cattle as well. Observant market analysts, including some members of the Cattle Raisers Association of Texas (but never enough livestock producers), noted that hogs represented the key to growth.[6]

H. E. Finney, general manager of the local Armour plant, suggested that the quickest way to get another packing plant in Fort Worth would be to ship three or four hogs to the market for every head of cattle. Swift officials agreed, and Louis F. Swift proclaimed that if Texans raised ten times as many hogs as at that time, the local market "would buy every one of them."[7]

No one can fault the Fort Worth Stock Yards Company officials for not trying to obtain more hogs at their market, for they used every promotional device known to advertisers in those early days of the twentieth century and even developed a few new ones. The stockyards launched a program in which the company would give monthly prizes of five registered boars, to the shippers of the four best carloads and one best wagonload of hogs. The producer had only to own the hogs and to have fed them for at least two months prior to sale. At the State Fair of Texas in Dallas, the Fort Worth Stock Yards Company offered a twenty-five-dollar premium for the grand champion boar and a twenty-five-dollar premium for the grand champion sow to encourage southwestern hog breeders. The company also cooperated with other organizations and stock journals in waging the hog campaign. The Cattle Raisers Association of Texas in the century's first decade continually told farmers in the *Stockman-Journal* how profitable hog raising could be. They even

6. "More Hogs Needed to Help Cattle Business," *Texas Stockman-Journal,* November 15, 1905, p. 8; "Encourages Movement among Cattle Raisers," *Fort Worth Daily Live Stock Reporter,* January 5, 1914.

7. "Raise More Hogs Says L. F. Swift," *Fort Worth Star,* March 23, 1907, quoted in Mack Williams, *In Old Fort Worth,* p. 73.

ran a special issue on hog raising.[8] The *Southwestern Farmer and Breeder*, also published locally, made a practice of printing names of individual ranchers or farmers who shipped to Fort Worth, the prices they received for cattle or hogs, and how they compared (favorably of course) with prices offered in Kansas City and Chicago.

The stockyards company fitted up a Cotton Belt Railroad to demonstrate different breeds of hogs. The stockyards encouraged the Missouri-Kansas-Texas and the Fort Worth and Denver City railway companies to do the same kind of educational campaign for farmers on their lines. The company also decided to bring in a number of high-grade gilts from Illinois and Missouri to sell at cost to stock farmers.[9]

Typical of the numerous advertisements used repeatedly by the company to urge hog raising was one which posed what it called the "Eternal Question."

With the Farmer—How to get the farm paid for, the children educated, the new house built, and some money in the bank?

With the Landowner—How to get the tenants to make the farm more productive?

With the Packer—How to get more hogs to meet the increased demand for pork products?

With the Stockyards—How to satisfy the packers' constantly increasing demand for more hogs?

With the Stockman—How to get another packing plant in Fort Worth?

The Answer is: Raise Hogs!
Raise More Hogs!!
And THEN SOME.[10]

The largest and most successful hog promotion effort of the company involved the fulltime activities of traveling promotional agent

8. "Now Will You Raise Hogs?"; "To Encourage Hog Raising," *Fort Worth Daily Live Stock Reporter*, September 10, 1909; *Texas Stockman-Journal*, February 24, 1909.

9. "Spreading the Gospel of Hogs," *Fort Worth Daily Live Stock Reporter*, July 21, 1910; "Missouri and Illinois Gilts To Be Distributed among the Farmers by Stockyards Co.," ibid., December 15, 1919.

10. Fort Worth Stock Yards Company Advertisement, *Texas Stock and Farm Journal*, January 1, 1909, p. 14.

and talker extraordinaire Charles C. French. His efforts through Texas and the South constituted a major aspect of a campaign for which Armour, Swift, and the Fort Worth Stock Yards Company jointly appropriated $100,000. They wanted to triple the hog supply in Texas within five years. They delayed in 1907 to see what the state legislature would do in its investigation of the market, but when it decided not to tax, they continued their plans.[11]

Convincing cotton farmers to change to hogs for their money crop was "almost a hopeless case," French believed, especially for farmers over age fifty. French therefore decided to start with the young-sters. He convinced A. W. Matthews, secretary-treasurer of the Fort Worth Stock Yards Company, to cooperate with his "herculean task." Studying the corn club idea that began spreading nationwide among young people in rural areas about 1908, French became convinced that a pig club idea would work, too.

Shortly after the turn of the century, at a time when agricultural colleges, farmers' institutes, and schools were developing a youth phase of their agricultural extension programs, public-spirited people in many places began home-project programs for rural youth. From 1908 to 1910, the number of boys' corn clubs grew steadily in rural communities. The clubs, which helped youngsters gain agricultural skills, eventually formed a nucleus for the 4-H Club organization.

French adapted the idea of the corn clubs for his hog promotion campaign. Because most county agents were agronomists, they did not support this adaptation; some even fought it. Nonetheless, French worked vigorously to establish pig clubs all over Texas and the South. For example, he visited towns along the line of the Fort Worth and Denver City Railway giving lectures to adults and establishing clubs for the youngsters. People began to call French a "pork evangelist."[12] Any farm youngster—whether from a well-off family or not—would be encouraged by French to borrow enough money at a local bank to purchase a bred sow. After the first litter arrived,

11. "Will Triple Hog Supply," *Texas Stockman-Journal*, May 22, 1907, p. 12; Board of Directors Meeting, Fort Worth Stock Yards Company, August 11, 1908, *Corporate Record*, p. 257.

12. Franklin M. Reck, *The 4-H Story: A History of 4-H Club Work*, pp. 93–94; "Arousing Interest in Hogs," *Fort Worth Daily Live Stock Reporter*, April 11, 1911.

the youngster would feed the piglets and, when they matured, sell them — at the Fort Worth market, naturally. Then the young pig farmer would pay off his loan at the bank, buy two bred sows, or more, and keep going. The situation made a businessman and swine producer out of the youngster, created a new customer for the small-town bank, and — what French mainly sought — produced more hogs for the Fort Worth market.[13]

When the Smith-Lever Act of 1914 created the U.S. Extension Service, cooperative extension work included the creation of pig, beef, corn, and other clubs, and the name 4-H soon appeared. Clubs spread all over Texas, Louisiana, Alabama, Mississippi, Oklahoma, the Carolinas, and the Dakotas. French continually explained: "The object of these clubs is to educate boys and girls correctly along livestock production lines." Quickly the USDA extended the clubs to thirteen states, and the *Live Stock Reporter* proudly claimed that the idea had spread to foreign countries. Naturally, that newspaper credited French and the Fort Worth Stock Yards Company with the pig club idea.[14] Franklin M. Reck, 4-H historian, has made clear, however, that the origin of the clubs represented too great a movement to be credited to any one man or any one community.[15]

French believed so strongly in the youth clubs that he quit the Fort Worth Stock Yards Company, October 1, 1915, and took a job as Superintendent of Livestock Development in Texas with the U.S. Department of Agriculture in its extension service at Texas A&M College. He told friends that he would be as close to the growth of the livestock business as before, if not closer. In his new job he assisted the eighty-five government farm demonstrators in various sections of Texas in organizing and building up different kinds of livestock clubs. In his new role French issued a statement that "more farmers raised hogs in Texas this year than ever before" and forecast that "a still greater number will raise hogs next year." He

13. "Boys Pig Club," C. C. French Manuscripts, p. 121, in *Research Data*, Fort Worth and Tarrant County, Texas, Federal Writers' Project, LXII, 24682–91.

14. "Extension Work 20 Years Old; Started in Texas by Knapp," *Weekly Live Stock Reporter*, May 17, 1934, p. 1; "C. C. French Discusses Growth of Hog Clubs," *Fort Worth Daily Live Stock Reporter*, March 31, 1915; "Pig Club Work Is Extended to Many Different States," *Fort Worth Daily Live Stock Reporter*, September 1, 1915.

15. Reck, *The 4-H Story*, p. ix.

added regretfully, however, that of the 525,000 farmers in Texas, 125,000 did not raise even one pig.[16]

As a favor to the Fort Worth Stock Yards Company, Floyd Sherwood, hog buyer for Armour, selected hogs to deliver to bankers in rural Texas towns, who then turned them over to youngsters at cost, taking their notes for a year. The Fort Worth Stock Yards Company first bred the sows to purebred boars. French argued that sometimes older, established farmers decided to raise hogs when they saw the success the boys achieved. French announced that on June 3, 1918, Texas boys clubs reached an enrollment of 28,388 participants and included clubs for corn, cotton, peanut, sorghum, potato, baby beef, sheep, dairy, and poultry, in addition to the pig clubs, which alone enrolled 9,241 members. If each club youngster raised two litters of pigs, averaging six per litter, and sold them at Fort Worth, the market would receive more than a hundred thousand additional hogs that year.[17]

French resumed his job as promotional agent for the Fort Worth Stock Yards Company around 1920. After he returned, even the aging L. V. Niles wrote from Boston asking, "How is Mr. French getting along in his plan of shipping the stock hogs to different parts of Texas?" In a single month French conducted fifty farmers' meetings in ten West Texas counties in conjunction with the West Texas Chamber of Commerce for a "poultry-dairy-livestock campaign." He showed moving pictures and slides to seven thousand people.[18]

Even during the Depression the Fort Worth Stock Yards Company still presented 200-pound bred gilts to several 4-H Club boys. The boys signed agreements by which they would return to the company from the first litter of pigs one gilt of the same weight as the one they first received. The boys also agreed to plant enough corn or grain to fatten two litters of pigs and to sell both litters to the Fort Worth Stock Yards through any commission company. The com-

16. "French Takes an Important Livestock Post with U.S.," *Fort Worth Daily Live Stock Reporter*, September 29, 1915; "Diversification Idea Is Lauded by French," ibid., November 5, 1915.

17. "Fort Worth's Showing Is Best of Any Trade Center," ibid., January 1, 1918; "Enrollment of Boys' Clubs Is Now 28,388," ibid., June 3, 1918.

18. L. V. Niles to W. C. Walker, May 10, 1921, Niles Folder, Dies Correspondence, FWSY Co. Coll. See also "Rural Campaigning in Western Texas," *Fort Worth Daily Live Stock Reporter*, January 4, 1923.

pany still worked with the 4-H in 1940. During that year they took boys from 4-H and the Future Farmers of America on tours of the stockyards and packing plants, showing and explaining the entire process so that they might even see the carcasses of their own cattle, hogs, or lambs hanging on the hooks soon after selling them. Cooperation with the youth clubs remained active through the 1950s.[19]

Although C. C. French and the Fort Worth Stock Yards Company made a major thrust in their hog promotion of 1909–10 and the years immediately following, they cannot take full credit for originating the pig club idea, nor for the official creation of the 4-H Clubs. Even so, the fulltime efforts of French as agent of the stockyards contributed greatly to the spread of these youth organizations in Texas and the South. What influence he and the stockyards exerted outside the state is impossible to measure, but within Texas certainly the 4-H movement would not have succeeded as well without their efforts. Although the motives of the Fort Worth Stock Yards Company and the packers to attract more hogs for their market may have been purely financial, their program nevertheless worked to the advantage of the youngsters. Many young men went at least partially into hog farming, gaining early business experience. For the stockyards' part, the promotional efforts of the company succeeded in creating the clubs and considerably increasing hog production in the state. Receipts climbed gradually, and the Fort Worth Stock Yards Company kept expanding its hog pens accordingly. Hog receipts finally reached a million in 1917 for the first time.[20]

Over the long term, though, farmers did not raise enough hogs to keep the two existing packing plants operating to capacity, and therefore no other large packers moved to Fort Worth. The Fort Worth plants needed five thousand to ten thousand hogs a day but often obtained only one thousand to three thousand. Operating at half capacity became standard. As a result, the Fort Worth market never

19. "Agreement for Swine 4-H Club Boys," February 4, 1933, Dies Correspondence, FWSY Co. Coll.
20. Board of Directors Meeting, Fort Worth Stock Yards Company, January 9, 1917, *Corporate Record*, Fort Worth, III, 108; "Fort Worth's Showing Is Best of Any Trade Center," *Fort Worth Daily Live Stock Reporter*, January 1, 1918; *Annual Report for 1917*, FWSY Co. Coll.

achieved the potential its owners saw in it, much less approaching the dream of being number one in the nation. In fact, the son of L. V. Niles once wrote, "In spite of the best efforts of Mr. French and everybody in general, it appears to be most difficult for the farmers of Texas to raise any considerable number of hogs."[21]

Someone estimated in 1909 that Texans were paying out $15 million annually for pork and pork products from other states. If this sum had gone to Texas stock raisers instead, "the effect on the state's prosperity would be marked. . . . There would be less talk about the price of cotton." Ironically, Fort Worth became the highest paying hog market in the nation and remained so for several years. The packers, the stockyards, and Mr. French were all trying.[22]

When there was a market that would buy all the hogs Texas farmers could produce and would pay a higher price than any other market in the country, why did Texas farmers not raise more hogs? The question may have been partially answered in an educational film narrated by actor Gary Cooper, called *Real West.* Cooper said that a Westerner did not want to do anything he could not do "from the hurricane deck of a Spanish pony."[23] In other words, Texans were cowmen, not hog men. Texas was part of the West, and in the West one rode a horse and raised cattle.

The Fort Worth Stock Yards Company probably would have been happy enough to let West Texas ranchers do as they pleased if East Texas farmers had raised hogs. Unfortunately for the Fort Worth market, although East Texans did not identify with the American West, they were southern enough in their heritage that cotton remained their king. Farmers had planted cotton as their money crop for generations and saw no reason to change, despite the massive promotional efforts of the Fort Worth market. A vast complex existed dedicated to the raising, ginning, marketing, and shipping of cotton—a complex that had been built up over generations. Any inclination to shift to hog production was cut short by the turn-of-

21. "Why We Need Hogs," *Fort Worth Daily Live Stock Reporter,* June 13, 1907; Harold L. Niles to W. C. Walker, November 29, 1926, Dies Correspondence, FWSY Co. Coll.

22. "Texas Should Be the Pork Barrel of the United States," *Stockman-Journal,* February 24, 1909, p. 1.

23. Gary Cooper, narrator, *Real West,* McGraw Hill Films, 1961.

the-century rise in the price of cotton after twenty years of decline. Moreover, tenancy was also on the rise in the area, and landlords generally pressed their tenants to stick with the proven money crop, cotton.[24]

Another major factor was the belief among many producers that since Texas was not a corn state it could not be a hog state either, for one needed corn to feed swine. Many farmers insisted that the Texas climate was too dry to be a corn-producing state. Humid weather in August and September was necessary for a good crop, and Texas generally experienced such conditions only two years out of five. Stockyards and packing officials denied that corn was a prerequisite for pork production. H. G. Kalhorn, hog buyer for Armour at the Fort Worth market, argued that Texas could produce hogs more economically than the corn-belt states because those states had such long winters and no grazing. Agents at the state agricultural experiment station proved that peanuts or cowpeas provided as good a feed for hogs as corn, and whereas Texas may not have had the soil or climate for corn, it did for peanuts. Armour officials suggested feeding kafir corn, milo maize, or Armour's 60 percent meat meal. They failed to convince enough Texas farmers.[25]

Fluctuating prices for hogs may have scared off some farmers. Or perhaps some Texans felt too independent to be tied down to hog raising. A farmer must take care of his hogs every day, but not his cattle, which can graze much of the time. Even with cotton, after planting his crop, the farmer enjoyed some days when he could turn to other things. In any event, and for whatever reasons, neither West Texas ranchers nor East Texas farmers ever turned as avidly to hog raising as the Fort Worth Stock Yards needed them to.

The Depression years marked a turning point in hog promotion efforts: the *Live Stock Reporter* stopped urging people to raise hogs. The pages never again carried on such an intense campaign, even though some of the 4-H pig work continued. The federal govern-

24. Samuel Lee Evans, "Texas Agriculture, 1880–1930" (Ph.D. dissertation, University of Texas at Austin, 1960), pp. 260–61.

25. Interview with Ted Gouldy, publisher *Weekly Livestock Reporter*, Fort Worth, Texas, October 29, 1979; "Fort Worth Plants Equipped to Kill 15,000 Hogs Each Day; Receipts Average around 8,000 Per Week," *Fort Worth Daily Live Stock Reporter*, October 7, 1913.

ment's New Deal hog reduction program attempted to raise prices by creating scarcity. In 1934 the Annual Report of the Fort Worth Stock Yards Company to stockholders commented, "We discontinued our efforts to increase the production of hogs in this state, which were inconsistent with the Government's program."[26]

On that note, the Fort Worth Stock Yards Company concluded a campaign that actually began in the nineteenth century and was carried on through the efforts of Charles C. French. With the demise of French's promotional program, Fort Worth abandoned her hopes of consistently ranking any higher than third or fourth in the nation among the major terminal markets. The company would settle for being during its peak years the largest market south of Kansas City and the largest market in the Southwest. Its grandiose dreams had been defeated, not by lack of cattle, but by too few carloads of squealing pigs.

26. *Annual Report for 1934,* FWSY Co. Coll.

Record-Breaking Years
1 9 1 1 – 1 8

FIVE THOUSAND PEOPLE gathered in the three-year-old coliseum at 9 A.M. on a crisp March morning in 1911 to see and hear former president Theodore Roosevelt at the National Feeders and Breeders Show being held at the stockyards. That was the current name of the fat stock show that had originated in 1896. Local cattleman Burk Burnett had hosted a breakfast for the former president at the Westbrook Hotel in downtown Fort Worth earlier that morning. When Roosevelt stepped on stage, he reminisced about earlier visits with his friend, "Colonel" Burnett. Roosevelt had once enjoyed a hunt with Burnett and Tom Waggoner on Comanche land the two ranchers leased in Indian Territory, and Burnett had visited at the White House when Roosevelt was president. The fare there was "not so good as that served from the chuck wagon while on the wolf hunt on Burnett's ranch," Roosevelt said.[1]

Roosevelt congratulated the people of Fort Worth on their show, their city, and their state. His praise for Fort Worth's market was probably not just political hoopla, either, for in 1911 Teddy was not running for anything. His enthusiasm reflected reality: things really were booming. In fact, board members of the Fort Worth Stock Yards Company had reason to rub their hands together in unabashed glee —or at least to congratulate themselves on their business acumen

1. "Theodore Roosevelt, Ex-President," *Fort Worth Daily Live Stock Reporter*, March 14, 1911, p. 1.

—at their monthly directors' meetings in Chicago during the second decade of the twentieth century. Receipts of animals in all categories continued to grow, and efforts by promotional agent Charles C. French to increase hog production seemed to be working.

The strength of big-business ownership, the company's well-organized promotional activities, and, later in the decade, increased demands brought on by World War I combined to make the ten years before 1920 memorable and profitable ones. In fact, when Edward Swift visited Fort Worth in February, 1911, he shared the largess with others by contributing $5,000 to a committee raising funds to purchase a site for a Methodist university. The Fort Worth Stock Yards Company and Armour and Company each contributed like amounts.[2]

There were a few setbacks to progress during the decade, however. Two fires ravaged the stockyards in 1911. The first, early on the morning of March 14, the very day that former president Roosevelt visited the Feeders and Breeders Show, destroyed the horse and mule barns. Between five hundred and six hundred horses died in the blaze, as did a hundred hogs and an unknown number of sheep. All the buildings on the south side of Exchange Avenue from Marine Creek to the swine sheds, including half the sheds, burned to the ground. Flames were fed by large stacks of hay in the barns. The stock show continued despite the disaster. W. B. King, manager of the Fort Worth Stock Yards Company, announced that the company would rebuild, this time with concrete and steel, fireproof buildings. On behalf of the company he also offered to pay for all hogs and sheep lost in the fire, even though lawyers indicated no legal obligation.[3]

A second fire erupted at the yards on Sunday afternoon, June 25, presumably started by a spark from a locomotive. Although a brick fire wall kept this second conflagration from spreading to the sheep pens, and possibly even the exchange building, the hog sheds and the greater part of the cattle pens burned. Only seventy-five to eighty head of cattle and fifty hogs perished in the blaze, but a thirty-mile-per-hour wind fanned the flames, causing a $175,000 to $200,000 loss.[4]

2. "Edward Swift Here," ibid., February 3, 1911, p. 1.
3. "Fire Destroys Horse and Mule Barns," ibid., March 14, 1911, p. 1; "Will Rebuild at Once," ibid., March 15, 1911, p. 1.
4. "Stockyards Swept by Disastrous Fire," ibid., June 26, 1911, p. 1.

ABOVE: Corner of Main Street and Exchange Avenue near the turn of the century. Courtesy Joe Weisberg Collection, Tarrant County Archives. BELOW: Union Stock Yards Hotel and Exchange Building during the fat stock show in 1901. Courtesy North Fort Worth Historical Society.

ABOVE: Interior of Fort Worth Livestock Commission Company, 1903. The man on the left is J. D. Farmer. Courtesy Genealogy and Local History Department, Fort Worth Public Library Collection, Amon Carter Museum. BELOW: Fort Worth Livestock Exchange Building, shortly after construction in 1903. Courtesy North Fort Worth Historical Society.

ABOVE: Livestock Exchange Building and Coliseum, where annual stock show was held, 1922. Courtesy North Fort Worth Historical Society. BELOW: Armour wagon in front of Exchange Building. Courtesy North Fort Worth Historical Society.

ABOVE: Niles City Town Hall, built 1912. Courtesy North Fort Worth Historical Society. BELOW: Stockyards baseball team, 1912: *(Back row, left to right)* Lefty Wright, Henry Klebold, Ward Farmer, Sammy Rogers, J. D. "Bus" Farmer, Raiford Ward, ———— Taylor, Katy Railroad, Frank Ely, manager; *(middle row)* Johnnie Bolinger, Harry Fifer, Clark Richards, unidentified; *(front row)* unidentified, Lester Thannisch, Lee Allen, Lou Watson, Bunk Thetford, Maurice Butz. Courtesy Larry Farmer.

ABOVE: Mule Alley, lined by brick horse and mule barns, which were constructed in 1912. Courtesy *Fort Worth Star-Telegram*. BELOW: Stockyards National Bank. Courtesy *Fort Worth Star-Telegram*.

The company began rebuilding immediately, and new hog sheds costing $60,000 soon replaced the old ones. The stockyards' interests planned new brick horse and mule barns to make everything south of Exchange Avenue fireproof, except for a small section of sheep sheds. The company also constructed fire walls in various divisions by using steel, concrete, and brick in place of timber.[5]

The new horse and mule barns, completed in March, 1912, stretched 540 feet by 350 feet and held as many as three thousand animals. Manager King had visited all leading markets for ideas to make the barns not only fireproof, but the most modern, sanitary, and well-ventilated public stables available. Costs reached $300,000. Feed storage houses, constructed like vaults, possessed automatic closing doors so sensitive that even the heat of a lighted match would activate them. The only lumber in the entire building consisted of gates, floors, and office fixtures. Local citizens began calling the new horse and mule barns "among the finest stables in the world."[6]

In addition to replacement costs, the board of directors authorized $30,000 to $40,000 to construct depressed runways and to reinforce concrete roofs over the hog division. The company authorized new dipping vats, as well as new covered pens, chutes, and docks at the north end of the southern cattle yards to replace those destroyed by the fires. The new vats became the best facilities in the country. A movie company took pictures of the first cattle to go through and planned to show the film at theaters throughout the nation to illustrate government inspection of cattle to prevent animal diseases.[7]

Fires were not the only hazard; a flood plagued the stockyards area when the Trinity River overflowed its banks late on June 9, 1915. Although the stockyards escaped actual flooding, the area was isolated from the city except for train service. Officials of the yards who lived in Fort Worth found it difficult to reach the yards. Also, local livestock producers who drove their animals to the Fort Worth yards or carried them in wagons could not reach the market. Hun-

5. "Fireproof Hog Sheds," ibid., August 30, 1911, p. 1.
6. B. B. Paddock, ed., *Fort Worth and the Texas Northwest*, II, 663.
7. Board of Directors Meeting, Fort Worth Stock Yards Company, July 17, 1911, *Corporate Record*, Fort Worth, 1st bound vol., p. 343; "New Dipping Vats Open," *Southwestern Farmer and Breeder*, August 11, 1911, p. 5.

dreds of men had to walk across the train trestle to get to work in the packing plants and yards.[8]

Despite these problems, livestock receipts in all classifications climbed during this second decade of the twentieth century, and previously set records began to tumble. The daily local market newspaper published a Mexican edition once a week to attract cattle raisers from south of the border, who looked to Fort Worth as their nearest U.S. market.[9]

The Brand Book of the Cattle Raisers Association, which agents used at the stockyards to examine brands to detect stolen animals, indicated that cattle came from Oklahoma, New Mexico, Kansas, and even as far as California. Big runs of cattle arrived by rail, with as many as eighty cars in the yards at one time. Not all cattle came by rail, however; some nearby cattlemen still trailed their herds to Fort Worth to save money. The company offered the services of drovers to these customers. In addition, a few motor trucks began to arrive with livestock during these years.[10]

As late as 1913 local citizens still "confidently expected" one, and possibly two, additional large packing companies to locate in the city. Several small, independent packers were operating, but not others of the Big Five, as citizens had hoped. Even so, part of the time the market claimed to be second in size in the United States. In 1913 alone the company spent $45,000 to grade, pave, and construct pens, $15,000 for a new office wing, and $8,000 for a roof over the pens in the dip division.[11]

By January, 1914, approximately one hundred regular buyers of cattle, hogs, sheep, and horses worked on the Fort Worth market, fifty of these for cattle. By the end of the year, market analysts saw that 1914 had been Fort Worth's best year yet. It was the only large market whose receipts had increased over the previous year's. Even adverse conditions such as foot-and-mouth disease in the north and

8. "Trinity Waters Flood Lowland: "Much Damage," *Fort Worth Daily Live Stock Reporter,* June 10, 1915, p. 1.

9. *The Book of Fort Worth: Who's Who in Fort Worth,* p. 23.

10. Brand Book, 1900–16, Cattle Raisers Association (handwritten), copy in possession of Louis Fields, Western Feeders Supply, Livestock Exchange Building, Fort Worth.

11. *Book of Fort Worth,* p. 23; Board of Directors Meeting, Fort Worth Stock Yards Company, May 16, 1913, *Corporate Record,* p. 369.

east and a tight money situation all over the country had not slowed its growth. Heavy receipts of Mexican cattle played a role in this success. Toward the close of 1914, an Armour official proclaimed that Fort Worth was "rapidly getting to be the greatest live stock center in the United States." He cited as major markets Fort Worth, Kansas City, Saint Louis, and Chicago.[12]

Also in 1914, General Manager W. B. King resigned. He had served in that capacity since 1902, having been a civil engineer and railroad builder before becoming manager of the stockyards. When he died nearly a year after his retirement, on October 11, 1915, practically the entire stockyards attended his funeral. J. A. Stafford, assistant general manager of the Fort Worth Stock Yards Company and manager of the National Feeders and Breeders Show, succeeded King as general manager on February 1, 1915. Stafford, a native Texan, had had ten years of railroad experience before he became traffic manager for Armour and Company in Kansas City and later at Fort Worth. Stafford enjoyed short tenure as general manager and was soon replaced by Al Donovan, who had started out years before as a messenger with Armour and Company. In Kansas City Donavon rose to manage the Armour Car Lines; in 1902 he came to Fort Worth as manager of Southwestern Mechanical Company, which repaired the packing companies' rolling stock, built steel and oil tanks, and manufactured packing boxes. In 1916 he resigned that position to become vice-president and general manager of the stockyards.[13]

Many foreign-born people, among them Serbians, lived near or worked in the stockyards and packing plants, and the events in their homelands which erupted into war in 1914, seemed close. The war created more activity at the stockyards, especially horse and mule sales, as foreign governments engaged in the Great War purchased cavalry animals. Thriving mule sales at the yards soon attracted at-

12. H. E. Finney, "The Fort Worth Market: Its Relation to the Livestock Industry of the Southwest," *Cattleman* 1 (December, 1914): 6.

13. "William B. King Dies at Early Hour Monday Morning," *Fort Worth Daily Live Stock Reporter*, October 11, 1915, p. 1. Also "Stafford to Manage Fort Worth Stock Yards," *Cattleman* 9 (February, 1915): 18; and "Al G. Donovan Dies at Home," clipping in W. L. Pier Correspondence, Fort Worth Stock Yards Company Collection, North Texas State University Archives, Denton (FWSY Co. Coll.).

tention. From her window one of the reporters of the *North Fort Worth News*, whose offices stood just west of the coliseum on Exchange Avenue, could often count among those buying mules as many as fifteen uniforms from as many nations. Mule buyers would practically play a tune with their bull whips as they drove the animals down the street. As drovers herded the mules down to auction, bypassers might have to wait a quarter of an hour for them all to clear the street.[14]

Within about an eight-month period from November 14, 1914, to July 29, 1915, warring nations of Europe spent more than $5 million in Fort Worth for horses and mules. The British and French governments also purchased cavalry animals at Kansas City, Oklahoma City, and Wichita. By June, 1915, foreign governments had bought an estimated two hundred thousand horses in all markets since the war erupted. A year later in June, 1916, local sources estimated that the total number of mounts shipped to Europe from Fort Worth alone reached one hundred thousand, for which local dealers had received $11 million. Fort Worth justifiably proclaimed itself the largest horse and mule market in the world during this period.[15]

Fort Worth also was calling itself the largest stocker and feeder market and the largest speculative market in the world. By 1916 the market could boast that more than a billion dollars had been paid for livestock at the Fort Worth market since 1903. Packing and allied industries distributed $3 million in wages annually and employed forty-seven hundred people. The activities of the year broke records in both receipts and prevailing prices.[16]

Even the U.S. government recognized the importance of the Fort Worth market, for the local office of the Bureau of Animal Industry, located in the livestock exchange building, became a distribution point for black-leg vaccine in 1916. Prior to this the Department of Agriculture had supplied the vaccine only from Washington. The

14. Interview with L. Harmon Rife, livestock producer, Dublin, Texas, August 13, 1976; interview with Mrs. Nita McCain, former owner of *North Fort Worth News*, Fort Worth, Texas, October 28, 1977.
15. "Notes on the War Horse Trade," *Cattleman* 1 (April, 1915): 14. See also "Horse and Mule Notes," ibid. 1 (June, 1915): 37.
16. "Commerce: Packeries Mean Three Million Dollars Paid in Wages Annually," *Fort Worth Record*, September 29, 1916.

following year in June the department opened a branch of the Bureau of Markets at Fort Worth in the exchange building. Office reports then could be published five days each week, giving complete information about fresh meat trade in the East, the demand, market conditions, and other information. The department issued other reports from New York, Philadelphia, Boston, Chicago, Kansas City, Omaha, and Portland.[17]

Because of the effects on the Fort Worth market, the daily war news made a special impression on local residents. North Side young men became the first to start military drills to get ready for army duty. Many felt that it would be a disgrace to wait to be drafted. By April 8, 1917, several hundred employees of the two packing plants and the Southwestern Mechanical Company started drilling twice a day, under the command of former students of military schools. Three airfields opened around Fort Worth to train Canadian pilots: Taliaferro, Barron, and Carruthers. After the United States entered the war, their names were changed respectively to Hickman Field, Everman, and Benbrook. Another effect of the war fever was that by 1917 nearly all German Americans in Fort Worth had taken out citizenship papers, probably to emphasize their loyalty.

The year 1917 became a record setter for the local market, chalking up marks that would stand for nearly thirty years. Increased war production pushed stockyards receipts to totals not surpassed until war conditions in the 1940s boosted livestock tallies even higher. Armour and Swift both enjoyed large Army contracts. Almost $250 million changed hands at the Fort Worth Stock Yards during 1917, breaking previous records. Daily receipts often surpassed 350 railroad cars. For the first time, cattle, exclusive of calves, reached and exceeded the million mark. Hog recruitment efforts also paid off, and swine receipts tallied a million in 1917. For 1917 Fort Worth's cattle and calf increase over the previous year surpassed that of any of the other big terminal markets, and the local yards became the only one to gain in hogs. Fort Worth ranked third largest in cattle in 1917.[18]

17. "Government Vaccine May Be Secured from Fort Worth," *Cattleman* 3 (August, 1916): 43–44; "Government Opens Market Bureau at Fort Worth," ibid., 4 (July, 1917): 15.

18. *Annual Report for 1917,* Fort Worth Stock Yards Company, FWSY Co. Coll.

By mid-1918 the war peak had passed and receipts of all species of livestock except horses and mules dropped from the same period a year earlier. However, Armour and Swift planned a combined expansion program of $800,000, with Armour spending $500,000 for a five-story building and Swift adding to facilities to increase its daily slaughter capacity from fifteen hundred to two thousand cattle.[19]

The cattle industry represented the largest business in Fort Worth. City leaders, including Amon Carter, who owned the *Fort Worth Star-Telegram*, determined to maintain that supremacy. Of course, Carter's own interest in increasing circulation for his paper publicized Fort Worth and its livestock market at the same time. With a circulation of sixty thousand by 1917, mostly in Fort Worth and West Texas, the *Star-Telegram* had become the largest newspaper in Texas, a distinction it would hold for nearly four decades. Carter reported the agricultural and livestock market news his West Texas readers wanted.[20]

One plan to get more West Texas customers for the Fort Worth market involved organizing the counties in West Texas that shipped livestock to Fort Worth into "one big family." The Fort Worth Chamber of Commerce, on which stockyards officials always served prominently, led in this effort, along with Amon Carter. The cities of Brownwood, Wichita Falls, and Ranger issued a joint call with Fort Worth on December 17, 1918, to formulate plans to organize. Representatives of thirty-seven counties met in Fort Worth December 21. Dr. C. C. Gumm, manager of the Fort Worth Chamber of Commerce, made a motion to organize a West Texas Chamber of Commerce. Visiting community representatives reacted enthusiastically to his suggestion and adopted it unanimously. The Fort Worth Chamber paid six thousand dollars for the preliminary meeting. Marion Sansom, Fort Worth cattleman, served on a committee to raise a permanent fund. Once organized, the first task of the new chamber became the study of possible solutions to agricultural and livestock problems.[21]

19. *Annual Report for 1918,* ibid.
20. Jerry Flemmons, *Amon: The Life of Amon Carter, Sr. of Texas,* p. 148.
21. Carl A. Blasig, *Building Texas,* pp. 152–53.

By creating a West Texas Chamber of Commerce, the Fort Worth businessmen also encouraged more participation from West Texas counties in the annual fat stock show. Carter naturally reported all show activities fully in the *Star-Telegram*. In a decade when livestock records were being set on all fronts, the show began to set a few records of its own. It had not always made expenses and had had to be subsidized by the stockyards company. In fact, in 1911 the board of directors of the company vowed to advance the show no more money after September 1 of that year. The extent of the show's problem became obvious when someone scheduled simultaneous riding and roping contests in an old ball park on the Texas and Pacific Railroad reservation. These amateur attractions always drew good crowds, while the stock show on the stockyards grounds failed to entice sufficient gate receipts to pay expenses.[22]

Wild West exhibitions were still enjoying their heyday nationwide in the 1915-16 period and generally drew big audiences wherever scheduled. Therefore, stock show officials, who had been operating at a deficit, decided to stage a Wild West attraction in 1916 in connection with the livestock exhibition. They invited Joe Miller of the 101 Ranch in Oklahoma to bring his Wild West show to the coliseum. The show that year "excelled all previous shows and for the first time in many years came through without losing money."[23]

At a citizens' meeting in the fall of 1916 the Chamber of Commerce discussed plans to change the name of the show to the Southwestern Exposition. Following the show in March, 1917, according to the terms of a contract made with the Fort Worth Stock Yards Company ten years earlier, the company would return stock subscriptions totaling $50,000 made by citizens of Fort Worth and prominent cattlemen of Texas. These had been made to persuade the company to build the coliseum for the show. The citizens wanted to make plans for the future of the show once the company no longer guaranteed to absorb any deficit. They proposed to create an exposi-

22. Board of Directors Meeting, Fort Worth Stock Yards Company, July 17, 1911, *Corporate Record*, 1st bound vol., p. 343.

23. "National Feeders and Breeders Show: Greatest Exhibition of Southwestern Livestock," *Cattleman* 2 (April, 1916): 15.

tion company and so appointed a committee of fifty-five prominent persons to solicit stock subscriptions and work out details.[24]

Col. Zack Mulhall and his daughter Lucille brought a Wild West show to the coliseum in 1917. Lucille was a daring bronco rider, for whom some claim the phrase "cowgirl" was coined; in fact, Will Rogers called her the "first cowgirl." The Mulhall troupe put on a performance with bronc riding, steer riding, and bulldogging, but paid all cowboys the same fee regardless of their efforts. Thus, it was more a demonstration than a competitive show.[25]

Either by the 1917 show or shortly thereafter, officials changed the name to Southwestern Exposition and Fat Stock Show. Cattlemen met in April, 1917, to plan a new organization, since the contract with the stockyards company had expired. The show would have to pay to the company an annual rental of $3,500 for the use of the coliseum and show grounds. The Fort Worth Stock Yards Company, however, agreed to spend $40,000 for additional accommodations to display sale bulls and for sheep and swine divisions inside the main show grounds. These animals had been scattered all over the stockyards in previous years.[26]

Late in 1917, Ray McKinley, editor and publisher of the *Daily Live Stock Reporter* and *Sunday North Fort Worth News*, lunched with Marion Sansom, stock show president, and A. B. Case, manager of Armour and Company in Fort Worth. McKinley saw the need for monetary incentive or competition to bring out the best in the Wild West show performers and suggested a competitive Wild West contest for the 1918 show. A committee later met to work out details and to find some way to distinguish the Fort Worth show from Cheyenne's "Frontier Days" and Pendleton's "Roundup." Claude Hamilton, a member of the committee, mentioned a Spanish word mean-

24. "To Enlarge Stock Show," ibid. 3 (November, 1916): 21. See also "Southwestern Exposition for Fort Worth," ibid. 3 (December, 1916): 5, and "Fort Worth Show Reorganized; Extensive Improvements Planned," ibid. 3 (May, 1917): 8.

25. "Background of Stock Show," *Fort Worth* 29 (January, 1954): 50; Don Russell, *The Wild West: A History of the Wild West Shows*, pp. 79–80; Tom B. Saunders, "How the Word Rodeo Originated as Applied to Western Events," *Quarter Horse Journal* 20 (June, 1968): 31.

26. "Fort Worth Show Reorganized," p. 8.

ing "to encompass or encircle," frequently used by cowboys to mean a roundup, cow work, or horse breaking, pronouncing it "RO-DAY-O." A member of the committee asked how it was spelled. Hamilton went to the blackboard and printed RODEO. Buck Sansom, son of Marion, spoke up and said, "That spells RO-dee-o!" The men liked the name and called their show "The Rodeo of the Southwestern Exposition and Fat Stock Show." The show on March 11–16, 1918, with its "rodeo," was the largest cattle show ever held until then southwest of Kansas City. Seven barns housed the show cattle, and officials increased pen yardage to take in all the pens of the Fort Worth Stock Yards Company south of the coliseum and east to the livestock exchange building. An estimated twenty-three thousand persons witnessed the event, which made history as the first indoor rodeo. The revamped show, after twenty-two years of nurturing by the Fort Worth Stock Yards Company, gave great promise of making it on its own.[27]

Stockyards officials could look back on the decade that began in 1910 with pride. Charles French's promotional campaign for hogs finally brought in a million swine in 1917, the same year that cattle receipts also reached the million mark. World War I demands made Fort Worth the largest horse and mule market in the world, and the stockyards company completed its contract with the stock show and saw it reorganized and rejuvenated by competitive contests called a rodeo.

Company officials were even happier as they reviewed the finances of the booming decade. Assets totaled nearly $4.5 million in January, 1912, and profits reached $151,534.48. The company paid quarterly dividends of $1.00 per share in 1912, but increased these to $1.50 per share during mid-decade. Twice in 1917 the board authorized extra dividends of $5.00 per share. When officials tabulated profits for the record-breaking year of 1917, they found them at $503,046.24. Quarterly dividends of $2.00 per share began in July, 1917. Assets of the company by that time had reached nearly $5 million.[28]

27. Saunders, "How the Word Rodeo Originated," pp. 31, 33; handwritten notes, Tom B. Saunders, Jr., Collection, Texas Christian University Special Collections; "Fort Worth Stock Show Will Be Bigger and Better," *Cattleman* 4 (March, 1918): 183; "Fort Worth Show—History of First," *Fort Worth* 49 (January, 1973): 22.

28. Annual Stockholders Meetings, 1912–18, and Board of Directors Meeting,

The success of Fort Worth as a livestock market center located within the heart of cattle country brought both pride and profit to the many persons responsible for its existence. Those who labored at the market and lived in the "company town" adjacent to it may have felt somewhat differently, but they nevertheless knew they were a part of something important happening to Fort Worth.

February 1, 1917, and December 4, 1917, Fort Worth Stock Yards Company, *Corporate Record.*

Niles City, U.S.A.

1911–23

EVERY MORNING AT 5:30 A.M. a Swift employee sounded a whistle to notify Swift workers in the North Side area with a shrill and demanding blast that a new work day had dawned. No working family within miles of the stockyards district needed to set alarm clocks, so loud and dependable was that Swift morning call. All who awoke to its sound each day knew that for better or for worse, they were stockyard people. The few blocks of Exchange Avenue that held the hotels, saloons, coliseum, exchange building, stockyards, and packing houses formed the heart of a company town during the days of the city of North Fort Worth and later of Niles City.

Nearby Fort Worth residents and businessmen enjoyed daily benefits from the lively market center in their midst. Consequently, the relationship between the stockyards district and the city of Fort Worth was characterized more by cooperation than by conflict during their many years of dealing with one another. Even the happiest of associations, however, cannot avoid occasional problems. The greatest of these came in the early 1920s when the city of Fort Worth decided not to deny itself any longer the substantial tax revenues of the separate stockyards district. The background of this struggle, which ultimately saw the cities clash in a hard-fought court contest, dates back at least a decade.

In 1889–90, when city leaders were constructing the packing plant and the Union Stock Yards, the area encompassing the stockyards was known as Marine, because of Marine Creek running through it. A brief land boom occurred and a few houses appeared, but when the packing company failed, some houses were deserted. Only about five hundred people lived in the community when Armour and Swift began work in March, 1902. When a vote came in November, 1902, to incorporate a large area north of the Trinity River as North Fort Worth, the action absorbed the old town of Marine. Boundaries of North Fort Worth included Marine Creek on the north, the Trinity River on the south, the Santa Fe tracks on the east, and Grand Avenue on the west.

Predictably, most candidates for the new community's city council owned commission firms or held other stockyards interests. James D. Farmer, a partner in a commission firm on the yards, became the first mayor of North Fort Worth. He owned land in the area and encouraged development by lending money to newcomers to build houses if they would come to North Fort Worth and work in the packing plants. The local newspaper, the *Daily Live Stock Reporter*, owned by the stockyards, reflected the interests of its owners when it criticized the city health officer of North Fort Worth, Dr. Charles Galloway, for complaining that the packers dumped refuse near the business district. Out-of-town visitors to the area, there to sell livestock, reported an "awful smell." Dr. Galloway informed a convention of health officers in Austin that he could not enforce sanitary regulations against the packing houses and stockyards, though, because the board of aldermen would not back him up. Moreover, when the packers and the stockyards company complained of high tax bills and offered to pay cash immediately if the aldermen of North Fort Worth would lower the bills to an amount specified by the companies, the aldermen unanimously complied.[1]

The state legislature at this time could merge incorporated cities whenever it chose. Fort Worth Mayor W. D. Harris and the city commissioners urged State Representative Louis J. Wortham of Fort Worth to push for annexation of North Fort Worth for the additional tax base. Since the smaller city did not have a state legislator living in its midst to advise them of developments, the bill annexing it

1. Interview with J. D. Farmer III, Fort Worth, September 12, 1983; interview with L. Harmon Rife, Dublin, Texas, August 13, 1976; "Ridiculous Statements by North Fort Worth Health Officer," *Fort Worth Daily Live Stock Reporter*, May 3, 1906; North Fort Worth, *Minutes of Town Council*, December 9, 1902, I, I.

to Fort Worth came as a complete surprise. Although North Fort Worth officials resisted, they lost, and the annexation occurred on March 11, 1909. Mayor John F. Grant of North Fort Worth became a special member of the Fort Worth city commission. W. D. Davis, who previously had served as mayor of North Fort Worth, later ran for mayor of Fort Worth and eventually served four terms, thus indicating the influence of the livestock business on the larger city. Davis was a "leading commission man on the North Fort Worth market."[2]

One area adjacent to and including the stockyards and packing plants did not fall under Fort Worth's jurisdiction in 1909 when North Fort Worth did. A Fort Worth committee on city boundaries, consisting of an aging B. B. Paddock, Clarence Owsley, and F. M. Rogers, recommended leaving a sizable area of trackage property outside the city limits to induce factories to locate close to downtown and yet be exempt from city taxes. The Chamber of Commerce advertised in many national trade journals, offering factory sites free of city taxes to manufacturing firms. Too few factories came to the area to compensate for the loss of tax revenues, however, so in 1911 the city decided to annex that strip as well. To forestall annexation, the stockyards' interests decided to create their own city. As early as November 23, 1909, the directors of the Fort Worth Stock Yards Company discussed incorporating a "village comprising the stockyards and packing houses" and even authorized twenty-five thousand to thirty thousand dollars to construct more rentable houses. They eventually owned seventy rent houses; only a few private homes existed because stockyards and packing interests or other corporations owned most of the land.[3]

Thirty-three men met in T. E. "Dad" Carson's grocery store, 126 Decatur Avenue, on February 21, 1911, and voted unanimously to incorporate a new city. Some suggested naming it Carson City, but

2. North Fort Worth, *Minutes*, March 9, 1909, I, 369; "J. Ogden Armour in Wire Says Plant to Be Enlarged," *Texas Stockman-Journal*, April 22, 1908, p. 13.

3. "The Real Story of Niles City: Editor Started It as Tax Shelter," in Mack Williams, *In Old Fort Worth*, p. 67; Board of Directors Meeting, November 23, 1909, Fort Worth Stock Yards Company, *Corporate Record*, 1st bound vol., p. 294; Janie Reid, "Niles City" history essay accompanying Historical Marker Application for Texas Historical Marker, 1980.

Carson insisted that they name the new community for the man they deemed most responsible for bringing Armour and Swift to Fort Worth: Louville V. Niles. Near the turn of the century Niles had spent six months out of each year for two or three years in Fort Worth operating the old packing plant, and the men of the area had become more acquainted with him than with his Boston partner, Greenlief Simpson. Through the years Niles tried never to miss the annual stock show in Fort Worth, and he always checked on his interests while in town. He kept close contact with the stockyards. He wrote frequent letters inquiring about every aspect of operation: painting the rental houses, roofing buildings, mowing lawns, or whatever interested him.[4]

Four days after the 1911 meeting at Dad Carson's establishment, the men incorporated the city under state law as a village or town (defined by statute as between five hundred and a thousand inhabitants). Actually, the community of Niles City claimed only slightly more than five hundred residents, all working-class families.[5]

The one-half-mile square area that housed the packing plants and stockyards also included a police and fire department, artesian wells for water, electric lights, telephone and gas service, five schools (four white, one black), two grain elevators, a pottery works, a roundhouse for the Belt railroad, three grocery stores, and one drug store. Niles City was bounded by a north-south stretch of Marine Creek on the west, Twenty-ninth Street on the north, Harding Street on the east, and the Trinity River on the south.

In the new little community's first election, held on April 4, 1911, forty-three voters chose the elderly Carson as mayor and picked five aldermen. The aldermen decided in their June meeting that the ad

4. Niles City, *Minutes of City Council*, Judge's Order Copied in Minute Book, February 25, 1911, I, 2; "The Town of Niles," *Fort Worth Daily Live Stock Reporter*, February 22, 1911; L. V. Niles to W. C. Walker, April 18, 1921, and Harold Niles to W. C. Walker, December 7, 1926, Niles Folder, Dies Correspondence, Fort Worth Stock Yards Company Collection, North Texas State University Archives, Denton (FWSY Co. Coll.). In Boston, Niles, still active at age eighty-seven, reportedly went to his office as usual one December day in 1926 after a twelve-inch snow. He died two years later.

5. Letter from law firm of Cantey, Hanger & McMahon to C. J. Faulkner, general counsel, Armour & Co., April 17, 1930, with enclosed "Report of Special Master in Chancery about Stockyards National Bank v. City of Fort Worth," Dies Corr., FWSY Co. Coll.

valorem tax rate for Niles City would be .25 of 1 percent of the value of all real and personal property as of January 1, 1911. They estimated property values at between $25 million and $30 million and claimed to be the "richest little city per capita in the United States" because of the proportion of wealth in relation to size and population. Roy Vance, an officer of the Stockyards National Bank, served as town treasurer. Vance served the bank as cashier, then president during his tenure as treasurer for Niles City. The aldermen eventually purchased a lot and by March, 1912, built a brick-and-stucco city hall at a cost of $4,511.[6]

The little city a few years later even boasted a woman mayor, Mrs. E. P. Croarkin, whom the aldermen appointed late in 1920 after her husband, the mayor, had died. She maintained her home, cared for two small children, operated the post office and drug store, and performed her duties as mayor—in spite of her claim not to believe in woman suffrage. She told a Fort Worth newspaper reporter, "I believe that women are as capable as men in any position for which they fit themselves, but I do not believe that they should be continually trying to remind the world of this fact." Apparently she knew the art of diplomacy, too.[7]

The most famous event ever to occur in Niles City (other than the visit of former President Roosevelt two weeks after the city's incorporation) was the visit of famous tenor Enrico Caruso, who sang to a standing-room-only crowd of eight thousand on October 19, 1920, at the North Side Coliseum. Competing with intermittent thundershowers and the stomping and cheering of the crowd, Caruso gave a two-hour performance. The enthusiastic reception of his first and only tour of Texas impressed the forty-six-year-old world-famous tenor. "This is the first time I have ever been stampeded," he said of the foot-stomping welcome. "Wonderful audience. Wonderful audience." He apparently did not mind the Western reaction of whis-

6. Niles City *Minutes*, April 6, 1911, I, 6; ibid., June 28, 1911, I, 12; Law firm Cantey, Hanger & McMahon to C. J. Faulkner, April 17, 1930, p. 4 of enclosed report, FWSY Co. Coll; Niles City *Minutes*, December 16, 1911, I, 18.

7. "New Woman Mayor of Niles City Runs Home, City Affairs and Drug store: 'Not Too Busy,'" *Fort Worth Star-Telegram*, October 31, 1920 in "Niles City" File, *Fort Worth Star-Telegram* Reference Library. See also Niles City, *Minutes*, October 25, 1920, I, 206.

tling and throwing hats in the air either. All nine policemen from Niles City and their chief, Frank Averitt, were on duty to handle the crowd.[8]

Not all events in Niles City were as happy as the Caruso visit, however. One of the rare strikes at the stockyards itself began at noon June 12, 1918, when 130 employees of the Fort Worth Stock Yards Company walked out. Union officials at Chicago had called the strike to demand an eight-hour day, time and a half for overtime, double time for Sundays and holidays, and a flat increase of one dollar per day in salaries. The participants in the strike included dockmen, weighmasters, and cattle drovers. Butchers at the packing plants agreed not to kill livestock driven by non-union men. Stockyards officials, however, assured the press that the strike was not affecting the market and business would continue as usual. Commission men helped the stockyards company clear up the livestock receipts. Employees of the company returned to work on June 17, 1918, after a government mediator arrived and held several conferences with stockyards and union officials.[9]

The Stockyards Labor Council, set up by the Chicago Federation of Labor, A.F. of L., in 1917–18, had helped organize the packing-house and stockyards workers. The council became a source of intrigue, factionalism, and disruption. For a time its secretary in Chicago was William Z. Foster, who several years later became a Communist.

When switchmen on the Cotton Belt Railroad went on strike April 9, 1920, they left cattle stranded and affected every railroad that operated through Fort Worth. The Santa Fe sent on to Oklahoma cattle that had been meant for Fort Worth. The livestock market at the stockyards was at a near standstill for two or three days. An officer of the Belt Railway operated one engine, and at least twenty-one cars of livestock arrived at the yards by April 12. Swift still killed

---

8. Mae Biddison Benson, "8,000 Fort Worth Folk Break Decorum to Give Caruso Real Texas Cheer at Concert's End," *Fort Worth Star-Telegram*, October 20, 1920; "Caruso, World's Greatest Tenor Charms Hearers," *Fort Worth Record*, October 20, 1920; "Caruso Concert Crowd Taxes Accommodation of City Hotels," *Fort Worth Star-Telegram*, October 19, 1920.

9. "Stockyards Men Walk Out; Eight Hour Day among Things Desired," *Fort Worth Daily Live Stock Reporter*, June 13, 1918, p. 1. See also "Stockyards Men Return to Work Monday Morning," ibid., June 17, 1918, p. 1.

a few cattle, but Armour had shut down. Everyone went back to work by April 15.[10]

Labor relations in the packing industry, which owned most of the stockyards of the nation, continually worsened as the year 1921 progressed. Low prices forced the packers to reduce wages. Only mediation by the Secretary of Labor averted a strike March 23, 1921. No major strike had plagued the meat-packing industry since 1904. The Amalgamated Meat Cutters and Butcher Workmen of North America, chartered by the American Federation of Labor, had been attempting to gain recognition for their union since 1897.[11]

To try to avoid future problems, Louis F. Swift announced on May 23, 1921, a plan under which employees could elect representatives to an assembly where employees and appointed management personnel could sit down and discuss problems. Decisions of the group would be binding. Armour and Company adopted the plan as well. Local workers later claimed that the governing council idea failed because the employee representatives did not include enough members from the foreign-born workers.[12]

Local Armour employees accepted wage cuts of from three to seven and one-half cents an hour in November, 1921, but in December the union voted to call a nationwide strike because of more proposed wage cuts and to gain official recognition of their union. The strike involved forty-five thousand workers in fifteen states. Armour and Swift in Fort Worth both kept operating as usual because they filled the places of the striking workers "from a long waiting list."[13]

Fighting occurred, however, on December 6, 1921, between packing-house workers who continued to report and the strikers. A large group of strikers accosted Fred Rouse, a thirty-five-year-old black

10. "Only Live Stock to Reach Yards Saturday Comes Via Auto Truck," ibid., April 10, 1920, p. 1; "Strike Still On But Conditions Here Show Bit of Improvement," ibid., April 12, 1920, p. 1; and "Strike of Switchmen in Fort Worth Comes to an End," ibid., April 15, 1920, p. 1.

11. "Employees Accept Wage Reduction; Strike Averted," ibid., March 24, 1921, p. 1.

12. "Swift Employees to Share in Management Problems," ibid., May 24, 1921, p. 1; and "Recognition of Union Demanded by Employees of Packing Houses," ibid., October 12, 1921, p. 1.

13. "Packers Run Business as Usual, They Say Monday," ibid., December 6, 1921, p. 1.

worker, who then pulled a .32 caliber pistol and fired into the crowd twice. He hit two Swift strikers, brothers Tracey and Tom Maclin, the former in the leg and the latter in the chest. Niles City police arrested Rouse, but a mob of several hundred persons took him away and beat the black man unconscious. Officials placed Rouse in the City-County Hospital, (later renamed to honor John Peter Smith), where Rouse was listed in critical condition. Authorities planned to charge him with murder should Tom Maclin die. Five days later, as Rouse began to recover, a group of about thirty young men wearing handkerchief masks entered the hospital around II P.M. and took Rouse from the nurse who was guarding him. They carried him to a well-known hanging tree on the east side of Samuels Avenue, southeast of the stockyards area, and left his bullet-riddled body dangling. The two Maclin brothers recovered, but authorities never identified the young men involved in the lynching.[14]

As difficulties continued, both Armour and Swift filed injunctions in district court to have certain of the strikers cited for contempt of court, claiming that they were interfering with the rights of persons who had refused to strike. The strikers apparently had been stopping streetcars, entering them, and threatening employees of the packing plants with bodily harm if they continued to work. W. C. Summers, the Armour manager, claimed that "hundreds" were turned back from their jobs on December 13, 1921. The next day Fort Worth and Niles City police officers patrolled their respective boundaries with extra attention to prevent a recurrence of the previous day's incident.[15]

The judge ruled that the number of pickets must be reduced from the one hundred or more who had been accosting workers each day to a pair of pickets at each approach to the packing houses. Squads of men who had been visiting the homes of strikebreakers were ordered to cease the practice. The judge also held in abeyance contempt charges against twenty-three striking employees to see

14. "Strikers Obey Court Unionists Cease Picketing Pending Appeal Decision," *Fort Worth Star-Telegram*, December 7, 1921; "Weapon May Prove Owner Took Part in Rouse Lynching," ibid., December 12, 1921.
15. "23 Strikers Accused, Armour Moves in Halting of Cars," ibid., December 13, 1921. See also "Master Is Sitting in Swift Plea on Strike," ibid., December 15, 1921; "Workers Get to Packeries Unmolested," ibid., December 14, 1921.

how the agreement between strikers and packers worked out. Both sides agreed to the injunction, and picketing soon became a silent procedure in contrast to the noisy activities of the previous days.[16]

Arthur Meeker, vice-president of Armour and Company in Chicago, refused to negotiate with the union, claiming that the packers had agreed with their employees over wages through the employee representative plan. He claimed that the company and the majority of its employees were in accord and that only a few workers had walked out.[17]

The nationwide strike accomplished little, finally ending February 1, 1922. A major local result was that Fort Worth officials, claiming that the strike and its violence had proved the inability of the nine-man Niles City police force to handle the explosive situation, intensified their annexation plans for Niles City and its lucrative livestock industries.

Fort Worth officials took the first steps to annex Niles City and several other suburbs in 1919 when the local representative to the state legislature, Wallace Malone, introduced a bill that would permit a city of from 100,000 to 150,000 population to annex any neighboring city with less than 2,000 population. The bill failed because of organized opposition from the Board of Trustees of the Diamond Hill Independent School District, near Fort Worth. Malone reintroduced the bill in the Thirty-seventh Legislature in March, 1921. Because Niles City had only about 700 inhabitants, the local aldermen in 1921 extended the city limits to include Washington Heights, North Fostepco Heights, and Diamond Hill, thereby increasing the population to 2,600 and the size to 1.5 square miles. With the larger population, the proposed new bill would be irrelevant. To counter Niles City's action, Malone during a special session in the summer of 1921 amended his bill by substituting 5,000 for the 2,000 figure. Officials of Niles City, attempting to defeat the bill, voted five hundred dollars for three city representatives to go to Austin. Their efforts failed, however, and House Bill 126 passed and became law that fall. Malone later explained his campaign: "I introduced it [the

16. "Picketing by Banner Decided on for Strike," ibid., December 16, 1921; "Judge Not to Try 23 Picketers at Present," ibid., December 17, 1921.

17. "Nothing to Settle Packer Chief Says," *Fort Worth Daily Live Stock Reporter,* December 12, 1921, p. 1.

bill] because I thought it was about time those two packing houses that ran Niles City started paying the city of Fort Worth and the school system some money in taxes."[18]

Fort Worth called an election of her citizens in July, 1922, to annex Niles City and several other suburbs; Niles City residents had no chance to express their wishes. Since most of them worked in the stockyards or packing houses, they would probably have been influenced by their employers to oppose it. Thus on July 22, 1922, the city of Fort Worth officially annexed Niles City and its property valued at from 25 million to 30 million dollars. Niles City officials had argued that the town would receive no benefits from uniting with Fort Worth, for it already had its own water plant, sewage system, police, and school facilities. They called the annexation unconstitutional and invalid. The state legislature proclaimed the Malone Bill to be a general law, but Niles City protested that it was a local law aimed at their city. Niles City had not even been given thirty days' notice before its passage, officials complained.[19]

Mayor W. S. Gallaway of Niles City declared in November, 1922, that the city would carry its fight to the U.S. Supreme Court if necessary. To the smaller city's dismay, the district court had upheld the right of a larger city (Fort Worth) to annex adjacent territory and had ruled the Niles City's hurried expansion of her own boundaries to increase its population to 2,600 had been an intentional move to circumvent the law. The smaller city approved a motion at its aldermen's meeting on January 16, 1923, to file an appeals suit against the city of Fort Worth.[20]

The case between Fort Worth and Niles City opened February 22,

18. Niles City *Minutes*, April 25, 1921, I, 212–13; "Amending Act Authorizing Certain Cities to Amend Their Charters—May Extend Their Corporate Limits to Include Adjoining Territory," 1921 Tex. Gen. Laws, 1st spec. sess., ch. 49, sect. 1 at 153, 21, H. Gammel, *Laws of Texas* (1923); Niles City *Minutes*, August 8, 1921, I, 218; *Niles City* v. *City of Fort Worth*, No. 63225 Dist. Ct. of Tarrant County, 17th Judicial Dist. of Texas, October 8, 1923; Raymond Teague, "Niles City a Present from the Past," *Fort Worth Star-Telegram*, August 2, 1980.

19. Law firm Cantey, Hanger & McMahon to C. J. Faulkner, April 17, 1930, p. 3 of enclosed report, FWSY Co. Coll.; *Niles City* v. *City of Fort Worth*.

20. *Minutes*, November 3, 1922, I, 237. See also "Niles City Will Carry Annexation Fight to U.S. Supreme Court," *Fort Worth Star-Telegram*, November 12, 1922. See also *Washington Heights Independent School District et al.* v. *City of Fort Worth* 251 S.W. 341 (1923); and Niles City *Minutes*, January 16, 1923, I, 241.

1923, before the Texas Court of Civil Appeals at Texarkana. This suit was still pending in July, 1923, when the two communities reached a compromise. Niles City agreed to drop all annexation suits and become a part of Fort Worth if the latter would assume the debts of the smaller city, estimated at between $300,000 and $400,000, although some believed them nearer $65,000. Nearly $10,000 of the debts represented salaries to city employees not paid when Niles City funds ran short because big taxpayers withheld their tax money pending the settlement of the annexation contest. Attorney S. F. Houtchens of Niles City blamed the huge debt on bank warrants issued because "Niles made no effort to live within its income."[21]

The City of Fort Worth appeared unconcerned about the amount of the bank warrants, gloating instead that an additional 30 million dollars in property values would be added to its tax rolls. Niles City had valued the property at only 8 million dollars and had taxed accordingly. When the bank warrants continued to be ignored, however, the Stockyards National Bank, which held them, sued the City of Fort Worth for the money Niles City owed. Some of the Niles City warrants the Stockyards National Bank had paid were apparently Christmas presents to various persons and bonuses to the officers and employees of Niles City. In some instances they had paid for flowers, funeral wreaths, or donations. On the other hand, some were for paving streets, sewage disposal, and similar items. Apparently, Niles City taxes had remained so low that the city could not pay all its obligations, so the packers and stockyards interests (which also owned the bank) had simply arranged for the bank to pay them. While monthly expenses generally did exceed income, the costs, even with the Christmas bonuses, seldom seemed excessive. When one alderman attempted to get the city to pay for a telephone in the home of each alderman, the motion failed. The industrial interests that owned from 75 percent to 96 percent of the taxable property in Niles City consisted of Armour and Company and Swift and Company, with their subsidiaries: the Fort Worth Stock Yards Com-

21. Niles City *Minutes*, July 31, 1923, I, 253; ibid., February 15, 1923, I, 242; *Annual Report for 1923*, January 5, 1924, FWSY Co. Coll.; Niles City *Minutes*, February 3, 1923, I, 242. See also Teague, "Niles City a Present from the Past," p. 2.

pany; Libby, McNeill, and Libby Foods; and the Fort Worth Belt Railway Company.[22]

The Stockyards National Bank filed its suit against the City of Fort Worth July 21, 1924, but when the court finally reached a conclusion in 1930, it discarded some of the older claims because the statute of limitations had been passed. The court also disallowed any items authorized by the Niles City aldermen after July 22, 1922, considering these acts not legally binding since Niles City was already a part of Fort Worth. Of the $400,000 the Stockyards National Bank had been trying to collect, the Court allowed only $70,685.20, plus interest at 6 percent. The interest amounted to $32,000. Apparently the stockyards and packing interests had covered the warrants for the bank, for when Fort Worth paid the claim, they got the money. The stockyards company wrote off as a loss that portion of the $400,000 which they claimed was owed them but which they did not collect. The city of Fort Worth eventually paid a total of only $59,952.42 in warrants and interest divided among Armour, Swift, the Fort Worth Stock Yards, and Libby, McNeill and Libby.[23]

Disposition of the two-toned beige and brown stucco building that had served as town hall of "the richest little city" rested with the larger city, which sold it to private interests. The building subsequently served as a residence for several years; then after standing vacant for a time it became a syrup factory. It served as a Works Progress Administration canning plant during the 1930s. Owners rented it out as a duplex to war workers in 1943. After again letting it stand vacant a number of years, the owners demolished the building in 1975 to make room for a parking lot, a decision that inspired citizens of the area to form the North Fort Worth Historical Society to prevent the demolition of other historic buildings.[24]

22. Niles City *Minutes*, December 20, 1917, I, 142; ibid., September 29, 1919, I, 180; ibid., August 30, 1920, I, 204; Cantey, Hanger & McMahon to C. J. Faulkner, April 17, 1930, and enclosed report, p. 11, FWSY Co. Coll.

23. Cantey, Hanger & McMahon to Faulkner, p. 14; *Stockyards National Bank v. City of Fort Worth*, No. 67594, Dist. Ct. of Tarrant County, 48th Judicial Dist. of Texas, June 16, 1930; A. G. Donovan to F. W. Ellis, April 18, 1930, and Albert H. and Henry Veeder to A. G. Donovan, May 26, 1931, Dies Corr., FWSY Co. Coll.

24. "Ye Town Hall of Niles May Become a 'War Duplex,'" *Fort Worth Star-Telegram*, December 3, 1942, and "Niles City" File *Fort Worth Star-Telegram* Reference Library; and Janie Reid, "Niles City, Texas," p. 36.

Not all dealings between the packing and stockyards interests and the city of Fort Worth during the 1920s disintegrated into court battles, however. Fort Worth and her citizens remained proud of their livestock market. When Amon Carter invested in 1922 in that new source of news — radio — a cowbell became the sound symbol. His station was WBAP, an acronym for "We Bring A Program." The *Star-Telegram* by 1923 boasted a circulation of 115,000, making it the largest newspaper in the South.

Both pride in the market and its influence as the largest industry in Fort Worth brought about cooperative effort between the larger city and the stockyards. Because floods of the Trinity River generally affected the stockyards district, officials from the North Side became as interested in flood control for the city of Fort Worth as anyone else. Immediately following a disastrous flood of April 24–27, 1922, a citizen's committee met at the Fort Worth city hall to provide relief. No sooner had they put plans underway than a second flood came, May 8–11, 1922. Kennerly Robey, chief engineer for the Fort Worth Stock Yards, who earlier had designed the coliseum and rent houses, became chairman of a group of citizens petitioning for the Tarrant County Water Control District No. 1, the first of its kind in the state. By a four-to-one margin, Fort Worth citizens on October 7, 1924, voted to approve the district. Supporters hailed it as the first combination flood control and water supply plan in America. Engineers announced intentions to construct two lakes on the West Fork of the Trinity: Lake Bridgeport, located approximately fifty miles upriver, and Eagle Mountain Lake, closer to Lake Worth, which the city had completed a decade earlier. Robey served as consulting engineer for the district. In an election in October, 1927, voters approved $6.5 million in bonds for the projects.[25]

Reluctantly then, during the early years of the 1920s the Fort Worth Stock Yards Company and the packing plants came under the taxing jurisdiction of the city of Fort Worth. Twenty years earlier the city had made concessions to persuade the packers to relocate in their area, but by the 1920s city officials believed that the

25. "Final Report of Board of Engineers of Tarrant County on Flood Control and Water Conservation for Tarrant Co. Texas," 1925, FWSY Co. Coll. See also Tarrant County Water Improvement District Miscellaneous Material, ibid., Item 2, p. 1.

time for such generosity to the wealthy meat entrepreneurs had expired.

The State of Texas had ended any "coddling" of the local livestock industry in 1907 when its courts outlawed the Fort Worth Live Stock Exchange. The city and the federal government, however, both chose the early 1920s to make their restrictive moves. How much a national mood antagonistic to the meat trust influenced the attitude of city leaders probably cannot be determined. While federal regulation of the meat packers and stockyards had been a subject under consideration since the 1880s, the movement did not reach fruition for those seeking such restrictions until the early 1920s.

Government Regulation

1921-28

THE ROARING TWENTIES brought a loud outcry in the cattle industry, which reached all the way to the nation's capital and affected all major terminal markets, including Fort Worth. In fact, the 1920s became a turning point for Fort Worth's leading industry for a number of reasons, none more important than the federal regulation that became law shortly after the decade began. Throughout the nation new trends—economic and political—were emerging which affected agriculture. Many still considered the raising of livestock the predominant industry of Texas in the 1920s; Texas produced 11 percent of the cattle of the entire country, nearly as much as any other two states combined. Toward the close of the decade, however, cotton grew increasingly important, pushing livestock to second place.[1]

Farmers and other livestock producers all over the nation began experiencing problems as the decade opened. Livestock prices to the producers remained low, although a postwar inflation caused prices to soar for consumers. The drop in livestock earnings was caused by low beef consumption (a pattern developed during wartime conservation which held on for several years), rising beef production that surpassed population increases, a two- or three-year drought in the South, increasing meat imports coupled with decreasing exports, rising labor costs, and tax hikes. In addition, higher freight rates came at the exact time when declining product prices

1. George M. Lewis, *A Market Analysis of the Cattle Industry of Texas*, p. 15.

made shipment impossible. Readjustment after booming wartime conditions may also have contributed to the major price decline, for European demand remained low.

Fort Worth in the 1920s still considered itself predominantly a cattle town and bragged that more than two million head of livestock arrived at the Fort Worth Stock Yards annually. The stockyards area employed more than five thousand workers and turned out products valued at $120 million each year. The population of 1920 had quadrupled during the two decades since the arrival of Armour and Swift in 1902.

Another factor that affected the position of livestock as the state's dominant industry was the discovery of oil west and northwest of the city in 1919. Fort Worth soon became the promotional and developmental headquarters for the oil industry in north central Texas. By 1924 nine area refineries produced petroleum products valued at $52 million annually, making Fort Worth the "oil capital of North Texas." Possibly seeing themselves on the way to being a great metropolitan center, citizens approved the council-manager form of government in 1925.[2]

The stockyards interests became concerned over their connection with the meat-packing trust and the proposed federal regulation of the industry. Both producers of livestock and consumers often believed themselves to be at the mercy of the Big Five, who they claimed set prices and acted in collusion to limit competition. Complaints bombarded Congress for several years. The Cattle Raisers Association of Texas charged that in 1916 the Big Five's control of interstate slaughter at the twelve largest packing centers had accounted for 94.4 percent of cattle, 89.1 percent of calves, 94.3 percent of sheep and lambs, and 81 percent of all swine brought to these markets. Net earnings for Swift and Company, after paying out dividends each year of $5,250,000, amounted to $3 million in 1912; $4 million in 1913, $4.2 million in 1914, and $8.65 million in 1915. Armour reported net earnings of $7,599,907 in 1914 and $11 million in 1915. The public became incensed at these figures, especially when they learned that the packers owned the stockyards where most

2. T. C. Richardson, "Fort Worth, Where the West Begins," *Holland's* 54 (February, 1935): 29.

livestock was sold as well as the railroad cars that carried much of the nation's processed meat and even perishable fruits and vegetables. Many persons feared that the meat trust could control the food supply of the nation. Some even called for the "meat monopoly" to be operated as a public utility, leaving only small independent companies to continue as free enterprise.[3]

In defending himself against trust charges, J. Ogden Armour wrote, "Unfortunately a good many people will always believe anything that is persistently told them, particularly if it be about a corporation." He claimed that no monopoly existed and that the five largest packers handled less than 50 percent of the beef and packing industry of the entire country. He said that packers built and operated their own refrigerated railroad cars so that they would be available when needed, for the railroads could not be depended upon to supply them. Once they had the cars, the packers found it more profitable to ship fruits and vegetables on them at least a part of the time than to move empty cars. They bought and operated stockyards for basically the same reason, he said, to see that a market existed to provide sufficient animals for their packing plants to operate efficiently.[4]

Armour and Swift remained among the top five industries of all categories in the United States as the 1920s began. Swift admitted that his company's business volume was second only to that of United States Steel.[5]

Unquestionably, the Fort Worth Stock Yards Company formed an integral part of this meat-packing trust, since Armour and Swift each owned one-third of the shares of the company. In testimony before the Senate Agriculture Committee on January 25, 1919, J. Ogden Armour admitted that he had induced Swift to build at Fort

3. "Facts about the 'Big Five' Packers," *Cattleman* 6 (July, 1919): 11, 49. The twelve markets were Chicago, Kansas City, Omaha, Saint Louis, New York City, Saint Joseph, Fort Worth, Saint Paul, Sioux City, Oklahoma City, Denver, and Wichita. "The American National Convention," ibid. 2 (February, 1916): 24. See also Lewis Corey, *Meat and Man: A Study of Monopoly, Unionism, and Food Policy,* p. 236.

4. J. Ogden Armour, *The Packers, the Private Car Lines and the People,* pp. 28–29, 163, 298–99, 364.

5. Louis F. Swift, with Arthur Van Vlissingen, Jr., *Yankee of the Yards: The Biography of Gustavus Franklin Swift,* p. 5.

Worth and had promised him half of the business to keep him from building across the river at Dallas. Armour also contended that the arrival of the packers at a location "made" the markets, for until they constructed plants to purchase livestock, very little market existed. He said that total receipts increased at Fort Worth by 1600 percent within sixteen years after the opening of the packing plants, from 227,000 head to 3,540,000. Published accounts of livestock purchases of the two packers at the Fort Worth Stock Yards indicate that buyers for the two packers often contracted for almost identical amounts, particularly of cattle, each day over the years.[6]

Harry Butz, who served as head sheep buyer for Swift for over forty years, said that no one in the Swift plant ever told him how many sheep to buy or to limit his purchases. They knew he knew his job and the value of the sheep, so his superiors just let him alone. If he purchased more than the local Swift plant could slaughter, the company sent them to Swift plants farther north. He said a lot of competition existed with Armour and insisted the rivalry "couldn't have been any stronger."[7]

Roy Weeman, who worked as a cattle buyer for Swift most of his forty-nine years on the Fort Worth yards, from 1913 to 1962, denied that Armour and Swift got together to agree on what to buy. The commission men could sell to anybody, and there were always a lot of buyers—Cudahy, Wilson, Bluebonnet, and others. The packers could not just pay what they wanted to pay. A commission man was hard to get along with because he was fighting for the last nickel for his producers all the way. As a youngster working for Swift in 1913, Weeman had as one of his jobs sending the daily telegrams. According to him, the company did not "wire ahead" prices quoted to people on the Fort Worth market who were shipping on to Kansas City or places north.[8]

6. Typed list of stockholders of Fort Worth Stock Yards Company, April 1, 1923, Gary Havard Personal Collection, Fort Worth. See also U.S. Congress, Senate, Committee on Agriculture and Forestry, *Hearings on Government Control of Meat Packing Industry on S. 5305*, 65th Cong., 3d sess., 1919, pp. 664, 537, 666. See also "Livestock Buying for Yesterday," *Fort Worth Daily Live Stock Reporter*, July 6, 1917, p. 1; "Five Packer Buyers Daily Bid for Cattle," ibid., March 30, 1917, p. 1; "Buying Yesterday," ibid., May 23, 1911, p. 1.
7. Interview with Harry Butz, Fort Worth, September 9, 1983.
8. Interview with Roy Weeman, Fort Worth, September 12, 1983.

Others on the Fort Worth yards, such as order buyers and commission men, expressed the same opinion that no collusion existed.
Perhaps livestock producers living many miles from Fort Worth who
became unhappy at prices they received joined with other cattlemen in protesting against the Big Five, but local people defended
their market. One speculator explained philosophically the differ-
ences between producers and the Big Five. "It depends on which side
of the fence you are on. There was never a cattle producer who sold
at a high enough price to satisfy him or a packer who got it cheap
enough to make enough profit."[9]

A wealthy rancher from West Texas named Dominick Hart sold
his land, cattle, and sheep holdings and moved to Fort Worth in 1916
with the intention of building a slaughtering operation on the North
Side. He purchased at least three blocks of land on the west side
of Main between Twenty-fifth and Twenty-eighth streets and constructed a two-story slaughtering plant with walls two feet thick.
He built other brick structures for office space and a cooler. Hart
never operated his packing facility, however, for the stockyards company leased his buildings and used the larger one as a hay barn.
While Hart's grandson could not say for certain that packer influence
kept the elder Hart from opening his slaughtering plant, several old-
timers on the yards firmly believed that Armour and Swift had exerted pressure.[10]

The two packers proposed buying out the Hodge Stockyards at
Fort Worth, an important feeding-in-transit facility nearer the downtown railroads, in order to eliminate that competition. They held
back when their attorneys advised them that such a purchase might
be construed as a violation of the antitrust law. The packers later
accomplished the closing of the Hodge yards by making an agreement with the Missouri, Kansas, and Texas Railway not to ship their
cattle from Hodge by promising them preferred shipments from the
Fort Worth Stock Yards two days a week. "I feel quite sure you will
be pleased to know that this competition is going to be discontin-

9. Interview with Phil Weaver, Jr., Fort Worth, September 13, 1983.
10. Interview with Dominick Hart III, Fort Worth, September 21, 1983; interview with Fred Ryon, Fort Worth, September 14, 1983; interview with James Cantrell, Fort Worth, September 21, 1983.

ued," A. R. Fay of the Fort Worth Stock Yards wrote Louis F. Swift on June 29, 1917.[11]

For years the Fort Worth Stock Yards conducted operations like the big business of which it was a part. Swift bought shares of Fort Worth Stock Yards Company stock in the name of directors of the company, but on the death of any director the stock went to his successor on the board, not his personal heir. In transferring stock, officials changed the name on the certificate but notified the secretary that "this transfer involves no change of ownership whatever."[12]

In 1920 the stockyards company still owned some seventy rent houses for employees. The company owned twenty blocks of land from Twenty-third to Twenty-eighth streets west of Main Street, plus twelve blocks between Twentieth and Twenty-third on the east side of Main. They also held an additional three or four blocks north of Twenty-eighth Street. Throughout the decade the company gradually sold land, and by 1930 it owned only a little over two blocks.[13]

Late in 1921 the company created an Agricultural Livestock Finance Corporation with John Sparks, president of the Stockyards National Bank, as president. The new corporation, capitalized at one million dollars, began soliciting applications and subscription blanks from cattlemen. They mailed them to members of the Texas and Southwestern Cattle Raisers Association, the new name of the organization formed when the Cattle Raisers Association of Texas had merged with the Panhandle and Southwestern Stock Raisers Association earlier that year. Out of their need to maintain a steady supply of fattened cattle, the meat packers encouraged the incorporation of cattle loan associations to help finance the indus-

11. "Why the Packers Own Stockyards," *Cattleman* 6 (November, 1919): 49–51.
12. W. W. Sherman, assistant treasurer, to Henry Veeder, February 5, 1923, attached to Stock Certificate No. 52, Havard Collection.
13. Surveyor's Map of Stockyards Area, ibid.; O. W. Matthews to Henry Veeder, March 24, 1915, St. Louis and SW Railroad Folder, ibid.; copy of agreement to sell North Fort Worth Townsite Company to Fort Worth Stock Yards Company for $1, Unmarked folder, ibid.; Map of Property of the Fort Worth Stock Yards Company Showing Land Now under Mortgage and All Transfers to July 1922, Altered to December 1930, K. Robey, Engineering Department, City of Fort Worth, ibid.

try better. This introduced risks to the producers, however. When the market became unstable, packers who had liberally advanced money called in the loans, letting the producers suffer. John Clay, a former Scot and northwestern stockman who later began a nation-wide commission business, agreed that the finance companies the packers owned loaned "millions where thousands would have been ample." They took livestock as collateral.[14]

In addition to real estate and cattle loan corporations, the Fort Worth Stock Yards Company held major control of the Stockyards National Bank, the Belt Railway Company, the *Fort Worth Daily Live Stock Reporter* (which would become a weekly in the 1920s), and a utility company. Stockyards owners "always denied connections between interests," one official admitted to another in a telegram. L. V. Niles did not like ownership of the Stockyards National Bank by the Armour and Swift interests. The stockyards company, of which Niles was a substantial stockholder, put money in the bank at little or no interest. Niles owned no stock in the bank and believed the practice to be unfair to him.[15]

In attempting to curb similar activities of the meat trust nation-wide, reformers urged federal regulation of the industry. In arguing for such legislation in 1921, Sen. George Norris of Nebraska expressed outrage when he contrasted the sixty cents his wife had recently paid for a pound of bacon with the ten to twelve cents per pound farmers received.[16]

Agitation against the meat-packing industry had begun long before Senator Norris's cry in 1921. After the Senate investigation of the dressed beef industry in 1888, the Supreme Court ruled in an 1898 test case that the activities of commission men did not

14. Charter No. 37096, Agricultural Livestock Finance Corporation, filed November 7, 1921, Office of Secretary of State, Austin; "Empire Builder," *Fort Worth Star-Telegram*, October 15, 1921, and November 9, 1921, as cited in *Research Data*, Fort Worth and Tarrant County, Texas, Federal Writers' Project, XXXVI, 14314; John Clay, *My Life on the Range*, p. 358.

15. Telegram from O. W. Matthews to G. B. Robbins, July 12, 1913, Dies Correspondence, Fort Worth Stock Yards Company Collection, North Texas State University Archives, Denton (FWSY Co. Coll.). See also L. V. Niles to W. C. Walker, October 20, 1923, L. V. Niles Folder, ibid.

16. U.S. Congress, Senate, Senator Norris Speaking for the Meat Packing Bill, S. 3944, 66th Cong., 3d sess., January 22, 1921, *Congressional Record*, 60:1877.

constitute interstate commerce, a ruling that favored the industry. But in 1903 the United States filed a bill in equity to enjoin further conduct of an illegal conspiracy of the Big Five packers as a meat monopoly and issued an injunction that the courts later sustained.[17]

Large profits by the meat industry during World War I brought renewed cries for reform, even though the government was regulating the packers under the wartime Lever Act. High prices and excessive profits, which were published, generated complaints and drew accusations of unfair competition. The American Federation of Labor became irate at the Big Five's resistance to collective bargaining and decided to challenge. Sen. Robert M. La Follette encouraged Progressives to seek reforms, and President Woodrow Wilson called for stricter antitrust legislation.

Probably the most effective call for reform came from farmers and ranchers in the Western states, concerned over the low and fluctuating price of meat animals. Producers also feared that commission men, who rented office space in livestock exchange buildings owned by packers, might favor the packers in order to keep on good terms with their landlords.

As early as 1914 the American National Cattlemen's Association formed a committee to investigate the growth and control of the large packers. A committee reported in July, 1915, at a special Denver conference that in the marketing of livestock, supply and demand "has ceased to have very much to do with the matter of price making." A. E. DeRicqles, chairman of the committee, reviewed the industry-wide pattern of gradual acquisition by the packing interests of stockyards companies, exchange buildings, daily market newspapers, tanneries, belt railways, and loan companies.[18]

Early in January, 1916, the American National Cattlemen's Association held its annual meeting in El Paso and created another com-

17. U.S. Congress, Senate, *The Packers' Consent Decree: A History of Legislation Pertaining to the Meat Packers Leading Up to the Packers' Consent Decree of 1920 and Subsequent Thereto*, S. Doc. 324, 71st Cong., 3d sess., 1931, p. 2; *Hopkins* v. *U.S.*, 171 U.S. 578 (1898); *Swift* v. *U.S.*, 196 U.S. 375 (1905).

18. Charles A. Burmeister, "Six Decades of Rugged Individualism: The American National Cattlemen's Association, 1898–1955," *Agricultural History* 30 (October, 1956): 148; "Western Stockmen Discuss Marketing of Live Stock, Urge Secretary of Agriculture to Hold Public Hearing," *Cattleman* 2 (August, 1915): 5–6.

mittee to study marketing conditions. A pro-packer and an anti-packer faction existed within the American National as well as several of the other livestock organizations. But at the El Paso meeting, the majority passed a resolution to ask Congress to enact legislation to correct the abuses of the packers. In March of that year Congressman William P. Borland of Missouri introduced a resolution directing the Federal Trade Commission to investigate any violations of the antitrust laws by the big packers. Borland said, "Indications are . . . that the Standard Oil Company in its palmiest days never had as complete a system of controlling the supply and price of a great necessity of life as has now been developed by the packers' trust."[19]

Packers tried to forestall such investigations by meeting with livestock associations. Officials of four of the Big Five came to Fort Worth in May, 1916, to meet with a committee of members of the Cattle Raisers Association of Texas. Their efforts failed, however, and the committee still recommended that the American National Cattlemen's Association continue its investigation.[20]

As a result of these calls for an investigation, on February 7, 1917, President Wilson requested the Federal Trade Commission to investigate the packing industry to determine if agreements in restraint of trade or other monopolistic practices existed. After several months of hearings, investigations, and five volumes of collected material, the Commission concluded, "It appears that five great packing concerns of the country—Swift, Armour, Morris, Cudahy, and Wilson—have attained such a dominant position that they control at will the market in which they sell their products, and hold the fortunes of the competitors in their hands."[21]

Some estimates placed as high as five hundred the number of subsidiary companies in which they held joint stock, agreements, communities of interest, or family relationships. In one chart, the Federal Trade Commission report listed thirty-one major stockyards,

19. "To Investigate Packers," ibid. 2 (March, 1916): III.
20. "Conference with Packers Fails," ibid. 3 (June, 1916): 5.
21. U.S. Congress, House, *Food Investigation: A Message from the President of the United States Transmitting Summary of Report of the Federal Trade Commission on the Meat Packing Industry*, H. Doc. 1297, 65th Cong., 2d sess., 1918, p. 3.

showing percentages of ownership by the Big Five. The dominant companies controlled over 50 percent of all but two of the yards cited, and the percentage of ownership for most stood at over 80 percent, or even over 90 percent. The two packers located at Fort Worth owned 66⅔ percent of the Fort Worth Stock Yards. The FTC also charged the Big Five with making agreements to buy cattle in specified percentages. The investigation also revealed the big packers engaged in extensive foreign meat export activity. The FTC recommended that the federal government acquire the railroads used to transport cattle, the stockyards, and the cold storage plants owned by the Big Five and operate them as a government monopoly.[22]

The FTC report cited the Fort Worth and Denver stockyards as markets where only two of the Big Five packers operated and claimed that they divided everything there fifty-fifty. They allowed independent packers, local butchers, and speculators to purchase up to (but not over) 5 percent of the livestock, which constituted too small a percentage of influence the market strongly, "much less fix the price." The FTC report asserted that at Fort Worth the two packers who owned the stockyards "have refused, contrary to the wishes of the citizens of Fort Worth to allow other packers to come in on the ground that there is not enough stock in that market to support another plant."[23]

Almost as an immediate result of the FTC report, President Wilson, under authority of a food control act passed the year before, issued a proclamation that as of July 25, 1918, all commercial stockyards, commission merchants, and livestock dealers must have a federal license. As could be expected, the local *Live Stock Reporter* defended the packers, blaming the high cost of living on the system of credit and the retail dealers. The editor also charged the consumers who wanted the best cuts of meat with causing the higher prices.

22. Ibid., pp. 4–5, 10, 16; U.S. Congress, House, *Report of the Federal Trade Commission on the Meat Packing Industry*, H. Doc. 1297, 65th Cong., 2d sess., pt. 2, pp. 72–75; and U.S. Congress, Senate, Report of Victor Murdock, Acting Chairman of the Federal Trade Commission Who Appeared before the Senate at Their Request, S. Res. 114, 66th Cong., 1st sess., July 31, 1919, *Congressional Record*, 58:3419.

23. "Government Control of Stock Yards, Refrigerator Cars and Cold Storage Plants, Recommended," *Cattleman* 5 (August, 1918): 21. G. O. Virtue, "The Meat Packing Investigation," *Quarterly Journal of Economics* 34 (August, 1920): 626.

Packers made a profit of only two cents on each dollar, the editor explained.[24]

Roy C. Vance, cashier of the Stockyards National Bank in Niles City, blamed the "caprice of politicians" for attacking a business simply because it had been successful and had attained tremendous growth, thanks to "economy and good business methods." Packers took the risks in establishing the banks, stockyards, and packing plants when the public did not want to invest; then when they became successful, they brought down the wrath of Congress, the attorney general, and others, Vance charged.[25]

A bill actually was introduced in the House of Representatives in November, 1918, authorizing government ownership of stockyards, exchange buildings, terminal railroads, rendering plants, market newspapers, and other market facilities, but some critics labeled the action as part of the war psychology. Once the war ended, the defeat of the bill became certain.

The livestock industry remained divided concerning the guilt of the packers and the need for strict regulation. One writer blamed the furor on wholesale grocers for publicizing the FTC report, although the "findings were never substantiated or made to form the basis of a real court action." Robert J. Kleberg, owner of the huge King Ranch in South Texas, opposed government regulation of packers, claiming that such regulation would be ruinous to packers, meat producers, and consumers.[26]

Fort Worth cattleman Marion Sansom favored the minority report of the Forty-fourth Annual Convention of the Cattle Raisers Association of Texas, which opposed the requested regulations. He told the convention he regretted that some had accused those who favored the minority report of being "bought" by the packers. He said that retailers, not packers caused the high beef prices to consumers, although he claimed he was not defending packers. Sansom argued

24. "Some Plain Facts Regarding the Packers and the Part They Are Alleged to Play in the 'H.C.L.' (High Cost of Living)," *Fort Worth Daily Live Stock Reporter*, August 6, 1919, p. 1.

25. Roy C. Vance, "A Banker's Viewpoint," ibid., August 8, 1919, p. 1.

26. Bertram B. Fowler, *Men, Meat and Miracles*, p. 128; and "Kleberg Says Placing of Packers and Their Agencies under Control of Government Will Be Ruinous to Packer, Meat Producer, Consumer," *Fort Worth Daily Live Stock Reporter*, August 6, 1919, p. 4.

that one could not get a larger market for beef by breaking up the packers, for they represented the only ones large enough to expand into a world market. A fellow Texas rancher, George Hendricks of San Angelo, asked Sansom in the meeting how "in the name of common sense" the proposed legislation would put the packers out of business. The majority report favoring the packer regulation passed 299 to 127.[27]

The meat industry formed the Institute of American Meat Packers, composed of at least two hundred small packers as well as the Big Five, to combat the anti-packer publicity and the proposed confiscatory legislation. The Institute, formed in 1919, grew out of the old American Association of Meat Packers created in 1906. The organization later became the American Meat Institute. To forestall any drastic regulation, the packers requested a meeting with U.S. Attorney General A. Mitchell Palmer in which they proposed to clean up the industry from within. They signed a consent decree in 1920, voluntarily agreeing to dispose of their interests in public stockyards, stockyards terminals and railroads, market newspapers, and cold storage warehouses and to relinquish the business in unrelated lines and the use of the distribution system for other than meat products. Many cattlemen became indignant at the deal they claimed the attorney general had made with the packers to avoid prosecution. Litigation began over the decree almost immediately and continued for a decade, during which time the packers did not comply with all its provisions. Moreover, others challenged the terms as well; the California Cooperative Canners' Association took the side of the big packers and argued that the order forbidding the cooperative to use the refrigerator cars belonging to the packers had, in a few months, ruined their fruit industry. Eventually the California canners and the Big Five lost, and the court ruled that the packers had to dispose of their stockyards and other interests before December 31, 1931.[28]

At the outset of the controversy, Armour and Swift began running full-page ads in the *Cattleman*, the monthly magazine of the

27. "The Forty-Fourth Annual Convention," *Cattleman* 6 (April, 1920): 68.
28. Senate, *Packers' Consent Decree*, p. 47. See also *U.S.* v. *California Canners Cooperative*, 279 U.S. 552 (1928); *Swift & Co. et. al.* v. *U.S.*, 276 U.S. 311 (1928), and *U.S.* v. *Swift & Co. et. al.*, 286 U.S. 106 (1932).

Cattle Raisers Association, to try to explain their position and to create good will. They protested that they were being misunderstood, that they helped the farmer on the world market. These full-page advertisements continued throughout the entire decade of the 1920s.

While litigation proceeded, those interested in regulatory legislation tried to get Congress to act. Neither the Sixty-fifth nor the Sixty-sixth Congress succeeded in passing legislation to regulate the packing industry, although congressmen listened to arguments on both sides during months of committee hearings. As the Sixty-seventh Congress met in the spring of 1921, feelings remained strong among many that the legislation could be passed, while the meat-packing industry opposed it as vigorously as ever. Representatives of various large organizations appeared before the House Agriculture Committee, chaired by Iowa Congressman Gilbert Haugen, to show their support for legislation to regulate the meat packers.[29]

Support for packer regulation came from a new organization created in 1919, the American Farm Bureau Federation. This federation was formed by local farm bureaus, which had been established to help underwrite the expenses of agricultural technicians from land-grant colleges to educate local farmers in better farming practices. The Smith-Lever Act of 1914, which helped create all those 4-H clubs, also authorized resident county agents to be financed by federal, state, local, and even private funds. Local and state farm bureaus allied with the land-grant colleges to help provide this aid, often on a membership-subscription basis.

In May, 1921, a group of twenty or twenty-five senators from agricultural states began meeting with the Washington agent of the American Farm Bureau Federation in his office. These western farm-bloc politicians made the decision to block adjournment until Congress passed agricultural legislation: a farm loan act, a grain futures act, and the Packers and Stockyards Act. The American Farm Bureau Federation and its Washington director, Gray Silver, exerted

---

29. U.S. Congress, House, Committee on Agriculture, *Meat Packer Hearings before the Committee on Agriculture on H.R. 14, H.R. 232, H.R. 5034, and H.R. 5692,* 67th Cong., 1st sess., 1921, p. 60.

much influence, and telegrams against adjournment poured in from farm areas.

The final law the Sixty-seventh Congress passed was a compromise House bill vesting packer regulation in the secretary of agriculture, rather than the Senate's bill, which would have given the Federal Trade Commission control. Congress titled Public Law 51, effective August 15, 1921, as "An Act To regulate interstate and foreign commerce in live stock, live-stock products, dairy products, poultry, poultry products, and eggs, and for other purposes." It became unlawful to engage in deceptive practices, to give undue preferences to persons or localities, to apportion supply among packers in restraint of commerce, to trade in articles to manipulate prices, to create a monopoly, or to conspire to aid in unlawful acts. Under the law, packers would be served with complaints of suspected violations, and hearings would be held. Stockyards had to file rates with the secretary of agriculture and could not make changes without ten days' notice. Hearings had to be held on new rates, and the secretary could suspend a rate schedule. In addition, packers, stockyards owners, and market agencies had to keep accounts and disclose them to the secretary. The Packers and Stockyards Administration, created by the act, also printed pamphlets and brochures to help livestock producers and livestock dealers know what the law meant to them. Later government officials charged that lawyers for the Big Five had helped write the final bill so that it would not regulate them too strictly.[30]

A court case immediately tested the constitutionality of the Packers and Stockyards Act. In challenging the law, the companies argued that the sale of livestock in stockyards did not constitute an integral part of interstate commerce and therefore was not a mat-

30. Packers and Stockyards Act, *Statutes at Large,* vol. XLII, chap. 64, pp. 159–69 (1921); U.S. Department of Agriculture, Packers and Stockyards Administration, *The Packers and Stockyards Act as It Applies to Livestock Dealers,* PA-808. See also U.S.D.A., Packers and Stockyards Administration, *Questions and Answers on the Packers and Stockyards Act for Livestock Producers,* PA-810; U.S.D.A., Packers and Stockyards Administration, *Livestock Payment Guidelines For Producers,* PA-923; interview with Mike Pacatte, Auditor, Packers and Stockyards Administration, U.S. Department of Agriculture, Fort Worth, Texas, July 27, 1977.

ter of national concern. Chief Justice William Howard Taft in his opinion explained that the act was a permissible regulation of a business affected by a public interest, as the court had ruled in *Munn* v. *Illinois* (1877). The stockyards, he said, were "great national public utilities" which served to promote interstate commerce in livestock and their public nature and national character combined to subject them to national regulation. He also maintained that the stockyards played a vital and direct part in interstate commerce. Thus the Court affirmed the Packers and Stockyards Act as constitutional. One historian of the meat industry indicated that in 1921 it suffered a net loss of nearly one hundred million dollars and the powerful packing houses were "fighting for their lives." Other estimates of losses run somewhat lower, much of it because of readjustments of demand after World War I.[31]

No drastic change happened for the stockyards of the nation, including the Fort Worth Stock Yards, right after the passage of the law because of the delaying litigation. The packers made no immediate moves to divest themselves of their stockyards. In fact, Henry Veeder, assistant secretary of the Fort Worth Stock Yards Company, wrote a Packers and Stockyards official in 1925 that the minute books of the Fort Worth Stock Yards were at his office in Chicago and the official could see them there. Veeder at that time served as vice-president of Swift and Company.[32]

A few fairly minor developments resulted from the law's enactment. H. J. Galloway of Washington, D.C., a special assistant to the U.S. attorney general, visited Fort Worth February 19, 1923, to inspect the yards and hear complaints. The Department of Agriculture ordered the Fort Worth Stock Yards to establish a new shipping division into which all cattle destined for interstate shipment might be gathered. The company had been trying to do this anyway. A disagreement between the American National Cattlemen's Association and the old line commission firms on the Fort Worth market

31. *Stafford* v. *Wallace*, 258 U.S. 495 (1922); Stanley I. Kutler, "Chief Justice Taft, National Regulation, and the Commerce Power," *Journal of American History* 51 (March, 1965): 658–59; Fowler, *Men, Meat and Miracles*, p. 141.

32. Henry Veeder to John T. Caine, III, Chief, Packers and Stockyards Administration, October 24, 1925, Dies Corr., FWSY Co. Coll.

over commission rates reached Secretary of Agriculture Henry A. Wallace for arbitration early in 1924.

One immediate result of the Packers and Stockyards Act was a new, packer-instituted practice of buying livestock directly from producers in the country rather than waiting until they arrived at the public terminal markets. Packers claimed that they could not get all the supplies they needed on the public markets. Producers charged that the packers bought directly in order to pay lower prices and also to avoid the federal regulations at the stockyards. With reduced competition for the cattle on the terminal markets where legitimate values were determined, prices plummeted just as farmers had feared. Packers buying hogs in the country surrounding the Fort Worth market claimed to pay "Fort Worth prices less freight," but such practices helped kill the hog market at Fort Worth, for the packer buyers could make deals with farmers, especially since they faced less competition.[33]

Many Midwestern farm groups agitated in the mid-1920s for amendments to the Packers and Stockyards Act to include provisions against this new practice of direct marketing. Others urged that jurisdiction of the Packers and Stockyards Administration be placed in the hands of the Federal Trade Commission rather than the Secretary of Agriculture, who many believed had acted too leniently. Some believed the law had failed, "so far as bringing to the farmers the relief which they hoped to get out of that sort of legislation." A lawyer representing the Kansas City Livestock Exchange, the Farmers' Union Associates, and the Missouri Livestock Producers Association argued before a Senate Committee that packers' direct purchases from a small, unregulated yard exceeded those at the public market in Kansas City by 80 percent.[34]

33. "'Direct Buying' Designed to Make Hogs Cheap" (Speech by J. E. Poole of Chicago at Annual Convention of Kansas Live Stock Association), *Weekly Live Stock Reporter*, May 9, 1929, p. 1; interview with Alonzo Keen, Fort Worth, Texas, August 28, 1983.

34. U.S. Congress, Senate, Committee on Agriculture and Forestry, *Amendment to Packers and Stockyards Act, 1921. Hearings Before Committee on Agriculture and Forestry on S.3841*, 68th Cong., 2d sess., 1925, p. 10; U.S. Congress, Senate, Committee on Agriculture and Forestry, *Hearings on A Bill to Amend the Packers and Stockyards Act S. 2089*, 68th Cong., 1st sess., 1924, p. 7.

Some farmers, however, liked the direct marketing system because they did not have to pay yardage or commission fees, as they would at the public yards, and so saved twenty-five to thirty dollars on each carload. They joined with the packers in opposing the amendment against direct marketing. Those favoring the amendment pointed out that the practice allowed big packers to manipulate prices, because the more stock they bought directly in their private yards, the lower the price would be on the public yards.[35]

Federal regulation of packers and stockyards affected the Fort Worth market eventually, but during the 1920s persons connected closely with the local market seemed to believe that the good days would go on for a while yet. The yards continued to break monthly and weekly records in July, 1919. During the first half of that year, Fort Worth had ranked sixth in sheep, sixth in cattle, fourth in calves, and eighth in hogs among the leading terminal markets. For the twelve months ending December, 1920, of the ten leading markets Fort Worth ranked sixth in cattle, fifth in calves, ninth in hogs, and tenth in sheep. Only three years later, however, a former trail driver and Texas commission agent reported that the cattle business was down and he expected the comeback to be slow.[36]

Optimism for the future continued at the Fort Worth Stock Yards, however, and the place never seemed to suffer from a lack of new ideas. In the fall of 1923, the company and commission firms set aside Tuesday and Friday of each week as "Stocker Days" and advertised this fact to shippers and buyers. They believed that within a radius of a few hundred miles of Fort Worth more stocker cattle existed than in any similar section in the entire United States. "Fort Worth is as much a stocker market as a packer market, but these possibilities have not been developed," one official stated. The market newspaper advertised the stocker-feeder idea with a box story on page one every day during September, 1923. Then Tom Wallace,

35. U.S. Congress, House, Committee on Agriculture, *Hearings Before the Committee on Agriculture, A Bill to Amend the Packers and Stockyards Act, 1921 H.R. 11384*, 69th Cong., 1st sess., 1926, p. 63; U.S., Congress, Senate, Committee on Agriculture and Forestry, *Hearings Before a Subcommittee of the Committee on Agriculture and Forestry on S. 3676 and S. 4387*, 69th Cong., 1st sess., 1926, p. 1.
36. George W. Saunders to T. B. Saunders, Jr., July 31, 1923, Tom B. Saunders, Jr., Collection, Box 1, Texas Christian University Special Collections.

head sheep buyer in Fort Worth for Armour and Company, suggested to C. C. French that each season feeder lambs be concentrated in Fort Worth for sale to northern buyers. Wallace wanted to build up a market at Fort Worth rather than allow buyers from the north to go personally to ranges in West Texas. Wallace believed that Texas constituted the greatest mohair- and sheep-growing section in the country and that Fort Worth could develop into one of the largest feeder lamb markets in the United States. Their plans succeeded, and by the 1940s the Fort Worth market was receiving more than two million sheep annually. Harry Butz, who served as head sheep buyer for Swift for nearly forty years, also helped build up the market.[37]

Terminal markets experienced larger cattle receipts in 1924 and 1925 because of a depression in the cattle trade following World War I. Producers had become accustomed to high prices during the war, but when they were no longer forthcoming, they kept their cattle from market for two or three years. When high prices failed to materialize and they could not afford to hold their stock any longer, they had to sell. Cattlemen held some animals back from market so long they were good only as canners. An agent of the United States Bureau of Animal Industry, Sterling Emens, said he never before saw as many aged steers on any market as he saw in Fort Worth during 1924 and 1925.[38]

Producers may have been hurting, but the Fort Worth Stock Yards Company succeeded admirably. The business paid an 8 percent return usually, but in 1925 the profits soared to 16 percent. The company paid quarterly dividends of two dollars most of the time throughout the decade. The boom year of 1925 even brought periodic extra dividends. Stockholders meetings, always held in Chicago, became mere formalities in the 1920s with no one present but the secretary and president, who held all the proxy shares of the

37. "Fort Worth to Be Made a Real Stocker Market," *Fort Worth Daily Live Stock Reporter,* August 23, 1923, p. 1; "Plans Suggested for Upbuilding of Fort Worth as Huge Market for Sale of Texas' Receipts of Feeder Lambs," ibid., October 27, 1923, p. 1.
38. Col. T. O. Walker, "Lessened Receipts But Better Prices Are Order for 1925 According to Final Figures Compiled by Statistician," *Weekly Live Stock Reporter,* January 28, 1926, p. 1.

absent owners and elected directors and voted dividends. That usually represented the only business conducted, and board meetings were held only once or twice a year.[39]

Unfavorable railroad rates hurt Fort Worth's receipts in mid-decade. Livestock shippers, commission men, and others formed the Live Stock Traffic Association of Fort Worth in 1923 to protest these rates, which drove cattle away from Fort Worth to other markets. The association filed an application in 1925 to the Texas Railroad Commission and finally got a favorable decision in April, 1927. The court ordered freight rates reduced by 15 percent starting June 1, 1927. The traffic association had argued that lower rates, even by a few cents, on long hauls could determine which plant would do slaughtering from certain sections. Because of freight rates, many packers found it more profitable to slaughter the great bulk of Texas livestock on the Missouri River and to the East rather than at Fort Worth. One of the packer representatives testified before the rate hearings that the northern plants operated near capacity, while the Fort Worth plants ran at about 50 percent. Producers testified that the more favorable adjustment in the longer haul rates resulted in forcing heavier receipts into northern markets, followed by immediate decline in prices, which in turn depressed prices at the intermediate markets. These transportation charges quite often determined the outlets for Texas cattle, giving other producing sections that had more favorable tariffs a competitive advantage over Texas producers.[40]

Labor problems apparently remained light during the 1920s decade except for the 1921 strike discussed previously. The stockyards company provided a group insurance for its employees as of September 4, 1926. General Manager A. G. Donovan contributed $250

39. Harold L. Niles to W. C. Walker, November 29, 1926, Dies Corr., FWSY Co. Coll.; Annual Stockholders Meeting, January 23, 1923, Fort Worth Stock Yards Company, *Corporate Record*, unnumbered vol. 1917–34, p. 76. See also the reports of the Annual Stockholders Meetings in that volume of the *Corporate Record* for the following years: January 16, 1924, p. 84; January 28, 1925, p. 92; January 12, 1926, p. 99; January 11, 1927, p. 113; January 10, 1928, p. 126; and January 15, 1929, p. 149; and the Board of Directors Meeting, December 23, 1925, p. 95.
40. L. V. Niles complained of this fact as early as October 18, 1921. L. V. Niles to W. C. Walker, October 18, 1921, Niles Folder, Dies Corr., FWSY Co. Coll. See also Lewis, *Market Analysis*, p. 170.

in the name of the company to the Open Shop Association of Fort Worth. In thanking him for his contribution, the secretary of the association gave his own agency credit for "the peaceful labor conditions which have existed here during the past several years."[41]

Another innovation Donovan tried at the local market in the mid-1920s consisted of radio coverage for its market reports. The Bureau of Agricultural Economics provided a livestock market news service, which Fort Worth market analysts bragged represented one of the most complete news services in the country. Service began October 1, 1925, in cooperation with Amon Carter's WBAP radio station, with market reports twice a day, at 10 A.M. and 2. P.M. The company provided a padded, well-equipped booth on the second floor of the Livestock Exchange Building for the broadcasts.[42]

Local stockyards workers often lived their daily lives, did their work, and remained unaware of federal legislation and court hearings that affected their industry until changes were implemented. One federal regulation everybody knew about, however, was Prohibition. In fact, the Texas and Southwestern Cattle Raisers Association held its convention one year in El Paso expressly so members could cross the border to Juárez, Mexico, for some "spirits." They endured teasing about their choice of convention cities but carried through nevertheless. Later, one of the calf men with the National Commission Company was trying to make a deal on the yards, and someone accused him, jokingly, of stretching the truth. "Now, you know where you go when you tell a lie, don't you?" he was asked. "I hope it's to Juárez," he grinned.[43]

Sometime during the Prohibition years the same fellow told his close friends on the yards that he knew a man who would sell him a five-gallon jug of whiskey. One of the stockyards employees said he could arrange to get the coliseum, which the stockyards company owned, for a big party. A crowd arrived that night and the hosts opened their five-gallon jug. The purchaser had of course tasted

---

41. A. G. Donovan to F. W. Ellis, December 12, 1925, Dies Corr., FWSY Co. Coll.; A. G. Donovan to several employees, September 4, 1926, ibid. See also C. O. Vinnadge to A. G. Donovan, May 16, 1927, ibid.

42. "Radio Gives News of Local Market," *Weekly Live Stock Reporter,* January 14, 1926, p. 1.

43. Interview, Roy Weeman, September 12, 1983.

and approved the whiskey before he bought it. Before many drinks had been poured, though, the thirsty party goers discovered that the good whiskey had been slipped down inside the mouth of the large jug in a smaller container. The remainder of the liquid was lake water.[44]

Prohibition, then, in the 1920s became a more noticeable federal restriction at the Fort Worth Stock Yards than the meat packer regulation. The decade ended before the actual implementation of the Packers and Stockyards Act, or before the binding provisions of the Packers' Consent Decree of 1920 changed much in Fort Worth, mainly because the latter agreement remained tied up in court appeals during that time. Armour and Swift each retained one-third interest in the stockyards company as late as May 1, 1928, although Armour shifted his stock by that date to a new company created for the purpose, General Stockyards. Correspondence indicates that Swift still owned one-third of the local sewage disposal plant in 1929.[45]

The crackdown on the Big Five meat packers, two of which owned the Fort Worth Stock Yards Company and numerous other interests in Fort Worth, represented the major event of the decade for all the nation's major stockyards, including Fort Worth. The packers were unable to increase their power any further, although in 1923 the Big Five were reduced to the Big Four when Morris was sold to Armour. Rather than sell stockyards interests, Morris chose to sell out its meat-packing operations instead.[46]

The value of government regulation did not immediately become apparent, but a feeling persisted that without it conditions would have been worse. Among the packers the attitude developed that with the proper ingenuity of corporation lawyers one could legally avoid a portion of the government controls. Regulation certainly hurt business, however, and eventually contributed to the changed methods of livestock marketing in this country.

Following the 1920s, the Fort Worth Stock Yards Company would

44. Ibid.
45. A five-page list of stockholders as of May 1, 1928, in front of Stock Certificate Book 1 to 250, Havard Collection. Also Swift and Company to W. C. Walker, October 14, 1929, Dies Corr., FWSY Co. Coll.
46. Interview with L. Van Kuhl, President, American Stockyards Association, Fort Worth, Texas, October 23, 1984.

experience a different relationship with its former mentors, Armour and Swift. The stockyards company existed before they took over control, and it continued after they relinquished direct ownership, but the loss of a rich benefactor undeniably alters one's circumstances.

Days at the Yards

1 9 2 8 – 2 9

STOCKYARDS GENERAL MANAGER AL DONOVAN made a quick tour of the busy yards one day, particularly to see how a carpenter was repairing the gates and some of the fences that needed new boards. He found a new two-by-four-inch plank a workman had just put up to replace one that had been whittled away. By the time he got there, however, he saw Charlie Daggett, son of Col. E. M. "Bud" Daggett, already whittling away on the new wood. Donovan figured that Daggett had been partially responsible for carving up the old one.

"Charlie," Donovan said, "I'll give you one hundred dollars for that knife of yours if you'll promise to give up whittling."

Without taking time to think about it much, Daggett answered, "Nothing doing, Al, you keep your hundred dollars and I'll hold on to my knife." It was enough to make Donovan's graying dark brown hair turn grayer.[1]

Daggett was not the only whittler. Carved-up wooden benches, gates, and fences all over the yards revealed the popularity of the pastime during the heyday of the stockyards, when private treaty sales prevailed. The independent commission man like Daggett was an intermediary between seller and buyer of livestock on the yards. When five hundred cars or more of livestock arrived daily, and approximately a hundred buyers roamed the yards, a lot of transac

---

1. "Whittlers Are Rough on Posts and Benches at Stockyards," *Fort Worth* 22 (January, 1948): 13.

tions occurred in a day. Nevertheless, participants in the process still took the time to dicker. The seller, for whom the commission man worked, wanted the highest price possible for the animal or animals belonging to him. The buyer wanted to purchase at the lowest price that he could, given the going market rates. The commission agent mentioned as high a price as he hoped he could get, and the buyer cited a low price that he wanted to pay for the animals. They both knew that if they really wanted to deal, they would meet somewhere in the middle. Meanwhile, in between the changes of offer, the two men pulled out their ever-present pocket knives and hacked on whatever wood they could find. They might have a leg propped up on the lowest rung of the fence, or be leaning against a gate with one arm resting on the top, but one hand always remained free to whittle. It gave the two men something to do to fill the silence while waiting for the other person either to raise his offer or lower it. Donovan knew the popularity of the whittling, so when he gave instructions to his carpenter to replace boards that had been carved to pieces, making them useless as gates or fences, he also instructed him to chip the leftovers into convenient sizes for picking up and holding in one's hand.[2]

"Throw some chunks of loose wood around," he told the worker. That helped some, but not much. Not everyone whittled, for some claimed to be too busy to do so, particularly heads of commission firms who stayed in the offices with the paper work much of the time. Enough whittlers operated to keep things carved up considerably.[3]

The conversation between Donovan and Daggett may not have occurred in 1928 or 1929, but it did happen at some time around then. Some of the other events in this chapter, too, may not actually have taken place during those two specific years. However, the years 1928 and 1929 represent a period of time in the heyday of the yards when the way of life characteristic of the large terminal markets still existed. The Great Depression had not yet struck, although farmers did suffer problems in the 1920s. Most animals still arrived in the yards by rail, although a few motor vehicles were beginning to ap-

2. Interview with William E. Jary, Jr., Fort Worth, July 12, 1983.
3. "Whittlers Are Rough," p. 13.

pear. Not until a decade later well over half would arrive by truck. Packers buying directly or auction barns in small country towns had not yet taken away the booming activity from the dozen or so large stockyards of the nation or changed them very much. Even the federally mandated order for meat packers to sell their stockyards, belt railroads, market newspapers, banks, and so on had not yet been completed, having been delayed by court litigation.

Therefore, at this point in the stockyards story it seems appropriate to describe the typical activity that existed during the time when the stockyards were to the cattle industry what Wall Street is to finance. A cattle market like the one at Fort Worth, handling over two million animals a year, drawing livestock from numerous other states as well as all of West and South Texas—remained big, booming, and busy. Stockyards manager Donovan always dressed in a suit and tie, looked the part of a businessman running the biggest business in town, and indeed the stockyards combined with the packing plants hired more employees than any other Fort Worth industry and generated more dollars.[4]

Cattle, hogs, sheep, horses, and mules arrived by rail twenty-four hours a day, seven days a week, so stockyards workers remained constantly on hand to unload. One of the six Belt Railway switch engines, which had the monopoly on handling the cars, picked up the various cars of the other railroad lines and brought them to the proper dock. Each of three docks—north, middle and south—could accommodate eighteen cars. All three docks stretched from Twenty-third to Twenty-eighth streets. With this many animals being unloaded at peak times, the bawling of cattle frightened by their unfamiliar surroundings was the common background for every conversation—unless one worked south of Exchange Avenue in the covered hog and sheep pens, with their own particular squeals and bleats. One adjusted to the noise and smell after a time and hardly noticed, but for a newcomer the animal aroma and sounds overwhelmed everything else. Surprisingly, though, sheep remained relatively quiet. After being sold they followed rather meekly behind

4. Interview with A. G. Donovan, Jr., Fort Worth, September 12, 1983; Jary interview, July 12, 1983; interview with Roy Weeman, Fort Worth, September 6, 1983.

a trained goat wearing a bell as he led them over the ramp to the packing plant to be slaughtered. For obvious reasons, the one or two trained goats used over the years for this purpose were called Judas goats. One was named Popeye.[5]

Anyone who climbed one of the two wooden viaducts or ramps that crossed over the railroad tracks to the packing plants could look back on a "sea of horns" in the cattle pens, for practically all the animals arriving in the early days, even into the 1920s, were horned cattle. One dealer remembers seeing a steer with horns so wide that his head would not come straight out of a railroad car. Stockyards workers had to turn his head and put one horn out at a time to get him out. Having to handle horned cattle often proved dangerous. Men have had their clothes practically torn off by cows that hooked their horns into them. Many of these horned cattle coming to the yards were extremely wild because farmers or ranchers would allow them to graze at pasture for three or four years and the animals were not accustomed to being near people. One day a bull jumped up on the corrugated tin roof on the shed behind the exchange building in which the more important employees like Donovan kept their automobiles each day. The hoof prints remained for quite some time.[6]

Also, most cattle arriving at the yards had to be quarantined. The section for dirty or ticky cattle in these early years remained much larger than the clean division farther north and west.

Trading began on the yards at six A.M. each day except Sunday. One old-timer explained, "You started when you could and quit when you couldn't," meaning they started bidding when they could see the animals at daylight and ended their day when they could not see to trade anymore. Monday always represented the biggest day of the week for receipts. A busy air pervaded the yards all morning as the team of buyers for each of the two local packing houses and out-of-state packer buyers as well as small independents scurried around to all seven divisions. Local packer buyers sent animals continually traveling over the ramps spanning the railroad tracks

5. Interview with Tommy Scribner, Fort Worth, September 19, 1983.
6. Interview with Phil Weaver, Jr., Fort Worth, September 13, 1983; interview with Claude Marrett, Fort Worth, September 12, 1983; interview with Roy Weeman, Fort Worth, September 10, 1983; interview with Ed C. Walsh, Jr., Fort Worth, September 13, 1983.

to reach the slaughtering plants. The two major packers purchased enough to ship out seventy-five to eighty railroad cars of processed meat each day. On days when a lot of stocker and feeder cattle had arrived on the market, dealers continued to trade even if the packers slacked off. Animals also continued to arrive that would be sold the following day. Anywhere from ten thousand to twenty-five thousand cattle and calves arrived each day during the summer and fall, when big runs were common. A lesser number of hogs and sheep came. Sometimes stockyards workers did not stop unloading until one or two A.M. The north rail dock would be full, with thirty or forty cars to unload, and about half that many on the south dock during boom periods. Sometimes stockyards workers kept a bedroll down on the docks and would sleep if they got caught up.[7]

What made stockyards work even busier was the added aspect of "feed and rest" cattle. A federal thirty-six-hour release law required railroads to unload animals from a cattle car before they had been on it longer than thirty-six hours and to feed and water them at a stockyards. Fort Worth accepted many "feed and rest" cattle on their way to northern pastures or markets. Sometimes stockyards workers would begin unloading cattle early and would unload nothing but "feed and rest" cattle practically all day. Then their task would reverse itself, and they would begin reloading the first ones, for by then they had rested the legally required length of time. Sometimes so many cattle came through needing to be fed that Ed O. Walsh, purchasing agent for the stockyards, feared he would run out of hay.[8]

Handling thousands of animals efficiently required much of terminal markets like Fort Worth. Scheduling of arriving railroad cars worked well, for agents called ahead to report how many carloads were to arrive. The railroad spokesman might tell the yardmaster at the stockyards, "We have some cattle and the time is about up," meaning they had been on board nearly thirty-six hours and had

7. Interview with Johnnie Stubbs, Fort Worth, September 15, 1983; Scribner interview; interview with William E. Jary, Jr., Fort Worth, November 11, 1981; transcript of oral interview by W. H. Barse, Jr., Fort Worth, 1977, in Junior League Oral History Collection, Oral Histories of Fort Worth, Inc.; interview with Alonzo Keen, Fort Worth, August 28, 1983; interview with Hutton Cox, Fort Worth, June 10, 1983; interview with Johnny Adams, Fort Worth, June 7, 1983.

8. Interview with W. M. Speck, Fort Worth, June 7, 1983; Adams interview; Walsh interview.

to be unloaded quickly. Of course, the stockyards' efficiency required long hours from their employees. When Bill Addieway first went to work for the stockyards company as a young man in 1926, he worked three days and two nights without stopping long enough to go home. His parents got worried about him, and his father came out to see what had happened.[9]

Even as late as 1928 ranchers within a thirty- to forty-mile radius of the stockyards still drove their cattle to the yards. Claude A. Tannahill and his neighbors in the western edge of Tarrant County would put their cattle together and with forty to sixty head leave home about 6 P.M. They would drive all night, stopping occasionally to rest, and arrive at the yards at daylight—assuming no early traveler in his Model T or Model A had scattered their animals. Some farmers even brought their hogs to market in wagons in the later 1920s, but most came by rail and a few by truck. One of the very first cows to arrive at the Fort Worth yards by truck was tied down on a flatbed truck made from a Model T. The vehicle had no sideboards. The cow's head was tied with rope and pulled one direction and her feet confined and stretched another. The men who unloaded her simply untied the ropes and got out of the way. "That was one mad cow," according to witnesses.[10]

Not all cattle arriving at the yards were for slaughter or "feed and rest." Stocker and feeder calves came frequently in the 1920s, as indeed throughout the years. Some days 60 percent of receipts were stocker and feeder cattle. Other days a majority of receipts might be for slaughter. Receipts obviously remained seasonal, with different types of livestock coming more heavily at different times. Fall of the year or early spring saw the heaviest runs of hogs. Most sheep came in April, May, or June, and cattle came in larger numbers in the fall.[11]

Animals arriving by rail were driven into pens just the right size to hold a railroad carload. The stockyards agent in South Texas had

9. Interview with Bill Addieway, Fort Worth, September 23, 1983.

10. Interview with Lester Kutch, Fort Worth, September 8, 1983; interview with Claude A. Tannahill, White Settlement, Texas, September 10, 1983; interview with J. D. Farmer III, Fort Worth, September 12, 1983.

11. Interview with Roy Weeman, October 5, 1983; Kutch interview; and interview with Harry Butz, Fort Worth, September 9, 1983.

been visiting ranches, urging them to ship to Fort Worth, as had commission company representatives. Each carload arrived consigned to a specific commission company that had pens in a division assigned to it. Bricks in the pens were laid crisscross, one face down and the next brick beside it with its edge up to keep the cattle from slipping in wet weather. Covered and enclosed wooden booths about twelve feet by twelve feet were built above the pens as a place for commission men to sit, store a little hay, hang up a saddle, and watch over what happened in their division. A lot of whittling over periods of time diminished the benches or railings on the booths. Eventually the stockyards company trimmed the edges of the benches, the upright posts, and any other exposed wooden edges they could with tin to deter the whittlers.

Stockyards employees kept watering troughs in each pen full and maintained bins of fresh hay for the animals. Sometimes they stacked hay on the wide walkways around the top of the pens. As workers drove cattle down the lanes between the pens to be weighed and sold, someone else stayed busy with a shovel cleaning up after them. The stockyards company later put out a little pamphlet, calling their arrangement for servicing livestock a "livestock hotel" in which the owners of the animals paid for their guests' expenses while in the yards. Some participants remarked that stockyards hay and other services did not come cheap, but the company obviously had to make a profit on them to pay all their workers. The stockyards had no involvement in sales, but simply provided the facilities for all the trading to occur and charged rent to commission companies and traders and fees for feeding and watering each animal. Packer buyers and the commission men usually kept horses which they rode when they went out on the yards; perhaps they rode them partly to keep from stepping where a stockyards worker with his shovel had not yet cleaned.

Sometimes the smoke from the nearby packing houses would hang low over the yards and cause a bad odor. Swift cattle buyer Roy Weeman remembers complaining loudly on those days about that "horrible smell from Armour." Of course, "it came from Swift too," he admitted with a grin.[12]

12. Weeman interview, September 12, 1983.

During the busiest days of the yards, the exchange building remained the focal point for all activity. After selling his livestock on the yards, one of the few producers who had come with his animals would go by the offices of the commission company that sold them to pick up his check. Most farmers or ranchers allowed their animals to be shipped by rail to the yards and anxiously awaited the results at home. As a service to him the commission company would telegraph this information and then mail his check the following day. Three telegraph services maintained offices in the building for that purpose: Western Union, Postal Telegraph, and Mackay. Commission men, traders, and others kept in touch with prices on the northern markets by telegraph, as well. Or they could visit the office of the U.S. Department of Agriculture's Market News Service, which also kept records of market activity on all the other major stockyards. In fact, if commission men, buyers, or others on the market got a breather, they liked to check the big board in the lobby, which listed receipts of all central markets in the United States each day for cattle, calves, hogs, sheep, horses, and mules. Only about twelve large markets handled most of the livestock of the nation, and Fort Worth ranked in a different position in each category. She fared consistently better in cattle than anything else. "Sometimes we handled as many cattle as anybody," cattle buyer Weeman claimed. Other terminal markets included Chicago, Omaha, Kansas City, Saint Louis, Saint Joseph, Saint Paul, Sioux City, Sioux Falls, Denver, South San Francisco, Portland, and a few others.[13]

Manager Donovan saw to it that the building and grounds showed the exchange building to an advantage. Shrubbery, palm trees, and a beautiful green lawn surrounded the building. The hardworking German fellow named Albert Whiff who mowed the grass could not speak English very well. He had a donkey and a wide mower. One time he requested "voots" for his donkey. When Donovan finally figured out what Whiff wanted, the manager contracted for inlaid leather boots made especially for the little animal. Whiff, a short, heavy-set man, would roll up his overalls nearly to his knees and trot along barefoot behind his little donkey as he mowed.[14]

13. Ibid.
14. Walsh interview.

Someone on the yards one day convinced Whiff that he ought to ask Donovan for more money because he worked so hard. The instigator watched the little German go inside the exchange building to hunt up Donovan in his office and ask for his raise. When Whiff came outside a few minutes later, he was asked how he fared.

"Did you get more money?"

"Naw," he grinned, "No more money, but I can take all the grass I cut as donkey feed." Donovan made shrewd deals.[15] Boots and grass for his donkey seemed to satisfy Whiff, for he worked very hard for many years. He was one of the few immigrants working for the stockyards itself; most obtained employment in the packing plants.

Al Donovan ultimately would manage the stockyards longer than anybody else, from 1916 to 1946, first as general manager and later as president. He let Harry "Cap" Henderson, superintendent, handle the two hundred or so stockyards workers. Henderson hired a lot of young men at thirty cents an hour in 1928 and let them work overtime so they could make more money per week. Henderson was a strict taskmaster with his men and would not let them smoke on the yards because of the hay all over the place. Disastrous fires had occurred too often at the yards already. The no smoking rule no doubt was company policy, but Henderson enforced it rigidly. He would not let the men drink on the job, either. Even though they respected him and knew he was boss, the men did not let Henderson successfully prohibit all vice, however. The younger stockyards workers got into the habit of meeting at some designated place on the yards after being paid on Saturday morning to engage in a nice sociable dice game. The fine for gambling if caught was $14.95, which represented more than a normal week's wages. The stockyards policemen seemed to have an uncanny way of finding out where the game was being held each week.[16]

Gambling, drinking, and visiting the prostitutes who lived in the hotels on West Exchange Avenue occupied the after-hours time of some of the workers. Many of the stockyards people, however, were family men who went straight home when their long day finally

15. Weeman interview, September 12, 1983.
16. Speck interview; Adams interview; Cox interview; Barse interview transcript, pp. 11–12.

ended. The wife of one commission man remembered her husband always working in his rose garden every day after work. She once told him he was watering the flowers too much.

"Listen, men have to do something," he told her. "Many stay at the yards and play poker, shoot craps, drink, and flirt with the hookers. Hadn't you rather I'd come home and work in the garden?" His wife thought a minute and said, "I guess those roses do need more watering than I thought they did."[17]

When a stockyards worker, commission man, or buyer encountered an unfriendly cow or bull, which occurred quite often, he had to climb a fence or gate in rapid time. Everybody "hoorawed" him and got a big laugh out of his narrow escape—that is, if he remained unscathed. The men were quick to sympathize if someone actually got hurt, however. When someone climbed a fence rapidly to avoid those threatening horns, he usually accumulated a good crop of splinters on his hands and body from all those hacked-up fences and gates. A pocketknife then came in handy to dig out the splinters.

One of the stockyards employees who did not have to worry about digging splinters out of his hands was a slight young fellow named John W. Dies. He had worked for the Texas and Pacific Railroad in Dallas during World War I. When the government took over the operation of the railroads during the war, officials sent him over to Fort Worth to help run the stockyards' Belt Railway. After the war, the Belt wanted to hire him full time, but he turned them down. They then offered him a position with the Fort Worth Stock Yards Company which owned the Belt, and he accepted it. Dies subsequently worked for the company for forty years, most of the time as secretary-treasurer.[18]

As a youngster and later as a teenager, Bill Jary worked for his father's commission business on the yards each summer. The elder Jary, who formerly had worked for his father-in-law, George W. Saunders, by 1928 owned his own firm. He had his young son Bill "chase tickets" on the yards. The pens were divided into seven sections, with commission companies and order buyers each assigned a portion of a section in which to put their livestock. The scale houses

17. Interview with Mrs. Clyde Kutch, Fort Worth, September 6, 1983.
18. Interview with Mrs. John W. Dies, Fort Worth, August 24, 1983.

were spread among these divisions. Young Jary would carry tickets from the scale back to his father in his assigned booth above the pens after the animal had been weighed. His father would then put the price on the ticket. A lot of young men got their start doing this kind of work for their fathers: J. D. Farmer II and J. D. Farmer III, for example. They would also spread out hay, water the stock, drive the cattle, and perform similar chores. In this way a second and then a third generation could almost literally "grow up" at the Fort Worth Stock Yards. The tickets the young men carried back and forth would have the total number of head sold in a group, the gross pounds, and the price. It would show from what ranch the animals came, the name of the commission company, and the buyer. The sale was complete when the animals stepped off the weighing scale.[19]

When he was in high school, Bill Jary worked in his father's office in the exchange building helping mail out the five thousand letters each week to customers of their company. He worked on the addressograph every Thursday during the summers. With each of the thirty-five to forty commission companies sending out a market letter to its customers every Thursday, the North Fort Worth branch of the United States Post Office received more than one hundred thousand pieces of mail that day. These newsletters informed customers of the current market prices for their animals. This information kept the sellers coming back to the yards and was one of the reasons why each of the companies could do between $20,000 to $30,000 in business each day during peak periods. On weekends agents from commission companies went out into the country to visit the customers who shipped to them and to meet others who might be wooed. They called their customers from Fort Worth to tell them when prices had jumped and when they should ship. People accused Charlie Daggett of not even needing a telephone to be heard clear out in West Texas when he talked long distance from the instrument in his office. He yelled so loudly that people heard him all over that wing of the exchange building.[20]

Employees and owners of commission companies did not go

19. Jary interview.
20. Ibid.; interview with Mrs. Bernelle Kutch, Fort Worth, September 19, 1983.

home at night until the day's work was completed. This included tallying all the paperwork for all the transactions that day, often without benefit of an adding machine, and writing checks, often accompanied by a personal note, to producers who had shipped in the livestock. Someone from the office mailed these each night on the way home. If it was too late for the mail to go out at the North Side Post Office, the carrier would mail the checks at the downtown branch. Mrs. Houston Hutchens, whose husband worked for fifty years on the Fort Worth market, most of the time in his own commission company, said her husband often came home at 11 P.M., midnight, or even 2 A.M.

"He was ready to go back the next morning," she said. "He loved it."[21]

So many commission companies competed on the Fort Worth market that heated incidents often occurred. Quite frequently agents would nearly resort to fisticuffs if someone took more than his allotted time at the weighing scale on a busy day. Any out-of-town visitor to the market might see men arguing vociferously and fear that a fight would break out any minute over a sale or a scale. But when the buying and selling ended and the men went through the turnstiles and entered the exchange building, or went to get a bite to eat together, they were still friends and the arguments were forgotten. In fact, years later participants would remember it as one big family. Many who worked on the yards together for forty or fifty years, or even saw a second generation grow up, became quite close.[22]

The ability of each commission man to judge cattle and please his customers and the service and satisfaction he gave, built loyalty among the producers who sent livestock to the market. This kept them coming back to the same commission company or order buyer. The men on the yards could look at an animal and tell within a few pounds what it weighed and what it would weigh when "dressed out" by the packing company. In fact, throughout the slaughtering process, packing companies kept separate records of the lots of livestock purchased by each buyer and determined how close actual yield came to his earlier projection of dressed-out weight. Anyone who

21. Interview with Mrs. Houston Hutchens, Fort Worth, September 9, 1983.
22. Weeman interview, September 22, 1983.

often missed it very far did not long remain a buyer for the company. Buyers also could look in an animal's eyes and tell if he had been wheat-fed or grain-fed in a feedlot. Wheat would produce a yellow fat on the animal that consumers did not like.[23]

The commission agent also shaped the cattle up, which meant that he put all those of the same size and grade together to sell because they would bring about the same price. He would be the judge of whether the cattle were ready for the packer or were feeders to be sold and fattened. Some could go either way, but he made the decision. Many believed that it took at least ten years' experience to accumulate enough knowledge to become a sharp salesman or buyer on the Fort Worth yards. The commission men knew the market value of all the animals, and the owners of the cattle naturally profited by their expertise. The market agency sometimes gave additional help to producers by lending them money in dry or otherwise bad years. This assistance often kept the cattleman as a customer by saving his business.[24]

Typical clothing worn on the yards consisted of medium-sized Stetsons or large straw hats in the summer, blue cotton shirts, and khaki pants. Men could purchase this kind of outfit at the White Front Clothing Store on Exchange Avenue for fifty cents for the shirts and a dollar for the pants.

"But you didn't necessarily pay what was marked," claimed William Barse, a long-time commission man; "you bid a little lower." The men were accustomed to bidding on cattle, so they bid on everything. Although a brief fad for overalls developed at the yards in the early 1920s, it soon died down and only farmers wore overalls. While some of the men claimed that good heavy shoes felt more comfortable on the uneven bricks of the pens than boots, most men at the yards still wore Western boots.[25]

Some of the people on the yards claimed the daily trading remained too serious and competitive a business for any shenanigans, but others could not restrain their natural instinct to enjoy a little

23. Ibid.; interview with C. M. "Pete" Wallace, Fort Worth, August 23, 1983; interview with Lee Carrell, Fort Worth, September 12, 1983.
24. Barse interview transcript, pp. 7–8.
25. Ibid., p. 10; Weeman interview, September 12, 1983; Carrell interview; interview with Bruce Davis, Fort Worth, September 13, 1983.

fun if the market slowed down enough to allow it. Someone in the exchange building had a huge paddle made for the purpose of saluting people on their birthday. The recipient of the "good wishes" had to be held down in the lobby by several husky fellows so he could get his paddling. One man went home on his birthday and claimed he was sick, but the well wishers went to his house and brought him back to administer his birthday licks. If they did not paddle someone, the pranksters might chase the object of their fun around with a whip snapping at his behind. Others saved up their celebrating for one or two times a year. The stockyards would have a combination square dance and round dance in the lobby of the exchange building during the Christmas holidays. Such brief respites from work had to serve for a long time usually. Men on the yards worked long hours and seemed to like being in the middle of the activity where millions of dollars worth of livestock changed hands daily.[26]

"My dad worked there before me and my brother. I grew up on the Fort Worth Stock Yards. It was my life." It does not matter which old-timer said this; many did. "If you find another cow person, you've found a friend. You can talk," said another.[27]

Although stockyards people might haze and harass their friends all in fun, they stuck together in times of adversity. The family aspect of the yards predominated. Many times they passed the hat around and "got up a list" to take care of the families of those who were ill or had died.

A special feeling existed at the Fort Worth Stock Yards, and perhaps at the other large terminal markets during their boom years. The private-treaty market system involving commission companies and the huge shipments of livestock by rail, which occurred during this special era in history, is unlikely ever to be duplicated. Just as railroads replaced steamboating in an earlier day, motor trucks eventually would replace the railroad as the major method of transporting the nation's goods — including livestock. When livestock did not have to move by rail, they could be carried anywhere, so the large terminal market centers designed mainly to receive rail shipments

26. Weeman interview, September 12, 1983; Addieway interview; Marrett interview.
27. Interview with J. R. Bettis, Azle, September 20, 1983.

began to decline. Packers and others began to buy livestock directly from the producer or in small-town auctions nearer the producing areas. By the 1930s this unique period of American livestock history, the terminal market heyday, in which Fort Worth played a major part, had begun its slow but inevitable change.

But the romantic spirit, Western character, and close camaraderie of stockyards people—that buoyantly alive feeling of being someone special—seemed as distinctive as the livestock markets themselves. That feeling among those special stockyards people lasted later than 1929, but it too was gradually altered—by mandated government changes in the way of doing things, by declines in rail receipts, and perhaps first of all by the Great Depression.

10

Depression Doldrums
1930–39

AN INCIDENT that old-timers still recalled vividly fifty years later ushered in the decade of the 1930s at the stockyards. About noon on August 9, 1930, a man carrying a satchel approached the desk of William L. Pier, president of the Stockyards National Bank. At that time the Fort Worth Stock Yards Company still owned the bank. The man demanded $10,000 in cash and informed Pier that he carried a bottle of nitroglycerin in his satchel. Fred L. Pelton, vice-president and cashier of the bank, engaged the man in conversation while Pier went behind the cages to ask the tellers to count out the money. Then Pier called the police, urging them not to run their siren and to wait for the man to leave the bank before apprehending him. When the police arrived, they either assumed that the man would already have left the bank or failed to get the message to wait, for they walked right inside. The bank robber, a thirty-year-old deranged man named Nathan Monroe Martin, saw the police and then dropped the two ounces of nitroglycerin on the floor.

The explosion killed Martin and Pelton instantly, scattering their bodies, bank furniture, and fixtures as well as money and checks throughout the room. Only two other persons suffered injury, but people heard and felt the blast a half-mile away. Some trees near the building lost leaves, and people outside the bank were hit by a shower of glass and other flying debris. The building, located just west of the coliseum on the north side of Exchange Avenue, suffered three thousand dollars' worth of damage. Contractors worked around the clock over the weekend to replaster the building, replace window panes, and clean up the mess. The bank opened as usual at 9 A.M. on Monday morning. Pelton, the vice-president, had been from Omaha, Nebraska, and his wife and child were visiting there at the time he was killed. Al Donovan, general manager of the Fort Worth Stock Yards Company and a director of the bank, accompanied Pelton's body to Omaha and represented the bank at his funeral.[1]

The decade of the 1930s, which the attempted robbery so dramatically introduced, saw erratic market receipts, plummeting prices, and federal programs designed to stabilize the market. Lower profits came to stockyard owners not only because of the national business decline, but also because the use of trucks and the expansion of feedlots nationwide began to break the power of the meat trust. Furthermore, packers completed their mandated task of selling their stockyards, railroads, banks, and other businesses.

Locally, a business newspaper reported that Fort Worth employment enjoyed a 10 percent advantage over the state as a whole, thanks in part to the activities encouraged by the livestock market. Capacity of the yards by 1930 reached 37,000 cattle, 20,000 hogs, 20,000 sheep, and 5,000 horses and mules. Thirty-nine commission companies handled the stock. Despite the increased handling capability, totals for 1930 reached only 637,515 cattle, 331,443 calves, 279,331 hogs, 432,082 sheep, and 27,047 horses and mules. Daily receipts fluctuated wildly; late in the decade a drought created daily cattle runs of from 12,000 to 15,000 head.[2]

Receipts of all classes of livestock except calves decreased in 1930. Of ten major national markets, Fort Worth ranked fifth in calves, seventh in cattle, and tenth in both hogs and sheep that year. The

1. "2 Killed, Two Are Hurt As Stock Yards Bank Robbed," *Fort Worth Star-Telegram*, August 9, 1930 (eve.). See also "Bomber Identified, Motive Sought," ibid., August 10, 1930; "Bombed Bank Open as Usual," ibid., August 11, 1930 (eve.); and "Bomber Anticipated Death, Note Reveals," *Fort Worth Record-Telegram*, August 11, 1930.

2. "Fort Worth Leads Cities in Employment," *Commercial Recorder*, February 2, 1933; *Annual Report for 1930*, January 10, 1931, pp. 4–5, Fort Worth Stock Yards Company, Fort Worth Stock Yards Company Collection, North Texas State University Archives, Denton (FWSY Co. Coll.); tape of a conversation between Ben Green, Bob Bramlett, E. A. "Dutch" Voelkel, Tom B. Saunders III, and Ted Gouldy, June 24, 1971 (tape in possession of Ted Gouldy, Fort Worth, Texas), tape 2, side 2.

stockyards tallied fewer receipts in cattle, calves, and hogs in 1931 than the previous year, but a record 1,173,326 sheep arrived, making 1931 the first time sheep surpassed a million. While receipts of hogs, sheep, horses, and mules increased in 1932, the 444,061 cattle marketed represented the smallest number of that species to arrive at Fort Worth since 1903. The year 1933 brought in an even smaller number of cattle, although calves, hogs, horses, and mules again increased.[3]

The feeder and breeder movement, a phenomenon which later grew to massive proportions and altered the entire livestock marketing process nationwide, had its Texas beginning as an official organization at the State Fair in 1929. The planting of feed crops and the "marketing" of such crops through livestock finished on the farm would restore the fertility of the soil and establish another permanent crop in addition to cotton, it was hoped. A. L. Smith, livestock specialist in the extension service of the Texas Agricultural and Mechanical College, reported in January, 1932, that Texas had nearly twice as many cattle feeders as the previous year and about 50 percent more cattle on feed. Farmers seemed to be turning to feeding their own livestock as a way to dispose of surplus grain.[4]

The Reconstruction Finance Corporation, instituted during the Hoover administration, established in the fall of 1932 a Regional Agricultural Credit Corporation with headquarters in Fort Worth and branch offices in San Angelo and Houston. Stockyards officials hoped that some of the funds could be used to feed livestock, thus encouraging people to purchase more feeder animals. Some of the cattlemen who lost money on their herds decided to raise sheep instead, which explains the much higher sheep receipts at Fort Worth a decade later.[5]

The depression affected the local market in more than decreased cattle receipts and falling prices. Certain economies had to be instituted. Effective February 1, 1932, the Fort Worth Stock Yards Company ceased its regular monthly contribution to the market news-

---

3. *Annual Reports for 1931, 1932, 1933,* January 14, 1932, January 12, 1933, January 12, 1934, FWSY Co. Coll.
4. "Texas Fast Becoming a Feeder State," *Cattleman* 18 (October, 1931): 5. See also "Livestock Feeding Increases in Texas," ibid. 18 (March, 1932): 7–8.
5. "Fort Worth Gets Credit Corporation," ibid. 19 (September, 1932): 8.

paper it had once owned and continued to subsidize, the *Weekly Live Stock Reporter*. It did plan to keep advertising occasionally, Donovan assured the editor. For several years the company had contributed five hundred dollars a year toward its support. Business and advertising receipts slowed down considerably for the newspaper, so much that they gave free full-page ads to the company in 1933 simply "to fill up space." As another cost-cutting measure, the directors of the company authorized the president to reduce the payroll expenses by 10 percent. "Cap" Henderson, yard superintendent, worked his men alternate days to keep more men on the payroll. He told them he wanted to enable everyone to be able to eat. One of the workers during those years does not remember anyone being laid off. Work tended to be highly irregular, however. Work depended on availability of railroad cars to unload. Men would work two or three hours in the morning, and then Henderson would send them home with instructions to come back for another couple of hours in the afternoon. If a man lived close by, that posed no problem. During a big run, stockyards employees might have to work all night.[6]

The Fort Worth Stock Yards Company maintained an intense advertising campaign during the depression years to try to encourage increased receipts. Full-page advertisements appeared in the *Cattleman* magazine and in annual rodeo programs, arguing the case for shipping to Fort Worth: its closeness, steady demand, accessibility by rail, and the real hometown service provided. In addition, the stockyards company and Armour and Swift each contributed five hundred dollars to the West Texas Chamber of Commerce for its promotion of the Fort Worth market in its member communities.[7]

In response to the problems common to stockyards nationwide

6. A. G. Donovan to Mr. McCain, January 21, 1932, Dies Corr., FWSY Co. Coll.; A. G. Donovan to W. K. Wright, June 22, 1933, ibid.; Board of Directors Meeting, Fort Worth Stock Yards Company, April 21, 1933, *Corporate Record*, unnumbered vol. 1917–34, p. 282; interview with Johnny Adams, Fort Worth, September 12, 1983; interview with Bill Addieway, Fort Worth, September 23, 1983.

7. Fort Worth Stock Yards Company Advertisement, *Cattleman* 19 (June, 1932): inside front cover; H. O. Hogue (Armour) to West Texas Chamber of Commerce, August 25, 1930; S. A. Middaugh (Swift) to West Texas Chamber of Commerce, August 7, 1930; A. G. Donovan (Stock Yards) to West Texas Chamber of Commerce, September 5, 1930, Donations Folder, Dies Corr., FWSY Co. Coll.

came the creation in 1933 of the American Stock Yards Association. Formed as a national trade association, the organization included as directors representatives of the stockyards companies at the leading markets of the country. The Fort Worth Stock Yards joined the association, but none of its officials served as executive officers during the organizational phase.

Cattlemen's organizations also worked together for solutions. Dolph Briscoe, president of the Texas and Southwestern Cattle Raisers Association in 1933 (and father of a future governor of Texas), urged that an orderly market program be instituted.[8]

Of course, federal reaction to the pressing depression problems of agriculture came mainly with Franklin D. Roosevelt's New Deal measures, most notably the Agricultural Adjustment Act (AAA). Affecting the local yards more than anything else were the hog-reduction program and the drought-inspired cattle purchase plan.

The company had launched "another campaign to import gilts from the North" during the summer of 1930 to encourage more hog production but reported that these efforts had met with little success because of "lack of feed, the present low market price for hogs, and farmers' inability to finance the purchase of the gilts." Once the hog-reduction program of the federal government got underway, the company discontinued its efforts to increase the production of hogs in the state. The company never really pushed hog production to any great extent again.[9]

U.S. Secretary of Agriculture Henry A. Wallace appointed Guy C. Shepard of Evanston, Illinois, to be administrator of the AAA program as it applied to packinghouse products. Shepard was a former vice-president of Cudahy Packing Company, who had retired in 1931 after forty years in the meat-packing industry. Thus an expert in pork merchandising would head up the government's hog-reduction program.[10]

At first, Texans viewed the government program with some trepidation. They basically preferred a philosophy of self-help and rugged individualism, although a few Populists believed the federal

8. "Government Action Needed," *Cattleman* 20 (August, 1933): 9.
9. *Annual Reports for 1930, 1934,* January 10, 1931, January, 1935, FWSY Co. Coll.
10. "Packer Administrator," *Cattleman* 20 (July, 1933): 27.

government had a responsibility to help. During the Hoover administration most of the state's elected leaders, such as Senator Morris Sheppard and Governor Ross Sterling, made pronouncements that seemed to oppose federal aid. Local and state sources did not provide relief during this period, either. By the time many Texans got over their aversion to the federal assistance that Roosevelt's New Deal provided, the situation had reached serious proportions. Although grumbling that the New Deal would destroy initiative, states' rights, and the American way, many abandoned their philosophy "temporarily" and accepted the assistance.[11]

When finally worked out, the emergency program for reduction of the nation's hog surplus meant that the AAA planned to buy four million pigs and one million sows within six weeks, beginning August 23, 1933. The program, recommended to the government at a meeting in Washington on August 10 by representatives of producers, processors, marketing agencies, and wholesale and retail meat dealers, saw its Fort Worth implementation begin on August 28. Secretary Wallace reported that the program nationwide would cost $55 million, which would be paid by a processing tax on hogs and pork imposed on all packers. Only federally inspected packers could purchase livestock in the government program, and they bought animals the regular way through commission firms. The government then reimbursed the packers for their costs. The Agriculture Department withheld the meat from entering regular market channels in order to prevent it from affecting prices. Prices of pigs varied by weight from $8.90 per one hundred pounds to $5.40.[12]

During the emergency six-week campaign ending October 7, 1933, the government actually purchased nearly 6.5 million pigs and sows. The plan cost $33 million—$30.5 million for the animals, and $2.5 for processing. The campaign, however, appeared to have little if any effect on hog prices during the last half of 1933. The government made a second purchase of 2 million more hogs between November, 1933, and September, 1934, and the program even continued

11.   Donald W. Whisenhunt, "The Texas Attitude toward Relief, 1929–1933," *Panhandle-Plains Historical Review* 46 (1973): 103–105, 111.
12.   "Government Buying 5,000,000 Hogs," *Cattleman* 20 (September, 1933): 9; "Emergency Hog Program Goes into Effect Monday," *Weekly Live Stock Reporter*, August 24, 1933, p. 1.

into 1935 among those farmers willing to sign contracts to sell.[13]

One story surfaced in the local market newspaper of a hog-reduction plan gone awry. W. J. Calhoun of Sherman agreed to get rid of two of the three sows he owned and so signed up in the government hog-reduction campaign in the spring of 1934. The third sow he kept, though, did the duty of three, for "she littered once, and 13 piglets blessed the home pen. She littered twice and septuplets arrived. She littered thrice, and 18 were added to the family." The reporter headed his story with the rhyme:

> This little pig went to market
> This little pig went too.
> This little pig stayed at home in the pen and found
>   she had plenty to do.[14]

At the Fort Worth yards, farmers marketed approximately eighty-four thousand pigs during the government hog-reduction program, which made 1933 receipts somewhat larger than usual. New canning plants opened on the North Side to take care of government-purchased meats, providing jobs to destitute individuals. A Texas Relief Commission canning plant opened December 18, 1933, at 2204 North Main for a trial run. Workers processed five thousand cans on the first day. The capacity output for the 572 workers could reach between fifteen thousand and twenty thousand cans daily, depending upon receipts. The plant worked four shifts of six hours each, with each shift employing about 100 women and 25 men. According to state requirements, the employees had to come from the city's relief rolls, and they were paid forty cents an hour. During at least a part of the time the building on Decatur Avenue that had been constructed as the city hall for Niles City served as a canning plant.[15]

Cattle raisers continued to complain of increased supplies and dropping prices, but many, like Dolph Briscoe of the Texas and Southwestern Cattle Raisers Association, did not feel that government

---

13. D. A. Fitzgerald, *Livestock under the AAA*, pp. 68–71.
14. "Pig Reduction Drive Not Such a Squealing Success on This Farm," *Weekly Live Stock Reporter*, May 17, 1934, p. 1.
15. *Annual Report for 1934*, FWSY Co. Coll.; "Canning Plant in Full Blast," *Commercial Recorder*, December 20, 1933, p. 1. See also "Beef Plant Will Use 525 Employees at 40¢ an Hour," *Commercial Recorder*, December 12, 1933, p. 1.

legislation to fix prices would work. The American National Cattle-men's Association opposed including cattle as a basic commodity under the AAA subject to its provisions and controls. As an alter-native, the association advocated legislation to restrict importation of beef and competing fats and oils, to raise the tariff on hides, to lower the costs of transportation and marketing, and to foster more orderly marketing. Congress deferred to them and did not include cattle in the AAA program. In 1934, however, drought conditions and government efforts to develop a production-control program co-incided. The worsening economic conditions and the AAA programs for other producers caused cattlemen to change their minds. At their annual meeting in 1934 the American National Cattlemen's Asso-ciation recommended that cattle be made a basic commodity. As a result, Congress passed the Jones-Connally Farm Relief Act, which amended the AAA to add cattle.[16]

The first announcement of a proposal to purchase cattle to aid the drought-stricken areas of the Great Plains came on May 14 and 15, 1934. The government initially authorized $50 million for drought relief and $200 million more to finance production control and surplus reduction and "to support and balance the market." The gov-ernment purchased the first cattle under the program June 12, 1934. An Emergency Appropriation Act approved June 19, 1934, provided funds. Eventually Congress would appropriate $63.4 million for cattle purchases in the program. Government agents made these purchases in the field and not in stockyards.[17]

Purposes of the Emergency Cattle Purchase Program included removing surplus cattle from the drought-stricken ranges, stabiliz-ing the beef market by removing the surplus, and providing more

16. Charles A. Burmeister, "Six Decades of Rugged Individualism: The Ameri-can National Cattlemen's Association, 1898–1955," *Agricultural History* 30 (Oc-tober, 1956): 149. The resolution was very controversial, however. See also Roger Lambert, "Drought Relief for Cattlemen: The Emergency Purchase Program of 1934–35," *Panhandle-Plains Historical Review* 45 (1972): 21; John T. Schlebecker, *Cattle Raising on the Plains, 1900–1961,* p. 139. The law was H.R. 7478 or Public Law 142, Chap. 103, Vol. 48, U.S. *Statutes at Large,* p. 528.

17. John D. Black, *The Dairy Industry and the AAA* (Washington, D.C.: Brook-ings Institution, 1935), p. 393 (this was H.R. 9830, Public Law No. 412. Chap. 648, Vol. 48, U.S. *Statutes at Large,* p. 1021). See also Edwin G. Nourse, Joseph S. Davis, and John D. Black, *Three Years of the Agricultural Adjustment Administration,* p. 106.

wholesome food for the needy. In addition, removing poorer cattle from the farmers' herds would improve their foundation herds for future production. Some controversy exists over whether these cattle slaughtered by the government in 1934 consisted only of poorer cattle or if better grades also were killed. Wayne D. Rasmussen, chief of the U.S.D.A. Agricultural History Branch believes that "most of the cattle sold were in bad shape." Some Texas farmers testify that at least some good, fat cattle were slaughtered. Apparently state practices varied, as did enforcement of the law. In Texas the Federal Surplus Relief Corporation became the buyer, and the Texas Relief Commission handled the canning and distributing. They gave six cans of beef consisting of one and one-fourth pounds of meat per can to a family of five each month. Relief officials intended that the canning plants (nineteen throughout the state, including Fort Worth) exist primarily to provide work for the unemployed. Consequently, inexperienced workers made plant operations costly, and a poor quality of meat resulted. Bone and hide frequently turned up in the canned beef.[18]

Locally, Dr. H. L. Darby of the Fort Worth office of the Bureau of Animal Industry became the inspector in charge. During the emergency campaign, the government bought cattle in 233 of 254 Texas counties, including Tarrant where the Fort Worth Stock Yards were located. Government officials purchased 8,154 cattle in Tarrant County and condemned 5,041 more. Statewide they accepted 1,292,339 cattle and condemned 677,048.[19]

Many Texas farmers refused to cooperate in the program and ridiculed their neighbors who did. Stories are told of strong men weeping as they watched the cattle condemned under the program being shot, and other outraged farmers and ranchmen refused to sell to Uncle Sam. The Swenson brothers at Stamford would not allow their cattle to be killed. They rounded up their surplus animals and shipped them to market, presumably Fort Worth, selling them at six dollars per head, half the price being paid by the government.

18. Irvin May, Jr., "Welfare and Ranchers: The Emergency Cattle Purchase Program and Emergency Work Relief Program in Texas, 1934–35," *West Texas Historical Association Yearbook* 47 (1971): 13–15. See also "Government Provides Drought Relief," *Cattleman* 21 (July, 1934): 5.

19. "Government Buying and a Cattle Shortage," *Cattleman* (March, 1935): 14.

Other cattlemen, however, reacted with gratitude to Uncle Sam, claiming that the program saved the industry. Among these was W. T. Coble, who succeeded Dolph Briscoe as president of the Texas and Southwestern Cattle Raisers Association in 1934 and served until the end of the depression. He said, "This program accomplished the saving of a large food supply which was necessary for the needy, furnished a market for cattle which could not have been found otherwise, and resulted in the removal of the surplus."[20]

Cattle indeed sold on the Fort Worth market at prices much lower than the government paid for scrub cattle. Market reporter Ted Gouldy remembered when a load of cattle brought only enough to pay for train freight, yardage fees, and the commission, with not even enough to pay for the hay they ate, much less to offer profit for the owners. The company tried to collect the money due them, however.[21]

One story that made the rounds at terminal markets represented a recurring experience. There was a shipper whose animals did not bring enough to pay the freight or stockyards charges. When informed he owed more money, so the Fort Worth variant goes, the West Texas goat raiser wrote back, "I don't have any money, but I can send you more goats."[22]

Prices remained so low that if a cow intended for slaughter had a calf while in the stockyards, Armour or Swift could find no market for the calf even after letting it nurse its mother for a couple of weeks at the yards. Someone could raise the calf, put feed in it until it weighed two or three hundred pounds, and still not be able to sell it for more than a dollar.[23]

Ironically, on the other hand, commission agent Tom B. Saunders III said he made proportionately, more money on cattle in the depression than he did in the 1940s or 1960s because he made fif-

20. Interview with Berta Rogers, Fort Worth, July 1, 1979. See also Mary Whatley Clarke, *A Century of Cow Business: A History of the Texas and Southwestern Cattle Raisers Association,* pp. 176–77.

21. Interview with W. M. Speck, Fort Worth, June 7, 1983.

22. Interview with Gary Allen, Fort Worth, February 24, 1982. A similar story is told in Charles L. Wood, *The Kansas Beef Industry,* p. 256, but he quoted James H. Shideler, *Farm Crisis, 1919–1923,* pp. 28–30, who got his information from the *Kansas Stockman* of September 1, 1921.

23. Interview with J. R. Bettis, Azle, September 20, 1983.

teen cents per head on a cow that sold for $20 in 1933, while in 1969 he made forty cents on a cow selling for $140. Interest rates were 3.5 percent in 1933, but they reached 8.5 percent in 1969, and it cost him more money to run his business at the later date.[24]

By June, 1934, the drought relief service, which originally had intended to purchase 40,000 cattle a week, was buying over five times that number. In the week ending August 11, the agency bought 588,000 head, and purchases remained at or above that level through the second week of September. They sent some cattle to relief agencies, some to commercial canners, others to pasturage, and killed and buried the rest. They let farmers salvage the hides of those they destroyed. By September, 1934, the administration began to worry about when and where the cattle purchase would end and tried to put a stop to the program. The public kept demanding large-scale purchases, so the government continued the program through January, 1935. During an eight-month period—from June, 1934, to January, 1935—the government bought almost 8.3 million cattle and provided to cattlemen and their creditors some $111 million. Most cattlemen seemed grateful, but they still refused to join a plan to control pork, grain, and beef output in the future and opposed the levy of any processing tax to recover part of the cost of their aid. By mid-decade rising cattle prices brightened the economic scene for Texas cattle producers, leading most to refuse any more government assistance.

Of the 8.3 million head purchased, the government bought nearly 25 percent in Texas and over 20 percent in the Dakotas. They condemned an overall 18 percent nationwide, but in Texas the proportion rejected reached 34 percent. The program reduced the number of beef cattle by 17 percent, which not only improved the market, but brought a better balance between feed and cattle. Had not drought relief taken center stage, the government might have worked out some feasible plan of benefit payments funded by a processing tax, but they abandoned any such plans in favor of the emergency aid. By 1935 herds had begun to improve.[25]

24. Tape of conversation between Green, Bramlett, Voelkel, Saunders, and Gouldy, tape 2, side 1.
25. Black, *Dairy Industry and AAA*, pp. 392–93. See also May, "Welfare and Ranchers," p. 18.

While some farmers in the Midwest thought that the drought was God's way of punishing Roosevelt for plowing under cotton and killing millions of little pigs in 1933, many more found the drought a convenient way to justify the government's increasing involvement in the agricultural economy. Some who opposed intervention, however, filed a case in a U.S. district court in Philadelphia in 1935, attacking the constitutionality of the Agricultural Adjustment Act. Six pork-packing concerns challenged the section establishing a processing tax on hogs and pork products. They called the law "an invalid means to accomplish an illegal end." The Supreme Court in a different case, *U.S.* v. *Butler*, eventually declared the Agricultural Adjustment Act unconstitutional. The processing tax was declared regulatory in nature. Congress later rewrote the law and reinstituted the AAA in slightly different form.[26]

The Southwestern Exposition and Fat Stock Show continued annual shows in the coliseum and exhibit buildings throughout the depression decade despite financial setbacks. Prior to the 1930 show, officials spent $250,000 on two new exhibit halls and other improvements, doubling the amount of room previously available. In 1931 all classes of livestock totaled 4,500 head, the largest number ever entered at a Fort Worth show. The next year officials broadcast over Amon Carter's WBAP radio a performance of the rodeo in its entirety, the first such broadcast anywhere in the country. The show that year, however, showed a $20,000 deficit, and exposition officials still owed three local banks outstanding debts of $55,000 from the previous construction. The Fort Worth Stock Yards Company accepted a note for $5,000 at 6 percent interest covering the rent due to the company for the coliseum and grounds.[27]

Show entries in beef cattle, sheep and goats, and hogs declined in 1933, but entries set new records in several smaller departments such as Hereford, Shorthorn, Angus, club calves, Jersey, Holstein,

26. Michael W. Schuyler, "Drought and Politics, 1936: Kansas as a Test Case," *Great Plains Journal* 15 (Fall, 1975): 6. See also "Pork Packers Get Restraining Order in Attacking AAA," *Commercial Recorder*, June 18, 1935, p. 1.

27. A. G. Donovan to William B. Traynor, March 24, 1932, Southwestern Exposition and Fat Stock Show Folder, Dies Corr., FWSY Co. Coll. See also Board of Directors meeting, April 21, 1933, *Corporate Record*, unnumbered vol. 1917–34, p. 282.

dairy club calves, and horses. That year officials offered a thousand seats to rodeo performances at what they called "Depression Prices," the lowest in history. That year the Fort Worth city manager, G. D. Fairtrace, suggested that the stock show of Fort Worth and the state fair of Dallas consolidate and hold both events at Arlington Downs, the new racetrack built by W. T. Waggoner, the stock show in the spring and the fair in the fall. Few took him very seriously, although space for the show was getting scarce on the North Side. By the close of the 1933 show with its $16,000 deficit, the officials owed the stock-yards $10,000 for two years' rent, plus $5,000 for the *Live Stock Reporter* building, which the stock show purchased in 1932 and tore down to make room at the entrance to the midway.[28]

Rent on the coliseum had been scheduled to increase in 1934 from $5,000 to $7,500, according to an earlier agreement, but the company maintained the rent at $5,000 through 1938 to help the show. Then the rental rate jumped to $8,000. In 1935 and for several years thereafter promoters held the World Championship Rodeo in Fort Worth in March as part of the annual events, allowing cowboys to be named to world titles.[29]

Texas also began planning its official centennial celebration, and the state legislature appropriated $3 million to be used by communities for appropriate activities. A delegation of Fort Worth citizens traveled to Austin in July, 1935, to try to obtain some of this money for a "gigantic new plant" to house the Southwestern Exposition and Fat Stock Show west of the city near Camp Bowie Boulevard at a cost of $1.5 million. The citizens wanted $300,000 from the centennial funds. City officials held a bond election in the fall of 1935 to approve funding for playgrounds, parks, and a coliseum and

28. "Entries for Fat Stock Show Set New Records," *Commercial Recorder*, March 1, 1933, p. 1. See also "Seats for Rodeo Placed on Sale at the Coliseum," *Weekly Live Stock Reporter*, February 25, 1933, p. 1; "Combine Stock Show and Fair," *Cattleman* 20 (July, 1933): 5; and A. G. Donovan to W. K. Wright, April 10, 1933, Southwestern Exposition and Fat Stock Show Folder, Dies Corr., FWSY Co. Coll.

29. A. G. Donovan to Southwestern Exposition and Fat Stock Show, April 14, 1934, Dies Corr., FWSY Co. Coll.; A. G. Donovan to John B. Davis, May 1, 1934, ibid.; A. G. Donovan to John B. Davis, June 10, 1935, ibid.; A. G. Donovan to C. F. Topping, October 19, 1940, ibid.; "Fifty Years of Rodeo in Fort Worth," bound rodeo programs for 1927–77, 1935 Program, I, 57, Local History Collection, Amon Carter Museum of Western Art, Fort Worth.

auditorium for the show to be built at the west-side site as their centennial project. North Side residents opposed the issue, because they did not want their area to lose the show. Twelve of these residents obtained an injunction to stop the sale of $687,500 of bonds, but the Texas Supreme Court finally ruled that the bonds to build the show facilities could be sold. The city had to submit the plans to the Public Works Administration for approval. Their proposal called for a centennial stock show auditorium, memorial tower, and coliseum at an estimated cost of $880,000 and six other exhibit buildings at $446,000. The story goes that Amon Carter almost literally had to twist a few arms in Washington, including President Franklin D. Roosevelt's, for Fort Worth to get the PWA money for the project. Washington officials called it "Amon's Cowshed." Carter urged that the complex be named after his good friend and the nation's beloved humorist Will Rogers, who had recently died in a plane crash.[30]

The stock show did not move to the new buildings as soon as they were completed, but the stockyards company made plans to sell their coliseum to the City of Fort Worth in 1936. Manager Donovan explained to the Chicago directors that the City of Fort Worth would maintain the buildings and that the sale was necessary to keep the show on the North Side.[31]

Although the coliseum cost $155,300 to build in 1908, the stockyards company declared the book value to be $232,128 less $60,257 depreciation. The city purchased the facility for only $100,000. The company also sold some show sheds, paving on the show grounds, the show office, and other improvements, and simply took a book loss for all in excess of $100,000. Company officials seemed satisfied, for they reduced their taxable property by $341,443.[32]

In September, 1936, the Fort Worth Stock Yards Company lent the stock show $6,666.67 to help it raise enough money to hold a cen-

30. "Delegation in Austin to Get Show Backing," *Commercial Recorder,* July 9, 1935, p. 1; *Lewis* v. *City of Fort Worth* 89 SW 2d 975 (1936). Also Jerry Flemmons, *Amon: The Life of Amon Carter, Sr. of Texas,* pp. 261, 390.

31. *Annual Report for 1936,* FWSY Co. Coll.

32. J. W. Dies to F. F. Murray, June 4, 1936, Dies Corr., FWSY Co. Coll. See also *Annual Report for 1935,* ibid., p. 6.

tennial celebration October 3–11. Show officials needed until 1939 to repay the loan.[33]

The more than 300,000 who attended the forty-first annual fat stock show in 1937, held in the usual stockyards area, broke all attendance records. Mrs. Franklin D. Roosevelt visited the stock show on March 12, 1939, as a guest of her son, Elliott, who lived in Fort Worth.[34]

The new Tarrant County Water Control District No. 1, first of its kind in the state, created under the major influence of Fort Worth Stock Yards Company engineer Kennerly Robey, completed its major projects in the 1930s. When completed in 1935, the two lakes created by the two dams on the West Fork of the Trinity River were among the ten largest artificial lakes in the country. Many Fort Worth officials even discussed a possible canalization of the Trinity River from the Gulf of Mexico to Fort Worth and argued that the two lakes would make this possible because they would provide enough water to operate canal locks.[35]

While these improvements helped the stockyards locally, a national problem remained. Armour and Swift faced court orders to divest themselves of direct ownership of the Fort Worth Stock Yards Company. In fact, as early as December 29, 1927, Armour officials requested that the Fort Worth Stock Yards Company transfer 9,230 shares of stock from J. Ogden Armour, Trustee, to F. W. Ellis. Ellis then on January 18, 1928, transferred the stock to a new corporation set up for that purpose: General Stockyards Corporation. By November 30, 1931, people still were signing dividends of Fort Worth Stock Yards Company stock over to General Stockyards Corporation. Two Armour brothers still served as directors of the Fort Worth Stock Yards Company late in the decade. When one of them requested that

33. Agreement from Southwestern Exposition and Fat Stock Show, September 14, 1936, signed by Van Zandt Jarvis and A. G. Donovan, Dies Corr., FWSY Co. Coll. See also J. B. Davis to Stockyards Co., March 29, 1939, ibid.

34. "'Bled' Sez," *Commercial Recorder*, March 23, 1937, p. 1; and "Mrs. Roosevelt to Attend Stock Show," *Weekly Live Stock Reporter*, March 9, 1939, p. 1.

35. T. C. Richardson, "Fort Worth, Where the West Begins," *Holland's* 54 (February, 1935): 29; "Deep Water Will Make City Giant Industrial Mecca," *Commercial Recorder*, November 19, 1931, p. 1.

the company deposit $50,000 in his Chicago bank, directors unanimously approved his request.[36]

In 1931 Armour and Company owned 59 percent of the stock of the Jersey City Stockyards and 30 percent of General Stockyards, including Fort Worth. Armour and Company sold to Stanmore Corporation, owned by Philip Armour, to Armforth Corporation owned by Lester Armour, and Valmay Corporation, owned by Mrs. May L. Valentine, mother of Philip and Lester. Justice Jennings Bailey of the District of Columbia Supreme Court on July 15, 1931, signed a court order that allowed the sale, claiming that "none of these parties hold any substantial voting interest in the Armour packing business."[37]

Finally, in compliance with the court order, the Fort Worth Stock Yards Company sold the Fort Worth Belt Railway on May 1, 1931, to the Missouri Pacific Railroad and the Texas and Pacific Railroad for $1.5 million. The company had planned to sell the railroad to the Texas and Pacific only, but the Missouri Pacific and others objected, fearing that the other lines would not obtain equal treatment. The Fort Worth Stock Yards Company sold the Belt Railway a tract of land later in the year, and Armour, Swift, and the stockyards company all received apportioned charges for hiring the land survey. A letter from the vice-president of the Texas and Pacific Railroad to A. G. Donovan in 1932 revealed how closely the stockyards and Belt railway had previously operated. The T&P official informed Donovan that the Belt would no longer share equally with the stockyards for the price of dues to the Fort Worth Club, the East Texas Chamber of Commerce, the West Texas Chamber of Commerce, the Fort Worth Chamber of Commerce, the hog campaign, the Telegraph News Service, the Purchasing Agent's Association, the North Fort

36. Certificates of Capital Stock, Fort Worth Stock Yards Company, Gary Havard Personal Collection, Fort Worth, Texas; Paul M. Johnson to Julian E. Simon, May 12, 1958, United Folder, Dies Corr., FWSY Co. Coll. See also A. G. Donovan to F. W. Ellis, January 10, 1931, in *Annual Report for 1930*, ibid. Ellis was president of the Fort Worth Stock Yards Company at this time. Certificates of Capital Stock, Fort Worth Stock Yards Company, Book 2 (1931), Havard Coll.; Laurance Armour, May 3, 1939, to A. G. Donovan, Dies Corr., FWSY Co.; A. G. Donovan to Laurance Armour, April 28, 1939, and September 11, 1939, ibid.

37. "Armour & Co. to Sell Market Holding," *Cattleman* 18 (August, 1931): 5. See also "To Sell Armour Holdings," *New York Times*, July 16, 1931, p. 11.

Worth Kiwanis Club, the Fort Worth Community Chest, *Traffic World,* and seven other newspapers and journals, as well as numerous other joint charges.[38]

A final ruling on the Packers' Consent Decree came June 16, 1932, directing Swift and Armour to transfer their shares to a trustee with the power and duty to dispose of their financial interests in all stockyards. Legal delays forestalled Swift's compliance with the order, at least regarding the Fort Worth Stock Yards, for an additional four years.[39]

In October, 1933, Henry Veeder, vice-president of Swift and Company, was still the assistant secretary of the Fort Worth Stock Yards Company. He refrained from signing a bank deposit form and asked the secretary to do it instead, "to avoid raising any question with the bank." Six months later Swift officials still gave the stockyards company directions concerning how to sign the payroll checks. J. Ogden Armour had resigned as a director of the Fort Worth Stock Yards Company as early as April 11, 1922, however.[40]

Another major holding of the Fort Worth Stock Yards Company, the Stockyards National Bank, merged with the Fort Worth National Bank (now Texas American/Fort Worth) as of October 13, 1934, as the company complied with the court order to divest itself of bank holdings. W. L. Pier, former president of the Stockyards National Bank, became a vice-president of Fort Worth National, and the former cashier of Stockyards became an assistant cashier at the larger bank. Pier later would become president of the Fort Worth Stock Yards Company and hold that position for fifteen years. The bank build-

38. Prospectus, United Stockyards Corporation $4,500,000 Fifteen Year Collateral Trust 4¼% Bonds, Series A, October 1, 1936, p. 17, Havard Coll. See also Board of Directors Meeting, March 11, 1931, *Corporate Record,* unnumbered vol. 1917–34, pp. 174–75; "I.C.C. Hearing Here Friday on Sale of Belt Ry.," *Commercial Recorder,* November 16, 1931, p. 1; "Fort Worth Belt Railroad," *Cattleman* 18 (November, 1931): 12; Brookes Baker to K. Robey, November 30, 1931, General Corr., FWSY Co. Coll.; J. A. Somerville to A. G. Donovan, September 29, 1932, Dies Corr., FWSY Co. Coll.

39. *U.S.* v. *Swift & Co. et al.,* 286 U.S. 106 (1932). A summary of forty years of litigation was included in *United States* v. *Swift & Co.,* 189 F. Supp. 885 (1960). See also Prospectus, United Stockyards Corporation, p. 3.

40. Henry Veeder to J. W. Dies, October 20, 1933, Dies Corr., FWSY Co. Coll.; A. G. Donovan to R. F. Murray, May 28, 1934, ibid.; Board of Directors Meeting, Fort Worth Stock Yards Company, April 11, 1922, *Corporate Record,* III, p. 251.

ing stood vacant in 1936, and the company hoped someone would rent it. In 1941 investors organized the North Fort Worth State Bank, and it occupied the old Stockyards National Bank quarters until 1949, when bank officials moved it to a new building four blocks away. It catered more to individual and industrial accounts than to the livestock trade.[41]

Swift created a new corporation, United Stockyards, to purchase all the stockyards stock owned by Swift and Company. It originated May 15, 1936, under the laws of Delaware. A federal district court in Washington on August 13, 1936, approved the sale of six stockyards owned at least partially by Swift to United Stockyards of Chicago. United Stockyards "was formed for the primary purpose of acquiring and thereafter holding the issued capital stocks and other securities of various corporations operating public stockyards at various points in the United States." The new corporation spent $8,873,340 to acquire shares in at least eight companies. Of the 110,000 shares outstanding of the Fort Worth Stock Yards Company stock, United bought 46,692 shares or 42.477 percent at $32 per share for $1,494,144. W. K. Wright, a former official of Swift and Company, became president of United Stockyards by October, 1936. Wright had entered the employ of Swift in 1917 as an assistant to Louis F. Swift. From 1922 to 1936 he headed stockyards operations for Swift. As of November 2, 1936, United became the holder of Fort Worth Stock Yards Company stock. During the nearly thirty-four years that Swift had owned one-third of the company, from January, 1902, through November 1, 1936, total dividends paid by the Fort Worth Stock Yards Company on its capital stock to Swift had amounted to $2,332,275. In a comparable time Armour and Company earned $2,357,025.[42]

41. "Stockyards Bank Is Merged with Strong Fort Worth National," *Weekly Live Stock Reporter*, October 18, 1934, p. 4; *Annual Report for 1936*, FWSY Co. Coll. See also W. L. Pier to John P. McQuillen, July 6, 1956, Pier Corr., FWSY Co. Coll.

42. Paul M. Johnson to Julian E. Simon, May 12, 1958, United Folder, Dies Corr., FWSY Co. Coll.; "Approve Sale of Swift Yards," *Fort Worth Star-Telegram*, August 14, 1936 (morn.), copy in "Swift" file, *Fort Worth Star-Telegram* Reference Library; copy of agreement between United Stockyards Corporation and Wesley K. Wright, September 29, 1936, Havard Collection; Prospectus, United Stockyards Corporation, October 1, 1936, pp. 2, 4, 15, ibid.; and Paul M. Johnson to Julian E. Simon, May 12, 1958.

Donovan received a message from a Swift official to discontinue remitting $500 per month to Swift and Company for legal service expense, as of November 4, 1936, but to send future financial statements and reports to W. K. Wright of United Stockyards. The stockyards company had been paying these monthly management charges to Swift for at least five years.[43]

Soon after the transfer of Swift's Fort Worth stock, United began buying up the rest of the stock in small amounts. Then on May 25, 1937, United Stockyards Corporation bought 39,178 shares of Fort Worth Stock Yards stock from General Stockyards Corporation, the shares that had once belonged to Armour.[44]

Not only Armour and Swift created new companies to own their stockyards; members of the Louville V. Niles family decided to transfer their shares to another organization, too. As early as 1928 the Hundreds Circle Trust had begun acquiring Niles's former shares, with the Niles heirs serving as trustees. Then in 1936 the Niles family sold 7,000 shares of Fort Worth Stock Yards Company stock to United Stockyards, but retained 2,000 shares. They indicated that they did not wish to terminate completely their association with the company, although United apparently wanted to purchase all their stock.[45]

To separate fully from the Fort Worth Stock Yards Company, the two Big Four meat packers had a few more tasks to complete. Armour and Company and the Fort Worth Stock Yards Company jointly owned a 1,280-acre ranch in Reagan County, which they sold in late 1938. They had already sold nearly 9,000 acres at $7.50 per acre three years earlier.[46]

Unlike many businesses that declared bankruptcy during the depression, the Fort Worth Stock Yards Company paid dividends during the entire decade, although sometimes small ones. Generally

43. Swift and Company to A. G. Donovan, November 4, 1936, Swift and Company Files, Dies Corr., FWSY Co. Coll.; Johnson to Simon, May 12, 1958.

44. Certificates of Capital Stock, Fort Worth Stock Yards Company, Book 7 (1936–37), Havard Coll.; ibid., Book 8 (1937–38).

45. Certificates of Capital Stock, Books 2, 12, Havard Coll.; Exhibit H-2-I, Registration Statement under Securities Act of 1933, as amended, p. 3, United Stockyards folder, ibid.

46. L. W. Marshall to John Dies, March 14, 1939, Dies Corr., FWSY Co. Coll. See also *Annual Report for 1935,* ibid., p. 4.

they paid quarterly dividends of two dollars until 1931, when they increased their shares from 27,500 par value to 111,000 without par value at a special stockholders meeting June 8. After that they paid a dollar fifty on the par value shares and thirty-seven and one-half cents per share on non-par value shares throughout most of the decade, with even a few extra dividends occasionally. Although the company made over a quarter of a million dollars' profit in both 1937 and 1938, workers asking for a raise during the depression were told the company could not afford it.[47]

The new labor union that emerged from the depression years, the Congress of Industrial Organizations, signed up the stockyards handlers union and by a vote of more than three to one gained recognition on September 20, 1938, as the sole bargaining agency for its class of employees at the Fort Worth Stock Yards Company. This action constituted the first major election involving the CIO in the Southwest cattle industry, according to Joseph Barrett of Chicago, regional director of the packinghouse workers organizing committee. Company officials believed that they could work harmoniously with the union. The stockyards still paid less than the local packers and less than the government paid the welfare workers in the canning plants. During at least part of the depression stockyards workers earned from thirty to thirty-six cents an hour. In August of 1939 the new union staged a four-day strike and obtained vacations and as much as a ten-cent pay hike for some workers.[48]

Cattle prices during the latter half of the decade began to pick up on the Fort Worth market. The company continued to give twenty-four-hour round-the-clock service in receiving the livestock, retaining an average of two hundred employees to do so. The company estimated that the value of cattle, calves, sheep, and hogs in 1935 equalled fifty million dollars, an increase of some ten million over the previous year. On a typical day cattle came from Arkansas, Lou-

47. Special Stockholders Meeting, June 8, 1931, *Corporate Record*, unnumbered vol. 1917–34, pp. 176–77; Board of Directors Meetings, 1930–39, ibid.; *Annual Report for 1937 and Annual Report for 1938*, FWSY Co. Coll.; Speck interview
48. "CIO Wins Poll at Stockyards," *Fort Worth Star-Telegram*, September 21, 1938 (morn.), in "Livestock" File, *Fort Worth Star-Telegram* Reference Library; *Annual Report for 1938*, p. 3, FWSY Co. Coll.; interview with Hutton Cox, Fort Worth, June 10, 1983; Speck interview; Adams interview.

siana, Oklahoma, and at least 42 percent of the 254 Texas counties.[49]

By 1936 Texas had become the largest producing state for both cattle and sheep. For one week in the spring of 1937 Fort Worth received
more sheep and lambs than any other principal market in the United
States. In fact, in May, 1937, for the first time in history, total receipts in Fort Worth tallied the largest in the nation, exceeding even
Chicago and Kansas City. The year 1937 proved to be the largest since
1917, for over three million head of all types of livestock arrived, with
more than 70 percent brought in by truck.[50]

By March 24, 1938, forty-two commission companies operated on
the Fort Worth market, and prices during the last half of the year
climbed higher than those during the first six months. Cattle passing through the Fort Worth Stock Yards were shipped to thirty-eight
states that year and producers selling to the local market earned
over ninety million dollars for their animals. In November, however,
the company decided to close the Saturday market in order to comply with the wage-hour act. Trade on Saturday had remained small
anyway.[51]

Optimism gradually returned to Fort Worth by the close of the
decade. Publicity about the city called the 253-acre yards the third
largest in the nation and cited the two packing plants as second
only in size to the home plants in Chicago. Rising livestock prices
helped create this enthusiasm.[52]

William L. Pier, former president of the Stockyards National Bank,

49. Fort Worth Stock Yards Company Statement of Average Number of Employees, January 1, 1935 to December 31, 1940, Fort Worth Livestock Handling Company Folder, Dies Corr., FWSY Co. Coll.; "The Big Corral," Fort Worth Stock Yards
Company Advertisement, *Cattleman* 22 (January, 1936): inside front cover.

50. Prospectus, United Stockyards Corporation, p. 17; "Livestock Receipts Soar,"
Fort Worth Chamber of Commerce News 11 (June, 1937): 4; "Fort Worth's Livestock Receipts for 1937 Largest in History," *Commercial Recorder*, July 18, 1939,
p. 7.

51. Typed list in Commission Firms and Dealers Folder, Dies Corr., FWSY
Co. Coll.; "Broad Demand towards 1938 Close," *Weekly Live Stock Reporter*, January 26, 1939, p. 1; Ed C. Walsh, *The Livestock Hotel* (Fort Worth: Fort Worth Stock
Yards Co., 1941), no page numbers, copy in T. B. Saunders Collection, Texas Christian University Special Collections.

52. "First Draft Copy of the Fort Worth City Guide, 1938–1939," as cited in
Research Data, Fort Worth and Tarrant County, Texas, Federal Writers' Project,
II, 20233. See also "Points of Interest Packing House District," as cited in ibid.,
VI, 22365.

and in 1939 a vice-president of the Fort Worth National Bank, served as chairman of the Agriculture and Livestock Committee of the Fort Worth Chamber of Commerce from 1936 to 1939. While in that position, he organized a committee of ten farmers representing ten counties surrounding Tarrant as an advisory group to the Chamber's Agriculture and Livestock Department. The purpose of this committee, naturally, was to help business at the stockyards. Pier, originally from South Dakota, was employed by the Stockyards National Bank in Omaha, Nebraska, before he came to the Stockyards National Bank in Fort Worth as vice-president in 1928. Pier became president of the Fort Worth Chamber of Commerce on February 6, 1939. Addressing the group a month later on the future of Fort Worth, he abounded in the optimism that many persons at the local market shared. He told his receptive audience that Fort Worth was "the best city in the best state in the best country in the world." As the city and the livestock market emerged from the throes of the depression to embark on a decade that would bring its largest receipts ever, such optimism seemed justified.[53]

53. "Agriculture and Livestock," *This Month in Fort Worth* 12 (July, 1938): 10; W. L. Pier to John P. McQuillen, July 6, 1956, FWSY Co. Coll.; "President Pier Addresses Membership Forum," *This Month in Fort Worth* 13 (March, 1939): 1

Wartime Changes

1 9 4 0 - 4 9

BEFORE HE WENT TO BED ONE NIGHT a farmer within a short driving distance of Fort Worth loaded his pickup truck with a steer so that he would be ready to drive in to the stockyards before daybreak the next day. The next morning the farmer slipped out of the house and started the motor so quietly that he did not disturb two chickens roosting on the sideboards of his pickup. Not until he arrived at the stockyards docks, let down the tailgate, and began unloading did the excitement scare off the chickens, which flew off squawking and frightened. While Farmer Jones unloaded his calf and lost his chickens on the dock, a curious ritual began in the exchange building. Every morning dealing occurred, representatives of each trader or speculator gathered in the large lobby before daylight, squatted down in a big circle, and tossed a coin for a position to begin the trading for the day. While some stockyards allowed traders to run for position to see who could reach the biggest and busiest commission agents first, the Fort Worth market for many years followed the practice of tossing coins for the first three chances to begin dickering at the pens of specific companies. After all the traders had tossed for their positions and looked at the animals of the particular company for which they had won the toss, then anyone could bid if the cattle had not yet been sold.[1]

These traders and order buyers created their own national orga-

---

1.   Interview with Mrs. Bernelle Kutch, Fort Worth, September 19, 1983; inter-

nization and attended conventions or sent delegates. Later the Packers and Stockyards Administration required that they be bonded and referred to all of them as "dealers," so that term came into more common usage than traders or speculators.

As each trader headed for the particular commission company to which his toss entitled him, he saw heavily loaded hay wagons being pulled slowly down the main alley which ran from Exchange Avenue to Twenty-eighth Street. Some of the approximately 250 stockyards workers were filling the pens on each side with fresh hay or delivering extra hay to the booths of the commission firms.

Head packer buyers sent their assistants down each alley to the several divisions to look over the fat cattle ready for slaughter. Roy Weeman, who became head buyer for Swift in 1940, remembered instructions from Swift manager John Holmes not to be too friendly with the Armour buyers, not to drink a lot of coffee with them or do anything that would cause suspicion that collusion in buying might be taking place. They did not want the agents from the Packers and Stockyards Administration after them. Ray Shelton, a young man just learning the ropes as an apprentice buyer for Armour, was having his own troubles getting the commission firms to take him seriously. He remembered bidding higher on some cattle than the buyer who eventually purchased them, but being ignored by commission men because he was such a young newcomer.[2]

Had the broadcast room over in the exchange building not been soundproof, bawling steers in the background would have provided just the proper sound effects for the new radio program that started in July, 1940. Ted Gouldy, market reporter for the *Fort Worth Star-Telegram*, was just beginning a broadcast Monday through Friday for the stockyards company and the approximately forty commission firms on the local market. He aired his fifteen-minute program at 12:45 P.M. on KGKO radio in Fort Worth. The company and the commission firms divided the costs fifty-fifty.[3]

view with Mr. and Mrs. Hilton Kutch, Azle, October 4, 1983; interview with Manson Reese, Fort Worth, October 29, 1983.

2. Interview with Roy Weeman, Fort Worth, September 10, 1983; interview with Ray Shelton, Fort Worth, October 27, 1983.

3. Board of Directors Meeting, July 24, 1940, *Corporate Record*, Fort Worth Stock Yards Company, V, pages not numbered; "Special Program on Live Stock

ABOVE: View at north end of stockyards from Twenty-eighth Street Viaduct looking south, 1935. Courtesy *Fort Worth Star-Telegram*. BELOW: Key stockyards figures, 1938: (*seated, left to right*) A. A. Lund, general manager, Armour and Company; Charlie Daggett; J. D. "Uncle Jim" Farmer; John Hall, general manager, Swift and Company; (*standing*) Bert O'Connell, head cattle buyer, Swift; George Scaling, head cattle buyer, Armour; Charlie Breedlove, Breedlove Commission Company. Courtesy Roy Weeman.

Inside Number One weigh scale, with Charlie McCafferty, Sr., seated at it. Courtesy North Fort Worth Historical Society.

ABOVE LEFT: Bert O'Connell, head cattle buyer for Swift and Company, 1910–40. Courtesy Roy Weeman. ABOVE RIGHT: A. G. Donovan, stockyards manager and president from 1916 to 1946. Courtesy Mr. and Mrs. A. G. Donovan, Jr. BELOW: Four head buyers from Swift, about 1945: (left to right) C. L. Hissrich, head calf buyer; Harry Butz, head sheep buyer; Claude Spurlock, head hog buyer; and Roy Weeman, head cattle buyer. Courtesy Roy Weeman.

ABOVE: Southwestern Exposition and Fat Stock Show grounds in 1942, the last time the show was held in the stockyards. Don Loyd Photo, courtesy North Fort Worth Historical Society. BELOW: Midway, between Coliseum and original Stockyards National Bank building, during stock show, 1941. Courtesy Genealogy and Local History Department, Fort Worth Public Library Collection, Amon Carter Museum.

ABOVE: Trucks waiting in line on Twenty-eighth Street on October 17, 1946. By ten that morning 1,121 trucks had unloaded. Courtesy *Fort Worth Star-Telegram*. BELOW: Commission company houses and walking ramp, above cattle pens, 1950s. J. D. Farmer II, J. D. Farmer III, and Don Alston, calf salesman for Farmer Commission Company, stand with young J. D. Farmer IV. Courtesy Larry Farmer.

New things were afoot more broadly than just on the Fort Worth yards; new beginnings seemed common in the city in 1940. In January the government mailed the first Social Security checks to the nation's elderly; in May Fort Worth women found nylon hosiery on sale in local stores for the first time; and in September local movie buffs witnessed the world premier of a film starring Gary Cooper, called *The Westerner*. Amon Carter hosted some of the notables who came to town, including Mr. and Mrs. Samuel Goldwyn and Bob Hope. Then in November the first young men on the stockyards received draft notices under the first peacetime conscription act in the nation's history.[4]

The Fort Worth Stock Yards Company even gradually began to change the spelling of its name, making *Stockyards* one word instead of two. For the sake of consistency, the one-word spelling will be used from this point to the conclusion of this volume, but the company itself never maintained such uniformity in the spelling of its own title. Also, a new program began of inviting boys in 4-H and Future Farmers of America to tour the stockyards and packing plants. Youngsters enjoyed the hospitality and atmosphere so much that participation doubled by the second year of the tours.[5]

Another addition for the Fort Worth Stockyards was a new company called the Fort Worth Livestock Handling Company. Officials organized it May 24, 1940, to do all the railroad loading and unloading previously done by the stockyards itself. Officers of the stockyards created the handling company after the court announced decisions in *Ex Parte 127 on the Status of Public Stockyards*. Under this ruling, the company, because of its ownership and operation of the loading-unloading function, probably would be classified as itself a railroad.[6] The firm's counselor pointed out that the Secretary of Agriculture already supervised the operations; the com-

---

to Be Put on 'Air,'" *Weekly Live Stock Reporter*, July 18, 1940, p. 1; and "Sound Effects," *This Month in Fort Worth* 14 (August, 1940): 5.

4. "Nation's Elders to Receive First Security Checks," *Commerical Recorder*, January 3, 1940, p. 1; "At Last—Nylon Reaches Hosiery Counter," ibid., May 15, 1940, p. 1; "Fort Worth Host to Many Notables," ibid., September 19, 1940, p. 1; interview with C. A. "Charlie" Prindle, Fort Worth, November 7, 1983.

5. "Cow Country Friends for the Future," *This Month in Fort Worth* 15 (November, 1941): 3.

6. Lester P. Shoene to A. G. Donovan, April 2, 1941, Fort Worth Livestock

pany did not want the Interstate Commerce Commission regulating it as well. Also, if classified as a railroad, the company might find its entire payroll subject to the Carriers' Taxing Act. Other large public stockyards—including Cleveland, Kansas City, Saint Louis, and Sioux City—also created handling companies as distinct individual corporations to avoid regulation of their markets by the I.C.C.[7]

Arrival of livestock by rail had been declining, but as long as some animals still entered the yards that way, federal regulation could affect the entire market. Following the creation of the new handling company, the Fort Worth Belt Railway (no longer owned by the stockyards) continued to do all switching to and from the docks, while the Livestock Handling Company loaded and unloaded the livestock from the cars and the Fort Worth Stockyards Company provided the feed and rest facilities and other services. Although the Livestock Handling Company remained in existence until October, 1981, the last livestock to arrive in Fort Worth by rail came in the early 1970s.[8]

The livestock industry employed five thousand workers and furnished a $6.25 million portion of Fort Worth's payroll in 1941. Texas ranchers and farmers marketed their 1941 animals for more net money than they had seen for several years. World War II, raging in Europe, had no appreciable effect on the Fort Worth market prior to the entry of the United States except that the sale of horses and mules boomed, and Fort Worth again became a leading market for these animals. Foreign governments were buying the animals, not so much for cavalry mounts as in World War I, but for a cheap source of food for their armies.[9]

Handling Company Folder, Dies Correspondence, Fort Worth Stockyards Company Collection, North Texas State University Archives, Denton (FWSY Co. Coll.).

7. Philip R. Wigton to F. C. Black at St. Joseph and John Dies at Fort Worth and enclosure, no date (June, 1943), Dies Corr., FWSY Co. Coll. Wigton was the lawyer advising the company. See also Board of Directors Meeting, April 25, 1940, Fort Worth Stockyards Company, *Corporate Record*, V, pages not numbered; "Proposed Reports in I.C.C. Cases Status of Public Stockyards," *Traffic World*, November 2, 1940, pp. 1077–78, clipping in Dies Corr., FWSY Co. Coll.

8. T. H. Hard to C. W. Emken, February 23, 1960, Dies Corr., FWSY Co. Coll.; Fort Worth National Bank to Fort Worth Stockyards, August 21, 1961, ibid.

9. "Cattle Growers Prosperous in 1941," *Weekly Live Stock Reporter*, January 22, 1942, p. 1; "Among the Three Largest Horse and Mule Markets in the United States" (Fort Worth Stockyards Company Advertisement), *Cattleman* 28 (September, 1941): inside front cover.

Once the United States entered the war in December, 1941, however, the demand for meat and meat products multiplied. The nation needed to feed its own troops and those of its allies. A consuming public that the American Meat Institute had convinced to eat more meat soon found steak and bacon scarce at a time when public markets like Fort Worth broke records for livestock receipts and as farmers and ranchers increased production.

As early as January, 1942, Fort Worthians felt the closeness of war as blackouts began. The worst flood the area had ever sustained diverted attention that spring, however, doing $1.5 million in damage. The flash flood hit North Fort Worth on Sunday evening, April 19, 1942. Then three hours later, a second wall of water, this one seven feet high, came down Marine Creek, and the stockyards area flooded a second time. A dam at a cement company had broken. Waters covered the lower end of the cattle yards and caused hundreds of losses in the horse and mule barns, sheep yards, and hog pens. Stockyards workers waded in water up to their waists trying to rescue animals.[10]

The *Weekly Live Stock Reporter*, housed in a building on Exchange Avenue, even missed two issues because of the flooding, and businesses in a six-block area of North Main and Exchange Avenue sustained damages. Merchandise from the stores floated away, and stockyards workers picked up debris all over the yards. They found gloves, boots, western wear, groceries, and whiskey bottles among the items that floated down the creek. Cleanup workers found carcasses of three mules under the debris in the lobby of the Maverick Hotel.[11]

Because beef producers had not yet increased their stock for war-

10. "Lights Out," *Commercial Recorder*, January 19, 1942, p. 1; Madeline Williams, "Menace of Marine Creek to Be Met by Bond Issue," *Fort Worth Star-Telegram*, October 11, 1950, p. 2.

11. "Announcement," *Weekly Live Stock Reporter*, May 7, 1942, p. 1; interview with Mrs. Nita McCain, Fort Worth, Texas, October 28, 1977; "Most Flood-routed Families Venture Back to Homes; Red Cross Survey Is Due Today," *Fort Worth Star-Telegram*, April 22, 1942, p. 1; "Flash Flood Hits North Side," *Fort Worth Star-Telegram*, April 20, 1942, p. 1; interview with W. M. Speck, Fort Worth, June 7, 1983; interview with Johnny Adams, Fort Worth, June 7, 1983; interview with Tommy Scribner, Fort Worth, September 19, 1983; interview with Bill Stevens, Azle, Texas, September 15, 1983.

time production, a beef shortage in 1942 caused a heavy slaughtering of unfinished, light cattle. The beef shortage resulted primarily from a sharp increase in consumer buying power brought about by the heavy concentration of laborers in war production plants. It was simultaneously affected by the swelling of the ranks of the Armed Forces to seven to eight million men. In 1940 the annual consumption of meat per capita in the United States was only 140 pounds, but in 1943 the amount allotted for men in the Armed Services reached 360 pounds per person. Cattlemen could not produce enough beef to meet the demand, and prices shot up.[12]

Because the draft took so many young men, the stockyards company found it difficult to keep workers, and this at a time when receipts would become the largest in history. They hired anyone they could. Some people worked two jobs, one at the stockyards and one somewhere else, perhaps defense work on another shift.

Producers marketed a million more head of livestock at the Fort Worth Stockyards in 1943 than in 1942, setting a new record with nearly 4.5 million head. Sheep receipts accounted for two million animals. For about five years Fort Worth had been developing into a booming sheep market. The war years would bring more than two million sheep each year into the yards. Stockyards workers remember one day when fifty-nine thousand arrived. Sometimes stockyards employees would work thirty-three straight hours unloading nothing but sheep.[13]

Although by the 1940s most sheep came by truck, some producers still shipped by rail. Sometimes it took four hours to unload two railroad cars of sheep because workers had to drag them out one by one. They considered themselves lucky if this did not occur during the busiest runs. The stockyards needed a Judas goat to lead the sheep out of the railroad cars as well as to slaughter, but they did not always have one handy. Fort Worth quite definitely had developed into the largest sheep market in the country. On some days

12. John T. Schlebecker, *Cattle Raising on the Plains, 1900–1961*, p. 170. See also W. L. Pier to *Fort Worth Star-Telegram*, June 29, 1943, Pier Corr., FWSY Co. Coll.

13. Tape of a conversation between Ben Green, E. A. "Dutch" Voelkel, Ted Gouldy, and Bob Bramlett, Fort Worth, June 24, 1971, (tape in possession of Ted Gouldy), tape 3. See also Adams; interview; interview with Hutton Cox, Fort Worth, June 10, 1983.

the yards received more sheep than the combined total of those animals in the eleven other major markets in the nation. In 1944 more
than 2.5 million sheep passed through the Fort Worth market. For
only the third time, in 1944 over a million hogs reached the market
in one year, and for the fourth time, a million cows. The grand total
surpassed 5.25 million animals, and 1944 remained the largest year
ever in the history of the market. Packers' purchases, including those
by Armour, Swift, and five smaller packers, amounted to less than
half the total receipts of the stockyards. Many animals supplied
stocker-feeder demands. Others traveled through Fort Worth by rail
to northern or midwestern ranges, and livestock handlers unloaded
the cattle, fed them, let them rest, and then loaded them back up
again.[14]

During the early war years, United Stockyards Corporation continued with plans to buy up all the stock of the Fort Worth Stockyards Company. In January, 1942, the larger corporation purchased
1,324 shares, and by December it was buying any stock it could, from
two shares to one hundred. United's decision grew out of the Federal Revenue Act of 1942, which contained relief provisions for corporations when 95 percent or more of all classes of their stock was
owned by a parent corporation. Such provisions afforded substantial income tax savings by permitting the filing of consolidated income tax returns. The Fort Worth Stockyards had outstanding 110,000
shares of capital stock, of which the parent company, United Stockyards Corporation, owned 80.571 percent in March, 1943. "If such
percentage of ownership be increased to 95 percent or more, this
corporation would be able to avail of the benefits of such relief provisions and would thereby be enabled to effect substantial income
tax saving," President A. G. Donovan wrote stockholders. United
needed to purchase 16,708 shares owned by others. Value of the stock
in March, 1943, amounted to $22.80 per share. The corporation of-
fered $23 to any who would sell and included an acceptance form
with Donovan's letter.[15]

14. Ibid; Adams interview; Jim McMullen, "Fort Worth Livestock Industry—
First in War and First in Peace," *This Month in Fort Worth* 18 (June, 1944): 5; "Comparative Statement of Five Competitive Markets for Twelve Month Period Ending December 31, 1945 and 1944," Dies Corr., FWSY Co. Coll.
15. Certificates of Capital Stock, Fort Worth Stockyards Company, Book II,

The appeal did not bring in quite enough shares, so at a stock-holders meeting October 28, 1943, officials reduced the capital of the Fort Worth Stockyards Corporation by $24,462.50, accounting for 1,957 shares without par value, and then retired those shares.[16]

At the next directors meeting on April 27, 1944, four of the seven directors met in Chicago to finalize plans for the complete liquidation and distribution of all property of the Fort Worth Stockyards Company. They voted to dissolve their corporation after selling all property and assets, to divide assets among those entitled to them, and to pay all debts and liabilities. By that time United held more than 98.5 percent of the capital stock. The holders of remaining shares agreed to sell. Directors decided to advertise for bids in newspapers in Chicago, New York, and Fort Worth for the sale of the property and assets and determined not to allow United automatically to purchase the property unless its bid actually was the highest. Stockholders also received a dividend of $1.50 per share as of April 27, 1944.[17]

Officials issued a public invitation on May 2 for bids for all property and assets of the Fort Worth Stockyards Company. The notice announced that no bid of less than $2.7 million would be considered. At a special stockholders meeting held a month later in Chicago, stockholders examined the only bid received: $2,791,000 from David Hunt of United Stockyards. The stockholders voted May 31 to accept it and to dissolve the corporation, "so the business of the Fort Worth Stock Yards Company officially ended and the corporation was dissolved." The stock of the Fort Worth Livestock Handling Company was to be transferred to United as soon as permission was obtained. Locally, operations continued much as usual, but soon Fort Worth Stockyards Company advertisements carried underneath the name of the company the statement, "a division of

---

Certificate 1201, Book 12, Certificates 1274, 1275, 1786, Gary Havard Personal Collection, Fort Worth; Letter to Stockholders of Fort Worth Stockyards Company from President attached to a March 30, 1943, waiver of notice form, Stockholders and Directors Corr., Dies Corr., FWSY Co. Coll.

16. Stockholders Meeting, October 28, 1943, Dies Corr., FWSY Co. Coll.

17. Ibid. See also letter to the Stockholders of the Fort Worth Stockyards Company from the Company, May 1, 1944, copy in possession of author. Directors present were A. G. Donovan, J. W. Dies, David F. Hunt, and W. L. Pier; those absent were Harold L. Niles, Louville F. Niles, and W. K. Wright.

United Stockyards Corporation." In 1944 United also acquired all the stock of the Milwaukee Stockyards Company and of the South San Francisco Union Stockyards Company.[18]

By 1945 only 15 percent of livestock shipments to the Fort Worth market arrived by rail. Buyers at the local market paid $145 million to ranchers and farmers for their livestock. Even so, livestock receipts for 1945 fell a little short of the record number marketed in 1944. The 4,787,660 that did arrive during 1945, however, made the second largest number of total receipts to be received in any calendar year at Fort Worth, and the 1945 sheep supply represented the largest number of sheep and lambs ever marketed in Fort Worth in one year: 2,713,524. Fort Worth remained the largest sheep market in the nation, but dropped to second in calves, fourth in horses and mules, and seventh in cattle and did not even make the top ten in hog receipts. Texas in the last year of the war produced nearly 10 percent of the nation's cattle and calves and almost 20 percent of the sheep and lambs.[19]

Government regulation of the livestock industry during World War II generally meant price ceilings set by the Office of Price Administration (OPA) of the War Food Administration. Market analysts believed that government regulation influenced price levels during the war more than seasonal or other normal price-determining conditions did. The War Food Administration extended price supports on certain weights of hogs to protect farmers from prevailing heavy discounts for swine weighing more than 270 pounds. Government regulations in 1945 greatly affected hog receipts and, to a lesser degree, cattle too. Sheep and lambs were not subject to price ceiling orders and were marketed under normal competitive conditions.

18. "Donovan Explains Stockyards Offer," *Weekly Live Stock Reporter*, May 4, 1944, p. 1; Stockholders Meeting, May 31, 1944, Stockholder and Directors Meeting folder, Dies Corr., FWSY Co. Coll.; "Do Your Part—Prevent Market Gluts" (Fort Worth Stockyards Company Advertisement), *Cattleman* 31 (July, 1944): inside front cover; *Annual Report*, United Stockyards Corporation, Year Ended October 31, 1944, United Folder, Dies Corr., FWSY Co. Coll.
19. "Comparative Statement of Five Competitive Markets for Twelve Month Period Ending December 31, 1945 and 1944," Dies Corr., FWSY Co. Coll.; U.S. Department of Agriculture, Agricultural Marketing Service, Salable Receipts of Livestock at Public Stockyards by Markets 1940–46.

Sources close to the stockyards called the period "the darkest days of the industry" when the regulated packers were forced to try to buy under OPA-compliance prices while most meat went to black market killers who paid excessive prices at small auction centers around the state. On the other hand, one historian of the cattle industry argues that government regulation worked well in properly distributing meat and in keeping prices down, and that cattlemen accepted the government intervention with little complaint. The cattlemen made handsome profits and remembered that government aid during the depression did not turn out too badly.[20]

The war had a great effect on one stockyards institution: the Southwestern Exposition and Fat Stock Show. John B. Davis, secretary-manager of the fat stock show, cancelled it in 1943 for several reasons. The city needed to direct all its efforts toward food production; out-of-town people faced transportation difficulties with gasoline rationing in effect; and some of the buildings customarily used for the show now housed industries engaged in "vital war work." In 1944 officials again could not hold the show in the stockyards area because Globe Aircraft Corporation leased all the North Side livestock buildings to manufacture war planes. Besides, the coliseum had not been used since the 1942 flood and had not been properly cleaned up. Thus, officials decided to move to the new $1.5 million Will Rogers complex in the west part of the city. The move when announced appeared to be only temporary because of the wartime conditions. However, attendance at the 1944 stock show exceeded all previous records, and the rodeo drew the largest crowd in history. Every evening performance was a sellout, and an extra performance had to be added at 1:30 A.M. Sunday so defense workers could see the rodeo. The stockyards company had even joined with other businessmen to help underwrite the cost of having the stock show in the new location up to a pledge of $2,000, but when the show made money, their contribution was unnecessary. In June, 1944, with Globe Aircraft Corporation still using the North Side site, directors

20. *Annual Report,* United Stockyards Corp., Year Ended October 31, 1945, United Folder, Dies Corr., FWSY Co. Coll.; "Hall Retires as Swift Manager at Fort Worth," *Weekly Live Stock Reporter,* July 3, 1947, p. 1; Schlebecker, *Cattle Raising,* p. 175.

decided to hold the 1945 show as well at the Will Rogers complex. Besides, the 1944 show in the new location had been "the most successful one ever held in Fort Worth."[21]

Nearly half a million persons attended the stock show in 1945, setting another all-time attendance record. Nearly every rodeo performance was a sellout. Thus it was no real surprise to many that the directors again voted in May, 1945, to hold the 1946 show at the Will Rogers complex. Nonetheless, it was a disappointment to the Fort Worth Stockyards Company, other livestock interests at the stockyards, and the citizens of the North Side area for the show to move away permanently after they had nurtured it for nearly fifty years. This move occured even though the show officials had in 1940 taken a fifteen-year lease of the North Side Coliseum and other facilities at $8,000 per year. Stockyards manager Donovan assumed that "the new lease-contract should eliminate in the future any question or suggestion as to having the stock show in the new location on the West Side, improvements of which were made in 1936." Donovan misjudged. The move took place anyway. Thirty-five years later some old hands still expressed regrets. "It's not the same show now. People used to come to the stock show from all over Texas to soak up the atmosphere. It's just a big show now. It was real then," one old-timer said.[22]

When the stock show celebrated its fiftieth anniversary at its new location across town in 1946, officials instituted another of the many innovative features that had characterized it through the years. They brought in a celebrated entertainer for a halftime performance. Gene Autry, one of the nation's best-known western singers, agreed to be the special attraction, one of the first such rodeo arrangements. Also featured were the Budweiser Clydesdales in "shining harness." Ed-

21. "Fort Worth Show Called Off," *Cattleman* 29 (January, 1943): 8; "Fort Worth Stock Show Dates Set," ibid. 30 (November, 1943): 47; "Greatest Southwestern Exposition and Fat Stock Show," ibid. 30 (April, 1944): 22; Homer Convey to A. G. Donovan, April 14, 1944, Southwestern Exposition and Fat Stock Show Folder, Dies Corr., FWSY Co. Coll.; "Will Hold Show in Coliseum," *Cattleman* 31 (June, 1944): 7; "Coliseum Selected as Site for 1945 Fat Stock Show," *This Month in Fort Worth* 18 (June, 1944): 8.

22. A. G. Donovan to C. F. Topping, October 19, 1940, Southwestern Exposition and Fat Stock Show Folder, Dies Corr., FWSY Co. Coll.; interview with Frank Kirli, Fort Worth, August 14, 1979.

gar Deen, secretary-manager of the show, who also was a city councilman, mayor pro tem, and sales manager of Armour and Company, had an idea to have one hundred Fort Worth businessmen patrol the grounds daily, extending greetings to visitors and offering assistance to any person who might need help. Officials called this 1946 show the "most successful in history" from the standpoint of rodeo entertainment, sellout performances, new record gate attendance, and quality of livestock. The Fort Worth Stockyards Company during these years sent a season pass for the stock show to the president or general manager of several other stockyards throughout the country as a goodwill gesture. Amon Carter was happy that the show was being held at the complex named after his friend Will Rogers. Earlier he had commissioned the granddaughter of Tom Waggoner, Electra Waggoner Biggs, a sculptress, to do a full-size figure of Will Rogers seated on his horse. General Dwight D. Eisenhower presided at the unveiling and dedication at the complex November 4, 1947, the sixty-eighth anniversary of Will Rogers' birth. Margaret Truman, daughter of President Harry Truman, sang "Home on the Range" at the ceremonies.[23]

The end of World War II brought a lot of young men back to Fort Worth and back to their jobs at the stockyards. Some worked for the company itself, others for their fathers in the family commission firm, or as traders. To the young men returning from war, the stockyards looked about the same—busy. Workers unloaded railroad cars or trucks frequently, more trucks than ever before. Every cubbyhole in the entire exchange building seemed full of offices. These were for more than forty commission companies, railroad agents, market reporters, feed stores, telegraph offices, Packers and Stockyards Administration officials, representatives of the cattle raisers' association, and even a barber shop.

Gaiety and exuberance returned. Christmas Eve was firecracker day as men dropped the fireworks down to the lower front lobby from the banisters of the second story. Young women working in the various offices could not leave their desks for fear someone would throw

23. "Back Stage at the Rodeo," *Fort Worth* 43 (January, 1978): 30; Capt. James R. Rash, Jr., "Fort Worth Jubilee," *Breeder's Gazette* III (May, 1946): 19; "Fort Worth's Fiftieth Annual Biggest and Best in Its History," *Buckboard* I (April, 1946): 6; interview with staff of Will Rogers Complex Office, Fort Worth, January 18, 1985.

a "chaser" firecracker at them. In fact, the stockyards area renewed its reputation as a rough part of town, and women did not walk unaccompanied down Exchange Avenue or even go into the lobby when the traders gathered for their early morning tossing for place. New Year's Day saw the annual dance in the lobby with numerous sets of square dancing going on simultaneously as different bands and callers were stationed in each wing of the building.[24]

Shenanigans continued out on the yards. A prankster might unsaddle someone's horse left unattended, put the saddle on a mule, tie the mule in the same spot, and go hide the horse.

By the mid-1940s commission companies or dealers had constructed more than forty enclosed booths above the livestock pens to provide the only shade around and protection from inclement weather. Men gathered in the booths to dicker, whittle, and oversee their livestock in their division.

Al Donovan retired from the Fort Worth Stockyards Company in January, 1946, after thirty years, having been president of the company from 1931 until 1944, when the company became a division of United Stockyards and he became division manager. At an appreciation dinner for Donovan at Hotel Texas (now renovated as the Hyatt-Regency), W. L. Pier, who replaced Donovan, said that according to his calculations some 75 million animals had passed through the stockyards during Donovan's thirty-year tenure. Harry Henderson, who had been superintendent all of Donovan's years on the yards, had retired in 1945. Ben T. Newby succeeded Henderson as superintendent.[25]

The new manager, Pier, while retaining close ties to livestock interests, had been a banker throughout his career. Since coming to Fort Worth in 1928 he also had been a member of the board of directors of the Southwestern Exposition and Fat Stock Show and had served as treasurer of the show for eight years.[26] Upon becoming di-

---

24. Bernelle Kutch interview.
25. "Pier is New Head of Stockyards Co.," *Fort Worth* 20 (February, 1946): 28; "Old Friends Pay Tribute to Donovan for 30 Years at Stockyards," clipping and photo in Mrs. J. W. Dies Scrapbook, Fort Worth.
26. "Pier Succeeds A. G. Donovan as Yards Mgr." *Weekly Live Stock Reporter*, January 16, 1946, p. 3. See also "William Lauren Pier," Vita in General Miscellaneous File Folder, Pier Corr., FWSY Co. Coll.

vision manager of the stockyards, Pier also became a director of the Fort Worth Belt Railway and received annual passes for his family on the Texas and Pacific Railroad, which owned the Belt. His position as division manager of the Fort Worth Stockyards Company meant that he also became a vice-president and director of United Stockyards, with the title president of the Fort Worth Stockyards.[27]

During a trying time in its history, the Fort Worth Stockyards Company came under the leadership of an efficient and kindly man. Pier faithfully and graciously answered every complaint by a shipper, inquiry by a school child who needed a report, or request for a list of commission men. He constantly was deluged with requests for money, for advertising, invitations to dinners, tours, rodeos, and fairs. He accepted some invitations and respectfully declined others. Bill Pier was a friendly, easygoing man in his late fifties—tall, slender, and slightly balding. While he always smiled and spoke to his workers out on the yards when he went there, he did not frequent the pens. He usually wore a suit, white shirt, and tie. He did not wear boots, so his Stetson hat represented his only concession to the Western image of the livestock industry. He left the daily operations to his husky assistant, Bill Joyce, and to Superintendent Newby.[28]

Pier accepted the leadership of the Fort Worth division of United Stockyards during the frustrating time of readjustment after World War II. In a speech to the Dallas Agricultural Club shortly after he took control, the new manager reviewed the problems of the local market. The beef cattle population of Texas was not increasing as rapidly as it should. About two million beef animals a year disappeared from Texas ranges, going either to grass in Oklahoma or Kansas or the feedlots in the North. "If these animals were all finished at home, Texas would soon be in the front rank of the nation's packing industry," Pier said. He believed the government should make adjustments to bring about better relations between livestock pro-

27. W. G. Vollmer to W. L. Pier, December 18, 1947, T & P Railway Folder, Pier Corr., FWSY Co. Coll. See also "W. L. Pier Manager of Fort Worth Stockyards to Retire Dec. 31," *Cattleman* 46 (December, 1959): 104.

28. Adams interview; Cox interview; interview with Charlotte Pier, Fort Worth, August 30, 1983; interview with S. S. Schultz, Fort Worth, August 28, 1983; interview with Paul Talles, Fort Worth, September 21, 1983.

ducers and processors. He wanted both to be able to make money unhampered by unwise regulations and destructive black market competition.[29]

By the time he made that speech, Pier had already faced his first crisis, for in mid-January, 1946, CIO stockyards and packinghouse workers had called a national strike. This coalition included the United Livestock Handlers of America at the Fort Worth Stockyards and the United Packinghouse Workers of America at Armour and Company. The Swift workers in Fort Worth were not affiliated with the CIO, belonging instead to an independent union, the National Brotherhood of Packinghouse Workers; they did not shut down. The twelve-day strike paralyzed the major markets, motivating President Harry Truman to issue an executive order to seize 137 packing plants and five public stockyards, including Fort Worth. The Secretary of Agriculture reopened the plants and yards and initiated certain regulations. The union at the local yards agreed to go back to work at the secretary's order, claiming that they were still on strike, but not against the government. They promised to await the decision of the fact-finding board. The National Wage Stabilization Board assumed jurisdiction and on April 29 ordered an increase in wages of sixteen cents per hour retroactive to January 26. The stockyards had been offering its workers a six-cent raise.[30]

Another major change for the yards came halfway through the year. The Packers and Stockyards Administration required stockyards to keep on file a copy of "Rules and Regulations of the Market" as well as tariff rate changes. On June 21, 1946, a new rule went into effect that provided for the Fort Worth Stockyards to operate from 8 A.M. to 3 P.M. A whistle would blow to start and end trading. No longer would the traders gather before daylight in the exchange building to start an early day; they would quickly toss for positions in the alleys just before the 8 A.M. whistle. Old-timers figured a real era had ended when trading became limited to the specified hours.[31]

29. "Texas Beef Big Business," *Weekly Live Stock Reporter*, May 2, 1946, p. 1.

30. W. L. Pier to Rowley W. Phillips, January 29, 1946, Pier Corr., FWSY Co. Coll.; *Annual Report*, United Stockyards Corp., Year Ended October 31, 1946, United Folder, Dies Corr., FWSY Co. Coll.

31. Interview with Dan Van Ackeren, Packers and Stockyards Administration, Fort Worth, September 15, 1983.

Besides the strike and the stricter trading times, the year 1946 was hectic because of the lifting and then restoring of price controls. While the controls were on, "the black market in meats was more often discussed and cussed than the weather," according to the market newspaper. The Office of Price Administration Act expired June 30, 1946. Producers, who had waited until after that date to move their animals to the stockyards, did so in unusually large numbers in July and August. Numerous workers and agents on the yards remember that all kinds of trucks, eighteen-wheelers, farmers' pickups, and trailers lined up and waited to unload at the stockyards docks in a line stretching bumper to bumper two abreast all the way down Twenty-eighth Street to Jacksboro Highway, a distance of over two miles. Some people at the yards got in their cars and drove down Twenty-eighth Street just to see how far the line of waiting vehicles extended. Prices stayed high for a while, but the market became so flooded that they soon dropped. The government then on August 20 ordered meat price ceilings and subsidies restored, which brought an outcry from the industry that all the evils of the black market might return. The government board freed most grains and all dairy products from renewed price control but placed price controls back on cottonseed products and soybeans as well as all meat and livestock.[32]

Local managers of both Armour and Swift expressed disgust at charges that big packers could operate at a profit under OPA ceiling prices but were just refusing to buy cattle. They both explained that it was impossible for them to purchase more than small numbers of cattle because stockmen were selling to unregulated markets in the country at higher prices than OPA regulations permitted. Packers would violate regulations if they paid those prices. Operators not regulated by the government remained ready and willing to pay the higher prices and therefore could buy most of the cattle. Meanwhile the two major packers at Fort Worth had to lay off workers because they could not buy enough livestock to keep the plants fully operational.[33]

32. "1946 Will Live Long in Memory of Cattlemen as Year of Much Turmoil," *Weekly Live Stock Reporter*, January 23, 1947, p. 1; Stevens interview; *Annual Report*, United Stockyards Corp., Year Ended October 31, 1946, FWSY Co. Coll.

33. "OPA Lawyers Get Challenge from Packers," *Fort Worth Star-Telegram*

When the controls ended permanently on October 15, livestock receipts boomed and prices shot skyward, to put the Fort Worth market back in the big-business bracket. Receipts had dwindled earlier in the year to only a trace of normal prewar totals. For the fourth consecutive year sheep receipts hit the two million mark, although the figures dropped from the previous year by over a third of a million head. For the third year in a row, the local market led the nation in sheep receipts and bragged that it represented the "nation's sheep capital." During one seven-day period that year at twelve major markets a total of 248,100 head of sheep arrived. Fort Worth received 157,535 of these and the eleven other markets combined received 90,565. Also, the horse market doubled over the previous year. The United Nations Relief and Rehabilitation Administration began buying mares to restock depleted areas of Europe, and packers bought fat horses for slaughter to reduce the food shortage in areas abroad. In addition, the market for riding horses in the nation's dude ranches boomed.[34]

Early in December, 1946, the Fort Worth Stockyards Company publicized another of its many firsts when an airplane hauled a load of twenty commercially grown calves for the first time from a livestock market in this country. A DC-4 transport plane took off from Fort Worth's municipal airport, Meacham Field, just north of the stockyards, and headed for New York. Within seconds after becoming airborne, the plane crossed the old cattle trail from which millions of head of stock had entered the Chisholm Trail in Indian Territory and headed for Kansas railheads. Bob Mason, vice-president of World-Wide Trading Corporation with headquarters in Fort Worth, bought the calves. They had been bred and fattened on the George A. McClung Ranch in Cleburne.[35]

(morn.), April 26, 1946, in Swift File, *Fort Worth Star-Telegram* Reference Library.

34. W. L. Pier to Harry Holt, February 27, 1947, and "Value of Fort Worth Yards Receipts Grow," clipping from *Abilene Reporter News*, Advertising Correspondence, Pier Corr., FWSY Co. Coll. See also Comparative Statement of Five Competitive Markets for Twelve Month Period Ending December 31, 1946 and 1945, Dies Corr., FWSY Co. Coll. See also enclosed ad with letter from Purchasing Agent for Fort Worth Stockyards to *San Angelo Standard-Times*, May 23, 1946, Advertising Correspondence.

35. "Texas Calves Cross Old Chisholm Trail in Plane," *Weekly Live Stock*

Manager Pier felt more optimistic about his market as 1947 began. He wrote that once the government lifted price controls, the meat on the hoof began to crowd the yards and allay the fears of many that the central market system of handling livestock was doomed. Pier, with his banking and business instincts, tried to operate more efficiently as he saw terminal markets in trouble. He began selling the fifty-five rent houses that the stockyards company still owned, mostly on Decatur Avenue, because the upkeep and depreciation made them a questionable investment. Maximum legal rent for their houses during World War II had been from thirteen to twenty dollars per month. Pier also cancelled ads in many stock journals; cutting back on advertising could hurt receipts, but with lower income Pier was forced to reduce expenses.[36]

Whether the efficient Pier or one of his associates discovered it is not known, but in 1947 the Fort Worth Stockyards Company suddenly realized that it was nine years older than officials thought. For forty-five years they had been dating everything from the time the packers Armour and Swift arrived in 1902, assuming that the company began on that date because the two packers bought two-thirds of its stock and reorganized it. Someone apparently found the original charter dated March 23, 1893, for the company revised its advertisements and stationery to reflect the 1893 date and began bragging that the market was fifty-four years old and had operated twenty-four hours a day most of that time. They still did not recognize the actual origin of the North Side market with the 1887 incorporation of the Fort Worth Union Stock Yards.[37]

The problem in the livestock industry at the beginning of 1948 was an "out-of-joint" condition between supply and demand, with demand high and the supply lacking. A short corn crop and high

---

Reporter, January 2, 1947, p. 1. See also "Twenty Bawling Calves Set New Aerial Record," *Fort Worth Star-Telegram* (no date), in Livestock File, *Fort Worth Star-Telegram* Reference Library.

36. W. L. Pier to David F. Hunt, February 14, 1947, Lease Folder, Pier Corr., FWSY Co. Coll. See also form letter from Lucien H. Wright, Area Rent Director of Office of Price Administration to C. Redmond, January 26, 1943, Dies Corr., ibid; H. M. Phillips to W. L. Pier, May 7, 1947, Advertising Correspondence, ibid.

37. "54 Years of Square Dealing" (Fort Worth Stockyards Company Advertisement), *Cattleman* 33 (April, 1947): inside front cover.

prices for all classes of feeds led to the short supply. In addition, an embargo against Mexican cattle because of hoof and mouth disease had been in effect for over a year, preventing annual shipments of approximately half a million head of Mexican cattle. Record employment rolls, high wages, and the ability of consumers to select and pay for the food they liked best caused the abnormal demand. Although Fort Worth's livestock market ranked first in the Southwest in 1948 and remained the largest south of Kansas City, aircraft had surpassed livestock as the city's number-one industry. Cattle and meat packing dropped to second place. The aircraft industry employed twelve thousand workers, while cattle and meat packing hired seven thousand. Eleven meat packers, small and large, operated in Fort Worth in 1949.[38]

Supplies of livestock on the local market declined in 1948 from the previous year. They dropped again in 1949, as over a million fewer head passed through the market than the year before. The biggest decline came in sheep receipts. Several years of drought conditions had depleted the herds. Then in 1949 adequate moisture for forage production induced producers to hold their stock for rebuilding. They thus marketed fewer animals in Fort Worth.[39]

Walter Rice became traveling field representative for the company during these years, a job similar to that of Charles C. French in the first three decades of the twentieth century. Rice traveled throughout West Texas during the last three years of the 1940s visiting small towns, judging livestock shows, and showing a film advertising the terminal market. When in Fort Worth, he handled 4-H and FFA tours. He also served as assistant livestock superintendent

38. "More Stock Problems Than Year Ago," *Weekly Live Stock Reporter,* January 22, 1948, p. 1; *Annual Report,* United Stockyards Corp., Year Ended October 31, 1948, United Folder, Dies Corr., FWSY Co. Coll.; *An Economic Survey of Tarrant County,* Prepared for the Texas and Pacific Railway Company by the Bureau of Business Research, College of Business Administration, University of Texas (June, 1949), p. 406.

39. *Annual Report,* United Stockyards Corp., Year Ended October 31, 1949, United Folder, Dies Corr., FWSY Co. Coll.; W. L. Pier to A. Z. Baker, March 13, 1950, Personal File, Pier Corr., FWSY Co. Coll.; Comparative Statement of Five Competitive Markets for Twelve Months Period Ending December 31, 1949 and 1948, Dies Corr., FWSY Co. Coll.

for the Southwestern Exposition and Fat Stock Show for several years.[40]

Two fires damaged company property in 1947 and 1948. On August 22, 1947, a fire that destroyed a part of the sheep division brought a net book-value loss of $86,964.90 to the company. Another bad fire did over $100,000 in damage to a hay barn on November 9, 1948. That hay barn burned for five months and two weeks, the fire finally extinguished in April, 1949. Officials attributed the duration of the fire to the thirty-seven thousand bales of stacked hay and alfalfa inside the barn, which continued to smolder until workers could remove them. Local firemen called the conflagration the longest fire in their memories.[41]

A flood in the spring of 1949 did more damage to the west part of the city of Fort Worth than to the stockyards area, although the water from the Trinity backed up Marine Creek. The company had to move the sheep, hogs, horses, and mules across Exchange Avenue to the cattle division. Paul Talles, a stockyards worker who later would become superintendent (1971–81), remembered wading waist deep in the hog and sheep pens to move the animals. Many were moved upstairs to the second floor. The water covered Exchange Avenue a few inches in some places, but it soon receded.[42]

In the late 1940s the major issue became the problem of decentralized markets in the various country town closer to the farms and ranches. Producers sold their stock there rather than at the larger public stockyards such as Fort Worth. A *Farm Journal* article announced decentralization as a fact as early as April, 1946, and reported that livestock receipts at the nation's foremost terminal

40. W. A. King to Walter Rice, July 9, 1953, W. W. Rice Folder, Pier Corr., FWSY Co. Coll.

41. W. L. Joyce to David F. Hunt, October 23, 1947, Fire Folder, Financial Records, FWSY Co. Coll.; *Annual Report*, United Stockyards Corporation, Year Ended October 31, 1948, p. 6; *Annual Report*, United Stockyards Corporation, Year Ended October 31, 1947, p. 5; David Hunt to W. L. Pier, March 8, 1949, Fire Folder, Financial Records, FWSY Co. Coll.; W. L. Pier to A. L. Olson, February 17, 1949, Advertising Corr., FWSY Co. Coll.; "City's Longest Five-Month Fire Finally Is Put Out," *Fort Worth Star-Telegram*, April 26, 1949, in Livestock File, *Fort Worth Star-Telegram* Reference Library.

42. Talles interview. W. L. Pier to R. B. Pendergast, May 20, 1949, Pier Corr., FWSY Co. Coll.

market, Chicago, tallied the smallest since 1879, although the volume of meat produced in the United States had reached the third largest in its history. During World War II, while the big packers sold in great volume to the government, openings developed for small independent packers to operate. Ordinary consumers during the war bought from these independents if they got meat at all. Smaller-scale butchers and packers thus obtained a foothold and a chance to develop, eventually obtaining government inspection and government grading. The scattered country auction barns in various Texas communities came along to accommodate them. The smaller auctions did not have to respect federal price controls, so farmers obtained higher prices there.[43]

In the 1930s and earlier the bulk of the livestock slaughter and packing took place in some twenty of the nation's larger cities, with Fort Worth ranking high on the list. As of 1946 thirty-five hundred meat-packing plants in all sections of the country, and twenty-six thousand other commercial establishments slaughtered the nation's meat animals. The trend also began in part when packers sought to sidestep mounting operating costs in the cities, to buy livestock more cheaply, and to take advantage of favorable freight rates by opening plants nearer the farms. Good highways and trucks accelerated this process. When Congress passed the Packers and Stockyards Act in 1921, sixty-seven markets were posted under the act. They handled from 90 to 95 percent of the livestock slaughtered under federal inspection. By 1946 the administration regulated 196 posted markets, and the number of animals going for slaughter under federal inspection at those markets had dropped to between 45 and 50 percent.[44]

The large terminal markets opposed the trend toward country auctions and argued that decentralization and "direct selling" to order buyers and packers' representatives resulted in lower prices to farmers in the long run. The practice continued, however, because government regulations affected only large markets and thus let any local

43. Tape of conversation between Green, Voelkel, Gouldy, and Bramlett, tape 3. Bob Bramlett was the one who spoke; interview with Ted Gouldy, Fort Worth, September 21, 1983.
44. L. T. Skeffington, "Where to Sell Your Livestock," *Breeders' Gazette* III (March, 1946): 8.

buyer or trucker pay what he pleased. In addition, farmers liked decentralization because it avoided shipping shrinkages and terminal market expenses and allowed farmers to dicker with buyers while they still had their livestock in their own possession. Also some farmers tried cooperative packing. Packers hurt the large markets like Fort Worth by sending their buyers to the smaller country yards, but they often could not obtain enough receipts to meet slaughtering needs at Fort Worth.[45]

Commission agents began going out of business as the central market declined. The yards dropped from its peak number of forty-eight companies, reached at one time in the 1940s. One agent wrote, "It looks as though the auction rings have got us, so I am trying to figure out some way that we can stay without starving completely." Other commission agents did not believe anything could ever replace the terminal markets. J. D. Farmer III remembers telling his dad the country auctions would take over. "He didn't believe it. He didn't *want* to believe it."[46]

W. L. Pier of the Fort Worth Stockyards began sending out pamphlets to producers and other friends of the local market warning of the "dangers" of direct marketing. The American Stockyards Association published a booklet arguing the case for terminal markets, entitled "Dollars and Sense in Livestock Marketing." They distributed it in bulk to member stockyards to give to producers at their market. In editorials, advertisements, and pamphlets, Pier argued the same case as other terminal market managers: the central market remained the only place where volume could be large enough to attract all kinds of buyers, and thus it was the only fair place for prices to be set. Dealers at the small auction markets based prices on the going rate at the nearest large terminal market, but if receipts at the large market declined radically, the competitive situation there would not be the fairest for price setting. Terminal market officials argued that in the long run it would be the cattle producer who would suffer. At the smaller markets an uninformed farmer faced an experienced, informed buyer and thus placed himself at a disadvan-

45. Weeman interview.
46. C. B. Johnson to Tom Saunders, June 28, 1949, 1940s Folder, Tom B. Saunders, Jr., Collection, Texas Christian University Special Collections, Fort Worth; interview with J. D. Farmer III, Fort Worth, September 12, 1983.

tage. Also, when packers bought directly from farmers, the packer buyers knew they could easily fill their daily supply, so they did not have to be as competitive or aggressive at the price-setting larger markets. Pier ordered ten thousand copies of a pamphlet entitled "Livestock Farmers in Fight for Existence" to mail out to producers. In this the author argued that direct buying would destroy the producers' greatest economic defense: their own competitive marketing system. Of course, the nation's large terminal markets, like Fort Worth, were fighting for existence.[47]

One situation that no doubt aided the nearby country auctions and hurt the local market was that the Fort Worth Stockyards closed for Saturday sales — at the request of the commission firms, so they did not have to work six-day weeks, and so that the stockyards did not have to pay overtime to its employees. The small country markets, on the other hand, usually operated on Saturday. Fort Worth was also probably hurt by the cancelling in February, 1949, of the yards' radio program when the noon hour, the ideal broadcast time, was reclaimed by the local station.[48]

During the summer of 1949, instead of estimating profits, Pier began sending in to United Stockyards weekly reports of losses — of anywhere from $1,500 to $5,000. But Fort Worth had not yet lost its status. Of 211 posted public stockyards in the nation late in 1949, the USDA classified only 12 as major markets, and Fort Worth remained one of these. It received the second largest number of sheep and lambs in the nation that year and remained the principal livestock market in the Southwest.[49]

Fort Worth still retained its pride in its "first love"—the cattle industry and packing plants, which had given the city its initial start toward prominence. Fort Worth's image of itself as the decade ended might have been of a cowhand sitting in the shade of an oil

47. Eugene Fish to W. L. Pier, April 13, 1946, Advertising Corr., FWSY Co. Coll.; A. Z. Baker, president, American Stockyards Association, to W. L. Pier, July 13, 1948, American Stockyards Association Folder, Pier Corr., ibid.; W. L. Pier to W. C. Crew, March 15, 1946, Advertising Corr., ibid.

48. Pier to Olson, February 17, 1949.

49. Report from W. L. Pier to David Hunt, Weekly Reports, July–September, 1949, Pier Corr., FWSY Co. Coll.; *Annual Report*, United Stockyards Corp., Year Ended October 31, 1949, ibid.

rig watching a B-36 airplane take off from Carswell Air Force Base or the "bomber plant." To keep any cowboy in that image in a future of increasing market decentralization and plummeting local livestock receipts, the Fort Worth Stockyards Company—that cowhand—had to stand up, load all his guns, and fight.

Promotional Efforts Accelerate
1950–59

YOUNGSTERS WANTING to learn the livestock business often obtained summer jobs on the yards. They learned that if the temperature soared to 100 degrees, it rose to 110 on the yards among the warm bodies of all those animals. They found out that hosing down the animals, and each other, on sweltering days became almost necessary for survival. And they also learned that tromping through the smelly alleys all day long was not glamorous work. "I ended up with a size bigger shoes and a size littler hat," one young man commented at the end of such a stockyards summer.[1]

They further learned that unless one worked for the stockyards company, he was not represented by a union. An employee of commission firms or traders enjoyed no forty-hour work week, no overtime, no sick leave, or other benefits. Like the livestock producers on the farms and ranches, most stockyards people remained highly independent, hardworking individuals. Their livelihood depended, among other things, on long hours of labor and even on something as unpredictable as Texas weather. During the 1950s decade both of these factors affected the stockyards, for Herculean efforts to promote the Fort Worth market coincided with the weatherman's slap in the face, a severe seven-year drought.

The Fort Worth Stockyards Company, like a stubborn cowboy,

1. Interview with Bill King, Fort Worth, November 3, 1983. A young man had told him this.

did not accept the decentralization threat to its market calmly but pulled out loaded pistols for a fight. Ammunition consisted of promotional gimmicks, multi-media publicity, and new organizations or programs. But before it could get off a telling shot, one quick blow damaged its ego.

The U.S. Department of Agriculture issued a press release on January 11, 1950, which referred to charges of "unfair and deceptive practices" in violation of the Packers and Stockyards Act on the Fort Worth market. This implied blanket indictment of all those on the market, "coupled with very light receipts," depressed everyone terribly. Division Manager W. L. Pier asked A. Z. Baker, president of the American Stockyards Association, to come to Fort Worth to speak to the livestock interests and cheer them up.[2]

The ranking Packers and Stockyards (P&S) Administration agent at the Fort Worth yards was Bill Ball, whose job was to look for violations of fair trade. Ball had headed the P&S district office in Fort Worth from his office in the exchange building since 1946 when he returned from a three-year stint in the Army. Before that he had worked for the P&S out of Kansas City for three years. Through his efforts and those of others the government filed charges that owners of commission firms used fictitious names so that they could speculate in livestock and that they encouraged their employees to speculate, hiring them at low salaries with that understanding. The government also charged that salesmen and commission employees worked closely with speculators, selling to them, and frequently reselling livestock daily for them. The P&S administration accused registered agencies of handling operations of other speculators who were not bonded or registered by using fictitious names and accounts. The government claimed that dealers, packer buyers, and other buyers did not operate independently of each other as the law required. The USDA also charged that some commission firms and dealers had failed to keep proper records. Certainly a potential for problems existed because a lot of commission men or traders had ranches and raised cattle. The Packers and Stockyards Act prohibited commis-

2. W. L. Pier to A. Z. Baker, March 7, 1950, American Stockyards Association Folder, Pier Correspondence, Fort Worth Stockyards Company Collection, North Texas State University Archives, Denton (FWSY Co. Coll.).

sion men or their employees from buying any livestock for their own accounts out of their shippers' consignments. Livestock exchanges on other markets regulated actions of members, but no exchange had existed in Fort Worth since the state of Texas had outlawed it in 1907.[3]

After the Packers and Stockyards Administration brought actions against eighteen firms and individuals, the firms discharged the guilty employees or required them to discontinue all dealer activities. The Fort Worth Stockyards Company issued a statement that the company did not buy and sell livestock and thus was not involved. They expressed relief that the government had charged only a small percentage of operators and asserted that the firms had eliminated all unfair practices. "We will, of course, continue to cooperate with the department and the market agency . . . to assure the patrons of the Fort Worth yards the fairest market conditions and safety," a spokesman for the market stated. Obviously, the bad publicity hurt the yards at a time when they were needing to create good will.[4]

Livestock interests created a new structure in April, 1950: the Fort Worth Livestock Market Institute. Its major task was to coordinate the promotional activity designed to create good will and increase market receipts. The institute was patterned after similar structures in Saint Paul and Sioux City. Organizers were Ted Gouldy, newspaperman; W. L. Pier, division manager and president of the stockyards; and J. C. (Buck) Weaver, of Cassidy Commission Company. Members of several other commission firms joined these men as directors. Plans called for the stockyards company to pay 50 percent of the cost of the institute and the member commission firms to pay the other 50 percent. Virtually all livestock commission firms, dealers, order buyers, and the company eventually joined. The institute spent only $5,079 in its first year, but by the end of the decade was paying

3. "U.S.D.A. Completes Investigation of Unfair Trade Practices at Fort Worth Stockyards," Carbon of News Release in Personal Folder, Pier Corr., ibid.; "U.S.D.A. Says Irregularities at Stockyards Corrected," *Fort Worth Star-Telegram*, January 12, 1950 (eve.), Livestock File, *Fort Worth Star-Telegram* Reference Library; interview with Bill Ball, Agra, Oklahoma, September 17, 1983.

4. M. J. Cook to E. S. Mayer, November 3, 1950, General File, Pier Corr., FWSY Co. Coll.; "Tribute Paid to Most Firms at Stockyards," *Fort Worth Star-Telegram*, January 13, 1950 (morn.), Livestock File, *Fort Worth Star-Telegram* Reference Library.

as much as $2,000 to $3,000 per month for advertising in newspapers and magazines, printed matter, radio coverage, dinners, equipment, management and secretarial costs, office supplies, postage, premiums, judging expenses, and wages. The institute sent weekly news releases to county papers over the territory adjacent to the Fort Worth market and to radio and television farm directors in the region. The institute immediately distributed free eighty columns by Ted Gouldy, and sixty papers in the market area picked them up and used them. Two or three years later Gouldy supplied at no cost to them a market summary called "Let's Talk Livestock" to more than three hundred newspapers in the state.[5]

The Agriculture and Livestock Department of the Fort Worth Chamber of Commerce in May, 1950, created another organization to foster interest in the local livestock industry, the Fort Worth Farm and Ranch Club. W. L. Pier, manager of the Fort Worth Stockyards, became vice-president of the new organization. Members met for a luncheon once each month to hear a speaker or see a film on some phase of agriculture.[6]

A cooperative public relations thrust, a Texas Livestock Roundup, occurred on November 2–3, 1950, sponsored primarily by the Chamber of Commerce and co-hosted by the *Fort Worth Star-Telegram*, the stockyards interests, and WBAP-TV. Experts in all phases of the livestock industry appeared on the program of the seminar, which more than one thousand ranchers and farmers attended. It became an annual event for several years.[7]

5. Charter No. 102374, Fort Worth Livestock Market Institute, filed March 27, 1950, Office of Secretary of State, Austin; W. L. Pier to W. E. Williams, May 4, 1950, Livestock Market Institute Folder, Pier Corr., FWSY Co. Coll.; "Financial Statement Covering Years Operations of Fort Worth Livestock Market Institute, Inc., from April 13, 1950 to April 12, 1951," Livestock Market Institute File, Pier Corr., ibid.; Fort Worth Livestock Market Institute, Inc., "Receipts and Disbursements for the eleven months ended February 28, 1959," Fort Worth Livestock Market Institute File, Financial Corr., ibid.; W. L. Pier to Roland B. Pendergast, October 5, 1950, Pier Corr., ibid.; "Your Fort Worth Live Stock Market Institute—In Action," An Outline of Activities April 1952–April 1953, Livestock Market Institute Folder, ibid.
6. "Ft. Worth Men Form Farm and Ranch Club," *Weekly Live Stock Reporter*, May 25, 1950, p. 1; "Farm and Ranch Club Formed," *Fort Worth* 25 (June, 1950): 21.
7. "Roundup Time Nov. 2–3 at Fort Worth Market," *Weekly Live Stock Reporter*, September 28, 1950, p. 1.

Several advisors outside the Fort Worth Stockyards suggested that the market try to re-create the livestock exchange that existed near the beginning of the century. Most other terminal markets had them. Pier would have to persuade the state of Texas to rescind its injunction against an exchange, which had come in the 1907 case of *The State of Texas* v. *The Fort Worth Livestock Exchange, et al.* To this purpose, Pier and his lawyer called on Texas Attorney General Price Daniel in Austin on May 5, 1950. They reviewed the 1907 injunction point by point, Pier arguing that it was obsolete because of the Packers and Stockyards Act. In five areas the suit enjoined the Fort Worth Livestock Exchange from doing what the Packers and Stockyards Act required it to do. For example, the 1907 injunction forbade the exchange to set prices and rates, but the P&S Act required it. Pier wrote that "the purpose of organizing the Exchange was to keep our own house clean and therefore make it unnecessary for the government to come in, as they have here recently, with various charges that have hurt the Yards and the commission men." Nothing came of the attempts to create a new exchange, however, for the Texas attorney general refused either to "approve nor disapprove" its organization.[8]

Among the public relations tactics of the stockyards were their continued tours for boys in 4-H or Future Farmers of America. When the youngsters brought in their cattle, the commission firms and the Fort Worth Stockyards Company paid for their hotel rooms at the Westbrook Hotel, and Armour and Swift invited them to a luncheon and tour of the packing plant. Files from the 1950s show numerous requests for such tours, some from as far away as Kansas. The livestock interests hosted twenty-eight groups of youngsters in one year. In addition, promotional field agent Walter Rice judged shows, and the stockyards helped furnish the ribbons.[9]

When Ted Gouldy's noontime radio program "Roundup Time" went back on the air in 1951, the network of high-power stations that carried it extended from Shreveport, Louisiana, along the Gulf

8. Julian E. Simon to W. L. Pier, May 15, 1950, FWSY Co. Coll.; Price Daniel to Julian E. Simon, August 1, 1950, ibid.
9. W. L. Pier to Buford Browning, February 19, 1948, Agricultural Extension Service Folder, Pier Corr., ibid.; U.S. Crippen to W. L. Pier, January 16, 1956, ibid.

Coast, down to the Rio Grande Valley. Gouldy broadcast the fifteen-minute program from the Roundup Studios in the Livestock Exchange Building. The program continued through the decade.[10]

Part of the promotional program included two films called *Today's Chisholm Trail* and *This Little Pig Went to Market*, which the American Stockyards Association produced. For over a decade the Fort Worth Stockyards Company loaned the films free to schools.

Despite optimistic publicity designed to bolster the market and indications that such tactics were working, one frustration after another seemed to plague the yards in the early years of the decade. During 1952 particularly, sheep, cattle, and swine diseases created problems. Compulsory dipping of sheep became a requirement on February 4, on orders from the Livestock Sanitary Commission of Texas. The campaign sought to eradicate sheep scab, a highly infectious disease caused by a tiny parasite. From time to time other states threatened embargoes on Texas sheep. The Texas Livestock Sanitary Commission and the Bureau of Animal Industry of the U.S. Department of Agriculture closed the hog and sheep divisions of the Fort Worth Stockyards on October 2, pending diagnostic tests on some hogs suspected of having vesicular exanthema, a swine disease that had swept through the Midwest in previous months. The testing procedure took seventy-two hours, so the yards remained closed to all hog shipments during that time. However, the USDA and state officials soon declared the Fort Worth Stockyards to be "clean yards."[11]

Labor problems repeatedly plagued the stockyards, and in the 1950s many persons viewed such troubles as evidence that communists had infiltrated the unions. The United Packinghouse Workers of America, of which the Livestock Handlers Union at the Fort Worth Stockyards was a member, had emerged in the midst of labor distress and disillusion during the depression and post-depression years. During the McCarthy era the communist issue, which had long beset the United Packinghouse Workers, became more publicized. Left

10. "Roundup Time, Texo Hired Hands Are in Fort Worth Stock Yards Studios Now," *Weekly Live Stock Reporter*, February 22, 1951, p. 1.

11. Ted Gouldy, "Swine Plague Brings First County-wide Quarantine in Texas, Tarrant County, Part of Parker Involved," ibid., October 16, 1952, p. 1.

wingers seemed to have more power in Chicago and New York than elsewhere, but they never completely controlled the UPWA.[12]

Perhaps as a response on behalf of management to hints of left-wing activities in the stockyards industry, W. L. Pier helped form and became a director of the Texas Better Business Bureau, an organization dedicated initially to helping "to reverse the trend of this country toward socialism." Pier also supported with a twenty-five dollar contribution a right-wing anticommunist group that sponsored a radio program called "Americans, Speak Up" and underwrote newspaper articles by John T. Flynn entitled "Behind the Headlines." Possibly to deter any labor unrest at the local stockyards, on March 21, 1951, the company began a pension plan for their employees.[13]

Approximately twelve hundred members of the United Packinghouse Workers of America walked off their jobs at Armour in Fort Worth on January 4, 1952, which, like any strike, affected the flow of livestock at the stockyards, even though Swift workers did not strike. The UPWA strike affected the Armour plants in Omaha, Chicago, Denver, Atlanta, and Sioux City as well. The strike revealed dissatisfaction with the line the current wage negotiations were taking, but quickly ended.[14]

A contract the company negotiated with the Livestock Handlers Union called for an additional holiday in 1952 besides July 4, Thanksgiving, and Christmas. The stockyards workers added Labor Day, and the stockyards closed on that day in 1952 for the first time in its history.

In 1954 Livestock Handlers Local 59 of the United Packinghouse Workers of America, CIO, seceded from the UPWA by an overwhelming majority vote and became an independent union because of what members called communist domination of the national organization. Lee Holley, secretary of Local 59 in Fort Worth, spoke for the members. They had formed a new Stockyards Workers Association

12. Theodore V. Purcell, *Blue Collar Man: Patterns of Dual Allegiance in Industry,* pp. 35, 38.

13. Form letter from W. L. Pier, January 13, 1950, Better Business Bureau Folder, Pier Corr., FWSY Co. Coll.; Robert L. Lund to W. L. Pier, April 26, 1951, ibid.; *Annual Report,* United Stockyards Corporation, Year Ended October 31, 1951, United Folder, Dies Corr., ibid.

14. "1,200 Strike at Armour," *Fort Worth Star-Telegram,* January 5, 1952, in Armour File, *Fort Worth Star-Telegram* Reference Library.

of America and were preparing a petition for the National Labor Relations Board, "as are other locals in Kansas City, Omaha, Saint Joseph, Mo. and Sioux City, Iowa, which have withdrawn from the UPWA for the same reason." The last straw for the stockyards workers came when the UPWA refused at a nationwide convention in Sioux City in May to adopt an anticommunist resolution. Also, the UPWA had refused to deny communists positions on the union staff and had defeated two militant anticommunists for important positions, including A. J. Pittman of Fort Worth. Pier continued to oppose strict union activity, as evidenced by a telegram he sent in 1956 to the attorney general of Texas, John Ben Shepperd, congratulating him on his efforts in behalf of the Texas right-to-work law.[15]

A business slump came early in the decade, so Pier cut down on the size of stockyards ads. At the suggestion of an editor, he tried to make them friendlier and less crammed with statistics. The treasurer wrote to magazine editors, "business has been terribly bad," in explaining why the ad he was sending was smaller than the previous year. The company continued to spend a large portion of its advertising budget through the Livestock Market Institute. The company even cut some monetary support from the West Texas Chamber of Commerce, which the stockyards interests originally had induced the Fort Worth Chamber of Commerce to create and support. Pier told the president of the WTCC that he had to reduce his usual $200 contribution to $100 because of increased expenses and income problems. The company also cancelled its usual full-page ad in the Southwestern Exposition and Fat Stock Show premium list. As another means of reducing expenses, the company forced its employees to retire at age sixty-five.[16]

The business problems of the Fort Worth Stockyards and packing interests did not prevent Armour and Swift from celebrating their

15. "Union Here Quits UPWA on Red Issue," May 29, 1954 (morn.), ibid.; "Stock Handlers File Petition with NLRB Here," *Labor News* (Fort Worth), June 3, 1954, clipping in Labor Folder, Pier Corr., FWSY Co. Coll. See also Moses Adedeji, "The Stormy Past: A History of the United Packinghouse Workers of America–C.I.O., Fort Worth, Texas 1936–1956 (Masters thesis, University of Texas at Arlington, 1975), pp. 75, 88–89; Telegram from W. L. Pier to John Ben Shepperd, January 3, 1956, copy in General Corr. File, FWSY Co. Coll.

16. H. M. Phillips to W. L. Joyce, March 14, 1949, Advertising Corr., FWSY Co. Coll.; letter and enclosed tear sheet of ad from Al Sledge to W. L. Joyce, ibid.;

fiftieth anniversaries in Fort Worth in 1952. A public relations agency planning the big celebration charged a fee of $600 and suggested a $7,100 budget for doing all the publicity, inviting movie stars to a premier in Fort Worth, printing movie-star buttons, and airing radio promotions. They also suggested that merchants in the North Side area have merchandise drawings and that everyone wear Western clothes. They sponsored a beard-growing contest and also placed loud speakers on Exchange Avenue playing old Western tunes. Swift and Armour conducted open-house tours of their plants. Armour bragged that its Fort Worth plant remained the fourth largest among thirty-four plants in the nation and employed twenty-five hundred workers in 1952.[17]

Nature, in the form of a drought, and the federal government, through its price controls, caused erratic receipts at the terminal markets, including Fort Worth, in the early part of the decade. The regulations came mostly because of the outbreak of the Korean war in June, 1950. President and general manager Pier complained, "It would seem that most increases in government regulations result in more costs and less efficiency." Pier reflected the opinion of many in the livestock industry.[18]

The government's Office of Price Stabilization (OPS) placed ceiling prices on meat and meat products at wholesale and retail levels as of January 26, 1951. This indirectly acted as a control on prices paid for livestock. Predictably, trading at the smaller country markets not posted by the Packers and Stockyards Administration expanded, while cattle and calf receipts at the regulated public markets limited by the OPS ceiling dropped. The packers increased their country buying in order to get the meat they needed. Then in May

---

W. L. Joyce to Sue Flanagan, April 28, 1952, ibid.; W. L. Pier to Ray Grisham, July 30, 1956, TCC Folder, Pier Corr., ibid.; W. L. Pier to W. R. Watt, July 30, 1958, Southwestern Exposition and Fat Stock Show Folder, ibid.; W. L. Joyce to H. E. Ratton, October 10, 1957, Pension Plan Folder, Dies Corr., FWSY Co. Coll.

17. "Suggested Outline For 1902-Golden Jubilee Celebration—1952, November 15, 1952, Fort Worth Stockyards," Jack T. Holmes & Associates, History FWSY Co. Folder, Dies Corr., FWSY Co. Coll.; "27,000 Enter Armour Gate at Open House," *Fort Worth Star-Telegram,* May 5, 1952 (eve.), Armour File, *Fort Worth Star-Telegram* Reference Library.

18. W. L. Pier to Wingate Lucas, June 29, 1949, General Correspondence Folder, Pier Corr., FWSY Co. Coll.

OPS Director Michael DiSalle set up a program that called for a rollback of cattle prices to pre–Korean War levels. Everett L. Dobbs, manager of the local Armour plant, laid off workers because of the dwindling availability of cattle at the Fort Worth Stockyards under the OPS regulations. He said that the average kill per hour before the regulations became effective had been sixty head. In the first week of regulations the kill dropped to eighteen head per hour. He predicted that even that figure would be cut by half during the following week. Swift faced a similar situation.[19]

Congress issued additional rollback orders to go into effect on August 1 and October 1. Cattlemen in Texas began presenting to Congress figures on the cost of production for raising calves on the range and argued that the rollback would force the feeder calves to sell below the cost of production. To try to sell before the new price rollbacks became effective, many producers brought stock into the yards in September, 1951. More than a thousand trucks unloaded 10,233 cattle on the single day of September 4. Just as in the 1940s, stockyards workers again saw trucks line up two abreast to the Jacksboro Highway two miles away, not to mention trucks coming from other directions. The rollback and the drought brought in so many animals that fall that Pier had to send a telegram to the chairman of the Interstate Commerce Commission to ask him to order the return of stock cars to the railroad lines in the Southwest.[20]

By the spring of 1952 heavy selling of cattle off drought-stricken ranges had cracked the market and sent prices shooting downward in a record slump. Cows for which men had paid up to three hundred dollars each would do well to bring one hundred dollars, even with calves by their sides. Because no grass existed on their ranges, cattlemen had to borrow money to buy feed. But the government price-support program on feed made its price outrageously high. By 1952 it was becoming a little easier for some in the industry to look to Washington for aid, and many producers began petitioning for

19. *Annual Report*, United Stockyards Corporation, Year Ended October 31, 1951, United Folder, Dies Corr., FWSY Co. Coll., pp. 3, 6; "Armour Lays Off More Employees," *Fort Worth Star-Telegram*, June 8, 1951 (eve.), Armour File, *Fort Worth Star-Telegram* Reference Library.
20. Note in Photographs File Folder, Pier Corr., FWSY Co. Coll.; telegram from W. L. Pier to W. M. Splawn, October 8, 1951, General Folder, ibid.

price supports for beef cattle. The Texas and Southwestern Cattle Raisers Association, the American National Cattlemen's Association, and most major organizations of beef stockmen opposed a support program, saying it would be impossible to administer and would mean the government would be running the cow business. Instead, they launched an "eat more beef" campaign intended to double consumption in ten years. The well-organized campaign sent literature to banks and utility companies to include in their monthly statements and mailed advertising mats to at least 522 Texas newspapers. In the first two years of the campaign, consumption of beef in Texas rose 33 percent.[21]

In late October, 1952, livestock interests won a battle in the sheep and mutton industry in a fight that had started the previous spring at Fort Worth. They enlisted the aid of U.S. Senator Lyndon B. Johnson of Texas and his assistant, Walter Jenkins, to end government grading of sheep. Harry Butz, who by the 1950s had been a sheep buyer for Swift for nearly forty years, claimed that young USDA graders right out of college were taking animals of exactly the same age and grading one a lamb and the other a yearling by the mandatory government grades. Prices varied depending on the government grades imposed, so these inconsistencies were important. Butz showed government agents his records on grading and pricing and thus helped to end the unfair grading system that caused uneven prices. Butz, Pier, and others at the market rejoiced that their complaints and requests for assistance had been answered satisfactorily as Senator Johnson intervened to remove the grading.[22]

Some cowmen wanted government support during the trying years of the drought. As a result the Truman administration proposed the Brannan Plan named for Secretary of Agriculture Charles

21. Remarks of Senator Lyndon B. Johnson, April 27, 1954, attached to Letter from Logan H. Walker to W. L. Pier, May 25, 1954, Pier Corr., FWSY Co. Coll.; Logan H. Walker to W. L. Pier, September 28, 1953, WTCC Folder, ibid.; Roy Parks to W. L. Pier, October 20, 1954, Texas Beef Council File, ibid.; "Beefing Up Beef Eating," *Fort Worth Star-Telegram*, December 1, 1957, clipping in Texas Beef Council File, ibid.

22. Ted Gouldy, "Industrial Wins Decontrol of Lambs, Mutton in Fight Started Six Months Ago at Fort Worth," *Weekly Live Stock Reporter*, October 30, 1952, p. 1; interview with Harry Butz, Fort Worth, September 9, 1983; interview with Ted Gouldy, Fort Worth, September 21, 1983.

Brannan. The plan included price supports, universal subsidies called incentive payments, government controls, production quotas, and marketing allocations. Bryant Edwards, president of the Texas and Southwestern Cattle Raisers Association, said the Brannan Plan was loaded with socialism. Edwards traveled to Washington to oppose it before the agriculture committees of both the House and Senate. He told Congressmen:

> We can imagine the graphic language that would have been used by one of our trail driving ancestors to a proposal of a subsidy by the government, and we can imagine what would have happened to some "economist" who would have had the temerity to tell an old cowman that the government or in particular the Secretary of Agriculture would tell him how many cattle he could raise or how many he could sell, or where and when he had to sell them — and the character of the cowman has not changed.[23]

When Dwight Eisenhower and his secretary of agriculture, Ezra Taft Benson, took office in January, 1953, the subsidy philosophy changed, and Eisenhower in February removed government price controls. The government granted loans on livestock and arranged for the sale of feed at reduced prices, but many producers still had to sell. Cattle and sheep receipts at Fort Worth tallied substantially higher than the previous year. In 1952 only 766,927 cattle had been marketed at Fort Worth, but 1,013,390 came in 1953. Sheep receipts totaled 920,006 in 1952 and 960,290 the next year. In July Benson declared Texas, Oklahoma, and Colorado disaster areas because of the continued drought. He increased the area in 1954. Even when the drought ended in 1957, farmers throughout the Southwest withheld their cattle from market in order to rebuild herds that had been liquidated or greatly reduced. Therefore the earnings of the Fort Worth Stockyards still suffered the effects of the dry spell as late as 1958. So many cattle producers lost money during the drought that many small operators went out of business. Representatives for feedlots also began buying more cattle.[24]

23. Mary Whatley Clarke, *A Century of Cow Business: A History of the Texas and Southwestern Cattle Raisers Association*, p. 192.
24. *Annual Report*, United Stockyards Corporation, Year Ended October 31, 1953, United Folder, Dies Corr., FWSY Co. Coll., pp. 3–4; "Comparative Statement of Five Competitive Markets for Twelve Months Period Ending Dec. 31,

In lieu of the direct cattle price-support program, the Eisenhower administration attempted to support cattle prices indirectly by purchasing more beef for foreign and domestic aid. Pier called the beef purchase program "the least painful thing that might be done in the present emergency."[25]

To aid sheepmen, Congress in 1954 passed the National Wool Act as an incentive plan to encourage greater wool production, with the hope that it would reduce a downward trend in sheep production. Farmers were raising fewer sheep than they had in the 1940s because of competition from New Zealand, Australia, and South Africa and because predators killed too many lambs. People who had once raised thirty thousand sheep cut back to fewer than one thousand, and the production trend moved back to cattle. Sheep receipts at the Fort Worth yards practically ended later, when Armour relocated its sheep slaughter to San Angelo and Swift to Brownwood to be closer to the sheep supply.[26]

While debate continued concerning government price supports and subsidies, the federal regulation of the stockyards industry, as enforced by the Packers and Stockyards Administration, remained in effect. In the beginning the act applied only to stockyards of over twenty thousand square feet. The legislation seemed to be adequate in the 1920s and 1930s, for most livestock passed through stockyards of this size, and most traveled by rail. Shifts in the marketing of livestock to country auctions and the decentralized purchase operations of packers after World War II made the act outmoded. Larger terminal markets like Fort Worth understandably saw themselves at an unfair disadvantage in the competitive fight with the country markets. By 1955 the country outlets had gained a slight edge over terminal markets in number of sales, 23 million to 21 million head. The larger stockyards felt particularly discriminated against when

---

1953 and 1952," Comparative Statements of Receipts Folder, ibid.; *Annual Report,* United Stockyards Corporation Year Ended October 31, 1958, ibid.

25. W. L. Pier to A. Z. Baker, October 20, 1953, American Stockyards Association Folder, Pier Corr., FWSY Co. Coll.

26. It was Title VII of Public Law 690, "An Agriculture Act to Provide for Greater Stability in Agriculture." U.S., *Statutes at Large,* LXVIII, 910–13. See also *Annual Report,* United Stockyards Corporation, Year Ended October 31, 1954, United Folder, Dies Corr., FWSY Co. Coll., p. 6.

a ruling by the Packers and Stockyards Administration became effective September 1, 1954, stating that commission companies could no longer finance traders. For years several large commission companies had "cleared" a clientele of traders, that is, paid for their purchases, handled the paper work, and so on. The government called such financing a conflict of interest.

Still the country auctions remained unregulated. By 1957 fourteen hundred to fifteen hundred country livestock markets operated in interstate commerce exempt from the act because they were less than twenty thousand square feet in size. To bring the Packers and Stockyards Act in line with the current practices, Congress amended it in 1958 to place under regulation all stockyards, regardless of size, engaged in interstate commerce. The American Stockyards Association favored the amendment so that all markets would compete under the same conditions. For example, part of the P&S regulations said an auctioneer could not himself buy or sell, but auctioneers had been doing this all the time in the country.[27]

The stockyards' publicity measures perhaps stirred other businessmen in the North Side area to make their own attempts to turn things around, for in September, 1955, a small group of North Side businessmen headed by Russell McElyea and DeWitt McKinley met at the Cattlemen's Steak House and drafted plans for a progress program for their area. They selected the name North Fort Worth Business Association. Headquarters would be the North Side Coliseum, which at that time McElyea was leasing from the city for Monday night wrestling. Their plans called for modern street lighting on North Main, hospital facilities for the area, an extension of Twelfth Street to University Drive, traffic outlets from downtown, additional parking, and attempts to attract more industry. McElyea did his part to bring interesting programs to the North Side, in 1956 arranging for a popular new performer named Elvis Presley to sing at the North Side Coliseum.[28]

27. The amendment was H.R. 9020, in U.S., *Statutes at Large*, LXXII, 1749–51; W. L. Pier to A. E. Brooks, March 8, 1956, General Corr., Pier Corr., FWSY Co. Coll.; mimeographed transcript of a Special Hearing to Texas Livestock Auction Owners, Roosevelt Hotel, Waco, Texas, January 6, 1957, p. 24; Miscellaneous Folder, Pier Corr., ibid.
28. R. G. McElyea to W. L. Pier, November 5, 1955, Personal File, Pier Corr., ibid.

The businessmen also soon conceived the idea of making the area into a Western-style tourist attraction like the New Orleans French Quarter, San Antonio's Alamo district, or a Western town like Virginia City. They asked the City of Fort Worth to provide $1.9 million to construct the Western village. Voters in a bond election November 18, 1958, turned down $1.25 million in bonds that would have provided a museum of Western art as a part of the attraction. Private funds for specialty shops failed to materialize as well, so the Western village had to remain a dream for about twenty-five years. As a compromise, then, merchants and businessmen spent their own money for new architectural fronts made of wood shingles and boardwalks on their buildings to give the area a Western look. Ironically, other communities that had played a part in the history of the cattle trade were voting "Yes" in the 1950s to plans to create Western villages, and Dodge City's Front Street, Abilene's Old Abilene, and Wichita's Cowtown soon began attracting tourists.[29]

The North Fort Worth Business Association sponsored a "Go Western Week" in 1956, as "a period dedicated to the recapture of a bit of the spirit of the old West and North Fort Worth's place in the metropolitan area's business picture." The occasion was the activating of the new vapor-mercury street lights along Exchange Avenue. Fort Worth Mayor F. E. (Jack) Garrison and L. N. Wilemon, of the North Fort Worth State Bank and president of the North Fort Worth Business Association, turned the lights on just after sundown. The people seemed to have so much fun during the festivities that the association decided to have a Western celebration every year. Accordingly, the next spring the association sponsored a "Pioneer Days" from May 30 to June 1, 1957, at the old North Side Coliseum. They brought back a rodeo to the coliseum for the first time in fifteen years. Western bands, square dancers, free variety acts, a carnival, and a giant parade accompanied the show.[30]

While area businessmen did their part to revitalize the stockyards district, the stockyards company continued its own efforts. To promote sales and interest, the Texas Hereford Association and

29. Fort Worth, City Council, *Minutes,* Vol. O-1, November 21, 1958, p. 306.
30. Jack Douglas, "Pioneer Day Festivities Mark North Side's Welcome to Lights," *Fort Worth Star-Telegram,* April 29, 1956, North Fort Worth File, Fort Worth Public Library.

the Fort Worth Livestock Market Institute jointly arranged a feeder calf show and sale featuring Herefords at the Fort Worth Stockyards on June 30, 1955. Judges selected the outstanding animals in various classes and awarded ribbons and prizes. Then the Texas Aberdeen-Angus Association joined with the stockyards to host their own feeder calf show and sale on July 8, 1955, with about two thousand calves. The show netted nearly $100,000 for producers and encouraged them to host several other such shows with the stockyards that season. The shows did so well that the two cattle associations and the Fort Worth Livestock Market Institute planned seven similar events the following year. They sponsored nine such special stocker and feeder sales in 1958, four of them with shows. Two were for sheep and seven for cattle. In connection with these shows the Livestock Market Institute tried prizes and drawings to get more traffic into their market. The institute advertised the special sales in seventy-three newspapers and magazines, placed paid announcements on eighteen radio and television stations, and sent news releases to 350 newspapers and magazines and sixty-three radio and television stations. The Fort Worth market got some of their ideas from other stockyards, such as Sioux Falls and Sioux City.[31]

Part of the stockyards company's promotional efforts involved market research to find out just what producers thought about shipping to Fort Worth. In March, 1955, several officials from the Fort Worth market traveled to College Station, Texas, for a quarterly directors meeting of the Texas Sheep and Goat Raisers Association. They also wanted to meet with a group of agriculture professors at Texas Agricultural and Mechanical College about market research. Representatives of stockyards in Houston and San Antonio also attended the meeting. They all urged the college professors to devote some time to the research of terminal markets.[32]

As a result of Pier's request, Texas A&M sent livestock produc-

31. Copy of a talk given by Ted Gouldy at a Marketing Clinic at Oklahoma A&M, "Special Events," enclosed with a letter from Ted Gouldy to Joe Whiteman, February 23, 1957, Pier Corr., FWSY Co. Coll.; John W. Bennett to W. L. Pier, October 16, 1959, ibid.
32. W. L. Pier to A. Z. Baker, March 18, 1955, American Stockyards Association Folder, Pier Corr., FWSY Co. Coll.; W. L. Pier and Ted Gouldy to Jack Sampier, June 12, 1956, Agricultural Extension File, ibid.; W. L. Pier to A. Z. Baker, November 16, 1953, American Stockyards Association Folder, ibid.

ers a questionnaire about the Fort Worth market. Some questions asked were: "Were you treated courteously? How long did you have to wait? What is your main reason for selling at Fort Worth? What day of the week is most convenient for you to deliver livestock to market? Do you have any suggestions for improving services at the Fort Worth market?" Manager Pier and market reporter Ted Gouldy were not too sure that their request for A&M to examine terminal markets meant so specific a study of Fort Worth because the publicity might prove embarrassing, but they decided to go along. They certainly wished they could pick the commission companies and the producers for A&M to interview, however.[33]

Unfortunately, Professor John G. McNeely took an extremely negative approach in an article he submitted to the *National Live Stock Producer* about his research on the Fort Worth yards. It proved so derogatory, that the editor offered to let the Fort Worth Stockyards make rebuttal statements before publication.[34]

McNeely's theme was that "people in the stockyards business are slow to change their ways." Small livestock producers represented the bulk of the trade. They wanted good food in a restaurant at reasonable prices, plenty of parking space, and clean and comfortable lounging areas for both men and women; "all of these services are lacking to some extent at the Fort Worth Stockyards." McNeely said that the prevailing system at the stockyards discouraged purchases by small buyers because commission men preferred to deal with packers and established dealers and even often refused to accept bids from outsiders. McNeely explained that the flow of livestock operated inefficiently because everything was laid out to receive livestock by rail from the east side of the yards, although nearly all cattle by 1955 came by trucks to the north end of the yards.[35]

Low volume during certain shifts and late in the week made it cost more to handle livestock during these times. One alternative

33. John G. McNeely to W. L. Pier, November 30, 1955, with enclosed questionnaire, Agricultural Extension Service Folder, ibid.; memo from Ted Gouldy to W. L. Pier, May 17, 1955, ibid.
34. J. W. Sampier to W. L. Pier, June 1, 1956, ibid.
35. John G. McNeely, "Stockyards Research Spotlights Industry Problems," *National Live Stock Producer*, pp. 1–2, clipping in Pier Corr., ibid.

would be to close the market during unprofitable periods, McNeely said. He believed that the stockyards and some commission companies needed advice in public relations. They preferred the farmer to stay away from the pens and alleys, whereas at local country auctions the farmer could stay, which led him to feel that smaller auctions appreciated his business more. McNeely suggested innovations such as identification badges for stockyards and commission company people and an invitation to buyers to have full privileges to bid on any and all livestock. He applauded the use of loudspeakers for paging at stocker and feeder sales and suggested they should be used more extensively.[36]

Pier asked Gouldy to help him frame the stockyard rebuttal to McNeely's article. They explained that the company had changed pen sizes many times to accommodate smaller shipments. They objected specifically to the sentence, "The current system at Fort Worth deliberately discourages smaller buyers," calling it an emotional expression. They accused McNeely of being biased against their market. The two men argued that most farmers did not know how buying was done and consequently the stock they might have wanted was usually sold before they could make an effort to buy it. Pier and Gouldy insisted that commission men did not refuse to accept bids from outsiders. They explained that if the stockyards closed down or charged higher rates for a particular day of low traffic, it would not only lose the advantage of being a twenty-four-hour market but also violate USDA rules. "Any suggestion that we would be more 'efficient' by rendering less service for higher rates is not apt to increase volume."[37]

After the rebuttal, McNeely toned down his report somewhat. Pier accepted his revised version of the article and did not send the further rebuttal remarks to the magazine editor. But in reaction to the criticism that the commission men did not want small shippers to buy, the stockyards and the commission firms put out a small booklet: *It's Easy When You Know How to Buy at Fort Worth.* They also turned the front lawn of the exchange building into a parking

36. Ibid.
37. W. L. Pier and Ted Gouldy to Jack Sampier, June 12, 1956, ibid.

lot for eighty cars in 1956 and built a lounge for shippers' families on the first floor.[38]

Because of his position at Texas A&M and his study of markets, Professor McNeely testified before a Senate subcommittee on Antitrust and Monopoly in the Meat Industry in June, 1956. He made three points: Armour and Swift were in a position to dominate livestock pricing in Texas; individual buyers for Swift and Armour could exploit the advantages given to them by this dominance; and the Packers and Stockyards Administration was not in a position to challenge their dominance. His information came mostly from his study of the Fort Worth market. He said that Armour and Swift buyers tended not to compete with each other, for one went down one alley and one another. The almost fifty-fifty division of the livestock bought each year "would be impossible to attain . . . strictly on a chance basis," he said.[39] Packer buyers and other traders on the market have disputed his conclusions, however, insisting that a great deal of competition existed. Representatives from fourteen packing plants purchased daily at Fort Worth as late as 1958, and nine of them were smaller than fifty employees.[40]

Charges that traders and commission companies discriminated against outside traders and small buyers apparently did have some merit. Some of those involved later admitted that they gave preference to regular customers they knew would be back on a day-to-day basis and whose checks they knew were good rather than dealing with an outsider who, they reasoned, might not be back and whose check might bounce. Had Fort Worth been allowed to create a livestock exchange, the favoritism might have been somewhat alleviated, for an exchange allows only members, who have been

38. John G. McNeely, "Research Results at Fort Worth," p. 4, Agricultural Extension Service File, ibid.; W. L. Pier to J. W. Sampier, June 15, 1956, ibid.; W. L. Pier to Jack Sampier, July 9, 1956, ibid.

39. Testimony of John G. McNeely, U.S. Senate Report, *Hearing Held Before Subcommittee on Anti-trust and Monopoly of the Committee of the Judiciary*, June 22, 1956, Washington, D.C., typescript in Agricultural Extension Service File, ibid., pp. 2, 14, 27.

40. Interview with Ray Shelton, Fort Worth, October 27, 1983; interview with Roy Weeman, Fort Worth, September 12, 1983; interview with Harry Butz, Fort Worth, September 9, 1983.

checked out, to buy and sell. Commission men would have felt safe dealing with any member of an exchange.

A longer published report of McNeely's Fort Worth study came out in 1959. McNeely found that many respondents preferred Fort Worth as a packer market but not as a stocker market. He made some recommendations including conducting personnel training, adding more yard telephones, building overhead walkways, controling dealers and speculators better, and increasing courtesy. The report concluded: "Probably no other major industry lacks so completely any control over its sales force as does the stockyards industry. While the Fort Worth Stockyards has a great investment in facilities, 29 individual commission firms are actually responsible for bringing in and maintaining business on the market."[41]

Despite some early ruffled feelings over the Texas A&M market study, the association between the stockyards and the college continued. Together they planned a series of Texas Livestock Marketing Clinics for terminal markets in Fort Worth. The one on March 20–21, 1959, was cosponsored by the Port City Stockyards in Houston and the Union Stockyards in San Antonio. The clinic attracted one hundred people who were interested in helping the markets keep step with changing conditions. Many persons came from out of state, representing stockyards in Omaha, Sioux City, Saint Joseph, and Kansas City. They analyzed their mistakes and discussed ways to avoid them. Most of the participants were optimistic that central markets could meet the challenge.[42]

Pier kept in touch with other terminal markets and exchanged letters and monthly livestock receipt statements with their presidents or general managers. They compared problems and traded ideas. Thirty-nine member stockyards of the American Stockyards Association relied on A. Z. Baker, its president, to keep them informed and to investigate attacks on their group. Fort Worth hosted the Twenty-fourth Annual Meeting of the American Stockyards As-

41. John G. McNeely and Jarvis E. Miller, *Fort Worth Stockyards — Operating Procedures and Problems*, pp. 18–19.

42. John G. McNeely to W. L. Pier, April 23, 1957, Agricultural Extension Service Folder, Pier Corr., FWSY Co. Coll.; J. C. Miller to W. L. Pier, December 31, 1957, ibid.; W. L. Pier to John Bennett, March 27, 1959, Pier Corr., ibid.

sociation on April 4–6, 1956. Toward the latter part of the decade some of the major terminal markets began to close, including South San Francisco and the Los Angeles Union Stockyards. At Fort Worth, commission firms slowly decreased to twenty-seven by January, 1958.[43]

Weekly reports during the decade showed periodic losses. Observers noted that if it had not been for the checks received from Armour and Swift for direct yardage payments, the stockyards might have closed. Fortunately, the original 1902 agreement had stated that so long as the stockyards continued to operate adjacent to the packing plants, all animals to be slaughtered on the packing plant property would pass through the stockyards and pay the customary yardage and other charges thereon. The stockyards had made this arrangement in exchange for giving Armour and Swift the land on which to build their packing plants, one-third of the Fort Worth Stockyards stock, and $300,000 in bonds. The stockyards therefore got a fee on all cattle going through Armour and Swift whether they passed through the stockyards or not.[44]

In May, 1952, the Fort Worth Stockyards executed a supplemental agreement with Armour, which reconfirmed that the packer would pay full yardage on livestock consigned direct to its Fort Worth plant. Armour acknowledged that the original commitments dated January 25, 1902, remained in effect. The packers had not realized how drastically marketing would change, but they abided by their agreement. In January, 1957, local Armour president Everett Dobbs, responding to his superiors' instructions to cut costs, asked Pier if the stockyards could reduce the charges. Pier not only refused but added that low receipts meant that the stockyards company might have to increase charges. Pier told Dobbs that packers were causing the poor showing on terminal markets by buying in the country at auctions. Then on May 14, 1958, the parent company of the Fort Worth Stockyards, United Stockyards, filed a suit in 67th District Court in Tarrant County demanding that Armour and Company live up to terms of the fifty-six-year-old contract and pay charges, delinquent

43. W. L. Pier to A. Z. Baker, American Stockyards Association File, Pier Corr., ibid.
44. The agreement was repeated in Fort Worth Stockyards Company *Corporate Record*, unnumbered vol. 1917–34, p. 233.

since March 15. United Stockyards dismissed the suit in November when Armour agreed to pay.[45]

Swift too became unhappy with the agreement that required payment to the stockyards for cattle that did not go through the yards. Hogs and sheep generally went through the stockyards, for Swift had no way to accept them directly, but cattle went directly to Swift. Swift began complaining in December, 1959, of having to pay the same charge on the cattle.[46]

The stockyards company unsuccessfully tried to get Morrell and Company to reopen a plant that they had closed on the North Side and even broached the idea of United's operating a feed yard near it. Plans did not work out. Morrell had become the nation's fourth largest meat packer by 1959 but had maintained only a small plant in Fort Worth.[47]

The story of promotional efforts at the yards during the decade of the 1950s would not be complete without a review of the methods commission companies had been using for many years. The core of each commission business (or order buyers and traders, for that matter) depended on mutual trust. Producers had to know and trust the commission agents in order to turn their livestock over to them for sale. To promote better communication, men left the yards early on Friday afternoon and drove to the country to visit their customers, meet new ones, and encourage shipment to their firm at Fort Worth.[48] "I hardly knew I had a daddy until I was twelve years old," one second-generation stockyards person said, "because he worked from daylight until dark at the yards every day and was gone all weekend to the country drumming up business."[49]

Besides visiting customers, commission company representatives

45. Paul M. Johnson to J. W. Dies, June 5, 1953, P & S Semi-annual Report Folder, Dies Corr., FWSY Co. Coll.; W. L. Pier to David Hunt, January 24, 1957, United Folder, Pier Corr., ibid.; *United Stockyards Corporation* v. *Armour and Company*, No. 8963-C, District Court of Tarrant County, 67th Judicial Dist. of Texas, May 14, 1958.
46. John M. Lewis to Harry J. Walsh, December 18, 1959, Miscellaneous, Pier Corr., FWSY Co. Coll.
47. John M. Lewis to John W. Bennett, November 19, 1959, ibid.
48. Interview with Bill Addieway, Fort Worth, September 23, 1983; interview with Bill King, Fort Worth, November 3, 1983.
49. Interview with Gary Allen, Fort Worth, November 3, 1983.

also continued to mail out a market newsletter to all their customers and wrote personal notes to them as they mailed their checks. Companies gradually cut back somewhat on advertising expense, however, just as the stockyards company did, as income dropped. Some commission men went all out in their advertising, though. Clint Shirley sometimes flew an airplane trailing a banner that read, "Ship to Shirley." He also placed the same slogan on a sign in the rear window of his car, which he could illuminate at the push of a button. Shirley's motto was, "No deal too big to handle and none too small to be appreciated."[50]

One last change in methods came late during this promotion-filled decade in an effort to compete successfully with the country auctions. Private treaty buying and selling had always been the practice at terminal markets, but the Fort Worth Stockyards decided to provide an auction as well. Ted Gouldy, Bill Pier, and others traveled to numerous country auctions to get ideas and use the best of what they found. They heard an experienced auctioneer that they liked in East Texas and hired him. His name was Don Muirhead, and he stayed at Fort Worth twenty years. The company scheduled the first auction on March 5, 1959, in an old livestock exhibit building behind the coliseum that had been left over from the Southwestern Exposition and Fat Stock Show days (the building that later housed Billy Bob's Texas). They held an auction every other week for the first couple of months. To encourage more participation at the auction everyone who shipped any kind of livestock to Fort Worth from April 13 through May 7 was entered by his commission firm in a drawing. The stockyards and commission firms gave away two Whirlwind Feeders at the May auction. United Stockyards tried to buy back the cattle barn and the coliseum from the city of Fort Worth to use for the auction sales, but the company abandoned the idea and leased the exhibit building until the end of the year. Then the stockyards built its own auction barn just behind the northeast corner of the exchange building. By the end of May the auctions had become a once-a-week affair. Older members of the commission companies resisted the auctions, however, preferring private treaty

50. Interview with R. K. Dunlap, III, Fort Worth, August 30, 1983; interview with W. Z. "Doc" Wilbanks, Fort Worth, November 3, 1983.

sales. Producers complained that it took longer to sell cattle by auction at Fort Worth than in the country because there were more pens to drive the animals through. Also, in order to be fair, each commission company got equal time whether large or small, so buyers had to watch small lots or single animals auctioned alternately with larger lots.[51]

Another public relations organ used by the stockyards was the *Doane Agricultural Report,* which for several years the company paid to have mailed to 225 vocational agriculture teachers and extension service personnel all over the state. Numerous letters in stockyards files testify to the favorable response to this service. Also, as a goodwill gesture, the company sent presents such as pen sets to bank executives, commission men, newspaper editors, managers of local restaurants, order buyers, and anyone else associated with the market. During the decade the stockyards sent out Walter Rice and Glenn Shields practically full time to visit the local auctions and to hustle business from the country to the Fort Worth Stockyards. Sometimes yard foreman Leon Odom went out, too.[52]

Contending with government controls, erratic receipts, and serious promotional challenges could not dampen the lively spirit of stockyards people for very long at a time. There always seemed to be time and energy for horseplay. Let the fellows around one weigh house find a lull on a cold winter day to go inside to warm at one of the coal-burning stoves, and someone would gently slide open the door to the scale and run a huge Brahma bull inside just to make everyone scatter.

Common currency had it that "there are no people like cattle people." Ed Barnett and J. R. Bettis, who ran the branding concession, claimed that even though they ran fifty thousand cattle a year through the branding chute, they never got a bad check from a customer. The lively stockyards spirit remained competitive, however, for angry words and near fights, sometimes real fisticuffs, could erupt

51.   Interview with Don Muirhead, Waxahachie, October 25, 1983; W. L. Pier to F. Wallace Rothrock, March 26, 1959, Other Yards Folder, Pier Corr., FWSY Co. Coll.; Copy of Lease Agreement between City of Fort Worth and Fort Worth Live Stock Market Institute, April 3, 1959, Pier Corr., FWSY Co. Coll.
52.   Doane Agriculture Service Folder, FWSY Co. Coll.; John W. Bennett to W. L. Pier, August 12, 1959, United Stockyards File, ibid.

over a particular commission agent's or dealer's hogging a weighing scale.[53]

W. L. Pier resigned as president and general manager of the Fort Worth Stockyards effective December 31, 1959, and stepped down as vice-president of United Stockyards at the same time. United Stockyards, which owned twelve fairly large terminal markets (with Fort Worth about the second largest), experienced some changes of its own. In order to diversify into an industry that was not subject to direct governmental regulations, the corporation in 1956 acquired substantial controlling interests in the Federal Steel Products Corporation and the Zenith Steel Casting Company, both of which produced steel castings in Houston.[54]

United's coast-to-coast stockyards operations represented the largest single unit in the livestock marketing field in the world. By March 19, 1959, however, a large real estate conglomerate named Canal-Randolph had acquired 73 percent of United's Stock through stock purchases and thus had authority to operate United's properties. David Hunt, president of United since 1941 and a director since 1939, fought the takeover, but was in ill health and died April 11, 1959. Heading Canal-Randolph was Hanns Ditisheim of Chicago, who had come to the United States in the 1930s after a successful banking career in Switzerland. He chose his company's name from an intersection in Chicago at which he had turned a forty-year-old warehouse into a modern office building. Ditisheim remarked while on a visit to Fort Worth that "those who are unwilling to put forth this effort to revitalize must necessarily become casualties of progress." Ditisheim's remarks proved to be quite prophetic, for old-timers on the yards — as John McNeely of Texas A&M had noted — did not like to change.[55]

In contrast, younger men who foresaw the inevitable decentralization of livestock marketing and adjusted accordingly fared quite

53. Interview with J. R. Bettis, Azle, September 20, 1983; interview with Ed Barnett, Chico, October 25, 1983; interview with Joe Whatley, Fort Worth, October 5, 1983; interview with Bill King, Fort Worth, November 3, 1983.

54. *Annual Report*, United Stockyards Corporation, Year Ended October 31, 1956, United Folder, Dies Corr., FWSY Co. Coll.

55. Ibid., Year Ended October 31, 1959; "Stock Yards Boost for City Predicted," *Fort Worth Star-Telegram*, June 18, 1959, clipping in FWSY Co. Coll.

well. J. D. Vann and Bill Roach, both of whom had followed their trader-fathers into business on the Fort Worth yards, saw that the decreased pen space and increased cost of service at the Fort Worth yards would limit their trading capacity. Thus in the late 1950s they bought land just two or three miles north of the Fort Worth stockyards, built pens, sent out a network of buyers to the country auctions all over the state, and as Vann-Roach Cattle Company soon became one of the largest, if not the largest, order-buying firm in the nation, handling three hundred thousand animals a year.[56]

Despite labor problems, a drought, federal controls, and the growing threat of the decentralization of livestock marketing into smaller country auctions, the Fort Worth Stockyards fought a successful fight during the 1950s. Although government controls or the drought caused erratic receipts at times, the market did not actually decline appreciably from the beginning to the end of the ten-year period. The market accepted somewhat more than two million animals the last year of the decade, just as it had at the beginning.[57] However, impending events and problems were soon to deliver so severe a blow to the local market that livestock receipts would drop drastically.

56. Whatley interview; Shelton interview; interview with J. D. Vann, Saginaw, September 23, 1983.

57. United States Department of Agriculture, Agricultural Marketing Service, Livestock, Poultry, Grain and Seed Division, "Salable Receipts at Public Stockyards, 1950–1959."

Retrenchment and Decline
1960–69

"ONE THING AFTER ANOTHER chipped it [the trade] away until there wasn't much left." Thus a commission man aptly described what began happening at the Fort Worth market that caused drastic reductions in receipts during the 1960s. Even the faces changed somewhat at the yards, for old-timers who had worked there for forty or fifty years began retiring. Retirement parties characterized numerous days, with a cake in somebody's office, a notebook signed by one's friends, and a sadness that one more face would be missed. Two typical retirees were Bill Joyce, assistant division manager, who retired in 1963 after working for the stockyards company for forty-three years, and commission man Houston Hutchens, whose party that same year celebrated his fifty years of work in one office in the exchange building. Many did not retire: "Most just worked until they died, or just kept coming out here after their office closed." Retirements, decline, old-timers passing on, and even pessimistic newspaper stories in the *Star-Telegram* contributed to the depressed mood around the yards. Reporters came out periodically to take pictures of empty pens and to write cutlines asking questions like, "Will they be filled again?"[1]

Leon Ralls, who started work at the yards in 1934 and was still

1. Interview with Claude Marrett, Fort Worth September 12, 1983; interview with Mrs. William L. Joyce, Fort Worth, September 6, 1983; interview with Mrs. Houston Hutchens, Fort Worth, September 9, 1983; interview with Bill King, Fort

there fifty years later, remembered finding it amusing even to think that the first scattered auctions that sprang up in small towns surrounding Fort Worth might challenge the big terminal market. Most of the people on Exchange Avenue laughed. During the 1960s no one laughed anymore, for country auctions by then threatened the very existence of the central markets, including Fort Worth.[2]

Many misjudged the causes of the situation and did not immediately see the auctions as a trend sweeping the entire industry. Small producers complained of bad treatment on the Fort Worth yards, erratic prices, and high service charges, while the stockyards officials thought that by publicity, friendlier service, and promotional gimmicks they could revitalize their market. Decentralization of terminal markets into smaller country auctions nearer the producing areas was inevitable, however, especially in Texas with its great distances, and could not have been halted single-handedly by the Fort Worth Stockyards Company.

Over the years livestock marketing had changed drastically and altered the dominant position of the Fort Worth Stockyards Company in the Southwest. The direct marketing that had begun slowly in the 1920s had become established by the 1930s with an estimated thirteen hundred local auctions in existence. World War II brought a need for quick movement of large numbers of animals, many by rail; therefore, the trend toward decentralization was temporarily slowed. New markets continued to appear in the country, however, and the war only delayed the inevitable by a few years.[3]

Country auction markets flourished after the war for many reasons. The nation's goods, including livestock, no longer moved primarily by rail, but by truck, even small farmers' pickups, and later the gooseneck trailer, along new all-weather roads. The development and use of telephones and radio also stimulated direct marketing. Just as the development of central livestock terminals between the Civil War and World War I had been the result of the transportation

---

Worth, November 3, 1983; Stockyards Decline Folder, William E. Jary, Jr., Private Collection, Fort Worth.

2. Interview with Leon Ralls, Fort Worth, November 1, 1983.

3. Carl Henry Moore, "Future Trends in the Marketing of Livestock and the Distribution of Meats" (Ph.D. dissertation, Purdue University, 1948), p. 51.

and communication patterns of that period, so was the demise of the central market a half-century later.[4]

Local country auctions were not posted under the Packers and Stockyards Act, so promoters did not have to worry about regulations. Only eight markets including Fort Worth had been posted in Texas as of June, 1950. In addition, small country auctions multiplied as packers placed buyers at them, finding it cheaper to buy directly and kill locally in new plants they constructed nearer the livestock-producing areas. Obsolescence hit the older packing houses in the 1950s, as ceramic tile and stainless steel of the new one-story local plants replaced the whitewash and wood of older six-story structures such as the Armour and Swift plants in Fort Worth (both constructed in 1902).

A farmer found it more convenient to sell at a local auction than to risk the damage and shrinkage of traveling to the more distant larger market. Also, if the prevailing price was not to his liking, he could with little trouble take his livestock home and try again another day. At the local auction farmers felt that they obtained comparable returns and avoided paying high feed charges and commissions. They also bypassed the crowded conditions, delays, time lost in travel, and other problems often associated with the larger and more distant central market.[5]

The larger markets like Fort Worth attempted to refute the arguments producers cited for using the smaller local auctions. Stockyards managers argued that direct buying lowered prices to producers in the long run. The stockyards reminded farmers that all safety regulations of the state and federal government were enforced at the terminal market. Because commission firms posted large bonds, the farmer or rancher was protected against "dishonest and unscrupulous people." No government agency enforced such protections at the smaller country auctions.[6] Farmers might think it more convenient to sell at local auctions, but that convenience became costly

4. Herrell DeGraff, *Beef Production and Distribution* (Norman: University of Oklahoma Press, 1960), p. 149.
5. Edward A. Duddy and David A. Revzan, *Marketing and Institutional Approach*, p. 320; Edward A. Duddy and David A. Revzan, *The Changing Relative Importance of the Central Livestock Market*, pp. 79–81.
6. Fort Worth Livestock Market Advertisement, Miscellaneous Folder, Dies

because prices would not be set by a large volume of competitive bidding as on the larger markets. The central market determined prices, provided specialized banking and insurance service, and provided highly trained specialists to aid the uninformed producer. Also, larger markets had the power and influence to petition the government to make necessary grading changes or other regulatory adjustments, as Fort Worth had successfully done concerning sheep grades in 1952. Terminal markets provided market information and prices more readily than smaller scattered auctions. Off-grades of animals sold better and for higher prices at the large markets, where a volume of other, similar animals existed.[7]

Despite these arguments decentralization continued. The Big Four packers of earlier years, Armour, Swift, Wilson, and Cudahy, lost their dominant position in the meat-packing field. In 1916 the four firms had handled 53.9 percent of the commercial cattle and 51.2 percent of all the hogs killed, but these statistics declined by 1955 to 30.8 and 36.4 percent, respectively. Small producers continued to complain loudly that commission men discriminated against them and cheated them, favoring their regular, large-volume customers. Many of these small-scale farmers remained firmly convinced that the Fort Worth Stockyards declined in receipts because commission men cheated them when the agents handled their animals, so they stopped selling at Fort Worth. While some problems of switching animals and other irregularities did occasionally occur, as they did at all large markets, these smaller producers were hurt more by them because the errors represented a larger proportion of their total sales. Such word-of-mouth complaints spread and added to the decline of the market. Producers blamed the stockyards for any bad practice by commission men on its yards, but the company really had little control over these agents.[8]

Corr., Fort Worth Stock Yards Company Collection, North Texas State University Archives, Denton (FWSY Co. Coll.). See also "Livestock Prices Received by Farmers, U.S. Averages for All Grades, 1925–1977," Chart in *1979 Cattle Feeders Annual*, p. 57; "Safety For You" (Advertisement), *Weekly Live Stock Reporter and Texas Poultry News*, November 7, 1957, p. 10.

7. Ted Gouldy, "Greater Southwest Livestock Sales," in Tom B. Saunders, Jr., Collection, Texas Christian University Special Collections, Fort Worth, Texas.

8. J. M. Lewis to John W. Bennett, July 26, 1962, Sub-Progress Report Folder, Dies Corr., FWSY Co. Coll.

Once the subsidized voice of the stockyards, the *Weekly Live stock Reporter*, an independently owned newspaper in the 1960s fought its own battle for survival and won. Owner Ted Gouldy suc ceeded by expanding coverage to include the activities of the small country auctions. One auction at Brownwood, Texas, drew big buy ers after its promoters took out a full back-page ad in the *Reporter* Further problems for Fort Worth came because the Texas Railroad Commission rules prevented farmers from hauling other producers livestock without a permit, and no more permits seemed to be avail able. A lot of farmers had to pay heavy fines for hauling such live stock to Fort Worth, whereas they could move their friends' animal to the local auctions without penalty. Also, stockyard rates con tinually remained a problem. When the company needed more reve nue, it considered asking the Packers and Stockyards Administra tion to let it raise rates, but the rates remained even lower at the country auctions than at the terminal markets. An increase would be "like waving a red flag and result in giving the auctions more ammunition." Some customers complained that not all the scales at the yards were open for use and they had to wait. The company had curtailed some services and laid off employees as a result of reduced receipts.[9]

The Livestock Market Institute served its co-sponsors, the stock yards and commission firms, well during the entire decade of the 1950s. Ted Gouldy, newspaperman, market reporter, and radio pro gram host, served the institute as a part-time director for eight years then with a budget of $50,000 he assumed a full-time position as director in 1958. The stockyards manager at that time, Bill Pier wrote, "We feel that we are on the right track to get a job done that is badly needed." The stockyards still planned an "aggressive attempt to reclaim its position as a public livestock market."[10]

John M. Lewis had arrived from South Dakota as assistant mana

9. Interview with Tommy Brown, *Weekly Livestock Reporter*, Fort Worth July 11, 1979; W. L. Pier to David F. Hunt, February 9, 1956, FWSY Co. Coll.; George Cain to John M. Lewis, September 16, 1958, Commission Company File, Pier Corr. FWSY Co. Coll.; John M. Lewis to George Cain, September 19, 1958, FWSY Co Coll.

10. W. L. Pier to A. Z. Baker, May 27, 1958, American Stockyards Association Folder, Pier Corr., FWSY Co. Coll.

ger of the Fort Worth Stockyards only three weeks earlier and immediately became a vice-president of the institute. Two months later Lewis wrote:

> Our Market Institute has been a very weak organization. A recent re-organization of this group has engendered some enthusiasm and so far the organization is supporting a budgeted program nearly twice the size of any previous program. However, business on this market has not improved to the same degree that it has on other markets and there is a great likelihood that the contributions will fall off unless we can find new gimics [*sic*] to keep the enthusiasm alive.[11]

Ted Gouldy believed that in the 1950s the Livestock Market Institute proved effective and succeeded with what it intended to do — stir up interest in the local market. Lewis, Gouldy believed, felt that in stating policy the Market Institute was playing a role that properly belonged to the stockyards. Gouldy explained that the commission men would not let the stockyards speak for them, but would let the institute because they were a part of it. Gouldy resigned as manager of the institute on April 27, 1959, citing "press of other business," but explained later that Lewis seemed to want more control as the stockyards' representative. Gouldy ended his taped market reports for Western radio stations at the same time.[12]

Once Ted Gouldy gave up the job as manager of the institute, the large group of commission firms and the stockyards company apparently could not decide on another person to run it. The institute lasted another year after Gouldy resigned but discontinued its activities as of May 1, 1960, after the stockyards company and several of the larger commission firms withdrew. Publicity had not been as extensive in the previous year. Reasons for the ultimate decline of the institute seemed to be a clash of personalities, a difference in philosophies, and a feeling that it had served its purpose. Lewis had been dissatisfied that the stockyards paid half the cost of the institute but had only one vote at policy meetings whereas the large group of commission men had one vote per company. After

11. John M. Lewis to John W. Bennett, July 15, 1958, Other Yards Folder, Pier Corr., FWSY Co. Coll.
12. Interview with Ted Gouldy, Fort Worth, October 29, 1979.

the institute disbanded, the stockyards took the lead in advertising, while the commission companies continued to pay half the cost. Some institutes remained on other markets. Understandably, it became more difficult for the stockyards company to get the commission firms to contribute their share of the cost of advertising.[13]

John M. Lewis, a tall, balding man in his early fifties, had come to Fort Worth in May, 1958, as assistant general manager and vice-president with the understanding that he would replace W. L. Pier as president when Pier resigned on December 31, 1959. Lewis had been president and general manager of the Sioux Falls Stockyards Company in South Dakota, another property of United Stockyards. Lewis came to Fort Worth with the hope of really turning things around, trying new ideas, and getting more receipts. But he and his superiors at United did not measure correctly the prevailing attitude on the Fort Worth market. As a newcomer to a yards where most commission men and traders were second- or third-generation stockyards people, he faced an attitude that one must pay his dues on the local market before others would listen. Any newcomer would have faced resistance to quick changes. But he had another strike against him: Lewis's training and background had been as a construction engineer. He had served as a troubleshooter for United Stockyards, supervising the reconstruction of the Saint Paul Stockyards after a fire and rebuilding Sioux City after a disastrous flood. The Stockton yards also faced some construction problems that claimed his attention. The Sioux Falls job had been his first actual presidency. The stockyards there did quite well, so the company believed Lewis could turn things around in Fort Worth.[14]

Thus, Lewis was not as well received on the yards as Pier had been, and many commission men and dealers resented him as a "Yankee." They apparently forgot that Pier originally had been from South Dakota, too; he had become "Texanized" in their minds during his nearly twenty years in Fort Worth before assuming control of the stockyards. Lewis made some fairly quick changes, which officials at United approved but old-timers on the yards resented. He reduced fifty-five acres of railroad-car-size cattle pens to twenty-

13. Interview with Elmo Klingenberg, Fort Worth, August 4, 1981.
14. Interview with Mrs. John M. Lewis, Fort Worth, November 21, 1983.

five acres and replaced the stockyards working horses and mules with motorcycles or scooters. Conservative Texas livestock producers complained of a "sissyfied" atmosphere, and some began taking their cattle elsewhere. They preferred old cowhands on horses handling their stock to "teenaged shirtless longhaired kids" on motor scooters. They called the scooters the "last straw" in their list of complaints. Some stockyards employees, however, agreed that the scooters proved more efficient than horses. A motor scooter could operate twenty-four hours a day; the driver could then turn the switch and forget the vehicle until the next day, which he could not do with his horse. Also, scooters turned sharply and their noise even helped herd cattle.[15]

Before Lewis even took control, officials had been looking at a possible reduction of the cattle division north to Twenty-eighth Street and examining deeds to consider possible sale or other use of the land, so the reduction of the pens already had been planned. Nevertheless, many commission men and traders blamed John Lewis and his changes for the decline of the yards. Because their businesses were suffering from reduced receipts, they could not look at the situation objectively and wanted a scapegoat. "The people that's gettin' gored are the ones that scream, like a pig under a gate," is the way one old-timer colorfully put it. Some traders moved out of the stockyards, obtained land, and built their own pens on the outskirts of Fort Worth in the 1960s as the reduced pen space and increased costs of the Fort Worth Stockyards became prohibitive. That decreased receipts at the yards even more and caused some to contend that Lewis had run off the traders.[16]

Because of this antagonism, Lewis did not get much local cooperation from the independent commission men and dealers. Employees of the stockyards company remembered Lewis as a friendly, outgoing man and enjoyed working for him. However, a lack of com-

15. Interview with Al Todd, Fort Worth, August 5, 1981; interview with Charles McCafferty, Fort Worth, August 12, 1981; interview with W. M. Speck, Fort Worth, June 7, 1983; interview with Johnny Adams, Fort Worth, June 7, 1983.
16. R. W. Hunt to J. M. Lewis, October 8, 1959, Pier Corr., FWSY Co. Coll.; interview with Winfred Christian, Fort Worth, November 3, 1983. Numerous traders and commission agents expressed this attitude to the author but preferred not to be quoted.

munication and cooperation certainly existed among the commission companies, traders, and the Fort Worth Stockyards, which hurt the market at a time when everyone needed to be working together. The stockyards company quite definitely wanted more business, but some commission men perceived the attitude of the stockyards officials as: "We have a facility here and you can use it if you want to and not if you don't want to." Conversely, Lewis expressed disappointment that heads of commission firms did not seem interested enough in revitalizing their market to attend seminars, advertise as much as they once had, or visit in the country frequently to encourage business. He said that because the owners of several smaller commission companies did not rely on the proceeds of their firm for their sole living, they refused to "participate in collective effort to publicize our market and advertise what it can do for producers." While the stockyards was "dependent solely on the volume produced by our Market Agencies" it was forced to "gamble our entire investment of several million dollars on results produced by these unambitious firms some of which even display disloyalty to our marketing system." Of course, the commission men wanted more business, and some agents still visited in the country. They too felt the pinch and cut back on expensive advertising. The situation had developed into a hopeless misunderstanding among all concerned.[17]

Despite frustrations involving stockyards management and the decline of their market, local traders still saved time for shenanigans. When John Lewis was advertising for a secretary, one of the traders dressed up like a woman and applied for the job. The unsuspecting Lewis hired "her," but she stayed only a few minutes. Most people in the exchange building were in on the joke, and perhaps making Lewis the object of their prank reflected something more than hilarity.[18]

17. Speck interview; Adams interview; interview with Paul Talles, Fort Worth, September 21, 1983; interview with Patsy Cooper, Fort Worth, July 30, 1981; interview with Manson Reese, Fort Worth, October 29, 1983; Statement Prepared by John M. Lewis for National Commission on Food Marketing Hearing at Fort Worth, Texas, April 22–24, 1965, Mrs. John M. Lewis Collection, Fort Worth; Addieway interview.
18. Interview with Mrs. Bernelle Kutch, Fort Worth, September 19, 1983.

Ted Gouldy, who owned stock in United Stockyards, the parent company, suggested an idea to help the Fort Worth market. He said that the terminal markets should go with the trend toward decentralization instead of fighting against it. He suggested that the Fort Worth Stockyards set up branches at places like Ennis, Abilene, and San Angelo and assign commission men, office staff, and buyers to move around, visiting different markets each day of the week. He believed that this policy shift would result in the Fort Worth Stockyards' controlling the country markets instead of letting the small independent auctions prevail. He also tried to interest local businessmen and packers in moving out of the central business district and building efficient one-story plants at the edge of Fort Worth. United Stockyards did not pick up on his suggestions. Gouldy reminded anyone who would listen that when a trend starts, you either go with it or you die. Although the packers did build plants closer to the supplies, the central markets did not adapt to the decentralization trend. If United Stockyards had decentralized, as the packers had done during World War II, they could have beat out all the little "outlaw auctions," Gouldy said.[19]

Instead, the stockyards company continued its promotional activities, reinstituting a daily radio broadcast, which aired fairly regularly during the first half of the decade. A "good percentage" of the 250 members of the Farm and Ranch Club continued to meet regularly. Pioneer Days continued annually, and promoters even staged a reenactment of the Chisholm Trail drives in 1967. In addition, the stocker and feeder sales, held in cooperation with the Texas Hereford Association and the Texas Aberdeen Angus Association (later called simply the Texas Angus Association), attracted good crowds, with usually seven of each category scattered throughout the spring, summer, and fall. These sales generally brought in approximately 5,000 head each and sometimes 6,000 to 7,000. The Charolais-Cross Feeder Calf sale brought that breed into the stocker-feeder sale ranks on September 25, 1965, when 837 were offered. Some buyers came from out-of-state for these sales.[20]

Promotional gimmicks for these shows became more elaborate

19. Gouldy interview.
20. "Agriculture and Livestock," *Fort Worth* 38 (November, 1962): 11.

and sometimes included an all-expense-paid weekend in Fort Worth for some lucky rancher and his family. Sharing the cost of the award were the Fort Worth Stockyards Company, the North Fort Worth Business Association, and the Fort Worth Chamber of Commerce. Another prize offered one year, a Philco Home Entertainment Center, included a combination color television, AM-FM radio, and hi-fidelity record player. Another time, a livestock producer who had sold on the Fort Worth market won a free steel gate.[21]

Even though promotional efforts continued in the 1960s, so did retrenchment of the market. As of October, 1959, the stockyards employed 123 yard men for their 54 acres of cattle pens and 20 acres of sheep and hog pens. By June, 1961, Lewis had finished the demolition of 30 acres of cattle pens, cutting down the working area of the yards by 40 percent and eliminating four scales from the operation. Consequently, by the fall of that year the number of yard men had been lowered to 107. A year later he had eliminated three more positions. Because employees had received two raises in a year's time, labor costs kept rising, but receipts at the yards had dropped by approximately 170,000 animals. As a result, Lewis cut back to 84 yardmen by June, 1962. He explained to his superiors at United that any further reduction to save money "would not permit necessary operation of present facilities," for they were spread too thin already.[22]

A once-a-week auction, on Thursday, had been the practice since May, 1959, and on Friday, June 3, 1960, the new air-conditioned auction ring opened with great fanfare. The Fort Worth Chamber of Commerce Agriculture and Livestock Committee hosted a breakfast for four hundred cattlemen and business and civic leaders. The new facility, located behind the exchange building, offered theater-type seats, a ladies' lounge, and a snack bar. In addition, a closed-circuit TV system showed the lot sale number, the commission company handling the consignment, the owner, his address, and the

21. "V.I.R. (Very Important Rancher) and Family to Have Fun in Fort Worth in August! Winner to Be Shipper to August 9 Sale," *Weekly Livestock Reporter*, July 20, 1967, p. 2.

22. Typed Sheet in Labor Misc. Folder, Dies Corr., FWSY Co. Coll.; John M. Lewis to John W. Bennett, July 26, 1962, United Stockyards File, ibid.

number of cattle. The name of the buyer and the selling price were flashed on the screen following each sale.[23]

When large delegations of tourists came to town and visited the auction, someone usually would slip Auctioneer Don Muirhead the name of a prominent person in the group. Sometime while they were there he would say, "Excuse me, Mr. ———. Are you bidding, or are you just scratching your head?" It always brought a laugh.

Fort Worth was one of the first terminal markets to institute an auction. Some suggest that Fort Worth made mistakes, however. Instead of setting a special time for large lots of cattle or calves, they mixed them. Buyers wanting large lots had to sit for hours and see one at a time come up. Fort Worth became just another small auction, for buyers could go to the country and buy one at a time and not have nearly as much competition.[24]

The reduction of commission firms to twenty-two by 1961 reflected the market decline, for by that time only 42.3 percent of all federally inspected animals slaughtered nationwide were purchased at terminal markets, and only 29.2 percent of all hogs. Fort Worth was not the only market facing problems; the trend away from central markets was nationwide. A few fared better, however, such as Omaha, Saint Paul, and Oklahoma City.[25]

The year 1962 seemed unusual. Not only did the stockyards get national coverage on the *Today* television show and celebrate an anniversary of sorts, one of the big packers closed its doors and cut receipts to the market even more. When John W. Bennett, president of United Stockyards, made a visit to Fort Worth in January, 1962, he assured local people that the rumors that the Fort Worth market would close were false and called the auctions there "among the largest in the nation."[26]

Nevertheless, officials believed it might be a good idea to do some

23. "Fort Worth Stockyards Formally Opens Auction Ring," *Cattleman* 47 (July, 1960): 92.
24. Interview with Don Muirhead, Waxahachie, October 25, 1983; interview with Bill Ball, Agra, Oklahoma, September 17, 1983.
25. "Selected Papers on Marketing," Fifty-eighth Annual Meeting of the American Meat Institute, Chicago, Ill., September 22–25, 1963, p. 29.
26. "Stockyards President Visits Fort Worth, Market Future Bright," *Weekly Livestock Reporter*, January 18, 1962, p. 14.

market research similar to the study made by John G. McNeely of Texas A&M some seven years earlier. Consequently, the Fort Worth Stockyards hired a public relations firm to conduct a survey in February, 1962. Members of the firm personally interviewed 392 people — 302 who had not used the Fort Worth Stockyards in six months and 90 who had used it more recently. The firm learned that people who did not ship to Fort Worth cited as their reasons distance, disadvantages to small operators with a few head, and transportation costs. The people preferred an auction to a commission firm and suggested that the stockyards disseminate more information, solicit producers' business more actively, and do magazine and radio advertising. Livestock raisers apparently considered services and facilities of minor importance in selecting a way to sell their livestock, however, for the operations of the Fort Worth yards were generally believed to be in good order. Only a smattering of criticism surfaced. The overall conclusion of the study as to why people no longer shipped to Fort Worth: "The market has gone to the seller; he no longer has to go to the market." The local auctions attracted them more. Producers believed they could get the largest net return by selling at local auctions, directly to dealers, or to packers.[27]

On the June day when officials of the National Broadcasting Company's *Today* show filmed at the Fort Worth market, the stockyards company offered a $100 savings bond to the shipper with the largest consignment and one to the shipper coming the greatest distance. The company planned free drawings for dozens of other prizes, ranging from saddles to billfolds and boots. To host the guests, people wore pioneer costumes to a chuckwagon breakfast at the Livestock Exchange Building. Anchorman John Chancellor interviewed auctioneer Don Muirhead, and the show pictured the once-a-week auction as though it were a daily occurrence.[28]

By and large the most important event, though a disillusioning

27. "Study of Live Stock Marketing among Farmers and Ranchers in the Market Area of the Fort Worth Stockyards," Conducted for the Fort Worth Stockyards by Belden Associates, Dallas, Texas, March 1962, Study of Marketing Folder, Financial Reports, FWSY Co. Coll.

28. "NBC's 'Today' Show to Feature Texas Cattle at Special Calf Show at Fort Worth Mart June 22," *Weekly Livestock Reporter*, June 14, 1962, p. 1; Muirhead interview.

one, of the year 1962 was the closing of the large Armour packing plant. Rumors had been circulating for nearly four years that both major packers might shut down their operations, but part of this pessimism came from the drought that made receipts erratic in the 1950s. However, Armour had discontinued the slaughtering of hogs at Fort Worth on July 11, 1959, and ceased operations entirely at six of the company's other thirty-two plants that summer. United president John W. Bennett asked Pier, who was still manager at that time, to try to get Armour officials to reconsider. Bennett suggested that another plant had been successful when the labor union agreed to increase productivity if the plant would not cancel the slaughter. Pier's pleas failed to change Armour's plans. Then in 1962 came the announcement that Armour would cease cattle slaughter as of June 1, but might continue sheep. All activities halted as of July 26, however. Armour's demise made an impact on Fort Worth's economy, for the previous year the meat packer had handled a payroll of $10 million and had spent over $40 million for livestock purchases locally. Swift's figures were comparable, except that Swift spent an additional $10 million on livestock.[29]

Local newspaper writers assured Fort Worth citizens that the stockyards would not close, for most of the animals bought and sold were stockers and feeders, and the packers did not constitute major buyers anymore. Not everyone believed them. Armour cited its outdated plant, labor costs, and high administrative expenses as its major reasons for the closing. They could not compete with independent packers with non-union plants that offered lower wages and fewer fringe benefits to their workers. John Lewis reported that the closing of the Armour plant "can be expected to account for a loss of perhaps 100,000 head of cattle and as much as 300,000 of sheep in the ensuing year, plus some possible contingent loss of salable receipts."[30]

After Armour closed, followers of the local market wondered if the Swift plant would cease operations as well. However, the Na-

29. John W. Bennett to W. L. Pier, August 7, 1959, United Stockyards Folder, Pier Corr., FWSY Co. Coll.

30. Ted Gouldy, "Armour, Fort Worth, Will Close, Effect Minimal," *Weekly Livestock Reporter*, March 15, 1962, p. 3; John M. Lewis to John W. Bennett, July 26, 1962, United Stockyards File, Dies Corr., FWSY Co. Coll.

tional Brotherhood of Packinghouse Workers, Local No. 6, the Swift union, voted on December 15, 1962, to take a wage cut of approximately twenty cents an hour and yielded some fringe benefits in order to allow Swift to be able to compete better in the local market. The Armour union, the AFL-CIO United Packinghouse Workers, Local No. 54, had opposed a similar vote. Armour officials had not guaranteed the union that the plant would remain open for at least three to five years if they voted a pay cut. Their contract already called for a nine-cent raise, so workers had voted to continue the contract. But the concession by Swift's independent union saved jobs for the fourteen hundred employees of the Fort Worth Swift plant and averted closing of their slaughtering facilities for nine years. Some local citizens believed that the Armour plant could also have remained open if their union had granted similar concessions.[31]

Following the closing of the Armour plant, many of the businessmen of Fort Worth and many local citizens gave up on the stockyards district and turned their interests to oil, banking, and aircraft. They planned to make Fort Worth a big business center like Dallas. Apparently Fort Worth was forgetting its cattle roots, for in a *Guide to Historic Sites in Fort Worth and Tarrant County* published by the Tarrant County Historical Society in 1963, no mention at all was made of the stockyards and packing plants. The only cattle reference was to the Chisholm Trail that a century earlier had gone through the city. (Even that fact was technically incorrect, for the trail was not called the Chisholm until it reached Indian Territory.) Similarly, a Chamber of Commerce bulletin on Fort Worth's attractions published five years earlier had made no mention of the stockyards whatsoever. Numerous persons in the livestock industry believed that the Chamber of Commerce leaders wanted to "write off" the North Side, which was becoming dilapidated and crime-ridden. Bumper stickers appeared in Fort Worth proclaiming "Nowtown, not Cowtown." Lewis realized that his job included a public relations battle with downtown business leaders to convince them that

31. Interview with Eddie Humphrey, Fort Worth, January 19, 1982. Humphrey was a member of the Armour union and on the negotiating committee.

the potential for Fort Worth to be the center of the West Texas livestock industry still remained.[32]

To let the public know that the market did not close when Armour did and to generate some new business, fifteen commission firms (which did not represent all firms left on the market) joined together to promote some special days from August 13 to October 26, 1962, to celebrate the sixtieth anniversary of the market, again accepting the erroneous start-up date of 1902. On October 26 they held a drawing for a fully-equipped, air-conditioned Chevrolet pickup truck. The truck remained on display inside the exchange building during the promotion.[33]

Despite the loss of one of the Big Four meat packers, the Fort Worth Stockyards continued to be active. Its business came mostly from its special stocker and feeder sales and its addition of auctions, but it had lost out in volume of business to the country. A news story proclaimed the market leaders in 1963, in terms of top-dollar volume of cattle, hogs, sheep, and goats, to be Norfolk, Nebraska, Dodge City, Kansas, and two Texas auctions in Amarillo and San Angelo. In 1965 Fort Worth ranked eighteenth of fifty-three terminal markets in the nation overall, but fourth in sheep, seventh in calves, and seventeenth in cattle.[34]

John Lewis wanted to reduce the number of commission companies on the yards, mainly because the stockyards did not generate enough trade for all the firms on the market. His position became that on the death or retirement of the owner, that commission company was no longer in existence. "Any successor would be a new registration, and we will not accept new registrants." That position constituted another of the things that did not make Lewis too popu-

32. Interview with Ted Gouldy; W. J. Overman, *A Guide to Historic Sites in Fort Worth and Tarrant County;* "Fort Worth," Chamber of Commerce booklet published in 1958, in Clippings File, Pier Corr., FWSY Co. Coll.; interview with Bill Shelton, Chamber of Commerce president, Fort Worth, July 29, 1980; McCafferty interview; interview with Mrs. Russell McElyea, Fort Worth, September 8, 1983.

33. "'Public Market Days' Set Aug. 13–October 26 at Fort Worth, Truck Grand Prize," *Weekly Livestock Reporter,* August 16, 1962, p. 1.

34. "Two Texas Auctions among Nation's Market Leaders," ibid., February 6, 1964, p. 1; Roy Scudday, "Fort Worth Stockyards," *Fort Worth* 42 (May, 1966): 27.

lar on the yards. He had reduced the number of commission firms to sixteen in 1968 and to fourteen a year later. The stockyards company, however, bought one of the older commission firms, John Clay and Company, and operated it for most of the decade.[35]

Some expressed concern that when certain commission companies shut down, their closing accelerated the decline of the market because some producers who lived many miles away from Fort Worth had continued to ship to the same commission company they had used for many years. When that commission firm closed, the producer felt no loyalty to the market any longer and shipped closer to home. The commission companies that remained started moving their offices to a downstairs wing of the exchange building in the mid-1960s.[36]

The Fort Worth Chamber of Commerce did not totally abandon the livestock industry, although many stockyards people believed it did. In 1968 the chamber came out with "a new plan to recapture the image of Fort Worth, Texas as the livestock center of the Southwest," which it announced in mid-September. The plan called for offering a package of services and financial assistance to any group or individual breeder who wanted facilities for shows and sales of livestock in Fort Worth. The facilities the Chamber of Commerce offered, however, were the barns with judging and sales arenas owned by the city on Amon Carter Square at the Will Rogers Complex on the west side of Fort Worth. The city leased these facilities for one month each year to the Southwestern Exposition and Fat Stock Show. The programs may have helped Fort Worth's cattle image, but they obviously hurt the Fort Worth Stockyards Company's business by attracting away some buyers or producers who might otherwise have participated in the stockyards' own stocker and feeder sales.[37]

Market receipts did decline in the 1960s from the previous de-

35. J. M. Lewis to John W. Bennett, July 26, 1962, United Stockyards File, Dies Corr., FWSY Co. Coll.

36. Joint interview with Gary Allen, Bill King, Doc Wilbanks, Fort Worth, November 3, 1983; interview with Mr. and Mrs. Hilton Kutch, Azle, October 4, 1983.

37. City of Fort Worth, Contract No. 1947, Southwestern Exposition and Fat Stock Show Lease—Municipal Buildings West, January 14, 1948; "Fort Worth Chamber of Commerce Livestock Promotion Planned," Cattleman 55 (December, 1968): 64.

cade, primarily because of the closing of the Armour plant and the further acceleration of auction markets and feedlots closer to the source of supply. Efficiency cutbacks caused resentment among many long-time customers. At the beginning of the decade salable receipts of cattle, calves, hogs, and sheep reached 1,378,509. In 1965 total receipts reached 1,113,058 and in 1969, 1,045,158, but the receipts had dropped by one million head from the yearly totals of the 1950s.[38]

When the United States began importing beef from Australia, New Zealand, and Ireland, cattlemen complained in 1964 to President Lyndon B. Johnson about their plight. The Johnson administration insisted that the imported beef would be used only in school lunch programs and for the needy, but cattlemen believed that this action represented unnecessary government meddling with beef supplies. The problem of imported meat continued throughout the decade. Farmers also complained about the government program concerning feed grains, oil seeds, and the acreage set-aside system. Feeders blamed the feed grain program for high costs of cattle and lamb finishing by placing feed items at artificially high levels. Any program such as the foreign imports or feed supports that caused cattlemen to cut back on production also obviously hurt receipts and sales at the Fort Worth Stockyards.[39]

By and large, however, the new phenomenon of the 1960s became the expansion of feedlots, particularly in the Texas Panhandle. They accelerated the decentralization process that had made great gains already. In 1956 about 63 feedlots with capacities of over one thousand head existed in Texas. In 1964 this figure had grown to 207. A *Texas Feedlot Directory* in 1968 cited 185 entries, representing member feedlots at that time, but only a year later the number had increased to 280. First came irrigation of land in dry areas such as the

38. Salable Receipts of Fort Worth 1939–79, Market News Service, U.S. Department of Agriculture, Fort Worth Office, Livestock Exchange Building. Figures for the entire decade and for all the years in which records were kept are presented in the appendix. "Comparison of Receipts and Disposition of Livestock," Fort Worth Stockyards Company, monthly report for years 1964–70, copy in author's possession.

39. "Administration to Buy Beef for Schools, Needy Distribution, But Cattle Leaders Insist Imports Must Be Sharply Reduced," *Weekly Livestock Reporter*, March 5, 1964, p. 2.

Texas Panhandle, Arizona, and Kansas. Then farmers grew grain on this irrigated land. They needed cattle as a way to market their grain, so the feedlot phenomenon erupted.[40] Also, people began demanding better cuts of meat, for their affluent life-style permitted this luxury. An Assistant Secretary of Agriculture called it eating "higher up on the hog." Buyers for supermarkets did not know cattle as well as the buyers on the terminal markets, but they required choice cattle for their customers. The only way they could be assured of choice meat was to buy directly from feeders who guaranteed corn-fed or grain-fed beef. They could not obtain these choice animals from the cattle available at terminal markets, for most were grass-fed. Feeders contracted ahead of time for a fair market sale of their animals rather than gamble for a large profit or risk a disastrous loss depending upon the fluctuating price at the terminal market when their animals were ready to sell.[41]

One Amarillo banker described the feedlot business as a six-billion-dollar investment in feedlots, packing plants, farms, and other businesses allied with the feeding of cattle. The abundance of grain plus cooler temperatures in a high and dry area located equally between lucrative East and West Coast markets set a favorable scene for the production of beef on the high plains of Texas. The *Texas Business Review* estimated that 160,000 cattle were fed in 1955 in Texas, but by January, 1969, feedlots held approximately 1,452,000 cattle in the Texas Panhandle.[42]

The feedlot system made possible more stable supplies of finished livestock allowing the meat-processing operation to be stream-

40. Ed Uvacek, "The Dynamically Changing Industry," *Cattleman* 51 (August, 1964): 41; United States Department of Agriculture, *Number of Feedlots by Size Groups and Number of Feed Cattle Marketed 1962–1964* (Washington, D.C.: Statistical Reporting Service, Crop Reporting Board, June, 1966), pp. 2–3; "Texas Feedlot Directory," *Cattleman* 55 (November, 1968): 67–78; "Texas Feedlot Directory, 1969," *Cattleman* 56 (November, 1969): 107–14; interview with J. D. Vann, Saginaw, September 23, 1983.

41. Address by Earl L. Butz before the Annual Convention of the American Feed Manufacturers Association, Conrad Hilton Hotel, Chicago, May 2, 1957, mimeographed copy in Department of Agriculture Folder, Pier Corr., FWSY Co. Coll.

42. James E. Vance, "Lots and Lots of Cattle," *Fort Worth* 46 (February, 1970): 25; Raymond A. Dietrich, "The Texas Cattle Feeding Industry," *Texas Business Review* 43 (October, 1969): 293.

lined. Smaller, speedier plants located near the major livestock-producing areas maintained a distinct advantage over the older, slower, and larger plants. Getting livestock in the right numbers had always been a problem at the larger stockyards for meat packers, making their days either feast or famine in supplies. This problem of erratic receipts explained their low profit margins. A decade or two earlier the meat packers depended largely on often relatively small individual farmers for their livestock needs, but by the late 1960s larger percentages of their kill came as a steady flow from large feeding operations.[43]

What really caused the decline, then, of the Fort Worth market —and other large terminal markets like those owned by United— was decentralization, first toward local country auctions in small towns and then to the large feedlot operations in the heart of the grain- and cattle-producing areas. Despite the company's massive publicity efforts, which seemed to work in the 1950s (possibly only because the decentralization process had not yet been completed) and which continued into the 1960s, the stockyards officials at Fort Worth and the other terminal markets could not reverse the trend. Livestock marketing in the United States changed dramatically in the two decades following World War II.

Whether the Fort Worth market would have declined quite as rapidly as it did had not a "Yankee" division president been making quick efficiency changes which old-timers resented will remain a question in the minds of many local observers. At any rate, just "holding on" became the primary task of the Fort Worth Stockyards Company by the end of the decade.

43. Ted Gouldy, "New Moves by Diversified Firms to Gain Control of Packers Reported," *Weekly Livestock Reporter*, October 10, 1968, p. 4.

Holding On

1 9 7 0 –

"You Mean, they still sell cattle at the stockyards? I thought it closed years ago when the packing plants shut down." Such comments became common in Fort Worth during the 1970s even in areas of the city reasonably near the stockyards district. Just because North Side residents could not smell the distinct livestock "aroma" to which they had become accustomed, they thought that no more cattle, hogs, or sheep ever arrived. Three hundred thousand animals arriving over a period of a year just did not smell as strongly as had three million, or even two million.

The man who dealt with the livestock that did arrive was Elmo A. "Mo" Klingenberg, who replaced John M. Lewis as division president on July 30, 1971, upon Lewis's retirement. After he left the Stockyards, Lewis remained active in the industry, serving as president of the American Stockyards Association for four years. In that role Lewis acted really as a public relations man for all the member stockyards, lobbying for bills and traveling on their behalf.[1]

Klingenberg had grown up on an Illinois farm, studied livestock marketing and animal husbandry at the University of Illinois in the early 1940s, and become associated with United Stockyards in his home state after graduation. David Hunt of United Stockyards directed Klingenberg to Fort Worth in 1946 and told him to work there a couple of years. Because immediately after World War II Klingen-

1. Interview with Mrs. John M. Lewis, Fort Worth, October 28, 1983.

berg could not find a house to rent, he asked if he could stay longer to make it worth his while to buy. A quarter of a century later he remained in Fort Worth to take Lewis's place.[2]

Klingenberg worked his way up as day yard master, superintendent, vice-president, and, upon Lewis's retirement, division president. United Stockyards' designation of its stockyards managers as division president was somewhat confusing, particularly to the press, for sometimes both Pier and Lewis were referred to as manager and sometimes as president. Illustrating that a close loyalty still existed between the stockyards company and the Southwestern Exposition and Fat Stock Show, Klingenberg also became a director of the latter organization soon after becoming division president of the Fort Worth Stockyards.[3]

Mo Klingenberg seemed the strong, silent type of whom Westerners usually approve; he dressed the part in his boots and hat, did not wear a suit and tie, and certainly had resided in Fort Worth long enough to shed any "Yankee" image. Therefore, he did not face the same kind of problems as his predecessor. The altered market situation he inherited differed drastically from the one he encountered when he had arrived in Fort Worth twenty-five years previously, and so this constituted his real challenge. Things had progressed a little too far for any hope of reversal; he simply had to try to hold on to what he had.

Klingenberg's task was not made any easier by the shutdown of the local Swift and Company plant May 1, 1971, just two months before he assumed the presidency. The closing at least had been anticipated. Swift announced as early as 1968 its plans to close its all-purpose packing plants and had already ceased operations in Chicago, Saint Louis, Denver, Saint Paul, and Omaha. In announcing the Fort Worth plant's demise, Swift officials explained that the nearest big livestock growing areas existed in the feedlots of Lubbock, Amarillo, Abilene, and Muleshoe, Texas.[4]

2. W. L. Pier to R. C. Ashby, University of Illinois, May 23, 1946, Personal Folder, Pier Correspondence, Fort Worth Stock Yards Company Collection, North Texas State University Archives, Denton (FWSY Co. Coll.).

3. W. L. Pier to A. Z. Baker, November 16, 1953, American Stockyards Association Folder, Pier Corr., FWSY Co. Coll.

4. "Swift Promises Workers Help in Plant Shutdown," *Fort Worth Star-*

Union workers at Swift in Fort Worth voted 557 to 244 on April 19, 1969, in favor of another pay cut to keep the plant open until at least April, 1971. Swift promised to keep the plant operating until that time to provide jobs for a total of 1,130 hourly workers who were members of Local No. 6 of the National Brotherhood of Packinghouse and Dairy Workers. The workers would receive no more cost of living wage increases during the life of their contract, which extended to September 1, 1970. Many of the company's employees had been with them thirty-five years or more and would be unable or unwilling to transfer to other Swift plants.[5]

Then in October, 1970, Swift made the "long anticipated announcement" that they would shut down the following spring. Officials cited as factors in their decision their obsolete plant, changing patterns in livestock production and marketing, and the growth of independent packing operations that diversified the meat business.[6]

Obviously, an immediate problem for the Fort Worth Stockyards became the loss of revenue from Swift for the direct livestock shipments of each animal slaughtered under the terms of the 1902 contract. As for other market receipts, several independent buyers had dominated the cattle slaughter market for years, so stockyards officials expected that aspect to be little affected. The independents possessed speedier and more efficient plants and hired cheaper labor than Swift could employ because of its union. Consequently, as long as three years after the Swift closing, these smaller packers slaughtered as many as two hundred thousand animals each year in the Fort Worth–Dallas area. The demise of Armour and Swift, however, left unemployment and stagnant businesses in the city's North Side, for most of the former employees of the two plants lived in the area. Their closing also caused fewer producers to bring their cattle to Fort Worth to market, for they were not as aware of the small independents as they had been of the Big Two.[7]

Telegram, October 3, 1970, clipping in Swift File, *Fort Worth Star-Telegram* Reference Library.

5. "Union OKs Cut in Pay from Swift," ibid., April 20, 1969.

6. Ted Gouldy, "Closing of Swift Plants Will Bring Changes in Market Here," *Weekly Live Stock Reporter,* October 8, 1970, p. 3.

7. Linda Gilliam, "Northside Stockyard Area Weathers Hard Times, Hopes

Aerial view looking east. The Coliseum and Exchange Building are in the lower left corner; Armour and Swift plants, in the top center. Photograph by W. D. Smith, Inc., Commercial Photography.

ABOVE: John M. Lewis, president and general manager of Fort Worth Stockyards, a division of United Stockyards, 1959–71. Courtesy Mrs. John M. Lewis. BELOW: William L. Pier, president Fort Worth Stockyards, 1946–59. Courtesy Charlotte Pier.

Milton Hogan, Armour's head cattle buyer, stands at right in the pens.
Courtesy Mr. and Mrs. Hilton Kutch.

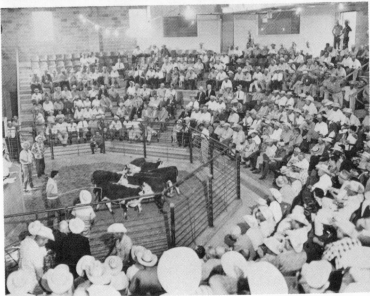

ABOVE: Covered sheep pens, 1972. Courtesy *Fort Worth Star-Telegram.*
BELOW: Inside an auction barn that was constructed in 1960. Courtesy
Fort Worth Star-Telegram.

ABOVE: Paul Talles, superintendent of yards, and Elmo Klingenberg, president, check market board, 1977. Courtesy *Fort Worth Star-Telegram*. BELOW: More people than livestock have come to the Fort Worth Stockyards in the 1980s. This crowd came for Chisholm Trail Days, June, 1983. Courtesy *Fort Worth Star-Telegram*.

LEFT: Elmo A. "Mo" Klingenberg, president of Fort Worth Stockyards, a division of United Stockyards, 1971–81. Courtesy Elmo Klingenberg. RIGHT: Gary Allen became president of the reorganized Fort Worth Stockyards in 1981. Lee Angle Photography, Inc., courtesy Gary Allen.

Unfortunately, fires destroyed the abandoned buildings of both Armour and Swift. The old Armour plant caught fire at II P.M. on May II, 1971, and soon more than one hundred firemen and between thirty and fifty pieces of fire equipment fought the blaze. Heavy wooden floors in the plant had accumulated a great amount of grease through the years, and that caused dense smoke over the area. Floors continued to smolder for a time, and the building was a total loss.[8]

Two fires plagued the abandoned Swift building. A brief fire on January II, 1974, lasted only three hours and involved the fourth and fifth floors of the plant. Apparently a cutting torch used by workmen in demolishing the building started it. Thirty-one firemen and eight pieces of equipment answered the call. The more disastrous Swift fire started May 30, 1975, and burned all night. Fire officials again believed that a demolition team's cutting torch started it. The fire burned for two or three weeks because it extended into the basement and tunnel, and no way existed for firefighters to get down there to extinguish it. Oil and grease also had saturated the thick floors. Again nearly one hundred firemen and twenty pieces of fire fighting equipment answered the call. A portion of this building remained standing as of 1987.[9]

During this second decade of decline in the market Klingenberg continued many of the same promotional tactics that had proven successful in the past. As of 1971 the special Hereford-Angus feeder calf shows and sales had been going on for seventeen years, and the stockyards planned eleven of the special shows that year. In previous years only seven had been held. To queries of how the market was faring in 1972, Klingenberg explained that the increased feeder and breeder shows had helped. He said he was taking a "positive approach on improving and expanding our services at Fort Worth."

Run High as Renovation Efforts Continue," *Dallas/Fort Worth Business*, March 27, 1978, p. 6.

8. "Packing Plant Blaze Reduced by Firemen," *Fort Worth Star-Telegram*, May 12, 1971 (eve.), Armour File, *Fort Worth Star-Telegram* Reference Library. See also Fred Blalock, "Boiling Flames Gut Old Armour Plant," ibid., May 12, 1971.

9. "Torch Is Blamed For Blaze," ibid., January 12, 1974, Swift File; Ken Hammond, "Firemen Battle 3-Alarm Swift Co. Blaze All Night," ibid., May 31, 1975.

Surprisingly, he reported that the hog receipts actually had grown after Armour and Swift closed because other buyers increased purchases and some new buyers appeared.[10]

A change, however, occurred in 1973 concerning the special monthly stocker and feeder shows, which the stockyards sponsored jointly with the Texas Angus Association and the Texas Hereford Association. As an economic measure the stockyards and commission companies decided to host the shows themselves rather than pay the fifty cents per animal sold to the two associations for doing the advertising and providing the ribbons and trophies. The stockyards people believed the two organizations were not doing as much advertising as previously. Both associations then withdrew from co-sponsorship of the sales because they saw no advantage to their organizations to continue the arrangement. Spokesmen of both groups explained that they no longer maintained any association with the Fort Worth Stockyards. "Purebred breeders never sell our cattle at a stockyards anymore, anyway," explained the secretary-manager of the Texas Hereford Association. "We sell at a ranch auction or by special agreement."[11]

The stockyards company and the commission companies did their own advertising and continued the special sales with much the same format of ribbons and trophies. "We saw no appreciable difference in the number of animals at the sales," Klingenberg said.[12]

The company held its first annual Performance Tested Bull Sale and Chianina Seed Stock Sale on January 27, 1973, at their auction arena with the help of the Aledo Custom Breeders organization. Also on September 14, 1974, Fort Worth Registered Horse sales began on the second Saturday of each month. By 1975 the company advertisements proclaimed that "in the last year the Fort Worth Stockyards has moved from a sellers market to a buyers' market attracting buyers with national outlets." The "Top Dollar" feeder and breeder

10. "Fort Worth Market Keeping Pace with New Livestock Era," *Weekly Livestock Reporter*, July 6, 1972, p. 2.
11. Interview with Gwen White, Texas Angus Association, Fort Worth, July 2, 1980; interview with Jack Chastain, Texas Hereford Association, Fort Worth, August 19, 1980.
12. Interview with Elmo A. Klingenberg, Fort Worth, August 6, 1981.

sales and shows continued the last Thursday of each month from May to November.[13]

Federal regulation always remained a concern in the livestock industry, although the Packers and Stockyards Administration seemed less effective than it had been in the 1940s, probably because it was spread thinner to cover many more auctions. The only new regulation that really affected stockyards during the 1970s was the 1976 amendment to the Packers and Stockyards Act, which made bonding mandatory for commission men at country auction markets and required for the first time that packers who purchased over $500,000 worth of livestock in a year post bonds. One provision allowed a farmer or rancher to obtain a lien or trust against a packer's assets if the packer failed to pay for the livestock. Not a P&S regulation but a government restraint, nevertheless, was the price freeze by the Nixon Administration in mid-June, 1973, which disrupted the livestock industry and as a result affected the Fort Worth market. John M. Trotman, president of the American National Cattlemen's Association, said that live cattle prices dropped nearly 30 percent from highs on August 17, 1973, the largest decline since 1950, at the beginning of the Korean War. As an explanation Trotman cited seasonality, the price freeze, and a surplus that caused the market price to drop even lower than the freeze price.[14]

William J. Kuhfuss, president of the American Farm Bureau Federation, at the organization's fifty-sixth annual meeting in New Orleans on January 6, 1975, expressed concern over recommendations of congressional leaders to bring back ceilings on food prices. "Government price ceilings at any level of the food pipeline put a lid on returns to farmers. Livestock producers still find themselves in a loss position due to the effects of the 1973 price controls," Kuhfuss said. "Cattle feeding operations have been cut severely." The Farm Bureau Federation was the largest general farm organization

13. "The Fort Worth Stockyards" (Advertisement), *Weekly Livestock Reporter*, January 2, 1975, sec. b, p. 12.
14. Interview with Mike Pacatte, Packers and Stockyards Administration, United States Department of Agriculture, Fort Worth, July 27, 1977; "Cattle Price Sag Biggest since 1950-Trotman," *Weekly Livestock Reporter*, October 11, 1973, p. 29.

in the nation, according to Kuhfuss, with 2.3 million member families, and it opposed farm subsidy programs. He continued, "Farmers and ranchers have a right to seek a fair return in the market place and a right not to be dependent on the federal treasury for handouts to supplement family farm income."[15]

Labor unrest also caused problems at the stockyards during the decade. Although the company had enjoyed more than thirty years of uninterrupted contracts with its employees, this pattern was broken on November 1, 1978, when twenty-seven livestock handlers and yard repairmen went on strike. They wanted a 25 percent raise the first year of a three-year contract. United Stockyards sent supervisors in from other areas to help keep the Fort Worth yards open. The commission men helped, and even Klingenberg's wife worked briefly at one of the yard's weighing scales. The yards did not stop operations, and the strike ended after about two weeks. The date for a special monthly stocker-feeder sale approached, giving both sides incentive to try harder to reach an agreement. Workers accepted the company's offer and returned to work Monday before the big sale on Thursday.[16]

Despite decentralization, United Stockyards still believed in the future of central, or terminal-type, livestock markets, for they purchased the stockyards at Omaha. It had not declined as much as Fort Worth, where the expansive geography of the state had a greater effect. United's eleven public stockyards handled about 30 percent of all livestock marketed through stockyards facilities, and its larger stockyards, especially Omaha, still affected the pricing structure nationally and were quoted frequently.[17]

A further indication that United and its parent company Canal-

---

15. "Congress Warned Price Controls Halt Needed Output," *Weekly Livestock Reporter*, January 9, 1975, pp. 1, 14.

16. "Stockyards Strike Stalemate Goes On," *Fort Worth Star-Telegram*, November 4, 1978, in Stockyards File, *Fort Worth Star-Telegram* Reference Library. This was the first strike against the stockyards since 1946.

17. James E. Vance, "Stockyards," *Fort Worth Star-Telegram*, December 19, 1976, in ibid.; interview with Elmo Klingenberg, Fort Worth, January 14, 1982. The eleven stockyards owned by United in 1984 included Stockton, Calif.; Sioux City, Iowa; Indianapolis, Ind.; Saint Paul, Minn.; Saint Joseph, Mo.; Omaha, Neb.; West Fargo, N. Dak.; Portland, Ore.; Sioux Falls, S. Dak.; Fort Worth, Tex.; and Milwaukee, Wis.

Randolph believed in their markets was a renovation project begun at the Fort Worth Stockyards in the latter part of the decade. In May, 1977, Klingenberg announced a $500,000 renovation program to include moving unloading docks for livestock from Exchange Avenue to a new site on the north side of the stockyards, remodeling pens, building new ones, constructing an overhead walkway from the new unloading area to the auction barn and Livestock Exchange Building, installing a new sanitary and storm drainage system, and providing a new parking area for livestock trucks. The project would take six months to complete. In addition, the Stockyards Development Corporation, a subsidiary of Canal-Randolph, announced on December 12, 1977, a $750,000 program to restore the historic Fort Worth Livestock Exchange Building to retain the original architectural style of the 45,000-foot structure, within which 29,000 square feet would be designated for leaseable office space. This project was completed by late 1978. The Stockyards company even moved out of the large office it had maintained for many years in the southeast corner of the first floor to a smaller office upstairs.[18]

The commitment of funds from the stockyards ownership came after two million dollars in public monies were spent in improvements along Marine Creek and Exchange Avenue as the city of Fort Worth began renovating and restoring the stockyards district. The stockyards company delayed its own project until drainage and other environmental requirements had been met. Their pen remodeling project basically represented a final transition from livestock shipments by rail to modern-day truck transportation. When completed, more than four hundred new and remodeled livestock pens lay centrally located in an area north of Exchange Avenue. The daily capacity for cattle was between 4,000 and 5,000 head and for hogs and sheep up to 2,000 head. When the renovation had been completed, the stockyards company sent out news releases to small weekly newspapers all over West Texas, and President Elmo Klingenberg sent a letter to patrons explaining the changes. As further evidence of the modernization, in 1979, for the first time, the company em-

18. "Fort Worth Stockyards Begin Renovation Program," *Cattleman* 64 (June, 1978): 72; "Fort Worth Exchange Begins $750,000 Renovation," ibid. 64 (February, 1978): 139.

ployed women to work in the yards. Women had been in the office for a long time, but not out on the yards.[19]

The decline in receipts at the Fort Worth Stockyards continued during the 1970s, dropping by 10 to 15 percent each year. Total receipts in 1970 reached 906,345, dropped to 371,342 in 1975, and slumped to 194,642 by 1979. At the beginning of the decade, drought conditions had hurt the industry, although the dry ranges caused increased marketing in 1971. That year shippers used the railroad for the last time to haul cattle into or out of the yards. At mid-decade the stockyards decided to spread sales out rather than try to sell all the cattle that arrived on Monday on that one day. The market had been receiving about half their week's receipts by noon Monday. They began assigning a number of drafts of cattle which each of the nine commission firms at the local market could sell on each of the four days of sales, Monday through Thursday. The firms met and worked out a rotation schedule that was fair to each company. By 1978 only six commission firms remained in business, and the stock pens, which once had covered 110 acres, had been reduced to 12. Then Farmer-Kutch Commission Company became inactive and formally closed out its business on July 27, 1981. Its name represented two of the oldest commission families on the market, those of J. D. Farmer and Jeff Kutch, formerly of Woody-Kutch Commission Company.[20]

The situation that existed at the stockyards late in 1981 only continued the problems of the seventies. Many Fort Worth residents, even those from the North Side, believed that the stockyards no longer operated as an active market. They assumed that all the renovation had been done because the market had closed and the Livestock Exchange Building was being leased out for office space, which, of course, some of it was. They figured that the cars in the parking spaces each day belonged only to office workers or tourists. New rumors circulated almost weekly through the exchange building, and stockyards employees would be asked periodically even by commission companies, "Is the stockyards closing down?" With only

19. Letter from Elmo Klingenberg to Stockyards patrons, April 6, 1978, copy in possession of author; interview with office staff, Fort Worth Stockyards Company, Fort Worth, February 19, 1981.
20. Comparison of Receipts and Disposition of Livestock, 1970–1979, United Stockyards Company, Fort Worth Division, Fort Worth.

ive commission companies in business in the late summer of 1981,
ew persons remained to hustle livestock business for the companies
or for the stockyards.[21]

With only five commission companies to share the cost of 50
percent of any advertising (with the stockyards paying the other 50
percent), each company bore a larger share than when split with
twenty-five or thirty commission companies in the 1950s. Thus the
stockyards found it difficult to persuade the companies to cooperate in advertising their market, although the companies advertised
some individually. Sales dropped considerably. The special stocker
and feeder sales of the last Thursday of the month generally brought
in four thousand animals during the summer months of 1980, but
in July, 1981—which should have been one of the best months—
only twenty-six hundred animals arrived.

Labor costs remained high, and the union contract called for the
company to guarantee its employees a forty-hour work week with
time and a half for overtime. Since Monday was a big day and the
other days slower, superintendent Paul Talles had to set his men
to work repairing fences and cleaning pens during the latter part
of the week, but he found it difficult to keep them busy.[22]

Because the company lost money in 1981, United Stockyards began
looking at numerous options. With division president Elmo Klingenberg scheduled to retire in the spring of 1982, some change would
be necessary anyway. Late in the summer of 1981 Klingenberg allowed Gary Allen of Foley-Allen Commission Company to announce
the major change in operations that Allen and his associates had
worked out with United Stockyards. The five commission companies remaining on the market agreed to dissolve and create one company. This new company officially registered itself as the Niles City
Cattle Company, Inc., doing business as the Fort Worth Stockyards.
The new company, operating under the old familiar name, leased
the auction barn, pens, and other yard facilities from United Stockyards, official owner of the old Fort Worth Stockyards Company.
Allen, as president, promised streamlined operations, more effi-

21. Interview with Kathy Rainey, Fort Worth Stockyards, Fort Worth, July 30, 1981.
22. Interview with Paul Talles, Fort Worth, September 21, 1983.

ciency, lower rates, and more competitive sales. With no union in volved, he could hire workers only on the days he needed them United agreed to install a new pneumatic tube system to send sale tickets to the office and back to save customers' time, to build a new trailer chute, and to enlarge the pens and watering facilities.[2]

Allen called the new venture the "most positive thing that ha happened in the last twenty-five years" and hoped to turn the trend toward decentralization around. He said that buyers within a 15c mile radius of Fort Worth often had to go to fifteen of the smalle auction arenas in one day to obtain enough livestock to fill thei orders. By lowering tariffs as much as 40 percent for larger truck loads of livestock, Allen planned to induce more producers to ship to Fort Worth.[24]

The five commission companies still in existence when they dis solved to aid Allen in the new venture were Foley-Allen, Carson John Clay, Farm and Ranch, and Leon Ralls. Of the owners, onl Allen and Ralls joined in the new company, along with some of th employees of the previous firms. The other owners retired. Gar Allen had been full-time on the yards since 1958 but had been on the yards off and on since age ten with his father and grandfathe who had begun Foley-Allen Commission Company in the 1940s. On of Allen's main problems would be the urban setting, for many ol farmers liked a rural atmosphere and disliked the freeways and tra fic they encountered in selling at Fort Worth.[25]

When the "new" Fort Worth Stockyards began operations Novem ber 1, 1981, several significant things occurred. After ninety-four years no terminal market existed at Fort Worth, for according to a Pack ers and Stockyards Administration definition a terminal marke must have more than one commission company to which to assig cattle, and only one company remained. Also, for the second tim in the history of the market, it would be managed by local livestoc personnel, even though the market had changed management o a lease basis rather than ownership. Since 1893 management alway

23. *Annual Report,* Canal-Randolph Corporation, 1982, copy in possessio of author; public announcement by Gary Allen, Auction Barn, Fort Worth Stoc yards, Fort Worth, August 19, 1981.

24. Ibid.

25. Interview with Gary Allen, Fort Worth, August 19, 1981.

had been out-of-state. Perhaps just as important, provisions had been made for the market to continue under the name of the Fort Worth Stockyards.[26]

After Gary Allen and his new company took over the management, mail deliveries became confused between the two businesses operating under the same name within the exchange building, for the older company still owned the building and facilities and maintained its office to oversee these interests. Consequently, the older company soon changed its office sign and stationery from Fort Worth Stockyards Company, a division of United Stockyards, to United Stockyards, Fort Worth Division, to avoid the confusion.

Gary Allen early in 1982 described himself as "well pleased" with the business and income for the first two months, although the winter season constituted the slower period for the market. His only disappointment was that he had not cut labor costs as much as he thought he could. By the end of that year Allen said that he was "gratified" that the stockyards had done 15 percent more cattle business that year than in 1981. In the summer of 1983 Allen signed a ten-year contract with United Stockyards to lease the stockyards facilities. He admitted, however, that the signing was more to offset the publicity about the Billy Bob's stockyards development program than an indication that he planned to be in business that long. News stories of Billy Bob's group of investors who planned to lease stockyards land for a $45 million Western tourist attraction made people assume that the active livestock market had closed. Allen received thirty to forty telephone calls a day after the development stories appeared in the newspaper, asking if he was shutting down. Traffic from Billy Bob's night club already hurt the Sunday night unloading of animals for a Monday sale, for truckers often found it difficult to get through to the unloading docks. Yet Allen wanted to stay and keep an active stockyards open.[27]

"As long as I'm making money, well, can squeeze out a little profit, I'll be here," he said. Allen and his coworkers admitted that they had other financial interests than the stockyards and remained in

26. Interview with Dan Van Ackeren, Packers and Stockyards Administration, Fort Worth, December 16, 1981.
27. Interview with Gary Allen, Fort Worth, January 20, 1982; interview with Gary Allen, Azle, June 14, 1983.

business there because it had always been their way of life and they enjoyed it.[28]

Canal-Randolph Corporation, owner of United Stockyards and of the land and facilities of the Fort Worth yards, divested itself of its United stock in 1984, and United became independent again. United leased all of its Fort Worth real estate to Triad Corporation, the Billy Bob's investors, giving the lease held by Gary Allen and the Fort Worth Stockyards the status of a sublease under Triad. On December 31, 1984, United Stockyards closed its Fort Worth office, with the retired Elmo Klingenberg kept on retainer to see after its facilities in Fort Worth.[29]

Then Gary Allen surprised nearly everyone and sold out his stock in the Niles City Cattle Company dba Fort Worth Stockyards as of December 31, 1985, to Hampton Butler, who had been one of his employees since 1981. Butler had been a fixture on the yards since 1961, when he had gone to work for Drive-In Commission Company. He had assumed the management of John Clay Commission Company in 1973 and operated it until 1981.

In order to cut costs Butler cut cattle sales back to Monday only, plus the last-Thursday-of-the-month sale, and condensed hog sales to three days instead of four. He employed twenty people, about half of them full-time. January, 1986, began with more cattle arrivals than usual, but sales proved extremely light in the late spring because of excessive rains. Nevertheless, he operated in the black and determined to continue the live market as long as he could profitably do so. He planned to sign one-year leases with stockyards investors who held the lease from United.[30]

While Sunday traffic at Billy Bob's Texas has continued to hamper cattle producers unloading at the docks on that day for the Monday sale, both Butler and the Billy Bob's investors have been determined to work out the parking problems. It has been in both their interests to keep an active market going in the stockyards area.

Thus a company calling itself the Fort Worth Stockyards con-

28. Collective interview with Gary Allen, Bill King, Doc Wilbanks, Fort Worth, November 3, 1983.

29. Interview with L. Van Kuhl, Fort Worth, October 23, 1984; interview with Kathy Rainey, Fort Worth, January 28, 1985.

30. Interview with Hampton Butler, Fort Worth, June 10, 1986.

tinues to operate in updated and renovated facilities on the city's close-in North Side. Since 1887 the market has undergone six changes of ownership, since 1893 under the same name. While tourists have begun to arrive in larger and larger numbers wanting to see a live cow or two, not even 100,000 animals now pass through the market yearly. Since cattle are sold only on Monday, it is no wonder that few people ever hear a bawling cow any more or smell the distinctive odor that once clearly identified the site as a stockyards. Tourists had become more visible than livestock on Exchange Avenue by the mid-1980s.[31]

31. The Fort Worth Stockyards' six changes of ownership include the 1893 purchase of the Fort Worth Union Stock Yards by Simpson and Niles, the 1902 reorganization giving two-thirds ownership to Armour and Swift, the 1944 complete purchase of stock and dissolving of the corporation by United Stockyards, the 1959 takeover of United by Canal-Randolph, the lease-agreement in 1981, and Hampton Butler's purchase of Allen's company.

15

A City's Heritage

AN OLD-TIMER who had spent nearly fifty years as a trader at the Fort Worth Stockyards described how bad a place it was to work—swelteringly hot in summer, with animal pens steaming from the crowded, milling bodies, and miserably cold in winter, when ice sometimes formed on the boardwalks, fences, and the animals themselves. But before he finished his conversation he remembered the people he knew there and the associations he formed. Because he knew he worked with the "finest people in the world," he concluded, "it was a great place to work." Reminiscing about their years at the yards usually affected people that way.[1]

Many who worked there, whether as independent traders, commission agents, buyers for a packer, or stockyards company employees, stayed forty or even fifty or more years. They loved it and agreed that it was a "great place to work."

Thus, an influence on thousands of individual lives might be the most valuable heritage the stockyards leaves. However, the impact the Fort Worth Stockyards Company and its related livestock industries made on metropolitan Fort Worth is clear and undeniable. They made a city: Cowtown! DeWitt McKinley, a former mayor, once stated, "The roots of Fort Worth are on the North Side of that river

---

1. Interview with Manson Reese, Fort Worth, October 29, 1983.

and I think we would be foolish to neglect or forget the heritage that we have."[2]

Relatively little history had been recorded about the North Side area of Fort Worth until a renewal came in the mid-1970s. Most of the blue-collar workers living there had little time or inclination for historical appreciation, and the out-of-state big business interests that owned the major industry in the area remained aloof from preserving local history. Most of the city's recorded history reflected the downtown area rather than the stockyards district, even though the latter represented a more significant past. Much interest in preserving the history and heritage of the stockyards began in 1975, however, when Charlie McCafferty and other North Side residents formed the North Fort Worth Historical Society, prompted by watching the old city hall of Niles City on Decatur Avenue being demolished to make way for a parking lot. McCafferty called the North Side "the heart and the muscle of Fort Worth" because the larger city would not have reached its metropolitan status had it not been for the livestock interests of the stockyards district. McCafferty became the first president of the North Fort Worth Historical Society, and the group began working to get historical markers for various buildings and locations and cooperating with other organizations to promote the area. In 1978 the society received a one-thousand-dollar grant from the National Trust for Historic Preservation to aid its efforts. The society's plans for Texas' Sesquicentennial year of 1986 called for the dedication of one historical marker each month in the area.[3]

The massive redevelopment effort that finally took place in the stockyards district in the late 1970s could not have been accomplished through the actions of the historical society or North Side residents alone; they needed the help of the city of Fort Worth. The North Fort Worth Business Association had been urging redevelopment for years and had set as their goal "a struggle for rebirth and a halt to decay."[4]

2. Jon McConal, "North Side Beating Image after Doldrums of Mid-1950s," *Fort Worth Star-Telegram*, August 13, 1978.
3. Raymond Teague, "N. Side Organizes History," ibid., September 23, 1976 (morn.).
4. Mary Abrego, "A Struggle for Rebirth and a Halt to Decay," *Northwest Passage*, April 7, 1976, p. 5.

Fort Worth officials divided the city of Fort Worth into geographical areas for planning purposes in the 1960s and in 1971 completed the Northeast Sector Plan, encompassing the stockyards area. At that time they recommended that the stockyards be redeveloped to aid the economy:

> The core area contains the highest concentration of features which may be restored and redeveloped as a tourist and commercial center. . . . The area's key features are the buildings and industries which have most significantly influenced the Fort Worth economy.[5]

In the 1970s Fort Worth began falling rapidly behind Dallas, Fort Worth's rival city across the Trinity, in convention bookings, so Fort Worth had to try to compete. When Fort Worth finally decided to try to reverse and halt the tide of unemployment and decay, it represented the first really concentrated redevelopment effort undertaken by the city.[6]

By 1972 the City Planning Department labeled about four hundred acres as the Stockyards Intensive Study Area. It contained 150 businesses, many of them agribusinesses, including the Fort Worth Stockyards Company. The area encompassed Meacham Field on the north, Samuels Avenue on the east, downtown on the south, and a jagged line on the west as far as Rosen. Then in April, 1972, the Fort Worth City Council appointed a sixteen-member Stockyards Area Restoration Committee to supervise both private and public redevelopment. Jack Shannon of Shannon's Funeral Home on North Main, his family long-time residents of North Side, chaired the committee. Included were other leading members of the North Fort Worth Business Association. This Stockyards Area Restoration Committee (SARC) in 1973 raised money for an economic-feasibility study, which concluded that a redevelopment effort was a "viable venture." A Stockyards Area Redevelopment Office opened July 19, 1974, in ceremonies at the Livestock Exchange Building, and Wilford "Butch"

5. Fort Worth, Texas, *Northeast Sector Plan*, Vol. II: *Fort Worth General Plan*, (1971), p. 77.
6. Interview with Jim Wilson, Economic Development Coordinator for the City of Fort Worth, 1977–80, Fort Worth, January 6, 1982.

Saxton became senior planner on the stockyards project. More than $400,000 in federal renovation funds from the Economic Development Administration for a Public Works Impact Program was available at that time. Congressman Jim Wright, who later helped obtain additional federal funds, spoke at the ceremonies. The projects at that time consisted of restoring the Marine Creek area, building a park, constructing three miles of bike trails, and renovating the city-owned North Side Coliseum. By 1975 the Economic Development Administration designated the North Side as a Special Impact Area, which allowed for additional federal funding. The Stockyards Restoration Project at that time became an official Bicentennial Project for the city. Promoters that year successfully persuaded the National Register of Historic Places to add the stockyards area to its prestigious list.[7]

The Fort Worth Economic Development Policy Board agreed unanimously on June 7, 1977, to recommend that the stockyards area receive $2 million in public works funds from the U.S. Economic Development Administration; the City Council later also approved application for the funds. The stockyards area, with a 19-percent unemployment rate, topped a list of seven sections of Fort Worth which had high unemployment and could benefit from federally financed construction work. The stockyards headed the list because street and sidewalk improvements there coincided with a long-time goal of many persons seeking to rejuvenate a historical city and because it would most benefit the neighborhood. Soon fifteen hundred feet of East Exchange Avenue had a brick surface, which had been the original covering, instead of the more recent asphalt paving. The project also reconstructed sidewalks of several streets in

7. Wilmer D. Mizell, Assistant Secretary for Economic Development, U.S. Department of Commerce, to Mayor R. M. Stovall, City of Fort Worth, April 24, 1975, copy in Jim Wilson's Office, City Hall; Fort Worth, City Council, *Minutes,* April 3, 1972, p. 2; "Evaluation of Fort Worth Stockyards Restoration Potentials—Phase I," prepared for Fort Worth Stockyards Restoration Committee by Economic Research Associates, Los Angeles, California, July 26, 1973, p. II-2; interview with Jack Shannon, Fort Worth, January 14, 1982; "Fort Worth Stockyards Area Redevelopment Project, Summary of Public Expenditures for the Period July 1972 through September 1978," list on file in office of Jim Wilson, City Hall, Fort Worth. See also Fort Worth, City Council, *Minutes,* November 18, 1974, pp. 466–67.

the area and placed decorative antique lighting as well as street furniture and landscaping. Workers also landscaped Marine Creek from Exchange Avenue to Twenty-third Street.[8]

By early 1978 some $4.4 million of public funds, mostly from the Economic Development Administration, had attracted nearly $7 million in private investment and created at least 660 new jobs in the area. North Siders gave a big party in the Horse and Mule Barns on October 20, 1978, to thank Congressman Wright for his help. City officials agreed that because of Wright's influence Fort Worth had received "millions of dollars of funds and grants." That year the city hired a public relations firm to promote the redevelopment activities. They adopted the Longhorn steer as the logo for the area in all its publicity and advertising. Rodger Line, the city manager of Fort Worth during much of the early stockyards restoration, called the overall project one of the "real success stories of the city-federal-private sector partnership program."[9]

Funds from a National Endowment of the Arts Grant and matching funds from the Fort Worth Junior League, with some additional administrative money supplied by the League — all totaled, $10,000 — allowed a one-year adaptive re-use study in 1978. Texas Heritage, Inc., the North Fort Worth Historical Society, and the Fort Worth Chapter of the American Institute of Architects used the funds to make an inventory of all historically and architecturally significant structures and sites of the North Side.[10]

Concurrent with the city-sponsored Stockyards Redevelopment Project came a renewed city-wide interest in the stockyards area and in the city's Western roots, so in 1977 the Chamber of Commerce sponsored a Chisholm Trail Roundup. Events scattered all over town included a Western writers' workshop at Texas Christian University, a roundup ride for several miles from south of town on horseback, and several activities at the Tarrant County Convention Center. The Chisholm Trail Days moved to the stockyards area, became an anticipated annual event the second weekend in June, and in 1980

8. Ibid., June 16, 1977, pp. 490–91.
9. Wilson interview; Rodger N. Line, to author, March 8, 1982.
10. *North Fort Worth Architectural/Historical Survey and Adaptive Reuse Studies*, pages not numbered. See also Stan Baker's Report to the North Fort Worth Historical Society, Auction Barn, Stockyards Area, November 17, 1978.

it coincided with Flag Day on June 14. The North Fort Worth Historical Society raised a flag on the cupola of the exchange building for the first time in forty years.[11]

Pioneer Days also continued and gained impetus as more and more Fort Worth residents set aside the third weekend in September each year for the annual festivities, which had begun in 1957. Each year it included a Pioneer Days Queen contest, art exhibits, booths of crafts and gift items, ethnic food concessions, a chili cook-off, and beginning in 1978 a "Stockyards Stampede," a 4.5-mile run, which also became an annual event. All contestants in the Stampede received T-shirts, and proceeds went to the American Cancer Society. Other regular Pioneer Days activities included shootouts, wagon rides, a carnival, Western bands and singers, historic bus tours, and a major parade with riding clubs, bands, floats, and queen contestants. The North Fort Worth Business Association rarely made any money from Pioneer Days in the early years and indeed usually donated about twenty thousand dollars to stage it. For the 1984 Pioneer Days, which promoters called the Twenty-fifth Annual (having skipped a couple of years), they invited Western stars Ben Johnson, Clint Walker, James Drury, Buck Taylor, Chuck Connors, and Dale Robertson as judges of a National Gunfight/Stunt Competition. The North Fort Worth Historical Society cooperated with both Chisholm Trail Days and Pioneer Days to provide children's activities in a huge tent called the Little Buckaroo Corral.[12]

Further evidence of interest in providing entertainment and preserving the city's Western heritage in the stockyards area came in October, 1975, when Steve Murrin became manager of the North Side Coliseum, the building the Fort Worth Stockyards Company had constructed in 1908 for the stock show. Murrin signed a contract with the City of Fort Worth to lease the structure, created Cowtown Coliseum Consortium, Inc., and brought rodeo back to the North Side on October 9–11, 1975. Murrin's father had worked on the yards for a cattle buyer from 1903 to 1918 and had later raised cattle. The

11. "Flags Flags Flags," *Tarrant County Historical Commission News* 1 (July, 1980): 5.

12. Robert Seltzer, "Restoration Reveals Pioneer Spirit," *Fort Worth Star-Telegram*, September 27, 1979 (morn.). See also "200,000 People to Plunge into Fun of Pioneer Days," ibid., September 22, 1984 (morn.).

rodeo, staged twenty-week seasons for eight years, but beginning in the spring of 1983, organized a few special rodeos and awaited news of further restoration grants and redevelopment plans for the coliseum before continuing its schedule.

The Cowtown Marathon, ranked as the best marathon in the state by *Running Through Texas* Magazine, began in 1979 and is held in February each year. A sheriff on horseback fires a gun to start the race in the stockyards area, and it ends back at the Cowtown Coliseum twenty-five miles later.

With an annual Cowtown Marathon in February, Chisholm Trail Days in mid-June, Pioneer Days late in September, rodeos, and other events like Christmas in the Stockyards (held for the first time in 1984), the eyes of the city were certain to be found on the stockyards district more frequently than in the past. When the Tarrant County Historical Society published a new *Historic Guide* in 1984, it devoted an entire chapter to the stockyards. Their previous guide twenty-one years earlier had ignored it.[13]

The success of the stockyards area in revitalizing itself as a business community dedicated to preserving the Western heritage in the 1980s finally depended almost solely upon the willingness of private businessmen to invest and get involved. The area provided an excellent business community, for it lay within five minutes of both downtown Fort Worth and a municipal airport. The area held the potential for industrial growth because little residential development existed. Commercial establishments promoting tourism would be favorably received as well.

The most ambitious Western-style tourist enterprise to start in the stockyards district was Billy Bob's Texas, which opened in April, 1981. With 127,000 square feet, it was billed as the largest night club in the world, surpassing Gilley's in Houston by a few hundred feet. The night spot accommodated between 5,000 and 6,000 customers and brought in well-known country-and-Western singers. The club featured live bulls and professional bull riders. The owners renovated a building behind the coliseum that the city of Fort Worth had built as a show barn for the stock show more than forty years earlier. It

13. Ruby Schmidt, ed., *Fort Worth and Tarrant County: A Historical Guide*, pp. 27–30.

was the same building in which the stockyards held their first auctions in 1959.

To provide further private development money, local supporters looked to Canal-Randolph, the New York- and London-based real estate development corporation that owned United Stockyards, the parent company of the Fort Worth Stockyards Company. It also held acres of what once had been cattle pens and the land along Exchange Avenue where the brick horse and mule barns and the decaying sheep and hog pens stood. Residents hopefully anticipated the construction of a big Mule Alley shopping mall, utilizing the existing structures, but Canal-Randolph remained publicly non-committed. Fort Worth Chamber of Commerce President Bill Shelton believed that smaller investors who might enter business in the area were holding off and waiting to see what Canal-Randolph would do. After a long wait, Canal-Randolph signed a memorandum of intent with a group of Fort Worth businessmen on July 16, 1982, which would transform the area into a nostalgic and authentic Old West entertainment and tourist attraction.[14]

Late in 1983 five private investors announced their plans for a $45 million, eighty-six-acre Western entertainment complex calculated to draw from 2.5 to 4 million persons during a four-month summer season. They planned parking facilities, a restaurant, an international market, an amphitheater, and the renovation of the horse and mule barns. Obtaining federal funding for public grants to renovate the city-owned Cowtown Coliseum and do some street work got delayed, and some investors dropped out. When Canal-Randolph divested itself of its United properties, it cancelled its participation. The continuing investors, Billy Bob Barnett, co-owner of Billy Bob's Texas night club and William Beuck II, a developer, reevaluated and scaled down their plans. They realized that the major value of the area was its Western authenticity. For nearly a century it had been a working cattle and horse area. They decided to keep the area architecturally and operationally authentic and design it for the repeat person rather than primarily for the one-time tourist. In 1984 they persuaded the Texas Longhorn Breeders Asso-

14. Interview with Bill Shelton, Fort Worth, July 29, 1980; *Annual Report,* Canal-Randolph Corporation, 1982, copy in possession of author.

ciation to move their headquarters to the area and to establish a museum. In anticipation of this, the breeders dedicated the largest bronze structure in the world — several Longhorn cattle — on the site in December, 1984. The facility actually represents the national headquarters for Longhorn breeding.

The investors also decided to work to increase cattle sales and to broaden the scope to include ranch sales and youth activities. Moreover, the existing Cowtown Coliseum, where the first indoor rodeo in the world was held in 1918, provides the potential for competition in horse activities, such as rodeo and cutting horse events.

Western retail and manufacturing also will be broadened. Business offices of music production companies are being encouraged to move to the area. "We're not trying to create an amusement park anymore. Tourists are more interested in the real thing, not something contrived," explained Bill Beuck.[15]

The $23 million first phase of the new locally financed development plans began April 1, 1985, with the construction of twenty-eight acres of landscaped and secured parking. Plans also called for the city of Fort Worth to spend $2.8 million to renovate the coliseum.

Beuck and fellow businessmen interested in the tourist and entertainment development of the area took a positive step forward in April, 1985, when Triad, Inc., and Stockyard Investment Inc. created "Stockyards '85" to raise capital. Principal investors in the two partner corporations included Beuck, Billy Bob Barnett, Don Guggenheim, Don Jury, and Bill Lund. They hired Robert Walters, a banker with twenty-five years' experience, principally with Nowlin Savings in Fort Worth and Ben Franklin Savings in Houston, to head the new Stockyards '85 as the president and chief executive officer.

Under Walters's direction the stockyards development has moved at a more rapid pace. While the Triad corporation employed about two hundred persons in April, 1985, within a year Stockyards '85 hired a large staff of key individuals with experience in entertainment and employed approximately eight hundred persons by summer of 1986. Construction began on the Brown Derby restaurant and the renovation of the Commerce Street exhibit buildings in July, 1985, and was completed and opened by July, 1986. Inside the exhibit

15. Interview with William Beuck II, Fort Worth, February 19, 1985.

buildings a Mexican restaurant called Sam's Place, the Silver Spur Saloon, and various speciality shops also opened in the summer of 1986, completing Phase I.

Phase II of their plans include the renovation of the horse and mule barns and construction of a year-round arena, to seat sixty-five hundred persons, for larger events than could be accommodated in the coliseum. Completion of Phase II was projected for 1987 or 1988.[16]

An exciting kick-off event for the opening of the new facilities of Phase I occurred June 1, 1986, when festivities took place in the newly restored city-owned coliseum to rededicate the facility and unveil a historical marker commemorating the historic events that had taken place in the building since its original 1908 opening. The ceremony marked the beginning of more than a month of activities that culminated in the arrival of the Sesquicentennial Wagon Train, which ended its six-month trek through Texas at the Stockyards in Fort Worth on July 3.

Among the activities in June, 1986, were a Winston Tour Rodeo June 5–8 with more than 130 of the nation's top pro rodeo cowboys and cowgirls competing for over $150,000 in prize money. The Stockyards Weekly Rodeo continued every Friday and Saturday night in June and would continue through November. In addition, the tenth annual Chisholm Trail Roundup took place at the stockyards June 13–15.

That promoters of the Sesquicentennial Wagon Train chose to schedule the conclusion of their six-month saga in the Fort Worth Stockyards proved significant. It illustrated that when many people think of Texas, they visualize cattle and a Western heritage. The Fort Worth Stockyards epitomizes both.

That increased commercial activity and tourism represented a significant future for the stockyards area began to be obvious as early as the mid-1970s, when small businesses that had been there twenty or thirty years, such as Ryon's Saddle and Ranch Supplies or M. L. Leddy and Sons Boots, reported an increase in business volume. In 1976 a restaurant chain known as the Old Spaghetti Warehouse spent $3 million to renovate and decorate the old Swift and Company office

16. Interview with Robert Walters, Fort Worth, June 2, 1986.

building, opening on June 1. Joe Dulle, a brother-in-law of Steve Murrin, managed the White Elephant Saloon, the Lone Star Chili Parlor and Beer Garden, and the Stockyards Drug Store, all of which saw greatly increased business. Investors began renovating the old hotels such as the Hereford, the Maverick, and the Right Hotel, reopening the Right late in 1983 as the elaborate Stockyards Hotel.[17]

Tourism would catch on in the area, many promoters believed, because the district possessed three excellent selling points: it was old, authentic, and Western. The bars of Exchange Avenue once separated the cowboy from his money, but by the mid-1980s stockyards-area business establishments planned to relieve area residents and tourists of their cash instead. Thus the area had changed from a major cattle center to a major tourist attraction and recreational complex because of the real history that took place there.

That livestock interests provided a vital beginning for the growth of Fort Worth from small community to thriving metropolis is brought out by those who have studied the growth of Fort Worth since its origin in 1849 as a military outpost on the bluff overlooking two forks of the Trinity River. One historian cites several stages of development in the growth of the city: military outpost, county seat of Tarrant County, oasis on the cattle trail, coming of the railroad, development as a livestock processing center, development of West Texas oil fields, military installation during World War I, and aircraft manufacture and diversified industry. One writer, however, narrowed the city's growth to four dates that stood out in Fort Worth's first one hundred years: the coming of the Texas and Pacific Railroad on July 19, 1876, the laying of the cornerstone of Armour's and Swift's plants on March 13, 1902, the discovery of oil at Ranger on October 27, 1917, and the ground-breaking for Consolidated Vultee Aircraft Corporation on April 18, 1941. In any list of milestones livestock-related items will dominate the first half, and by that time Fort Worth had become an important city. Early city promoter B. B. Paddock stated, "All agree that the factor next in importance to the

17. Sharla Marks, "The Stockyards Are Alive and Well," *Fort Worth* 52 (December, 1976): 39; "Fort Worth Yards New Face Begins to Take Shape," *Weekly Livestock Reporter*, April 29, 1976, p. 30.

railroads in conferring prosperity and substantial greatness on Fort Worth has been the creation of a live-stock market through the instrumentality of stock yards and packing houses."[18]

The livestock industry was the greatest single industry of the nation during the last years of the nineteenth century and until World War I, so Fort Worth built its base alongside. In the twelve years preceding World War I the livestock market poured $550 million into the city's economy. During the war a million dollars a week entered the pockets of producers of cattle, hogs, sheep, horses, and mules at the Fort Worth Stockyards. Throughout the 1920s and 1930s livestock and meat processing remained "the largest industry of Fort Worth."[19]

Even late in the 1940s an advertisement for Texas Electric Service Company showed a picture of the "canyon" between the tall buildings of Seventh Street in downtown Fort Worth and proclaimed in the cutline, "Cattle Helped Build This Canyon." The advertisement continued with information that the West Texas livestock industry, along with oil and farm products, was "the foundation of Fort Worth's business and industrial prosperity." Even in the 1950s the Fort Worth Chamber of Commerce called "cattle, grain, and oil" the city's "principal corpuscles." Writers still claimed by the 1960s that the "livestock industry of the Southwest, through its various ramifications contributes more wealth to the economy of the area than any other," citing transportation, feeds, grains, equipment, entertainment, and supplies, and in fact "every phase of business from finance to government. . . . It would be difficult to single out any business that is not touched by the livestock industry and profits therefrom." So even in a period of the stockyards company's own decline, the city and the industries that grew from the impetus of the stockyards and meat packing continued solidly. Through the

---

18. Robert H. Talbert, *Cowtown-Metropolis: Case Study of a City's Growth and Structure*, pp. 22–23; "50 Years Ago Fort Worth Began Flirting with Meat Packers," *Fort Worth* 26 (March, 1951): 32. See also "Fort Worth," *Cattleman* 33 (March, 1947): 145–46; B. B. Paddock, ed., *A Twentieth Century History and Biographical Record of North and West Texas* I, 198.

19. Clarence Arnold Thompson, "Some Factors Contributing to the Growth of Fort Worth," Master's thesis, University of Texas at Austin, 1933, p. 79.

years Fort Worth developed other industries, but "cattle carried it from 1900 through World War II." Thus, "the cattle industry is credited with providing the foundation for Fort Worth."[20]

In comparison with livestock markets nationwide, the Fort Worth Stockyards performed well. It remained the largest marketing center in the entire Southwest for at least sixty years of its existence and the largest south of Kansas City for the same time. Soon after its establishment as a packing center, Fort Worth began to challenge the mighty Chicago, and some thought Cowtown might even surpass the Windy City. At some periods Fort Worth tallied second only to Chicago in cattle and calf receipts. To attract hogs, Fort Worth remained the highest-paying hog market in the country for a number of years. By World War I Fort Worth developed into the largest horse and mule market in the United States, which meant the largest in the world, as Fort Worth sold animals to domestic and foreign governments for their cavalry. During some months of 1914 more than $100,000 per day changed hands at the stockyards. The horse and mule market continued to hold up well even into the 1920s. Although receipts of various categories of livestock varied from year to year, Fort Worth generally ranked fifth or sixth in cattle and calves, and often the total receipts of the market made it third or fourth overall, particularly throughout the 1930s. Then by World War II Fort Worth developed into the largest sheep market in the nation and world and remained so during most of the 1940s. Quite clearly, then, the Fort Worth Stockyards and meat-processing plants functioned as the major industry of Fort Worth for at least a half-century, threatened the big market centers of the nation, and ranked consistently in the top four or five as a market nationally.[21]

The most obvious result of this achievement is that it made Fort

20. "Cattle Helped Build This Canyon," Texas Electric Service Company Advertisement, Fort Worth 21 (October, 1947): 6; "This Is Fort Worth, Texas," ibid., 26 (November, 1951): 7; "A Salute to the Livestock Industry," Weekly Live Stock Reporter, July 14, 1966, p. 1; Linda Gilliam, "Northside Stockyard Area Weathers Hard Times; Hopes Run High as Renovation Efforts Continue," Dallas/Fort Worth Business, March 27, 1978, p. 6; "Entertainment—Stock Show," in "Star-Telegram Country," Fort Worth Star-Telegram Special Section, August 2, 1981.

21. "Fort Worth Now Second to Chicago in Calves Receipts," Texas Stockman-Journal, January 1, 1908, p. 3; "Horse Trade Now Brings In More Than $100,000

Worth forever into Cowtown. First the trail drivers who came through Fort Worth for a supply stop on their way to markets in Kansas and then the men with vision who brought the railroads, stockyards, and packing plants contributed the title to the frontier community. Fort Worth later became an industrial giant but retained its image as a Westerner who, if he walked away somewhat from the stockyards district, nonetheless was still wearing a cowboy hat and boots. With all the redevelopment, now Fort Worthians are walking back to the stockyards for entertainment, again in boots and hat. A newspaperman put it well: "We were born 'Cow Town' and as 'Cow Town' we will become immortal." A Fort Worth boy dating an Oklahoma girl in the 1940s asked her to write him a letter and put Cowtown for Fort Worth in the address. Even in that day before zip codes, he got his letter with no delay.[22]

One measure of the importance of the livestock market at the Fort Worth Stockyards is the number of other livestock-related industries and organizations generated by it. These include numerous milling firms, many for livestock and poultry feeds, which made Fort Worth the milling center of the Southwest. The city remained the nation's second-largest grain center into the 1970s. Two of Fort Worth's oldest banking institutions, the First National (now Interfirst) and the Fort Worth National (now Texas American Fort Worth), originated around the cattle business. In the 1970s a new aspect of livestock's impact on Fort Worth appeared when the metropolitan banks began seeking to finance the booming feedlot production of beef. Several laboratories in Fort Worth experimented with serums to prevent animal disease and thus made the city a leader in research and development of animal pharmaceuticals. Other allied industries included boot and saddle makers, manufacturing facilities for cat-

---

Daily," *Fort Worth Daily Live Stock Reporter,* November 5, 1914, p. 1; Thompson, "Some Factors Contributing to the Growth of Fort Worth," p. 122. See also Verna Elizabeth Berrong, "History of Tarrant County from Its Beginning until 1875," Master's thesis, Texas Christian University, 1938, p. 61; *An Economic Survey of Tarrant County,* Prepared for the Texas and Pacific Railway Company by the Bureau of Business Research, College of Business Administration, University of Texas, June 1949, p. 4.

22. "Cowtown," *Cattleman* 14 (January, 1928): 13–14; interview with Irene Francis, Fort Worth, August 21, 1979.

tle trailers, Western apparel shops, and livestock fencing and watering equipment.[23]

First among the organizations the stockyards either created or fostered at its market, one must place the annual Southwestern Exposition and Fat Stock Show. It has been impossible to put a dollar figure on the economic importance of the show to Fort Worth, but the Chamber of Commerce has estimated that more than $100 million is spent by visitors each year during the twelve-day show. The show has been recognized as one of the four major stock shows of America and is, according to Delbert Bailey, the show's publicist, "without a doubt Fort Worth's biggest annual event." The show chalked up a record gate attendance in 1987 of 741,200. It features the largest quarter horse gathering at any North American livestock show and is one of the top three rodeos in the nation. It boasts of being the world's first indoor rodeo and the oldest continuously held annual livestock show in the nation. The Will Rogers Memorial Center Cultural District's one hundred acres, forty-five of which are under roof, make the combined livestock and museum facilities the largest municipally owned facilities of their kind in the United States.[24]

Numerous livestock organizations located their headquarters in Fort Worth in the early days because of their close connection with the local market. These include the American Paint Horse Association, the National Cutting Horse Association, the Texas Angus Association, the Texas Hereford Association, the Texas Longhorn Breeders Association, and the Texas and Southwestern Cattle Raisers Association. The *Weekly Livestock Reporter*, the largest livestock newspaper in the Southwest, began in 1896 as the subsidized publication of the Fort Worth Stockyards Company. The 4-H and Future Farmers of America movement in the state benefited

23. Interview with Wayne C. Jordan, Senior Vice-President, Agricultural Loan Department, Fort Worth National Bank, Fort Worth, January 6, 1982; "World's Largest Serum and Vaccine Plant Locates Here," *Fort Worth Daily Live Stock Reporter*, November 20, 1918, p. 1.

24. Interviews with Delbert Bailey, Southwestern Exposition and Fat Stock Show Publicity Director, Fort Worth, August 11, 1981, November 15, 1983, and February 18, 1985.

greatly from the pig clubs C. C. French organized from 1909 to 1914.[25]

In addition, the West Texas Chamber of Commerce, the first regional chamber in the world, exists as an organization because the Fort Worth Chamber of Commerce started it, largely to develop the relationship between West Texas communities and Fort Worth with its livestock industry. The stockyards also influenced highway construction into Fort Worth to aid the transportation of livestock to their market. In the early days the company encouraged new railroad lines to come to Fort Worth. In addition, the stockyards engineer became the moving force behind the Tarrant County Water Control District No. 1, perhaps more to prevent so many disastrous floods in the stockyards area than to provide water reservoirs for a growing city. It was the first such district in the state.[26]

Despite all the important things the stockyard fostered, what it did not become may be just as significant historically as what it became. Fort Worth never became the number one market in the country, surpassing Chicago, even though the packers who owned two-thirds of it intended for it to do so. They constructed their most modern plants in Fort Worth, the heart of the livestock-producing area. Lack of sufficient hog receipts at the market kept other large packers from building plants in Fort Worth. Thus even cattle slaughter did not expand to its potential. Perhaps the fault lies with the packers who, seeing a lack of hogs in Texas, should have slaughtered only cattle at Fort Worth. They would not change their method of doing business to fit a different situation. Early-day editor Ray McKinley explained, "It is generally accepted that packing houses should kill five head of hogs for every head of cattle." Market growth would come to Fort Worth "when the farmers have been educated thoroughly." Unfortunately, not enough farmers ever became con-

25. Doug Perkins, "The Ranchers' Detective," *Fort Worth* 52 (January, 1976): 16.
26. R. Wright Armstrong, Amon G. Carter, Jr., J. B. Thomas, and W. L. Pier to Sherman Beasley, June 10, 1952, West Texas Chamber of Commerce Folder, Pier Corr. Fort Worth Stockyards Company Collection, North Texas State University Archives, Denton; W. L. Pier to J. A. Gooch, February 4, 1959, Chamber of Commerce Folder, ibid. See also W. L. Joyce to D. C. Greer, State Highway Engineer, January 18, 1959, Highways Folder, ibid.; W. L. Pier to Otto Frederick, October 21, 1948, General Corr. Folder, ibid.

vinced they should raise more hogs. Like the packers, they would not change. By being too much Cowtown—too focused on cattle—Texans limited their own potential in refusing to accept hogs, the product that would have induced more packers to come and would have made Fort Worth an even greater packing center in its early years than it became. The name Cowtown appealed more than Hogtown.[27]

Boston money organized the Fort Worth Stockyards Company in 1893, and Chicago money expanded the market in 1902 when the packers came. One must not forget, however, that the market nevertheless became uniquely Texan. "Texan" often means ruggedly individualistic, independent, slow to change, proud, and perhaps even stubborn. Had city fathers like B. B. Paddock, John Peter Smith, Khleber M. Van Zandt, and others not been so stubborn in just not giving up, Fort Worth might never have had a livestock market or a railroad at all. The wholehearted pride in their market that local citizens felt transferred itself to enthusiastic support of any endeavor associated with it, most especially the annual stock show. Fort Worth and Texans bragged about their market during its first half-century because much of the economy of the city revolved around it. But then in later years when things slowed down, the commission companies often complained about the Fort Worth Stockyards Company and its officials as big-business absentee owners; local companies retained independence and resisted change in their businesses. Texas farmers and ranchers through the years also remained independent and tied to tradition and as a result limited themselves and their own market. Then in the 1950s and 1960s they ceased to sell at the terminal market, where volume buying could have set higher competitive prices.

Texans thus contributed to the course their market followed, particularly the dominance by cattle. It is likely, however, that Texas never could have raised enough hogs to be the number one market, and that later nothing could have halted the movement toward decentralized local auctions or feedlots in Texas because of the large

27. Ray H. McKinley, "North Fort Worth Will Be Nation's Meat Market," *Fort Worth Daily Live Stock Reporter*, June 30, 1914, p. 3; "Dold Party Visits Local Yards; Is Highly Pleased," ibid., May 10, 1915, p. 1.

geographic area the state covers. Producers just naturally would drive shorter distances to market once trucks replaced rail shipments. Even so, the livestock producers who became the customers of the Fort Worth Stockyards and the Texans who worked there influenced it greatly, just as its existence altered Fort Worth's history and destiny.

Epilogue

CHANGES ARE OCCURRING RAPIDLY in the historic district of North Fort Worth known as the Fort Worth Stockyards. This area includes the facilities of the company, which still hosts a livestock auction each Monday, as well as the properties of business investors who own nightclubs, hotels, and restaurants. Each year brings innovations, historic celebrations, and changed renovation plans. The year 1987 certainly witnessed all of these.

One company that opened an office in the Livestock Exchange Building early in the year—Superior Livestock Auction—has been introducing major innovations to the stockyards. The company sells cattle in televised auctions transmitted by satellite all across the United States, Canada, and Mexico. Of the forty-six thousand animals sold on March 21, 1987 for over $2 million, 90 percent were purchased by telephone by buyers who viewed the sale, which originated in Billy Bob's Texas, over the closed-circuit cable network. The sale represented the largest one-day auction of cattle ever. Although the company is separate from the auction market still operating on the yards, the setting of the Fort Worth stockyards area seemed appropriate for the record-breaking activity.

The direction for future business development—for the purpose of attracting tourist dollars to the stockyards—seemed unclear late in 1987. The company calling itself Stockyards '85 owned by Billy Bob Barnett and his associates, held options on some property that once belonged to United Stockyards. Their plans have vacillated during the year between an open-air amphitheater and a collection of shops and restaurants in renovated Horse and Mule Barns. Which direction the private investments may take remains in question. Representatives of Lloyds of London even visited during the year to examine the facilities with the possibility of providing funding. The City of Fort Worth has applied for and received an $11.8 million grant from the Economic Development Administration, which it plans to use in the stockyards area. This is in addition to $15 million in grant monies already spent between 1974 and 1986. The city has considered either lending the new money to private investors or purchasing the Exchange Building and Exhibit Hall and maintaining them itself. An additional $20 million of federal funds has been appropriated to the Corps of Engineers to spend on flood-control projects in the stockyards. New jobs and additional activity can be expected in the stockyards once these projects are undertaken. However, because plans are incomplete, implementation may be delayed.

Unfortunately, increased tourist and business activity, although welcome and necessary to further development of the stockyards area, hamper livestock producers as they bring their livestock to the stockyards for sale at the Monday auction. Producers do not appreciate being asked to pay to park in Billy Bob's Texas night club parking lot. The differing activities in the area seem less conducive than in the past to traditional livestock sales. Consequently these sales continue to dwindle.

The most important event that occurred in 1987 in the stockyards was the centennial celebration on Sunday, July 26, when officials commemorated the landmark anniversary of the incorporation of the Fort Worth Union Stock Yards, the very first stockyards company to organize on the North Side. Mayor Bob Bolen of Fort Worth read a proclamation honoring the stockyards for its hundred years. Gary Havard presented the mayor with a copy of his original limited-edition stockyards poster. J. W. Burgess, grandson of one of the original stockholders, was introduced. Then Bolen, Billy Bob Barnett, and Hampton Butler jointly cut the huge birthday cake, which was served, with lemonade, to hundreds of spectators and guests.

The North Fort Worth Business Association's Pioneer Days on September 18–20 carried through on the one-hundredth anniversary theme. So too did the North Fort Worth Historical Society, which unveiled a historical marker (at the Horse and Mule Barns) on October 24 during the third annual reunion of old stockyards personnel.

For an old-timer that just reached one hundred, the stockyards appeared to have a lot of help celebrating a birthday, an appropriate tribute to the importance of its legacy to Cowtown.

Appendix

Total Livestock Receipts at Fort Worth Stockyards

r	Cattle	Calves	Hogs	Sheep	Horses and Mules	TOTALS
6[1]	29,411	–	86,480	3,912	1,297	121,100
3	375,779	70,999	150,527	125,322	10,094	732,721
4	549,772	93,022	280,840	103,650	17,895	1,045,179
5	663,660	148,427	462,766	125,270	18,033	1,418,156
6	603,615	234,269	550,661	97,514	21,303	1,507,362
7	707,631	314,442	486,679	112,853	18,507	1,640,112
8	839,774	229,591	702,844	120,489	12,435	1,905,133
9	883,353	314,022	868,333	188,006	20,732	2,274,446
0	784,987	285,545	541,190	162,980	34,445	1,809,147
1	690,840	192,713	556,201	186,535	37,361	1,663,650
2	775,321	263,958	387,579	283,914	49,025	1,759,797
3	965,525	219,629	403,761	327,527	56,724	1,973,166
4	990,763	185,536	515,003	407,796	47,712	2,146,810
5	794,505	149,926	463,879	363,003	53,640	1,824,953
6	905,345	175,177	968,024	430,911	79,209	2,558,666
7	1,646,110	313,427	1,062,021	405,810	115,233	3,542,601
8	1,384,594	280,515	762,486	334,596	78,881	2,841,072
9	1,031,343	235,292	588,004	453,292	60,363	2,368,294
0	875,476	258,847	412,637	393,927	45,362	1,986,249
1	572,496	410,903	382,348	357,094	13,086	1,735,927
2	759,927	324,274	510,362	324,870	28,610	1,948,043
3	946,553	311,376	485,895	385,780	58,437	2,188,041
4	1,048,966	342,559	392,414	372,515	46,071	2,202,525
5	1,059,983	309,815	312,019	314,234	34,233	2,030,284

[1]These figures for 1896 are for six months from December 1895 to 1 June 1896. "Fort Worth Market," *Texas ck and Farm Journal*, 5 June 1896, p. 7. No other statistics are available for these years 1897–1902.

Year	Cattle	Calves	Hogs	Sheep	Horses and Mules	TOT
1926	943,774	240,871	217,139	445,208	27,343	1,874
1927	956,135	330,305	338,055	444,541	42,555	2,111
1928	885,902	325,217	431,635	457,788	43,429	2,143
1929	761,798	327,334	401,740	539,687	42,304	2,072
1930	637,513	331,443	279,331	432,082	27,047	1,707
1931	597,586	243,368	216,347	1,173,326	13,052	2,243
1932	444,061	209,097	255,202	1,197,570	16,730	2,122
1933	416,975	223,070	497,873	778,806	23,276	1,940
1934	756,619	381,017	403,716	596,616	30,240	2,168
1935	749,227	368,661	290,505	646,664	47,485	2,102
1936	657,650	373,865	372,004	609,733	51,867	2,065
1937	908,677	491,890	350,637	1,280,807	44,010	3,076
1938	763,774	448,785	278,614	1,378,268	33,460	2,902
1939	620,062	422,041	355,111	938,729	30,570	2,366
1940	523,748	377,054	446,960	1,085,610	27,510	2,460
1941	590,784	372,358	519,967	906,379	21,900	2,411
1942	829,832	404,659	647,818	1,367,123	21,783	3,271
1943[2]	879,685	377,050	1,001,484	2,098,479	26,649	4,383
1944[3]	1,046,116	482,068	1,092,086	2,657,226	−	5,277
1945	1,078,633	565,825	492,119	2,714,414	−	4,850
1946	923,344	505,548	580,930	2,337,668	−	4,347
1947	1,083,412	474,153	728,189	1,770,614	−	4,056
1948	868,892	337,036	812,742	1,593,146	16,407	3,628
1949	634,245	251,072	638,518	952,090	12,855	2,488
1950	584,633	279,556	717,106	1,068,003	8,916	2,658
1951	638,583	350,823	800,245	869,399	7,813	2,666
1952	766,927	297,578	796,951	920,006	3,596	2,785
1953	1,013,390	313,092	543,317	960,290	2,602	2,832
1954	894,631	275,166	507,942	1,083,198	1,124	2,762
1955	818,077	222,605	651,817	1,137,193	704	2,830
1956	912,272	244,210	678,599	1,169,859	614	3,005
1957	610,908	187,370	567,107	919,515	674	2,285
1958	424,873	166,529	225,633	943,006	606	1,760
1959[4]	458,963	160,711	430,552	1,074,897	982	2,126
1960[5]	482,947	103,109	128,147	664,306	−	1,378

[2] Figures for 1903–43 came from *Annual Reports,* Fort Worth Stockyards Company, Fort Worth Stocky. Company Collection, North Texas State University Archives, Denton (FWSY Co. Coll.).

[3] Even with Fort Worth breaking all records in 1944 with over 5 million total receipts, the market ranked only sixth in the nation. The first five were Chicago, 10,701,059; Omaha, 7,689,358; St. Paul, 6,829, Kansas City, 6,119,258; and St. Louis, 6,026,457 (Advertising-Clippings, W. L. Pier Correspondence, FWSY Coll. Horse and Mule figures are missing for 1944–47).

[4] Figures for 1945–59 came from "Comparative Statement of Five Competitive Markets for Twelve Mc Period Ending December 31, 1944–1959" (Dies Corr., FWSY Co. Coll.).

[5] Figures for 1960–63 are salable receipts rather than total receipts. When the Stockyards Company mc its office to the second floor of the Livestock Exchange Building in 1978, its records of those years were stroyed. The Market News Service of the United States Department of Agriculture reports salable rece only. They began this practice in 1940. Prior to that their reports are for total receipts.

ır	Cattle	Calves	Hogs	Sheep	Horses and Mules	TOTALS
1	413,620	67,695	97,714	715,783	—	1,294,812
2	329,262	68,179	82,684	734,490	—	1,214,615
3	294,354	84,860	73,543	432,134	—	884,891
4[6]	315,759	105,698	253,173	624,539	—	1,299,169
5	281,648	104,875	230,216	496,319	—	1,113,058
6	236,309	112,419	211,597	429,402	—	989,727
7	209,950	121,606	283,511	557,481	—	1,172,548
8	195,343	120,934	388,774	447,522	—	1,152,573
9	169,791	122,035	360,650	392,682	—	1,045,158
0	140,660	109,809	301,828	354,048	—	906,345
1	121,145	102,054	180,251	143,885	—	547,335
2	122,457	96,497	74,428	17,378	—	310,760
3	129,510	83,798	64,642	11,647	—	289,597
4	130,464	81,995	80,421	10,177	—	303,057
5	189,810	90,045	84,381	7,106	—	371,342
6	123,018	80,795	76,674	5,373	—	285,860
7	138,821	72,666	94,379	4,208	—	310,074
8	137,458	63,718	86,000	2,636	—	289,812
9	89,958	38,717	64,695	1,272	—	194,642
0	53,667	46,681	81,267	1,441	—	183,056
1	65,659	14,458	54,165	668	—	134,950
2	80,326	2,423	38,873	1,132	—	122,754
3	69,350	1,903	34,063	1,056	—	106,372
4	77,466	2,554	40,249	1,276	—	121,515
5	54,499	1,303	31,318	1,036	—	88,156
6	35,214	—	21,530	437	—	57,181

[6]Comparison of Receipts and Disposition of Livestock, 1964–86, Fort Worth Stockyards Company, Fort ▸rth, Texas.

Bibliography

PRIMARY SOURCES

Manuscripts and Collections

Amon Carter Museum of Western Art. Fort Worth. Local History Collection. "Facts about Fort Worth and Adjacent Country," Columbian Souvenir Edition, 1893. "Fifty Years of Rodeo in Fort Worth," 5 vols. of bound rodeo programs, 1927–77.

Bruner, Lee, and Mike Kern. "An Analysis of Mule Alley Art Center in the Fort Worth Stockyards Redevelopment Program," mimeographed, University of Texas at Arlington, 1979.

Dies, Mrs. J. W., Scrapbook. Fort Worth. Clipping and photo, "Old Friends Pay Tribute to Donovan for 30 Years at Stockyards," from *Fort Worth Star-Telegram*.

Fields, Louis. Personal Collection. Fort Worth. "Brand Book, 1900–16." (handwritten) Cattle Raisers Association.

Fort Worth Public Library. Fort Worth. Federal Writers' Project, 70 vols.: *Research Data*, Fort Worth and Tarrant County, Texas. North Fort Worth Clipping File, North Side Collection. Peak, Howard W., "My Recollections of Fort Worth," scrapbook of newspaper clippings of articles he wrote for the *Fort Worth Star-Telegram*.

Fort Worth Star-Telegram Reference Library. Fort Worth. Armour File. Livestock File. Niles City File. North Side File. Packing Industries File. Stockyards File. Swift File.

Fort Worth Stock Yards Company. Fort Worth. Comparison of Receipts and Disposition of Livestock, 1964–87. *Corporate Record*, 1893–1940 (recently donated to North Fort Worth Historical Society).

Hart, Dominick, III. Personal Files, Fort Worth. Clipping about his grand-father from *Texas Goat Raiser.*

Havard, Gary. Personal Collection, Fort Worth. Fort Worth Stockyards Company Certificates of Stock and other Records.

Jary, William E., Jr. Personal Collection, Fort Worth. Jary Commission Company and Stockyards Files.

Lewis, Mrs. John M. Personal Collection. Fort Worth, Texas. Notebook. Statement Prepared for National Commission on Food Marketing Hearing at Fort Worth, April 22–24, 1965.

North Fort Worth Historical Society. "Mule Alley Barn Party," printed program for North Fort Worth Historical Society, October 20, 1978. "North Fort Worth," mimeographed progress report of the North Fort Worth Historical Society, prepared by Brenda Kelley, March 10, 1978. Visitor Information Center Report, 1981.

North Texas State University Archives. Denton, Texas. Fort Worth Stock Yards Company Collection (FWSY Co. Coll.).

Stockyards Redevelopment Corporation Office. Fort Worth. Files on Stockyards Redevelopment.

Tarrant County Historical Commission Files. Fort Worth.

Tarrant County Junior College, Northeast Campus. Hurst, Texas. Local History Collection. Weekly Account Book of a packinghouse worker and his family.

Texas Christian University Special Collections. Fort Worth. Tom B. Saunders, Jr. Collection.

Texas and Southwestern Cattle Raisers Foundation, Waggoner Library. Fort Worth. Proceedings of Cattle Raisers Association of Texas, 1893–99.

Government Documents and Publications

Fort Worth, Texas, City of. Files of Federal Grants from Economic Development Administration in Office of Economic Development Coordinator: Stockyards Restoration.

———. *City Ordinances,* 1873–79.

———. Lease Agreement with Southwestern Exposition and Fat Stock Show for Municipal Buildings West, 1948–87.

———. *Minutes of City Council,* 1873–78; July, 1904; December 31, 1958; April 3, 1972; February 25, 1974; November 18, 1974; November 1, 1976; June 16, 1977; May, 1978.

———. Planning Department Records. *Northeast Sector* Plan. September, 1971.

Gammel, H. *Laws of Texas*. 1898.
———. *Laws of Texas*. 1923.
Niles City, Texas. *Minutes of City Council*, 1911–23.
North Fort Worth, Texas. *Minutes of Town Council*, 1902–1909.
Tarrant County. Tarrant County Historical Commission. "Niles City," prepared by Janie Reid. Research paper accompanying Texas Historical Marker Application, Fall, 1980.
Texas, Department of Agriculture, and U.S.D.A. *1980 Texas Livestock, Dairy and Poultry Statistics*. Compiled by Texas Crop and Livestock Reporting Service. Bulletin 192. MAY, 1981.
Texas, Office of Secretary of State. Corporations Division. Agricultural Livestock Finance Corporation, November 7, 1921.
———. Corporations Division. Charter No. 37096. Fort Worth Livestock Market Institute, March 27, 1950.
———. Corporations Division. Charter No. 1490. The Fort Worth Packing Company, December 29, 1881.
———. Corporations Division. Charter No. 4581. The Fort Worth Packing Company, April 30, 1890.
———. Corporations Division. Charter No. 1490. The Fort Worth Packing Company, Amended, November 28, 1891.
———. Corporations Division. Charter No. 3772. The Fort Worth Refrigerating and Export Meat Company, June 16, 1888.
———. Corporations Division. Charter No. 3402. Fort Worth Union Stock Yards Company, July 26, 1887.
———. Corporations Division. Non-Profit Corporation Forfeiture. Fort Worth Livestock Market Institute, September 1, 1965.
U.S. Bureau of the Census. *Report[s] On the Production of Agriculture*. 10th, 11th, 12th. 1880, 1890, 1900.
U.S. Congress, House. *Cattle Tick Fever*. Prepared by W. M. MacKellar. H. Doc. 527, 77th Cong., 2d sess. Reprinted in "Keeping Livestock Healthy," *1942 Yearbook of Agriculture*, U.S. Department of Agriculture. Washington, D.C.: U.S. Government Printing Office, 1942.
———. *Food Investigation: A Message from the President of the United States Transmitting Summary of Report of the Federal Trade Commission on the Meat Packing Industry*. H. Doc. 1297, 65th Cong., 2d sess., 1918.
———. *The Range and Cattle Traffic of the United States*. Prepared by Joseph Nimmo, Jr. H. Doc. 267, 48th Cong., 2d sess., 1886.
———. *Report of the Federal Trade Commission on the Meat Packing Industry*. H. Doc. 1297, 65th Cong., 2d sess., 1918.
———. Committee on Agriculture. *Business Meetings on Packers and*

Stockyards Act of 1921, As Amended on H.R. 8410. 94th Cong., 2d sess., 1976.

——. Committee on Agriculture. *Hearings Before the Committee on Agriculture, A Bill to Amend the Packers and Stockyards Act, 1921 H.R. 11384,* 69th Cong., 1st sess., 1926.

——. Committee on Agriculture. *Hearings to Amend Packer Act.* 67th Cong., 2d sess.–70th Cong., 2d sess., 1922–28.

——. Committee on Agriculture. *Jurisdiction of Packers and Stockyards Act. Hearings before the Committee on Agriculture, House of Representatives, on H.R. 7743 and H.R. 8536.* 85th Cong., 1st sess., 1957.

——. Committee on Agriculture. *Meat Packer Hearings before the Committee on Agriculture on H.R. 14, H.R. 232, H.R. 5034 and H.R. 5692.* 67th Cong., 1st sess., 1921.

——. Subcommittee of the Committee on Agriculture. *Amend the Packers and Stockyards Act of 1921. Hearings before the Subcommittee on Livestock and Grains of the Committee on Agriculture on H.R. 6231.* 90th Cong., 1st sess., 1967.

——. Subcommittee of the Committee on Agriculture. *Amend Packers and Stockyards Act of 1921. Hearings before the Subcommittee on Livestock and Grains of the Committee on Agriculture on H.R. 8410 and Related Bills.* 94th Cong., 1st sess., 1975.

——. Subcommittee of the Committee on Agriculture. *Bonding of Packers under Stockyards Act of 1921. Hearings before the Subcommittee on Livestock and Feed Grains of the Committee on Agriculture on H.R. 4831 and H.R. 5749.* 87th Cong., 1st sess., 1961.

——. Subcommittee of the Committee on the Judiciary and Committee on Interstate and Foreign Commerce. *Meatpackers. Joint Hearings on Bills to Transfer to the Federal Trade Commission from the Department of Agriculture Jurisdiction over Unfair and Monopolistic Trade Practices on H.R. 5282 and Others.* 85th Cong., 1st sess., 1957.

U.S. Congress, Senate. *The Packers' Consent Decree: A History of Legislation Pertaining to the Meat Packers Leading Up to the Packers' Consent Decree of 1920 and Subsequent Thereto.* S. Doc. 324, 71st Cong., 3d sess., 1931.

——. *Profiteering.* S. Doc. 248, 65th Cong., 2d sess., 1918.

——. Report of Victor Murdock, Acting Chairman of the Federal Trade Commission Who Appeared before the Senate at Their Request. S. Res. 114, 66th Cong., 1st sess., July 31, 1919. *Congressional Record,* vol. 58.

——. Senator Norris Speaking for the Meat Packing Bill, S. 3944, 66th Cong., 3d sess., January 22, 1921. *Congressional Record,* vol. 60.

——. Senator Smoot Speaking against the Meat Packing Bill, S. 3944, 66th Cong., 3d sess., January 24, 1921. *Congressional Record,* vol. 60.

——. *Transportation and Sale of Meat Products.* S. Rep. 829, 51st Cong., 1st sess., 1890.

——. Committee on Agriculture and Forestry. *Amend the Packers and Stockyards Act, 1921. Hearings before the Committee on Agriculture and Forestry on S. 2123, S. 2621, and S. 3064.* 73d Cong., 2d sess., 1934.

——. Committee on Agriculture and Forestry. *Amendment to Packers and Stockyards Act, 1921. Hearings before Committee on Agriculture and Forestry on S. 3841.* 68th Cong., 2d sess., 1925.

——. Committee on Agriculture and Forestry. *Hearings before a Subcommittee of the Committee on Agriculture and Forestry on S. 3676 and S. 4387.* 69th Cong., 1st sess., 1926.

——. Committee on Agriculture and Forestry. *Hearings on a Bill to Amend the Packers and Stockyards Act,* S. 2089. 68th Cong., 1st sess., 1924.

——. Committee on Agriculture and Forestry. *Hearings on Government Control of Meat Packing Industry on S. 5305.* 65th Cong., 3d sess., 1919.

——. Committee on Agriculture and Forestry. *Hearings to Amend Packer Act.* 67th Cong., 4th sess.–70th Cong., 1st sess., 1927–28.

U.S. Department of Agriculture. Agricultural Marketing Service. "Salable Receipts of Livestock at Public Stockyards by Markets 1940–46."

——. Agricultural Marketing Service. "Salable Receipts of Livestock at Public Stockyards, 1950–59."

——. Market News Service, Fort Worth, Texas. "Salable Receipts at Fort Worth, 1939–1979."

——. *Number of Feedlots of Fed Cattle Marketed 1962–1964.* Washington, D.C.: Statistical Reporting Service, Crop Reporting Board, June, 1966.

——. Packers and Stockyards Administration. *Livestock Payment Guidelines for Producers.* PA-293. Washington, D.C., n.d.

——. Packers and Stockyards Administration. Fort Worth, Texas. Mimeographed List of Feedlots, 1979–80.

——. Packers and Stockyards Administration. *The Packers and Stockyards Act as It Applies to Livestock Dealers.* PA-808. Washington, D.C., n.d.

————. Packers and Stockyards Administration. *Packers and Stockyards Act, Fair Play in the Marketplace.* PA-1019. Washington, D.C., n.d.

————. *Packers and Stockyards Act, 1921, As Amended.* Washington, D.C.: U.S. Government Printing Office, 1977.

————. Packers and Stockyards Administration. *The Packers and Stockyards Act: What It Is, How It Operates.* PA-399. Washington, D.C., n.d.

————. Packers and Stockyards Administration. *Questions and Answers on the Packers and Stockyards Act for Livestock Producers.* PA-810. Washington, D.C., n.d.

————. Packers and Stockyards Administration. *Regulations and Statement of General Policy Issued Under the Packers and Stockyards Act, 1921 As Amended.* Revised June, 1974.

Correspondence

Binford, Bill, to Carolyn Snyder, November 10, 1980. In Clipping File at Stockyards Redevelopment Office.

Camtrell, Patricia, Certifying Clerk in Office of Secretary of State, Austin, Texas, to author, May 22, 1981.

Fort Worth Stockyards Company to Stockholders, May 1, 1944. Copy in possession of author.

Fort Worth Stockyards Company to Customers of the Market, August 19, 1981. Copy in possession of author.

Fort Worth Stockyards to Patrons, n.d. [January, 1982]. Copy in possession of author.

Hunnicutt, Col. S. L., to author, November 7, 1983.

Klingenberg, Elmo, President of Fort Worth Stockyards Company, to Stockyards Patrons, April 6, 1978. Copy in possession of author.

Line, Rodger N., to author, March 8, 1982.

Rasmussen, Wayne, Chief, Agricultural History Branch, U.S.D.A., to author, January 26, 1982.

Interviews

Adams, Johnny. Fort Worth. June 7, 1983; September 12, 1983.

Addieway, Bill. Fort Worth. September 23, 1983.

Allen, Gary. Fort Worth. August 19, 1981; January 20, 1982; February 24, 1982; June 14, 1983; November 3, 1983.

Allen, Pat. Fort Worth. November 8, 1983.

Bailey, Delbert. Publicity manager, Southwestern Exposition and Fat Stock Show. Fort Worth. August 11, 1981; November 15, 1983; February 18, 1985; October 20, 1987.

Ball, Bill. Agra, Oklahoma. September 17, 1983.

Barnes, Milton. Fort Worth. September 15, 1983.

Barnett, Ed. Chico, Texas. October 25, 1983.

Barse, W. H., Jr. Transcript of Oral Interview, Fort Worth, 1977. Oral Histories of Fort Worth, Inc. Fort Worth Junior League Oral History Collection.

Bettis, J. R. Azle, Texas. September 20, 1983.

Beuck, William, II. Fort Worth. February 19, 1985.

Bowles, Dr. Wilson. Veterinarian. Fort Worth. November 16, 1976.

Brown, Ron. Assistant Manager, Fort Worth Stockyards Company. Fort Worth. August 2, 1977.

Brown, Tommy. Reporter, *Weekly Livestock Reporter*. Fort Worth. July 11, 1979.

Butler, Hampton. Fort Worth. June 10, 1986.

Butz, Harry. Fort Worth. September 9, 1983.

Callan, Faris. Fort Worth. October 25, 1983.

Campbell, Paul. Reference Librarian, Fort Worth Public Library. Fort Worth. July 28, 1980.

Cantrell, James. Fort Worth. September 21, 1983.

Carrell, Lee. Fort Worth. September 12, 1983.

Chastain, Jack. Texas Hereford Association. Fort Worth. August 19, 1980.

Chester, Opal. Fort Worth. September 7, 1983.

Christian, Winfred. Fort Worth. November 3, 1983.

Cooper, Abney. Fort Worth. October 25, 1983.

Cooper, Patsy. Vice-President, United Stockyards, Fort Worth Division. July 30, 1981; November 17, 1983.

Cox, Hutton. Fort Worth. June 10, 1983.

Davis, Bruce. Fort Worth. September 13, 1983.

Dies, Mrs. John W. Fort Worth. August 24, 1983.

Dodson, Leonard E. Fort Worth. October 25, 1983.

Donovan, A. G., Jr. Fort Worth. September 12, 1983.

Donovan, Paul. Fort Worth. October 29, 1983.

Doyle, Dr. Frank. Fort Worth. June 22, 1978.

Dunlap, R. K., III. Fort Worth. August 30, 1983.

Farmer, J. D., III. Fort Worth. September 12, 1983.

Francis, Irene. Fort Worth. August 21, 1979.

Goforth, Robert. Fort Worth. November 7, 1983.

Gouldy, Ted. Publisher, *Weekly Livestock Reporter.* Fort Worth. October 29, 1979; September 21, 1983.

Harper, Mary. Fort Worth Chamber of Commerce. Fort Worth. July 27, 1980.

Hart, Dominick, III. Fort Worth, September 21, 1983.

Humphrey, Eddie. Former member of United Packinghouse Workers, Local 54 at Armour and Company. Fort Worth. January 19, 1982.

Hunnicutt, Lloyd G. Fort Worth. October 25, 1983.

Hutchens, Mrs. Houston. Fort Worth. September 9, 1983.

Jary, William E., Jr. Fort Worth. November 7, 1981; November 11, 1981; July 12, 1983.

Jordan, Wayne C. Senior Vice-President, Agricultural Loan Department, Fort Worth National Bank (now Texas American Fort Worth). Fort Worth. January 6, 1982.

Joyce, Mrs. William L. Fort Worth. September 6, 1983.

Keen, Alonzo. Fort Worth. August 28, 1983.

King, Bill. Fort Worth. November 3, 1983.

King, Don. Secretary-Treasurer, Texas and Southwestern Cattle Raisers Association. Fort Worth. November 27, 1981.

Kirli, Frank. Fort Worth. August 14, 1979; October 27, 1983.

Kirli, Frank. Transcript of Oral Interview, August 21, 1975. Oral Histories of Fort Worth, Inc. Fort Worth Junior League.

Klingenberg, Elmo A. Division Manager, Fort Worth Stockyards Company. Fort Worth. Numerous interviews, February–August, 1981; March 21, 1985.

Kuhl, L. Van. President, American Stockyards Association. Fort Worth. October 23, 1984.

Kutch, Jeff. Fort Worth. September 26, 1983.

Kutch, Lester. Fort Worth. September 8, 1983.

Kutch, Mrs. Bernelle. Fort Worth. September 19, 1983.

Kutch, Mrs. Clyde. Fort Worth. September 6, 1983.

Kutch, Mr. and Mrs. Hilton. Azle, Texas. October 4, 1983.

Lewis, Mrs. John M. Fort Worth. November 21, 1983.

Lindsey, Mrs. Ward. Springtown. October 29, 1983.

McCafferty, Charles. North Fort Worth Historical Society. Fort Worth. Numerous interviews, 1976–81.

McCain, Mrs. Nita. Former owner, *North Fort Worth News.* Fort Worth. October 28, 1977.

McElyea, Mrs. Russell G. Fort Worth. September 8, 1983.

McKinley, DeWitt. Fort Worth. August 23, 1983.

Marrett, Claude. Fort Worth. September 12, 1983.

Marshall, Marion L. Fort Worth. September 17, 1983.

Muirhead, Don. Auctioneer. Waxahachie, Texas. October 25, 1983.

Novacek, F. J. Packers and Stockyards Administration. Fort Worth. July 27, 1977.

Pacatte, Mike. Packers and Stockyards Administration. Fort Worth. July 27, 1977.

Pier, Charlotte. Fort Worth. August 30, 1983.

Prindle, C. A. "Charlie". Fort Worth. November 7, 1983.

Rainey, Kathy. Office staff, Fort Worth Stockyards Company. Fort Worth. July 30, 1981; January 28, 1985.

Ralls, Leon. Sales representative, Fort Worth Stockyards Company, Fort Worth. March 29, 1982; November 1, 1983.

Reese, Manson. Fort Worth. October 29, 1983.

Reid, Janie. Niles City Historian. Fort Worth. March 7, 1981.

Rife, L. Harmon. Dublin, Texas. August 13, 1976.

Rogers, Berta. Fort Worth. July 1, 1979.

Rogers, Grover. Former Swift employee. Fort Worth. Numerous interviews, 1979–82.

Rogers, Lee. Fort Worth. November 7, 1983.

Rogers, Vernon. Fort Worth. January 31, 1982.

Ryon, Fred. Fort Worth. September 14, 1983.

Schilling, Leonard. Mounted policeman on Stockyards beat. Fort Worth. April 18, 1981.

Schultz, S. S. Fort Worth. August 28, 1983.

Scribner, Tommy. Fort Worth. September 19, 1983.

Shannon, Jack. Chairman, Stockyards Area Restoration Committee. Fort Worth. January 13–14, 1982.

Shelton, Bill. President, Fort Worth Chamber of Commerce. Fort Worth. July 29, 1980.

Shelton, Ray. Fort Worth. October 27, 1983.

Snyder, Wayne. Stockyards Development Corporation. Fort Worth. August 10, 1981.

Speck, W. M. Former Stockyards employee. Fort Worth. June 7, 1983.

Stevens, Bill. Azle, Texas. September 15, 1983.

Stubbs, Johnnie. Fort Worth. September 15, 1983.

Talles, Paul. Former Fort Worth Stockyards Company superintendent. Fort Worth. September 21, 1983.

Tannahill, Claude A. White Settlement, Texas. September 10, 1983.

Tape of conversation between Ben Green, E. A. "Dutch" Voelkel, Tom Saunders III, Bob Bramlett, and Ted Gouldy. Fort Worth. June 24, 1971. Tape in possession of Ted Gouldy.

Team, Charles B., Jr. Fort Worth. October 25, 1983.

Todd, Al. Fort Worth. August 5, 1981.

Van Ackeren, Dan. Packers and Stockyards Administration. Fort Worth. December 16, 1981; September 15, 1983.

Vann, J. D. Saginaw, Texas. September 23, 1983.

Vaughn, Joyce. U.S. Department of Agriculture Market News Service. Fort Worth. August 17, 1979.

Vestal, Johnny. Fort Worth. September 12, 1983.

Wallace, C. M. "Pete". Fort Worth. August 23, 1983.

Walsh, Ed C., Jr. Fort Worth. September 13, 1983.

Walters, Robert. Fort Worth. June 2, 1986.

Wardlaw, Verner S. "The History of the Packing Plant Industry in Fort Worth." Written transcript of 1915 interview. Copy in author's possession.

Weaver, Phil. Fort Worth. September 13, 1983.

Weeman, Roy. Head cattle buyer for Swift. Fort Worth. September 6, 1983; September 10, 1983; September 12, 1983; October 5, 1983; October 7, 1983.

Whatley, Joe. Fort Worth. October 5, 1983.

White, Gwen. Texas Angus Association. Fort Worth. July 2, 1980.

Wilbanks, W. Z. "Doc". Fort Worth. November 3, 1983.

Wilemon, L. N. Fort Worth. August 23, 1983.

Wilson, Jim. Economic Development Coordinator, City of Fort Worth, 1977–80. Fort Worth. January 6, 1982.

Woods, Woodie. Mayor of Fort Worth, 1979–81. Fort Worth. January 19, 1982.

Speeches

Allen, Gary. Public Announcement in Auction Barn, Fort Worth Stockyards. Fort Worth. August 19, 1981.

Baker, Stan. Progress Report on Architectural Survey to North Fort Worth Historical Society. Fort Worth Stockyards Auction Barn. Fort Worth. November 17, 1978.

Beuck, William, II. Speech for North Fort Worth Historical Society. Fort Worth. August 11, 1983.

Kelly, Gordon. Speech in Horse and Mule Barns. Fort Worth Stockyards. Fort Worth. October 20, 1978.

Wright, Jim. Speech at White Elephant Saloon in Stockyards Area. Fort Worth. January 12, 1981.

Films

"The Heart of Cowtown." Tape-Slide Show Produced and Narrated by Gary Havard for the North Fort Worth Historical Society, 1980.
"Real West," Part 2. Narrated by Gary Cooper. McGraw Hill Films, 1961.

Newspapers and Periodicals

American Live Stock Journal. See *Breeder's Gazette.*
The Bohemian (Fort Worth), 1899–1902.
Breeder's Gazette, 1941–62. Name changed to *American Live Stock Journal* in 1960; original name resumed in April, 1962.
The Buckboard, 1945–48.
The Cattleman, 1914–81.
The Citizen (Fort Worth), 1903–1904.
Commercial Recorder (Fort Worth), 1931–50.
Fort Worth Daily Gazette, 1887–90.
The Fort Worth Daily Live Stock Reporter, 1904–24.
The Fort Worth Democrat, April, 1875, July–August, 1876.
The Fort Worth Gazette, March 10, 1876.
Fort Worth Morning Register, 1900, 1901. Title varies; sometimes *Fort Worth Register.*
Fort Worth Press, 1955, 1957–59, 1961, 1967, 1971, 1973, 1975.
Fort Worth Record, July 29, 1915.
Fort Worth Record-Telegram, August 11, 1930.
Fort Worth Star-Telegram.
New York Times, July 15, 1931.
North Fort Worth Sunday News, 1911.
Southwestern Farmer and Breeder (Fort Worth), 1905–1909, 1911–12.
Tarrant County Historical Commission News, 1978–81.
Texas Live Stock Journal (Fort Worth), 1880–1909. Name changed to *Texas Live Stock and Farm Journal* in 1892, to *Texas Stock and Farm Journal* in 1894, to *Texas Stock Journal* in 1900, and to *Texas Stockman-Journal* in 1904.
This Month in Fort Worth, 1941–80. Name shortened to *Fort Worth* in 1945.
Washington Post, June 18, 1921.
The Weekly Citizen (North Fort Worth), 1904.
Weekly Livestock Reporter, 1925–79. The former *Fort Worth Daily Live Stock Reporter,* which operated under several names: *Weekly Live*

Stock Reporter, 1925, *Weekly Live Stock Reporter and Texas Poultry News,* 1954–59, *The Reporter,* 1959–60, and *Weekly Livestock Reporter,* 1960–present.

Secondary Works

Books

Armour, J. Ogden. *The Packers, the Private Car Lines and the People.* Philadelphia: Henry Altemus Co., 1906.

Atherton, Lewis. *The Cattle Kings.* Bloomington: Indiana University Press, 1961.

A Bank and a Shoal of Time. Fort Worth: First National Bank, n.d. [1970s].

Barksdale, E. C. *The Meat Packers Come to Texas.* Austin: University of Texas, 1959.

Black, John D. *The Dairy Industry and the AAA.* Washington, D.C.: Brookings Institution, 1935.

Blasig, Carl A. *Building Texas.* Brownsville, Tex.: Springman-King Company, 1963.

Blum, John Morton. *V Was for Victory.* New York: Harcourt Brace Jovanovich, 1976.

Bogart, Ernest Ludlow. *Economic History of American Agriculture.* New York: Longmans, Green and Co., 1923.

The Book of Fort Worth: Who's Who in Fort Worth. Fort Worth: Fort Worth Record, 1913.

Brody, David. *The Butcher Workmen: A Study of Unionization.* Cambridge: Harvard University Press, 1964.

Brody, William. *Glimpses of Texas: Its Divisions, Resources, Developments and Prospects.* Houston: A. C. Gray & Co. Printers, 1871.

Clancy, Foghorn. *My 50 Years in Rodeo.* San Antonio: Naylor Co., 1952.

Clarke, Mary Whatley. *A Century of Cow Business: A History of the Texas and Southwestern Cattle Raisers Association.* Fort Worth: Texas and Southwestern Cattle Raisers Assn., 1976.

Clay, John. *My Life on the Range.* Chicago: Privately printed, 1924.

Clemen, Rudolf Alexander. *The American Livestock and Meat Industry.* New York: Ronald Press Co., 1923. Reprint. Johnson Reprint Corp., 1966.

Corey, Lewis. *Meat and Man: A Study of Monopoly, Unionism, and Food Policy.* New York: Viking Press, 1950.

Cox, James, ed. *Historical and Biographical Record of the Cattle In-*

dustry and the Cattlemen of Texas and Adjacent Territory. 2 vols. With a new introduction by J. Frank Dobie. 1895. Reprint. New York: Antiquarian Press, 1959.

Dale, Edward Everett. *The Range Cattle Industry.* 1930. Reprint. Norman: University of Oklahoma Press, 1960.

Danborn, David B. *The Resisted Revolution: Urban America and the Industrialization of Agriculture, 1900–1930.* Ames: Iowa State University Press, 1979.

DeGraff, Herrell. *Beef Production and Distribution.* Norman: University of Oklahoma Press, 1960.

Dobie, J. Frank. *A Vaquero of the Brush Country.* Dallas: Southwest Press, 1929.

Dollar, Charles M., gen. ed. *America: Changing Times,* vol. 2. New York: John Wiley & Sons, 1979.

Douglas, C. L. *Cattle Kings of Texas.* Dallas: Cecil Baugh, 1939.

Down Historic Trails of Fort Worth and Tarrant County. Fort Worth: Dudley Hodgkins Co., 1949.

Drago, Harry Sinclair. *Great American Cattle Trails.* New York: Dodd, Mead & Co., 1965.

Duddy, Edward A., and David A. Revzan. *The Changing Relative Importance of the Central Livestock Market.* Chicago: University of Chicago Press, 1938.

———. *Marketing and Institutional Approach.* New York: McGraw-Hill Book Co., 1953.

An Economic Survey of Tarrant County. Prepared for the Texas and Pacific Railway Company by the Bureau of Business Research. Austin: University of Texas, College of Business Administration, 1949.

Evaluating Fort Worth Stockyards Restoration Potentials — Phase I. Prepared for Fort Worth Stockyards Restoration Committee. Los Angeles: Economic Research Associates, 1972.

Facts and Figures: City of Fort Worth, Texas. Fort Worth: City Council, City of Fort Worth, 1966.

Fischer, John. *From the High Plains.* New York: Harper & Row, 1978.

FitzGerald, D. A. *Livestock under the AAA.* Washington, D.C.: Brookings Institution, 1935.

Flanagan, Sue. *Trailing the Longhorns: A Century Later.* Austin: Madrona Press, 1974.

Flemmons, Jerry. *Amon: The Life of Amon Carter, Sr. of Texas.* Austin: Jenkins Publishing Co., 1978.

Forney, John W. *What I Saw in Texas.* Philadelphia: Ringwalt and Brown, 1872.

The Fort Worth National Bank Century One: 1873–1973. Fort Worth: Fort Worth National Bank, 1973.

From Ox-Teams to Eagles. Texas and Pacific Railway Co., n.d. [ca. 1946].

Fowler, Bertram B. *Men, Meat and Miracles*. New York: Julian Messner, 1952.

Gard, Wayne. *The Chisholm Trail*. Norman: University of Oklahoma Press, 1954.

Garrett, Julia Kathryn. *Fort Worth: A Frontier Triumph*. Austin: Encino Press, 1972.

Greater Fort Worth, 1907. Fort Worth: A. Owen Jennings, Publisher, 1907.

Green, Ben. *Wild Cow Tales*. New York: Alfred A. Knopf, 1971.

Gressley, Gene M. *Bankers and Cattlemen*. Lincoln: University of Nebraska Press, 1966.

Griswold, A. Whitney. *Farming and Democracy*. New York: Harcourt, Brace and Company, 1948.

Hall, Colby D. *Gay Nineties*. San Antonio: Naylor Co., 1961.

Hanes, Bailey C. *Bill Pickett, Bulldogger*. Norman: University of Oklahoma Press, 1977.

Havard, Gary L., and Don A. Ryon. *Cowtown, U.S.A.: A Concise History of the Fort Worth Stockyards*. Fort Worth: Identity Arts, 1976.

Heckler, Edwin L. *The Meat Packing Industry*. Boston: Bellman Publishing Co., 1944.

Hicks, John D. *Republican Ascendancy 1921–1933*. New York: Harper & Bros., 1960.

History of Texas, Together with a Biographical History of Tarrant and Parker Counties. Chicago: Lewis Publishing Co., 1895.

History of the Cattlemen of Texas. Dallas: Johnson Printing & Advertising Co., 1914.

Houck, U. G. *The Bureau of Animal Industry of the United States Department of Agriculture: Its Establishment, Achievement and Current Activities*. Washington, D.C.: Privately printed, 1924.

Howard, Robert West, and Oren Arnold. *Rodeo Last Frontier of the Old West*. New York: New American Library, 1961.

Josephson, Matthew. *The Robber Barons*. 1934. Reprint. New York: Harcourt Brace Jovanovich, 1962.

Kennedy, Michael S., ed. *Cowboys and Cowmen*. New York: Hastings House, 1964.

Knight, Oliver. *Fort Worth: Outpost on the Trinity*. Norman: University of Oklahoma Press, 1953.

Kutler, Stanley I. *The Supreme Court and the Constitution*. New York: W. W. Norton & Co., 1977.

Lee, Hong Y., and John S. Perrin. *Interregional Analysis of Texas Swine-Pork Industry.* Lubbock: Texas Tech University, 1975.

Leech, Harper, and John Charles Carroll. *Armour and His Times.* New York: D. Appleton-Century Co., 1938.

Leuchtenburg, William E. *The Perils of Prosperity, 1914–1932.* Chicago: University of Chicago Press, 1958.

Lewis, George M. *An Analysis of Shipments of Texas Sheep and Goats.* Austin: University of Texas, 1930.

———. *A Market Analysis of the Cattle Industry of Texas.* Austin: University of Texas, 1928.

Lincoln, C. C. *The Cattle Raising Industry of the Southwest.* Los Angeles: Security Trust and Savings Bank, 1921.

McCoy, Joseph G. *Cattle Trade of the West and Southwest.* Kansas City: Ramsey, Millet and Hudson, 1874. Reprint. Ann Arbor: University Microfilms, 1966.

McNeely, John G., and Jarvis E. Miller. *Fort Worth Stockyards — Operating Procedures and Problems.* College Station: Texas Agricultural Experiment Station, 1959.

Miller, Sidney L. *Tomorrow in West Texas.* Lubbock: Texas Tech Press, 1956.

Miller, W. Henry. *Pioneering North Texas.* San Antonio: Naylor Co., 1953.

Myres, Sandra L., ed. *Force without Fanfare: The Autobiography of K. M. Van Zandt.* Fort Worth: Texas Christian University Press, 1968.

A 1903 Packing House. North Fort Worth, Tex.: Armour and Co., 1903.

Nordyke, Lewis. *Great Roundup: The Story of Texas and Southwestern Cowmen.* New York: William Morrow & Co., 1955.

North Fort Worth Architectural/Historical Survey and Adaptive Reuse Studies. Fort Worth: Motheral Printing Co., 1980.

The North Fort Worth Story. Fort Worth: North Fort Worth Business Assn., n.d. [1960s].

Nourse, Edwin G., Joseph S. Davis, and John D. Black. *Three Years of the Agricultural Adjustment Administration.* Washington, D.C.: Brookings Institution, 1937.

Nourse, Edwin G., and Joseph G. Knapp. *The Co-operative Marketing of Livestock.* Washington, D.C.: Brookings Institution, 1931.

Official Souvenir Programme, Twenty-ninth Annual Convention, Cattle Raisers Association of Texas, Fort Worth, Texas, March, 1905. San Antonio: Milt S. Mooney Publisher, 1905.

Official Souvenir Programme, 33d Annual Convention Cattle Raisers

Association of Texas, Fort Worth, Texas, March 1909. San Antonio: Milt S. Mooney, 1909.

Oppenheimer, Harold L. *Cowboy Arithmetic: Cattle as an Investment.* Danville, Ill.: Interstate, 1964.

Orear, Leslie F., and Stephen H. Diamond. *Out of the Jungle: The Packinghouse Workers Fight for Justice and Equality.* New York: Hyde Park Press, 1968.

Osgood, Ernest Staples. *The Day of the Cattleman.* Chicago: University of Chicago Press, 1929.

Overman, W. J. *A Guide to Historic Sites in Fort Worth and Tarrant County.* Fort Worth: Tarrant County Historical Society, 1963.

Overton, Richard C. *Gulf to Rockies: The Heritage of the Fort Worth and Denver–Colorado and Southern Railways, 1861–1898.* Austin: University of Texas Press, 1953.

Paddock, B. B. *Early Days in Fort Worth, Much of Which I Saw and Part of Which I Was.* N.p., n.d.

———, ed. *Fort Worth and the Texas Northwest,* Vols. 1–4. Chicago: Lewis Publishing Co., 1922.

———, ed. *A Twentieth Century History and Biographical Record of North and West Texas,* 2 vols. Chicago: Lewis Publishing Co., 1906.

Peak, Howard M. *The Story of Old Fort Worth.* San Antonio: Naylor Co., 1936.

Pirtle, Caleb, III. *Fort Worth, the Civilized West.* Tulsa: Continental Heritage Press, 1980.

Porter, Roze McCoy. *Thistle Hill: The Cattle Baron's Legacy.* Fort Worth: Branch-Smith, 1980.

Powell, Cuthbert. *Twenty Years of Kansas City's Live Stock Trade and Traders,* Kansas City, Mo.: Pearl Printing Co., 1893.

Powell, Fred Wilbur. *The Bureau of Animal Industry: Its History, Activities, and Organization.* Baltimore: Johns-Hopkins Press, 1927.

Powell, T. J. *Samuel Burk Burnett: A Sketch* (Fort Worth: Fort Worth Public Library, 1916).

Proceedings of the National Live Stock Exchange at Fort Worth, Texas, October, 1896. Chicago: Harvey L. Goodall, Printer, 1896.

Proceedings of the 1970 Beef Cattle Conference, October 29, 1970. Lubbock: Texas Tech University Animal Science Department, 1970.

Prose and Poetry of the Live Stock Industry of the United States. 1905. Reprint. New York: Antiquarian Press, 1959.

Purcell, Theodore V. *Blue Collar Man: Patterns of Dual Allegiance in Industry.* Cambridge, Mass.: Harvard University Press, 1960.

Race, Lila Bunch. *Pioneer Fort Worth, Texas: The Life, Times and Families of South Tarrant County.* Dallas: Taylor Publishing Co., 1976.

Reck, Franklin M. *The 4-H Story: A History of 4-H Club Work.* Ames: Iowa State College Press, 1951.

Rohrer, Wayne C., and Louis H. Douglas. *The Agrarian Transition in America: Dualism and Change.* New York: Bobbs-Merrill Co., 1969.

Russell, Charles Edward. *The Greatest Trust in the World.* New York: Ridgway-Thayer Co., 1905.

Russell, Don. *The Wild West: A History of the Wild West Shows.* Fort Worth: Amon Carter Museum of Western Art, 1970.

Saloutos, Theodore, and John D. Hicks. *Agricultural Discontent in the Middle West 1900–1939.* Madison: University of Wisconsin Press, 1951.

Sanders, Leonard, and Ronnie C. Tyler. *How Fort Worth Became the Texasmost City.* Fort Worth: Amon Carter Museum of Western Art, 1973.

Savage, William, Jr., ed. *Cowboy Life: Reconstructing an American Myth.* Norman: University of Oklahoma Press, 1975.

Schlebecker, John T. *Cattle Raising on the Plains, 1900–1961.* Lincoln: University of Nebraska Press, 1963.

Schmidt, Ruby, ed., *Fort Worth and Tarrant County: A Historical Guide.* Fort Worth: Texas Christian University Press, 1984.

Schroth, Thomas N., ed. *Congress and the Nation.* 3 vols. Vol. 1: *1945–1964.* Washington: Congressional Quarterly Service, 1965.

75 Years of Kansas City Livestock Market History. Kansas City: Kansas City Stock Yards Co., 1946.

Shannon, Fred A. *The Farmer's Last Frontier: Agriculture, 1860–1897.* New York: Farrar & Rinehart, 1945.

Shideler, James H. *Farm Crisis, 1919–1923.* Berkeley: University of California Press, 1957.

Skaggs, Jimmy M. *The Cattle-Trailing Industry between Supply and Demand, 1866–1890.* Lawrence: University Press of Kansas, 1973.

Smith, Sam. *Things I Remember about Early Days in History of Fort Worth.* Fort Worth: River Oaks Printing, 1965.

Soule, Gardner. *The Long Trail.* New York: McGraw-Hill, 1976.

The Stock Manual. Fort Worth: George B. Loving, Publisher, 1881.

Stockyards Area Restoration. Fort Worth: Fort Worth City Council, n.d. [early 1970s].

The Story of Fort Worth from Outpost to Metropolis. Fort Worth: Fort Worth National Bank, 1965.

Swift, Louis F., with Arthur Van Vlissingen, Jr. *Yankee of the Yards: The Biography of Gustavus Franklin Swift.* Chicago: A. W. Shaw Co., 1927.

Talbert, Robert H. *Cowtown-Metropolis: Case Study of a City's Growth and Structure.* Fort Worth: Leo Potishman Foundation, 1956.

Taylor, Edith Wharton. *Money on the Hoof—Sometimes.* Fort Collins, Colo.: Old Army Press, 1974.

Terrell, J. C. *Reminiscences of the Early Days of Fort Worth.* Fort Worth: Texas Printing Co., 1906.

Texas: A Guide to the Lone Star State. Compiled by Workers of the Writers' Program of the Work Projects Administration in the State of Texas. American Guide Series. New York: Hastings House, 1940.

The Texas-Oklahoma Cattle Feeding Industry Structure and Operational Statistics. College Station: Texas A&M University Agricultural Experiment Station. Bulletin B-1079. December, 1968.

Towne, Charles Wayland, and Edward Norris Wentworth. *Cattle and Men.* Norman: University of Oklahoma Press, 1955.

Ward, Celeste. "Fort Worth: A Cowtown Success, Its Stockyards and Packing Industries, 1870–1903." In *E. C. Barksdale Student Lectures in History, 1975,* edited by Roger Townsend. Arlington, Tex.: University of Texas at Arlington, 1975.

Welch, June Rayfield. *People and Places in the Texas Past.* Waco: Texian Press, 1974.

Williams, Mack, ed. *In Old Fort Worth.* Fort Worth. News-Tribune, 1977.

Wood, Charles L. *The Kansas Beef Industry.* Lawrence: Regents Press of Kansas, 1980.

Working, Elmer J. *Demand for Meat.* Chicago: University of Chicago Press, 1954.

Wortham, Louis J. *A History of Texas,* Vol. 5. Fort Worth: Wortham-Molyneaux Co., 1924.

Articles

Abrego, Mary. "A Struggle for Rebirth and a Halt to Decay." *Northwest Passage,* April 7, 1976, p. 5.

"A Bill to Make the Packers Be Good." *Literary Digest,* February 5, 1921, pp. 10–11.

Burmeister, Charles A. "Six Decades of Rugged Individualism: The American National Cattlemen's Association, 1898–1955." *Agricultural History* 30 (October, 1956): 143–50.

Butcher, Lee. "Holy Cow, A Livestock Exchange Is Renovated." *Texas Business* 2 (February, 1978): 14.

Caldwell, Edwin L. "Highlights of the Development of Manufacturing in Texas, 1900–1960." *Southwestern Historical Quarterly* 68 (April, 1965): 405–31.

"Caruso, World's Greatest Tenor Charms Hearers." *Fort Worth Record*, October 20, 1920 (morn.), p. 2.

Cauley, Troy Jesse. "Early Business Methods in the Texas Cattle Industry." *Journal of Economics and Business* 4 (May, 1932): 461–86.

———. "Longhorns and Chicago Packers." *Texas Monthly* 5 (January, 1930): 54–62.

Cheshire, Ashley. "North Fort Worth Comes Back." *Sunday* supplement to *Dallas Times-Herald*, January 23, 1977, pp. 4–5, 7, 12.

"City Packing Industry to Get Honors." *Fort Worth Press*, October 11, 1951, p. 36.

Clark, Dave. "Dallas–Fort Worth." *Flying Colors* 7 (October, 1978): 19–23.

Clark, J. Stanley. "Texas Fever in Oklahoma." *Chronicles of Oklahoma* 29 (Winter, 1951–52): 429–43.

"Col. C. C. French Funeral to Be Saturday." *Fort Worth Star-Telegram*, August 6, 1937 (eve.), p. 8.

"The Coliseum," *The Commission* 4 (June, 1983): 3.

"Cowtown Rodeo Gains Professional Status." *Exchange Quarterly Publication of North Fort Worth Business Assn.* (Spring, 1980): 1.

"Cowtown Rodeo Going Pro in March." *News-Tribune*, February 2, 1979, p. 13.

Davis, G. Cullom. "The Transformation of the Federal Trade Commission, 1914–1929." *Mississippi Valley Historical Review* 49 (1962): 437–55.

Destler, Chester McArthur. "The Opposition of American Businessmen to Social Control During the 'Gilded Age.'" *Mississippi Valley Historical Review* 39 (May, 1953): 641–72.

Dietrich, Raymond A. "The Texas Cattle Feeding Industry." *Texas Business Review* 43 (October, 1969): 293–99.

"Dreams Really Do Come True . . ." *Cowtown Dispatch* (August, 1983): 5–6.

Dugas, Vera Lee. "Texas Industry, 1860–1880." *Southwestern Historical Quarterly* 59 (October, 1955): 151–83.

"$500,000 Stockyards Renovation." *Azle News-Advertiser*, May 4, 1978, sect. 2, p. 9.

Flemmons, Jerry. "Fort Worth Cultural Acropolis of the Southwest." *Southern Living* 8 (October, 1973): 85–92.

"Fort Worth: The Gateway to the Panhandle." *Frank Leslie's Illustrated Newspaper* 71 (September 27, 1890): 7, 13.

Freund, Carl. "Stockyards Renovation Faces Reagan Fund Cut Plans," *Dallas Morning News*, February 10, 1981, sect. a, p. 20.

Gard, Wayne. "Retracing the Chisholm Trail." *Southwestern Historical Quarterly* 60 (July, 1956): 53–68.

Gilliam, Linda. "Northside Stockyard Area Weathers Hard Times; Hopes Run High as Renovation Efforts Continue." *Dallas/Fort Worth Business* 27 (March 27, 1978): 6–8.

Gordon, Jack. "Opera Star Set Fort Worth Agog." *Fort Worth Press*, August 12, 1975 (clipping in Jary files, page cut off).

Gouldy, Ted. "Fort Worth Important Livestock Market." *West Texas Today* (August, 1956): 12.

Gressley, Gene M. "The American Cattle Trust: A Study in Protest." *Pacific Historical Review* 30 (February, 1961): 61–77.

Haley, J. Evetts. "Texas Fever and the Winchester Quarantine." *Panhandle-Plains Historical Review* 7 (1934): 37–53.

Harrison, D. S. "A Texas Hog Campaign." *Texas Magazine* 2 (October, 1910): 19–22.

Havins, T. R. "Livestock and Texas Law." *Yearbook of the West Texas Historical Association* 36 (1960): 18–32.

———. "Texas Fever." *Southwestern Historical Quarterly* 52 (July, 1948): 148–62.

"Heritage on the Hoof." *Dallas* 55 (October, 1976): 26–27.

"Historic Livestock Exchange Building Undergoing $750,000 Restoration Plan." *Azle News-Advertiser*, December 29, 1977, sect. 1, p. 9.

"House Packer Bill Passed by Senate." *New York Times*, June 18, 1921, sect. 1, p. 2.

Johnson, Arthur M. "Anti-trust Policy in Transition, 1908: Ideal and Reality." *Mississippi Valley Historical Review* 48 (Winter, 1961–62): 415–34.

Johnson, Keach. "Struggle in the Stockyards: The Rise and Fall of the Cooperative Livestock Commission Co." *Arizona and the West* 18 (1976): 315–32.

Knight, Oliver. "Fort Worth's First 100 Years." *Texas Industry* 15 (June, 1949): 17–19, 38–39.

Kutler, Stanley I. "Chief Justice Taft, National Regulation, and the Commerce Power." *Journal of American History* 51 (March, 1965): 651–68.

Lambert, Roger. "Drought Relief for Cattlemen: The Emergency Purchase Program of 1934–35." *Panhandle-Plains Historical Review* 45 (1972): 21–37.

"Livestock Receipts Soar." *Fort Worth Chamber of Commerce News* 11 (June, 1937): 4.

Lobrovich, Mitch. "Last of the Cowboy Towns." *Vista* 16 (August, 1980): 22–25.

"Louville V. Niles Dies in Wellesley." *Boston Transcript*, July 19, 1928. Xerox of clipping in possession of author.

May, Irvin, Jr. "Welfare and Ranchers: The Emergency Cattle Purchase Program and Emergency Work Relief Program in Texas, 1934–35." *West Texas Historical Association Yearbook* 47 (1971): 3–19.

"Meat for America." *T&P Topics* (August, 1955): 4–11.

Miller, Mrs. C. R. "How Texas Handles Cattle." *Leslie's Weekly* 102 (January 25, 1906): 76.

"New Dress for an Old Landmark." *Observer*, September 28, 1978, pp. 1, 3.

1979 Cattle Feeders Annual. Amarillo: Texas Cattle Feeders Association, 1979.

Noey, Ben. "Business, Patrons Enjoy Rejuvenation." *North East Weekly Student*, April 2, 1981, p. 7.

Nordyke, Lewis. "Industry Likes Fort Worth." *Texas Parade* 19 (January, 1959): 5–12.

"North Side Cattle Auctions Have a Bawl in New Quarters." *Observer*, April 30, 1978, sect. a, p. 10.

Novak, Ralph. "Stockyards Are Dying." *Fort Worth Press*, July 5, 1971, p. 6.

"The Packers State Their Case." *Literary Digest*, October 4, 1919, pp. 14–15.

Paddock, B. B. "The Night the Spring Palace Burned." In *In Old Fort Worth*, ed. by Mack Williams. Fort Worth: *News-Tribune*, 1977, pp. 79–80.

Paukner, Frankie. "Fort Worth Stockyards' Rejuvenation Said Combination of Imagination, Conservatism." *Dallas/Fort Worth Business*, November 27, 1978, p. 5.

Perkins, Frank. "How 'Calf Fries' Made Debut on Fort Worth Menu." *News-Tribune*, April 24, 1981, p. 28.

"Proceedings of the Eighth Annual Convention of National Live Stock Association." Denver, Colorado. January 10–13, 1905.

"Projection." Tarrant County Junior College Newsletter, February 13, 1978, p. 1.

"Quanah Parker, Great Chief of the Comanches," *Fort Worth Record*, March 17, 1907, p. 1.

Reeves, Frank. "History of the Texas Hereford Association." *Texas Hereford* 8 (May, 1959): 120–36.

Reid, Janie. "Niles City." History essay accompanying application for Texas Historical Marker, 1980.

————. "Niles City, Texas." 1980 Program for Texas Cowboy Classic, Windy Ryon Memorial Arena, Saginaw, Texas, May 30–June 1, 1980.

Reinert, Al. "The End of the Trail." *Texas Monthly* 6 (November, 1978): 168–77, 297–301.

Renner, G. K. "The Kansas City Meat Packing Industry Before 1900." *Missouri Historical Review* 55 (October, 1960): 18–29.

Richardson, T. C. "Fort Worth, Where the West Begins." *Holland's* 54 (February, 1935): 7, 27, 29.

Royles, Milton C. "The Stockyards Story." *Fort Worth* 44 (December, 1968): 56–63.

Schuyler, Michael W. "Drought and Politics, 1936: Kansas as a Test Case." *Great Plains Journal* 15 (Fall, 1975): 2–27.

"$750,000 Pumped into Livestock Building Facelift." *Observer*, December 15, 1977, p. 59.

"60 Years of Big Business." *Parade*, November 13, 1977, p. 15.

"Sixty Years of Corporate Ups, Downs and Outs." *Forbes* 120 (September 15, 1977): 127–48.

Skaggs, Jimmy. "Hip Pocket Businessmen: The Cattle Trailing Contractors." *Great Plains Journal* 10 (Fall, 1970): 1–10.

"Stockyards Area Greets President." *Cowtown* 1 (December, 1980): 1.

"Stockyards Project Update." *Cowtown Dispatch* (November, 1983): 5.

Taylor, Sheila. "Taking Stock of Cowtown's Heritage." *Dallas Morning News*, October 17, 1979, sect. c, p. 3.

"Texas Cattle," *Democrat* (Fort Worth), April 21, 1875, p. 3.

"Texas Now Has More People Than Cattle." *Texas Pioneer* 10 (September–October, 1931): 17.

Thomas, Les. "The West Still Lives in Fort Worth." *Southern Living* 14 (June, 1979): 78–81.

"To Sell Stockyards Holdings." *New York Times*, July 16, 1931, p. 11.

Travis, Edmunds. "Fort Worth's Big Water Plan." *Bunker's Magazine* 2 (July–December, 1928): 40–53.

Trimble, Bob. "Hometown Auctions Slice into Cattle Business in Fort Worth." *Fort Worth Press*, August 31, 1961, p. 35.

———. "Is Commission Man on the Way Out as Cornerstone of Market?" *Fort Worth Press*, September 1, 1961, p. 18.

———. "That Traditional Bovine Title May be Slipping—And Here's Why." *Fort Worth Press*, August 29, 1961, p. 7.

"Twenty-Seventh Annual Meeting of the Cattle Raisers Association of Texas." El Paso, 1903.

"Uncle Sam to Control the Packers." *Literary Digest*, July 2, 1921, p. 16.

Virtue, G. O. "The Meat Packing Investigation." *Quarterly Journal of Economics* 34 (August, 1920): 626–85.

Whisenhunt, Donald W. "The Texas Attitude toward Relief, 1929–1933." *Panhandle-Plains Historical Review* 46 (1973): 94–III.

Williams, Mack. "Gains Seen for North Side." *News-Tribune,* September 29, 1978, pp. 1, 30.

Wilson, James A. "Cattlemen, Packers, and Government: Retreating Individualism on the Texas Range." *Southwestern Historical Quarterly* 74 (April, 1971): 525–34.

Wirtz, Michael S. "Cowtown Stockyards." *Westward* Sunday Supplement to *Dallas Time-Herald,* December 7, 1980, pp. 46–53.

"World's Renowned Tenor Arrives in City for Concert." *Fort Worth Record,* October 19, 1920 (morn.), p. 1.

Young, Stephanie. "Sansom House Reflects By-gone Era." *Northwest Passage,* February 28, 1977, p. 4.

Theses and Dissertations

Adedeji, Moses. "The Stormy Past: A History of the United Packinghouse Workers of America — C.I.O. Fort Worth, Texas, 1936–1956." Master's thesis, University of Texas at Arlington, 1975.

Atkinson, Eva L. "Kansas City's Livestock Trade and Packing Industry, 1870–1914: A Study in Regional Growth." Ph.D. dissertation, University of Kansas, 1971.

Bennett, Rossie Beth. "History of the Cattle Trade in Fort Worth, Texas." Master's thesis, George Peabody College for Teachers, 1931.

Berrong, Verna Elizabeth. "History of Tarrant County from Its Beginning until 1875." Master's thesis, Texas Christian University, 1938.

Duncan, Patricia Lenora. "Enterprise: B. B. Paddock and Fort Worth — A Case Study of Late Nineteenth Century American Boosterism." Master's thesis, University of Texas at Arlington, 1982.

Evans, Samuel Lee. "Texas Agriculture, 1880–1930." Ph.D. dissertation, University of Texas at Austin, 1960.

Harkins, Thomas A. "A History of the Municipal Government of Fort Worth, Texas." Master's thesis, Texas Christian University, 1937.

Hendricks, Delia Ann. "The History of Cattle and Oil in Tarrant County." Master's thesis, Texas Christian University, 1969.

Hooks, Michael Q. "The Struggle for Dominance: Urban Rivalry in North Texas, 1870–1910." Ph.D. dissertation, Texas Technological University, 1979.

Keaveney, Sister Mary Ailbe. "The Depression Era in Fort Worth, Texas, 1929–1934." Master's thesis, University of Texas at Austin, 1974.

McArthur, Daniel Evander. "The Cattle Industry of Texas, 1685–1918." Master's thesis, University of Texas, 1918.

Miles, James C. "Fort Worth and World War I." Master's thesis, Southern Methodist University, 1946.

Moore, Carl Henry. "Future Trends in the Marketing of Livestock and the Distribution of Meats." Ph.D. dissertation, Purdue University, 1948.

Thompson, Clarence Arnold. "Some Factors Contributing to the Growth of Fort Worth." Master's thesis, University of Texas, 1933.

Index